DEVELOPING SUBJECT KNOWLEDGE ACROSS THE PRIMARY CURRICULUM

DEVELOPING SUBJECT KNOWLEDGE ACROSS THE PRIMARY CURRICULUM

EDITED BY
JEN AGGLETON

3rd Floor
HYLO
103–105 Bunhill Row
London, EC1Y 8LZ
UK

2455 Teller Road
Thousand Oaks
California 91320

10th Floor, Emaar Capital Tower
2 MG Road, Sikanderpur, Sector 26
Gurugram, Haryana – 122002
India

8 Marina View Suite 43-053
Asia Square Tower 1
Singapore 018960

Editor: Amy Thornton
Senior project editor: Chris Marke
Cover design: Wendy Scott
Typeset by: C&M Digitals (P) Ltd, Chennai, India
Printed in the UK

Library of Congress number: 2026934483

British Library Cataloguing in Publication Data

A catalogue record for this book is available from the British Library

ISBN 978-1-0362-3093-7
ISBN 978-1-0362-3092-0 (pbk)

CONTENTS

ABOUT THE AUTHORS

Dr Jen Aggleton is a Senior Lecturer in Education Studies at the Open University (OU), where she has taught across undergraduate and initial teacher training programmes. She is co-chair of the Education, Childhood, Youth and Sport EDI Champions group, focusing on anti-racist and inclusive approaches to teaching and assessment. A former primary teacher and qualified librarian, Jen spent many years teaching and running school libraries in Hampshire and Cambridgeshire before moving into academia. Her research centres around education, communication and media, with publications covering topics such as developing literacy skills through videogames, reading illustrated novels and children's participation in libraries.

Matt Borg is a Senior Lecturer for Initial Teacher Education and Mathematics lead at the University of Huddersfield's School of Education. He has worked in education for over 20 years, teaching across primary and higher education sectors. Before joining Huddersfield, Matt lectured at the University of Derby and taught in schools in Sheffield, where he led science and maths. His research interests include creativity across the curriculum, beginning teacher identity and supporting dialogic pedagogy. He has contributed book chapters on adaptive teaching in primary schools. Matt provides science training for schools in Sheffield, focusing on substantive and disciplinary knowledge, and also serves as a school governor.

Jane Calcutt has worked in many primary school settings over 25 years while completing practitioner research at Master's and Doctorate level. She has experience teaching Early Years through to Key Stage 2 leading on subjects including PSHE, history, art and PE. Jane is a qualified Mindfulness in Schools primary programme teacher, Massage in Schools Association instructor and Neuro-Linguistic (NLP) Coach in Education. Jane currently teaches undergraduate and postgraduate primary teacher and education programmes at Edge Hill University with a focus on children's behaviour, mental health and wellbeing. Research interests include social and emotional learning and utilising mindfulness for supporting social justice principles. Current projects include investigating student teacher personal and interpersonal development for enhancing professional resilience.

Dr Jane Carter was a primary classroom teacher for many years before joining University of the West of England (UWE) as a Senior Lecturer teaching on undergraduate initial teacher education to education doctoral programmes. Jane was awarded the HEA National Teaching Fellowship in 2013 which led to a research project in rural and city schools in the USA. Since then, Jane has been engaged in a number of projects focusing on all aspects of literacy, with a particular interest in the teaching of reading including approaches to engaging all children and families. This work includes exploring community funds of knowledge and anti-racist pedagogies that can help the understanding of inclusive language and literacy learning

Helen Crawford is Lecturer in Early Childhood Education at University College London (UCL) Institute of Education. She is chair of the Historical Association primary committee and a member of the editorial board for Primary History. A qualified Early Years and primary teacher, Helen worked in primary schools for 18 years as a teacher, history subject leader and senior leader. She is a series editor of Cambridge Primary Humanities, author of Oxford International Primary History series (OUP) and a consultant for BBC Bitesize™ primary history.

Gavin Davenport is a former games developer who worked for companies like Atari and Gremlin Interactive before becoming a primary teacher. From 2005 to 2023, he taught and led computing across multiple schools and a large multi-academy trust (MAT), emphasising creativity across the curriculum. He supported national cultural institutions in developing their educational offerings before becoming a Lecturer in Education at Edge Hill University, where he leads Computing for Primary QTS courses. Gavin is a National Centre for Computing Education (NCCE) Senior Professional Development Lead, an Apple Certified Teacher and an NCCE course author. He has written on digital literacies for *Hello World* magazine and is a doctoral researcher examining the interaction between digital literacy and digital poverty.

Dr Kathrina Farrugia-Kriel is a dance scholar, educator and author. Her books include *Princess Poutiatine and the Art of Ballet in Malta* (2020), *The Oxford Handbook of Contemporary Ballet* (2021), *The Oxford Handbook of Ballet Pedagogy* (2026) and *The Oxford Handbook of Musical Theatre Choreography* (in progress). Following her dance teacher training, Kathrina pursued a career in higher education, from graduate teaching assistant to Head of Research. Her responsibility for dance pedagogy covered mentoring in assessment of teaching placements (public, private and community sectors) and overseeing the curriculum for education studies and equality, diversity and inclusion (EDI, including anti-racist and inclusive approaches to dance teacher training) for BA and MA degrees in Dance Education. Over the past 20 years, she has taught research in dance, ethics of researching dance education with children and young people, as well as practice as research and action research in dance and musical theatre. Kathrina is a Senior Fellow of Advance HE and volunteers at Grayswood Church of England Primary School, teaching dance to the Early Years (ages four to seven).

Ailsa Fidler is a Senior Lecturer in Primary Education at Liverpool John Moores University where she leads primary history across all routes as well as a module focused upon Climate Change and Sustainability Education (CCSE). She is a member of the Historical

Association's primary committee and the Primary History editorial board. Ailsa qualified as a primary teacher in 1993 and worked in a range of schools and roles before entering initial teacher education. She is an Associate Fellow of UCL's Centre for CCSE and a member of the advisory panel for UCL's Holocaust Education Centre's work on the Kindertransport.

Dr Catherine Foley is Associate Professor of Mathematics Education and Head of Initial Teacher Education at the University of Reading. She began her career as a primary teacher and subject leader before becoming a local authority mathematics consultant. After working for the Primary National Strategy (PNS) she moved to her current role in initial teacher education, teaching across undergraduate and postgraduate programmes on mathematics education, research methods and climate and sustainability education.

With a lifelong passion for outdoor learning, environmental sustainability and wildlife conservation, she has loved being part of the team working with beginning teachers to incorporate climate and sustainability into their teaching, and has recently taken on a university-wide role leading education for sustainable development.

Phil Griffith is currently a Senior Lecturer in Music for Bath Spa University. He lectures for both the Secondary Music and Primary PGCE music provisions. Phil is the Academic Tutor for the PGCE Secondary Music course and the Music Specialism tutor for the Primary PGCE. Previously, Phil taught music at secondary level in Bristol, has been an external assessor for the Teach First route into secondary music teaching and occasionally an external second marker for the undergraduate Composition and Arranging modules at London School of Theology. Phil has been a choir leader and a church music director. He is a pianist, singer, composer and arranger, with a wider interest in hymnody, both old and new.

Rebecca Harris is Professor of History Education at the University of Reading. They taught history in secondary schools for 16 years and have been involved in history teacher education for both secondary and primary teachers for 25 years. They have researched issues to do with school history, particularly focused on students' engagement with the curriculum and history teachers' choices about the curriculum. Besides numerous academic articles, they have produced *The Guided Reader to Teaching and Learning History* (2013) for Routledge, and a range of professional articles in *Teaching History* and *Primary History* for teachers. They have a broad range of experiences linked to history education, both in terms of practice and research.

Sean Harris is an internationally recognised education leader committed to tackling educational inequality. He is Director of People, Learning and Community Engagement (PLACE). PLACE grew out of an ambitious mission, to understand more deeply and respond more meaningfully to the needs of the children, families and communities that are served through Tees Valley Education, a multi-academy Trust in the North East of England. A doctoral researcher, he explores co-production in place-based school approaches. He is a Fellow of the Chartered College of Teaching and was awarded the 2024 Fair Education Alliance and Bloomberg Innovation Award. Sean received Let Teachers SHINE funding for poverty-informed curriculum design. He contributes to research with Child of the North and works alongside schools across the UK to help them develop poverty-informed practices. His Substack™ of over 11,000 regular readers explores many of these issues.

Dr Claire Hawkins, a former secondary teacher, has experience across both primary and secondary teacher education. She has been Course Leader for undergraduate and postgraduate Secondary ICT/Computer Science with QTS programmes. She was Subject Leader for Primary Computing and Primary Foundation Subjects at Edge Hill University. Claire has co-authored two key texts featured on initial teacher education computing reading lists: *Teaching ICT* (2009) and *Teaching Computing* (2015). Currently, she serves as the Faculty Lead for Online and AI Pedagogy contributing to institutional policy in this area. She researches pre-service primary teachers' adjustment to the computing curriculum and their use of generative AI.

Phillippa Heath, Head of Learning and Engagement at the Museum of English Rural Life (MERL), University of Reading, has over 20 years' experience in museum and gallery education. In that time she has worked in diverse organisations including the National Portrait Gallery, Orleans House Gallery, Museum of Richmond, the Churchill Museum and Cabinet War Rooms, the Holocaust Educational Trust and the V&A's former Theatre Museum; she is passionate about bringing the past to life and making heritage accessible and inclusive – in particular for those who experience the greatest barriers to participation. In her current role she oversees the schools learning and community engagement programmes which welcome over 10,000 participants annually to the museum to discover, create, enjoy and be inspired. The schools programme has been awarded the Sandford Award of Museum Education. Part of the recent focus has been exploring how the museum collections can support schools in climate and sustainability education. In 2024 Phillippa was also a finalist for the Museums Association's national Museums Change Lives Award.

Emma Jones is an experienced primary SENCo and SEND consultant. She holds a PGCert NASENCo, a PGDip in Mental Health in Education and an MEd in Inclusive Education and the L5 Specialist Dyslexia Teacher qualification. This comprehensive background gives her a strong, practical understanding of key theories, research and debates concerning special educational needs. Having taught students from Early Years to Year 8, Emma is highly skilled at empowering teachers across all subjects and curriculum stages to effectively teach and support diverse learners.

Matthew Knight is the Ecology and Sustainability Lead at Shinfield St Mary's Church of England Junior School. Having spent 11 years teaching and leading ecology and sustainability to children in a primary school, Matt has built up a plethora of resources and project ideas. He has worked with fellow researchers and scientists from the University of Reading and UWE to help shape the future of climate learning. He has published in primary science journals on his specialism of aquaponics, a sustainable food production system. Aside from teaching and leading professional development within and beyond his school, Matt works for the environmental charity the Tree Council as regional lead for the education department and is also a co-founder of the community orchards and gardens charity Freely Fruity.

Dr Elizabeth Malone is a Reader in Education, Practice and Citizenship at Manchester Metropolitan University and a National Teaching Fellow, celebrated for her compassionate leadership in advancing teaching excellence and inclusive curriculum design. Her research and practice centre on innovative approaches to education and curriculum development. Elizabeth serves on the National Executive of the Association for the Study of Primary Education (ASPE), where she advocates for evidence-informed teaching and learning. Her career spans a range of leadership and academic roles, including Head of Primary Programmes at Liverpool John Moores University, where she oversaw and coordinated primary initial teacher training. A specialist in foreign language education, Elizabeth has studied the subject at every level, holding a BA (Hons) in French, PGCE (QTS) in French, MA in Education (French), PGCERT in Teaching and Learning in Higher Education (Key Stage 2/3 French) and a PhD entitled 'An ethnographic case study of foreign language education'. She has written extensively on the topic through peer-reviewed journal articles, podcasts and reports for national boards.

Dr Sarah Marston is the Head of School at the Institute of Education and a strong advocate of Education for Sustainable Development. Sarah is a co-author of the University of Reading's Climate Education and Sustainability Initial Teacher Education framework and Deputy Team Leader of the submission regarding the framework which was awarded the Advance Higher Education Collaborative Award for Teaching Excellence 2024. Sarah has also co-authored journal articles regarding the embedding of the framework in the educational sector and is a member of and collaborator with the University of Reading's National Climate Education Action Plan (2021) network. Before working in higher education, Sarah worked as a senior leader in secondary schools and is inspired to develop young people's skills and knowledge across the curriculum in order to empower them to make global change for the future.

Dr Marc Turu Porcel is the Subject Leader for Initial Teacher Education at the University of Huddersfield's School of Education and Professional Development. Originally trained as a teacher and educational psychologist in Catalonia, he has taught across primary and secondary sectors. Prior to his current post, Marc served as a lecturer and course leader at Leeds Beckett University. His research interests focus on school staff wellbeing, professional development and organisational culture.

He has contributed to various publications, including chapters in *Becoming a Teacher-Researcher* (2024) and articles in journals such as *Learning and Teaching*. Marc actively contributes to the academic community as an advisory board member of the Academy of Education and Social Sciences Review and serves as a school governor.

Dr Jo Anna Reed Johnson's passion for education for sustainable development and systems thinking stems from her Engineering Master's degree from Cranfield University and PhD in Education for Sustainable Development from Manchester Metropolitan University. Her role as School Director of Climate and Sustainability at the Institute of Education has allowed her to be instrumental in the development of an initial teacher education framework for climate and sustainability education as part of the National Climate Education Action Plan (2021). She was the Team Leader for a National Collaborative Award for Teaching Excellence from the Advance Higher Education Academy in 2024 for Climate and Sustainability Education in Initial Teacher Education. Jo Anna has published extensively within journals, conference publications and practitioner-focused texts.

Malcolm Richards is a Senior Lecturer in Education and co-lead of UWE Bristol's Equity in Education research strand. His research interests include schooling in rural areas, critical pedagogies, funds of identity methodologies, anti-racism and social justice in education, Global Majority people, experiences and cultures in teaching, and international approaches in anti-racist teacher education and development.

Simon C. Ripley is a Lecturer of Education at the University of Sunderland with over 25 years of experience in all phases of education. He focuses on improving outcomes for learners with special educational needs and disabilities (SEND) and those categorised as 'disadvantaged'. Simon is an advocate of social justice and its role in education. He has extensive experience in school leadership, including improving the quality of teaching and learning, and as Headteacher of an all-age special school. He is currently working towards his Doctorate, which focuses on classroom interactions between teachers and learners with SEND. Simon is proudly neurodivergent, a fact actively reflected in his work and approach to education.

Rachel Sidoli is a part-time Curriculum Tutor with the Primary PGCE Wales team at the Open University and a primary practitioner with 20 years of classroom experience. She currently serves as her school's Humanities lead and Eco-schools coordinator. Academically, Rachel holds a degree in Ancient History and Philosophy, an MA in the History of Philosophy (specialising in political and ethical theory) and a further MA in English Studies. She is currently pursuing a Professional Doctorate in Education, researching the enactment of subsidiarity within the Curriculum for Wales framework. Since joining the OU, she has contributed to an international handbook chapter on literacy teaching and a BERA blog on teacher and pupil mental health.

Eilidh Slattery is a Lecturer in Arts Education at the Royal Conservatoire of Scotland. Her research focuses on supporting primary teachers to develop their use of dance and creative movement. She received Athenaeum Award funding for a large-scale project exploring teachers' experiences with dance education in Scottish primary schools. Eilidh trained as a dancer and dance teacher before qualifying as a primary school teacher. In primary education, she held roles including class teacher, specialist teacher, principal teacher and acting headteacher, while also delivering dance-focused professional learning. Before joining the Royal Conservatoire of Scotland in 2019, Eilidh was a Lecturer in Teacher Education at the University of Dundee, working across Initial Primary Teacher Education programmes.

Teresa Smith is a Lecturer on Initial Teacher Education courses at the University of East Anglia. She holds lead responsibility for Primary Art and Design and is the Lead Tutor for Professional Studies, SEND and Inclusion. Previously, Teresa was a class teacher in Norfolk, specialising in primary art education, an area she honed through museum and gallery education roles. She is a strong advocate for art's power to reach and include all children and maintains close links with gallery education departments. Her research focuses on creativity in the primary classroom, the use of artists and galleries in schools, and the concept of artist–researcher–teacher identity explored through her personal art practice, as well as her teaching.

Reece Sohdi began his career in education after earning a degree in Performing Arts, developing a deep appreciation for the power of creativity, self-expression and storytelling in learning. Before becoming a teacher educator, he worked in educational and community settings, using drama, movement and music to build confidence and communication in children and young people. He has a particular passion for supporting learners with SEND, developing inclusive, play-based approaches that centre creativity. In his current role as a Senior Lecturer in Initial Teacher Education, he supports trainee teachers in embedding creative, inclusive and learner-led pedagogies. His work focuses on the intersection of performing arts, social justice and communication, emphasising fostering voice, self-regulation and wellbeing through creative expression.

Joanne Stuart is a Headteacher and Director of Trust Improvement at Tees Valley Education in the North East. She is dedicated to improving teaching and learning, with a love of English in particular, and has over 20 years of experience. She is passionate about making a difference to children's lives and strives to make the world a little better than how she found it! Joanne is a Trustee in another MAT and works alongside a number of organisations to support system change.

Emma Thomas is a Senior Lecturer at UWE and a specialist in primary humanities. She teaches across undergraduate and postgraduate teacher training programmes and is the co-founder of the Joy Trail curriculum model. Her research centres on Black joy, where she works to disrupt dominant narratives about people, places and spaces. Having recently completed her Master's in Education, which explored 'joyful encounters with social justice projects', she is now undertaking a Doctorate in Education. Emma also works as an educational consultant, supporting schools to design bespoke curricula rooted in local contexts, community heritages and meaningful place-based learning.

Dr Karan Vickers-Hulse is Associate Director of Education at UWE Bristol with expertise in initial teacher education, particularly professional identity, equity and social justice. Her current research examines the experiences of pre-service teachers from minoritised groups, focusing on how race, sexuality, disability, neurodiversity and gender identity intersect in training and school placements. She is also researching how to embed social and emotional learning into ITE. Active in anti-racist education and social justice research, she publishes on identity, praxis and curriculum reform. Through teaching and leadership, she promotes reflective, equity-driven practices that support teacher resilience and challenge systemic inequalities.

Dr Sarah Whitehouse is a Senior Lecturer at UWE Bristol and Programme Leader for the International Doctorate in Education. She specialises in the teaching of sensitive and controversial issues, with research grounded in anti-racist practice and educational equity. An expert in primary geography and history, she contributes widely to national and international debates, publications and projects in these fields. Sarah is an active researcher and experienced doctoral supervisor, supporting EdD and PhD students in developing critical, creative and transformative approaches to educational research. Her work focuses on leadership, social justice and embedding anti-racist and inclusive practices across educational systems.

Dr Jordan Wintle is the Associate Head of the School of Education, Health and Science at the University of Gloucestershire. He brings nine years of experience in physical education (PE) teaching and 12 years in teacher education, having worked across primary and secondary settings to promote inclusive and innovative practice. Jordan's doctoral research explored the implementation of meaningful PE and curriculum change in UK schools, emphasising features like fun, choice, challenge and relevance to shape positive pupil experiences, especially for those traditionally marginalised in PE. Dr Wintle regularly contributes to practitioner development, national conferences, peer-reviewed publications and policy conversations, bridging research and practice to help educators design purposeful learning experiences that build physical literacy and foster a lifelong connection to movement.

Elizabeth Yeomans is a Senior Lecturer at Liverpool John Moores University in the School of Education and the Subject Lead for Religious Education. She teaches both undergraduate and postgraduate students on the primary education programmes. Before becoming a lecturer, she was a primary school teacher and a Lead Teacher in RE, supporting local schools with curriculum planning and teaching. She has always had an interest in RE and social justice, studying Theology for her BA at the University of Nottingham and completing a Master of Arts in Education with the Open University. She is a member of the Liverpool Institute for Education, and an Open University Master's Affiliate. Lizzie is passionate about supporting student teachers to become dialogic and trauma-informed primary teachers.

PART 1

UNDERSTANDING SUBJECT KNOWLEDGE

1
DEVELOPING SUBJECT KNOWLEDGE: AN INTRODUCTION

JEN AGGLETON

Developing children's knowledge is one of the fundamental purposes of primary education. However, the process of developing that knowledge is far from simple. The practice of education is a complex one, where educators continually make choices about what knowledge their learners will explore, how they will introduce that knowledge and how they will respond to individual children and the context that they are working in. While this can seem like a daunting prospect, especially for those new to educational practice, it is also an extremely exciting one. Whether you are working within a rigid formal school curriculum with high levels of guidance and requirements, creating your own curriculum from scratch, or somewhere in between, all educators have agency to make choices about what and how they will teach, and those choices matter. Enabling a child's learning is a gift, both to the child, and to the educator.

You may have noticed that this book is not simply about *subject knowledge*, but *developing subject knowledge*. The focus here is on the action of development. This means exploring both what knowledge to teach and how educators can develop the subject knowledge of learners and themselves. These facets are inherently intertwined.

Education scholar Robin Alexander (2004) identified that in order to make pedagogical decisions (decisions about how to teach), educators draw on a range of knowledge: their knowledge about subjects and how to teach them, of the curriculum they are teaching in, of assessment and of how children learn. To this I would add that educators also draw on their own values – what they believe is important both in terms of what children learn and how children should experience education. These values influence everything from the elements of subjects that are prioritised, to the resources used and the unspoken expectations of the hidden curriculum, such as when children are allowed to express their views or how they should behave.

On top of all this, none of these elements is stable. Educators constantly respond to the continually changing needs of individual learners; the financial and managerial contexts in which they work; dynamic local and global events such as climate change, conflict and technological breakthroughs; changing governments and national curricula; and the constant progress of human knowledge, which means that subject knowledge development is never complete. All these factors impact on the choices educators make about how to develop subject knowledge and what knowledge to teach, as represented in Figure 1.1.

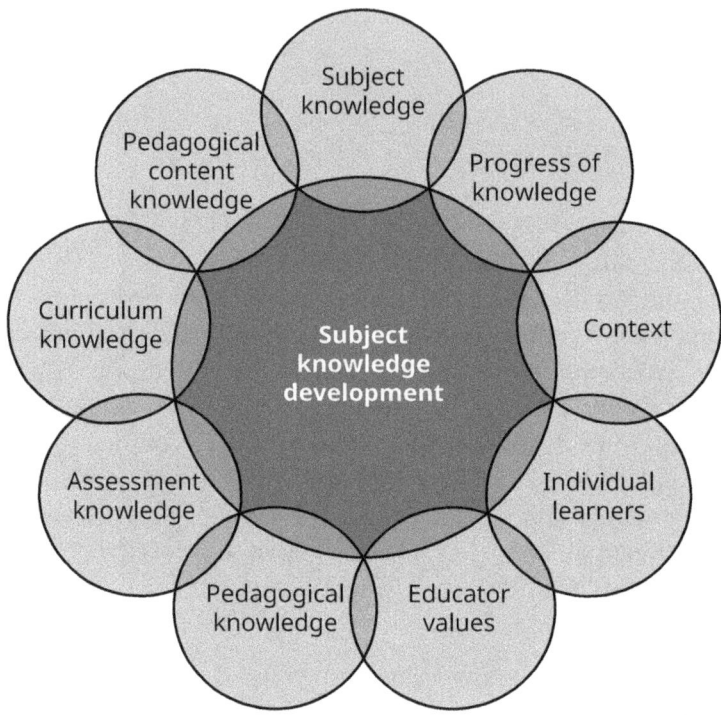

Figure 1.1   Subject knowledge development

Reflecting these different facets, within this book you will find a range of approaches to the development of subject knowledge. These approaches engage with different elements of the knowledge development process, and the unique requirements of different subjects. Different types of knowledge require different approaches to teaching, as do different learners and different contexts. Therefore, as an educator you will always need to adapt your teaching to your own circumstances. Reflection questions in each chapter will help you with this process by encouraging you to engage critically with the ideas presented. You will also find a number of case studies, through which you can explore how these ideas may be put into practice and consider what could work in your own setting.

Just as with educational practice, the writing of the authors in this book is informed by their own perspectives, including their professional expertise, their extensive knowledge of research and practice, and the values they hold. You can read about the expertise of the authors in their biographies, and this information may help you to better understand the perspectives they are writing from. All of the chapters have a strong educational research evidence base. However, a crucial principle of educational practice is that there is no single correct way to teach. One of the most valuable things you can do as an educator is to explore a range of different perspectives and approaches, be open to debate and new ideas, and use these to continually develop your own values, perspectives and practice. I therefore recommend you consider these chapters as a 'jumping off point', from where you can explore topics further if you so choose. You will find recommended further reading in each chapter to help you to progress with your explorations.

Part 1 of this book explores not individual subjects, but broad themes which are crucial to the development of subject knowledge. There are chapters on creating curricula that are poverty-informed or anti-racist, developing the knowledge of children with special educational needs and disabilities, and about how interactions can be used effectively to develop subject knowledge. These chapters reflect the importance of ensuring we view the children we teach as people, rather than as empty vessels into which we impart knowledge (Freire, 2000). Alongside this, it is crucial to acknowledge that teaching practice does not happen in isolation. I often hear people making a distinction between 'school' and 'real life', but this divide does not exist. Our schools are part of our communities, and what and how we choose to teach both responds to and has impacts beyond the learners in front of us into society and beyond. Education is never neutral, so as educators we have a professional responsibility to be mindful of the choices we make and the implications of these choices. We also have the great privilege of being part of a profession with the potential to contribute to the transformation of the lives of our learners, communities and societies for the better. Regardless of whether you are an experienced educator or just taking your first steps into educational practice, these chapters offer thought-provoking insights into how your professional decision-making can support children to flourish.

While formal curricula may have set guidance about which knowledge should be 'covered' in individual subjects or areas of learning, in practice the development of knowledge does not respect these boundaries. Children bring their own knowledge, interests, questions and challenges to education, and so do educators. Learning is a social process that, at its best, is co-constructed between learners and educators. Educators frequently learn as much from the children they teach, and the communities they work in, as the children learn from the educators. For that reason, while this book has a focus on primary education within the four nations of the UK, reflecting the locational expertise of the contributors, it does not simply reflect current statutory curricula for those nations. Rather, the authors have taken a broader view, presenting what they believe to be the key *content knowledge* (sometimes called substantive knowledge), *practical knowledge* (sometimes called disciplinary knowledge or skills) and *pedagogical content knowledge* (knowledge of how to teach a subject) important to teaching their subject at the primary educational phase.

In Part 2, you will find chapters covering a range of subjects. Many of these are included in national curricula, and there are also chapters covering subjects which might not be statutorily required, but are, nonetheless, highly important to living well within our world. These include climate and sustainability education, and citizenship and ethics. Recognising the value of both discrete and interdisciplinary approaches to education, you will also find plenty of information on links between content in different subjects, or how pedagogies associated with specific subjects can be used to great effect in others. While the chapters in Part 2 are organised into individual subjects for ease of access to information, which you can dip in and out of at need, you may also find it useful to read across chapters and identify common themes, concepts and principles that can inform how you approach your practice.

While many chapters make links to English or mathematics, you will not find specific chapters dedicated to these subjects. This is not because these are not important and useful subjects, but rather a recognition of their currently privileged position within teacher education and educational publishing. Trainee teachers usually spend many hours exploring these subjects with experts, and there are numerous fantastic books on developing subject knowledge in English and maths. It is often the case that far less time and publishing space are given to other curriculum subjects, but this does not mean that those subjects are not equally valuable. There is just as much joy to be found in seeing the outcome of a science experiment or scoring a goal in PE as there is in sharing a story or solving a mathematical equation. Through the exploration of languages, religious education and the arts, we can learn more about ourselves and the other people we share the planet with, improving understanding, empathy and communication. Studying the humanities can help us learn how to make decisions about how to live in our own time and place, while a knowledge of digital technologies, health and wellbeing, and design can give us the tools we need to achieve our goals. There are many other subjects that could have been included here, but that would have resulted in a far longer (and much more expensive!) book. In light of those practical decisions, it felt only right that English and maths should cede their space to other topics.

No matter how much we learn, there is always more to know. Human knowledge is vast and constantly evolving – therefore continuing to develop your own subject knowledge is a key responsibility for any educator. It is also one of the great joys of teaching that we have not only the opportunity, but also the expectation to continually learn new things. In the final part of this book, you will find a chapter introducing the *subject knowledge development cycle*. This cycle is a reflective tool you can use to assist you in your onward learning journey. You can use it to identify when and why you might need to develop your knowledge further, what processes and resources you can use to develop that knowledge effectively and how to assess the impact of that new knowledge on yourself, your practice and the children you teach.

It is both a great delight and a challenge of primary education that we work with children across a wide range of curriculum subjects. While this can at times feel intimidating, it also enables us to feed the curiosity that both we and our learners have about the world, and to develop our knowledge in ways that are both professionally and personally satisfying.

I hope that you will find this book a useful and inspiring tool to inform your practice, helping you to use your agency as an educator to make decisions about what subject knowledge to teach, and how to teach it. These choices have a great impact on our learners and on our societies, and you are at the heart of that transformational process.

REFERENCES

Alexander, R. (2004). Still no pedagogy? Principle, pragmatism and compliance in primary education. *Cambridge Journal of Education*, *34*(1), 7–34.

Freire, P. (2000). *Pedagogy of the oppressed: Thirtieth anniversary edition* (M. B. Ramos, Trans.). Bloomsbury. (Original work published 1968.)

2

POVERTY-INFORMED PRIMARY CURRICULUM: A PRACTICAL GUIDE FOR EDUCATORS

SEAN HARRIS AND JOANNE STUART

THIS CHAPTER

This chapter explores the ideas that:

- *poverty and inequality are growing*: they can impact curriculum access, opportunity and the experience of children throughout it

- *curriculum is a social and political force*: schools can use curriculum to challenge structural inequality and respond to poverty

- *an equitable curriculum is needed*: educators need to consider what pupils know and how poverty shapes learning; an equitable curriculum is possible and is important.

KEY TERMS FOR THIS CHAPTER

Equity: in the curriculum means recognising that not all pupils start from the same place and taking action to address that. Unlike equality, which offers the same to everyone, equity responds to individual and community needs by removing barriers and providing targeted support. It is about designing learning and opportunity in ways that are fair, just and inclusive, especially for those who face systemic poverty-related barriers to learning.

Co-production: a relational process where professionals, learners, families and communities can work together as equal partners to design, deliver and refine practices. It values lived experience and expertise equally, helping to build trust, shared ownership and more responsive solutions. In curriculum development, co-production can help ensure that what is taught is relevant, respectful and rooted in specific contexts.

Misconception: misunderstandings or incomplete knowledge held by pupils (or sometimes educators) that can distort further learning. In the context of poverty, misconceptions can also refer to deficit narratives, such as the assumption that low-income families lack aspiration, which can shape curriculum choices, expectations and interactions in negative ways. Tackling misconceptions, we argue, is both a pedagogical priority for educators and a social justice imperative.

Poverty: a plethora of research and literature has attempted to define poverty. For the purpose of this chapter and in our work as educators, we state that poverty should be seen as more than a lack of income. Poverty encompasses the constrained access to material resources, opportunities and experiences needed to participate fully in society and also in curriculum. This can also be compounded by intergenerational hardship, limited access to housing, transport and nutrition, and by persistent structural inequalities. Poverty restricts what feels possible, not what is hoped for.

Poverty-related barriers to learning: we use this term to define the challenges that arise when children and young people experience the effects of poverty on their ability to engage fully in curriculum and education. Examples can include limited access to food and nutrition, unstable housing, reduced access to transport, restricted digital access, unmet physical or mental health needs and fewer opportunities for enrichment. These barriers are sometimes invisible in curriculum planning, yet they can profoundly shape what pupils can attend to. Addressing them requires educators and curriculum leaders to understand the structural nature of poverty and design learning with inclusion, access and support throughout curriculum.

INTRODUCTION

This chapter is designed around four interwoven threads that together build a rationale for, and practical guide to, a poverty-informed curriculum. These threads are:

- misconceptions and knowledge gaps;

- enrichment and equity;

- curriculum as civil and social architecture;

- responding to context and lived experience.

Each of these threads offers a distinct lens through which to consider how curriculum can be shaped to meet the needs of pupils experiencing poverty. However, it is important to recognise that a truly equitable curriculum cannot be developed in isolation. It must be informed by the wider themes explored across this book as a whole and grounded in a deep understanding of individual contexts and learners. No single chapter can fully capture the complexity of this topic. Instead, this contribution should be seen as part of a broader, ongoing conversation; one that requires sustained reflection, collaboration and a commitment to justice in curriculum design and delivery.

Rather than offering a one-size-fits-all approach, in this chapter we draw on case studies, practitioner insights and research from the Tees Valley Education academies to show how these principles are brought to life in real-world contexts. Our aim is to support you to reflect on how these principles and processes have been applied elsewhere – and to inspire you to adapt and apply these approaches within your own practice. We want to help readers to consider how others have applied the principles and processes explored in much of this chapter. We encourage you to engage reflectively with each thread; considering how the concepts might resonate within your own context, challenge assumptions, or inspire different approaches. The chapter is intentionally bespoke in its design, recognising that poverty and curriculum are experienced differently in different contexts. Our aim is not to prescribe, but to provoke and guide purposeful curriculum thinking rooted in justice and care, especially for pupils facing poverty-related barriers to learning.

WHY A POVERTY-INFORMED CURRICULUM IS NEEDED

Curriculum is not neutral. It is never just a compilation of knowledge or a sequence of lessons; it can be a cultural, social and political force. In the context of growing and enduring inequalities, the curriculum becomes one of the most powerful levers schools have to create opportunity, challenge structural injustice and respond meaningfully to the lived realities of poverty. This chapter begins with a call to rethink what we teach, how we teach it and who we imagine our curriculum is for.

Recent years have seen a consistent rise in poverty and disadvantage across many communities in the UK and globally. However, rather than anchoring this chapter in the most current datasets, which are often rapidly outdated, contested, or limited in scope, we made a deliberate choice not to cite specific figures. This is not to underplay the urgency of the issue, but to emphasise the importance of local understanding and contexts. Researchers, school leaders, and curriculum designers should access and interpret data with care, recognising its nuances and caveats within the specific contexts they serve. This is especially important when considering the value and place of curriculum in schools.

Poverty is more than a datapoint. It cannot be neatly captured by eligibility thresholds or funding criteria. It is dynamic, lived and deeply personal; shaped by geography, identity, policy and time. It influences how children and young people begin their day, how they engage with learning and how they see themselves reflected in curriculum both in schools and throughout other educational settings. Yet, for too long, educational discourse has leaned on reductive proxies to attempt to understand and respond to poverty and disadvantage, such as the use of free school meals and pupil premium eligibility in England and Wales. While these indicators may offer a starting point, they risk flattening the complexity of disadvantage and distancing educators from the learners behind the categories. Various commentators have highlighted the limitations of using criteria and datasets such as these as a core proxy for identifying and responding to poverty across education settings (Gorard, 2016; Montacute and Cullinane, 2021; Rowland, 2021). To respond meaningfully to poverty in education, educators must go beyond the binary of 'eligible' or 'not eligible'. This, of course, is not straightforward as educators must develop a deeper, more relational understanding –one that sees poverty in its local and lived dimensions. Only then can educators begin to shape a curriculum that speaks to the realities of children's lives, rather than one that merely acknowledges their absence from national averages or attainment gaps. Sobel (2018) argues that teachers should view the attainment gap through the lens of their school's wider community, recognising that effective responses emerge when schools develop community-focused approaches tailored to their local context.

One clear way to do this is to think deliberately about poverty and curriculum – not only in terms of design or intent, but in its human impact. For pupils experiencing poverty, curriculum can widen the gap or work to close it. It can reproduce the inequalities of the outside world or offer counter-narratives that validate lived experiences and open up possibilities. When shaped with care, with context and justice at its core, curriculum becomes a site of hope in schools and across classrooms.

This chapter does not rehearse the latest poverty statistics. Instead, it is anchored in the belief that those working in and with schools already know that poverty is real and urgent in the communities that they serve. What is needed is shared language, informed strategies and practical examples that help educators and curriculum leaders to shape a curriculum responsive to the challenges pupils face, especially those in poverty or from low-income backgrounds. Central to this is rejecting deficit narratives and recognising the assets, knowledge and potential that pupils facing poverty can bring with them.

By positioning the curriculum as a place where equity can be enacted, this chapter invites teachers and leaders to reflect on how poverty is experienced within their setting and how curriculum decisions can either entrench or disrupt that experience. It begins with a simple but provocative premise: that what we choose to teach, and how we teach it, matters profoundly in the lives of our pupils. This is especially important for children and young people facing poverty and inequality.

WHAT RESEARCH AND EVIDENCE SUGGEST

This section distils a selection of research and theory that has shaped our approach to building a poverty-informed curriculum. It is not an exhaustive literature review, nor is it intended to cover all available evidence on curriculum and poverty. Instead, it offers a curated overview of key ideas and frameworks that have influenced our work as school and curriculum leaders. We encourage readers to explore the wider body of literature in more depth and to critically engage with how research can inform, not dictate, practice.

WILIAM (2013): *PRINCIPLED CURRICULUM DESIGN*

Dylan Wiliam explores the purposes of curriculum and education in his work. He outlines four broad aims of education and curriculum intent:

- *personal empowerment*: helping individuals live fulfilling lives;

- *cultural transmission*: passing on the best that has been thought and said;

- *preparation for employment*: equipping pupils for the labour market;

- *preparation for democratic citizenship*: fostering engagement and critical thinking.

Wiliam argues that curriculum decisions inevitably prioritise one or more of these aims, whether consciously or unconsciously. Therefore, educators must be intentional about what and whom their curriculum serves, especially in contexts of structural inequality.

Of course, this is no straightforward task. However, we have found Wiliam's thinking useful in helping us consider whose knowledge and experiences are central to the curriculum and whose are omitted. We explore this further in the case studies in this chapter.

Another important thread in Wiliam's thinking is the integration of democratic and participatory learning to support agency and civic identity. For Wiliam, this can be an important outcome of effective curriculum design and delivery. We have also found it a useful caution against over-emphasising 'economic productivity' as the main driver of curriculum, particularly in schools serving areas of significant poverty where children face poverty-related barriers to learning.

MYATT (2018): *GALLIMAUFRY TO COHERENCE*

Mary Myatt critiques curriculum that feels like a 'gallimaufry', a confused jumble, and makes a compelling case for a more structured, knowledge-rich approach that builds deep understanding over time. Her work is especially valuable in emphasising that curriculum must be ambitious for all learners. Myatt also highlights the importance of revisiting and deepening key concepts and knowledge regularly, reminding educators to resist the temptation to view curriculum or content as ever 'done' or 'complete'.

Myatt argues that teachers and educators need intentional time and space to reflect on curriculum content, not just focus on lesson delivery. At the heart of her approach is a belief in the dignity of children and the moral responsibility educators have to treat pupils as capable thinkers throughout the curriculum journey.

This research has helped to shape our thinking in designing curriculum with poverty in mind. It challenges educators to be wary of fragmented or superficial curricula that fail to foster lasting depth and understanding. There is a natural temptation to fill the curriculum with a wide range of topics, activities and ideas, but Myatt's work serves as a valuable reminder that learning is unlikely to stick or hold meaning unless it is underpinned by thoughtful planning, careful sequencing and purposeful design.

Importantly, Myatt's work also infers caution against equating equity with simplification. An equitable curriculum is not about making learning easier or diluted for pupils facing barriers such as poverty, disadvantage, or additional needs. Rather, it is about ensuring all children, including those facing poverty-related barriers to learning, have access to the same ambitious content as their peers.

Myatt's work is also helpful in highlighting the importance of supporting teachers – particularly those newer to the profession – to build professional confidence in sequencing learning and articulating the rationale behind it: why this knowledge, why now? It underscores the need to strengthen coherence between curriculum, pedagogy and assessment in order to reduce the hidden barriers that can disproportionately affect disadvantaged learners.

JENSEN (2009): *TEACHING WITH POVERTY IN MIND*

Poverty is not simply a social or economic issue; it can influence all aspects of a child's life, including dimensions such as health, relationships, emotional wellbeing and learning. Recent research indicates that poverty can have an impact on cognitive development and the learning brain. However, it is vital to approach this body of research with care and nuance. Not every child experiencing poverty will be impacted in the same way. The effects of persistent poverty and inequality are shaped by a complex interaction of factors including individual resilience, family support, cultural context and wider community influences.

The work of Eric Jensen is a useful starting point in that it draws together insights from neuroscience, psychology and classroom research to explore how poverty can impact brain development and, consequently, learning. Educators should be cautious about assuming that all children experiencing poverty will show the same patterns of development or that a single aspect of poverty is solely responsible. Differences in language, reading and learning are more often the result of a complex mix of factors and the length of time children are exposed to them, rather than poverty in isolation. Recognising this complexity helps ensure responses are thoughtful, individualised and rooted in understanding rather than assumption.

Jensen argues that educators must understand the neurological and environmental impacts of poverty, such as chronic stress, disrupted attachment, poor nutrition and limited language exposure, not as fixed deficits but as challenges that schools can help to mitigate. Insights include how sustained stress can impact working memory and how limited sleep and nutrition can limit executive functioning. Jensen also explored how limited early language experiences can suppress vocabulary and verbal reasoning development. These factors combine to make self-regulation, focus and academic stamina harder for many children facing poverty – not due to lack of ability, but due to systemic barriers beyond their control.

Jensen advocates for what he calls 'brain-friendly' classrooms and curriculum, where safety, consistency, high expectations and relational warmth support the neuroplasticity and resilience of pupils affected by poverty. He also highlights the value of purposeful learning environments as a means of actively reversing some of the negative impacts of early adversity.

In relation to curriculum and poverty, this might mean embedding overexposure to difficult or complex concepts and subject knowledge. Planned repetition and retrieval of complex content can support pupils with memory and recall. The research is useful for advocating the need for carefully pacing new learning and working hard as educators to avoid cognitive overload, particularly when introducing unfamiliar knowledge to pupils that educators know face poverty-related barriers to learning. The research is also useful for reminding school and curriculum leaders to avoid deficit thinking, recognising that difficulties with regulation or curriculum engagement can stem from unmet needs as opposed to simply being a case of apathy or poor motivation in pupils. Jensen's work is also useful for helping educators avoid simplistic or punitive responses to poverty. Instead, it encourages a practical and optimistic mindset for educators. Curriculum and classroom pedagogy can be leveraged to foster equity and inclusion.

TREANOR (2017): CAN WE PUT THE POVERTY OF ASPIRATION TO BED NOW?

Morag Treanor's (2017) analysis of data from the *Growing Up in Scotland* study provides a powerful counter to the myth that families living in poverty lack aspiration. Drawing on longitudinal data across multiple cohorts, the research examined parents' hopes for their children's futures, their confidence in influencing their children's education and the impact of time spent in poverty on educational experiences.

This research is useful for illustrating how parents across all income levels often want the best for their children. However, those facing persistent poverty and hardships are often less familiar with available opportunities or how to support their children in accessing them. This gap is not a reflection of low ambition, but rather of limited access to the networks, information and resources that support educational and life success. Treanor concludes that the idea of a *poverty of aspiration* is a harmful myth. It shifts responsibility for educational outcomes away from government, policy-makers and schools and onto families and young people themselves. Rather than tackling the structural causes of inequality, the myth reinforces a deficit view that blames those experiencing hardship.

In terms of curriculum and pedagogy, we have found it helpful to use Treanor's work as a caution against basing curriculum intent or design on myths such as the idea that the communities we serve have inherently low aspirations or ambitions. Treanor's research highlights that poverty restricts what feels possible, not what is hoped for. This distinction matters, especially for educators responsible for designing and delivering curriculum knowledge. If educators assume a lack of ambition, they may offer a narrowed or overly remedial curriculum, rather than one that opens doors and builds opportunity.

A poverty-informed curriculum should therefore be deliberately expansive, exposing pupils to powerful knowledge, diverse role models and opportunities that extend beyond their immediate experiences. It should equip learners and families with the language, understanding and confidence to navigate systems, including post-16 pathways, that may otherwise feel out of reach. The earlier we are able to do this in education, the better. Treanor's work is also helpful in reminding educators of the need to engage with families rather than making assumptions, ensuring that our curriculum is built on equity rather than myths or misconceptions about what low-income families or children do or do not have.

In the sections that follow, we explore how the research discussed above can inform both the design and delivery of curriculum. We make no claim that these are quick fixes or silver bullet solutions. Rather, we present them as practical mechanisms that, when used alongside other approaches outlined in this book, can help to ensure fairer, more equitable access to the curriculum, particularly for pupils experiencing poverty-related barriers to learning.

REFLECTION 2.1

- What assumptions, spoken or unspoken, do you think exist in society about children, young people and families experiencing poverty?

- How might these assumptions shape how learning, behaviour, or 'potential' are perceived in your context or the type of education settings you want to serve?

- Where might curriculum, resources or activities unintentionally reinforce deficit narratives?

CASE STUDY: TEES VALLEY EDUCATION – MISCONCEPTIONS AND EQUITABLE CURRICULUM ACCESS

Misconceptions are not just accidental errors that a pupil will make; they can be deeply rooted, shaped by experience, prior knowledge and social context.

In our work with Tees Valley Education (TVEd), a multi-academy trust in the North East of England, we have explored how poverty-related barriers can intersect with learning and how curiosity, rather than assumption, can help educators understand and respond to these challenges more effectively through curriculum design and delivery. This work is based on specific action research that was developed with generous funding from SHINE, a charity based in the North of England that supports educators to innovate their own ideas for tackling educational disadvantage in schools. This work has been grounded in the belief that poverty does not cause misconceptions, but it can create conditions in which misconceptions are harder to identify and address, especially if curriculum is not designed with these challenges in mind.

Teachers across TVEd primary schools collaborated with Evidence Based Education (EBE) and the Chartered College of Teaching through the *Let Teachers SHINE* programme. This £18,000 action research grant supported teachers to investigate the nature and origins of misconceptions, and how curriculum, pedagogy and professional learning might better anticipate and respond to them. The aim of the research was to support teachers and pupils to understand *why* learners misunderstand and support them to plan accordingly, particularly when working with pupils who may face poverty-related barriers to learning.

WHY MISCONCEPTIONS MATTER IN CURRICULUM DESIGN

A core insight from this work has been the importance of proactively building common and persistent misconceptions into curriculum planning, not as an afterthought, but as part of the fabric of high-quality instructional design. Using insights from lessons and discussions with pupils, teachers were supported to anticipate where pupils might struggle and co-create strategies for clarifying and revisiting complex ideas.

Misconceptions were explored not as failures, but as opportunities for deeper understanding.

This was particularly powerful when paired with structured professional development in schools. Through workshops, coaching and enquiry cycles, teachers developed habits of asking:

- what might pupils misunderstand, and why?

- are there local, cultural, or socioeconomic factors influencing this?

- how can I teach this content more deliberately to avoid misinterpretation?

For example, in one case, a teacher planning a lesson on religious concepts used the Latin root *incarnatus* ('made flesh') to explain Christian theology. To make it memorable, they linked it to *chilli con carne*. It backfired. Pupils began associating the incarnation with chilli. Far from a trivial anecdote, this revealed how well-intentioned but oversimplified analogies can embed misconceptions, especially if pupils do not have the prior knowledge to correct or challenge them.

This experience prompted staff to rethink how language precision and cultural assumptions can influence meaning-making. Teachers were able to help illustrate that curriculum design must go beyond coverage and content, it must anticipate misinterpretation and build in clarity.

TACKLING POVERTY WITH CURIOSITY, NOT ASSUMPTION

Throughout the SHINE project, a recurring theme has been the danger of making assumptions about what pupils do or do not know, particularly when poverty is involved. For example, pupils from lower-income households may have had fewer opportunities to engage with certain vocabulary, visit specific historical sites, or access science enrichment. But this should not lead us to lower expectations or reduce complexity. Instead, it means we need to build in support that is deliberate, precise and rooted in what pupils bring with them.

A misconception-aware approach to curriculum design at TVEd includes:

- planning for preconceptions and common errors across subjects;

- including teacher-friendly prompts in lesson plans: e.g. 'Watch out for ...' or 'Likely misconceptions ...';

- using analogies and real-world links, but stress-testing them for clarity;

- pairing high challenge with structured scaffolds, particularly for pupils who may lack background knowledge but not ability.

This approach can benefit all pupils, but is particularly vital for pupils experiencing poverty, who may need more support in connecting new knowledge to prior experiences, or decoding abstract concepts that rely on assumed cultural capital.

SHARED LANGUAGE AND CONCEPTS

At TVEd, we have also been working to create a shared language and approach to misconceptions across classrooms. Through professional development, coaching sessions and action research, staff have begun building a shared repository of common misconceptions and strategies across subject areas. These are embedded into planning documents and staff resources, making it easier for teachers, especially early career teachers, to be responsive and confident in their delivery. This school-wide approach helps break down isolation, ensuring that the expertise of experienced colleagues is shared rather than siloed. It also reflects one of the most powerful lessons of the project in that curriculum design cannot be divorced from the realities of pupils' lives.

Too often, work around poverty and education can slip into deficit thinking, focusing on what children lack. This project has helped to flip that narrative in the Tees Valley and communities that TVEd serves. Rather than assuming poverty or disadvantage equates to disinterest or inability, we have seen how curiosity, shared enquiry and sensitive planning can further unlock understanding. It has supported curriculum leaders to be intentional about recognising that misconceptions are not simply problems to be fixed, but signals to be read – clues to how pupils are trying to make sense of the world around them.

Misconceptions are, in many ways, acts of curiosity. When we plan curriculum with that in mind, educators do not just correct errors, but are able to build richer, deeper and more meaningful learning experiences for every child. In doing so, educators help to make curriculum both accessible and equitable.

REFLECTION 2.2

- How has your thinking about the relationship between poverty and ambition changed after engaging with this chapter so far?

- In your role (or future role), how might you challenge deficit narratives and promote high expectations?

CASE STUDY: BRAMBLES PRIMARY ACADEMY – EQUITABLE CURRICULUM OPPORTUNITY

This case study provides an actionable example of how extracurricular opportunities can form a vital part of curriculum design and delivery, particularly in schools serving communities affected by poverty-related barriers to learning. It also highlights how such opportunities can be intentionally designed with equity in mind, ensuring that all children, regardless of income or background, can access and enjoy rich educational experiences. This is an important part of ensuring that children can access subject content and many of the broader opportunities explored in other chapters throughout this book.

At Brambles Primary Academy, part of TVEd, curriculum thinking goes beyond subject content as it does in many other settings. It also encompasses how children experience school and how social, cultural and economic barriers shape that day-to-day experience. One such example is the school's innovative approach to World Book Day, reimagined through a poverty-informed lens that has deepened engagement, belonging and inclusion.

THE COST OF EXTRACURRICULAR ACTIVITIES

Traditionally, World Book Day invites pupils to dress up as their favourite book characters, a joyful tradition, but one that can carry hidden costs. Shop-bought costumes and accessories can be expensive for low-income families, placing undue financial pressure on families, particularly amid growing costs in other areas of life. This can create barriers to participation, introduce stigma, or cause some children to miss out altogether.

As Headteacher Stuart Mayle puts it, 'It is our absolute responsibility to consider the impact this can have on our communities.' That sense of responsibility has motivated educators at Brambles Primary Academy to move beyond well-intentioned gestures and design an approach that aligned more fully with their curriculum intent and the realities of their community.

Rather than asking families to purchase costumes or dress up with homemade costumes, educators in the school provides each pupil with a plain white t-shirt and access to fabric markers – materials already available in school. Children are invited to design their own book-themed shirts at home, supported by their parents and carers, in the lead-up to World Book Day. It is important that this is implemented in such a way that it does not assume children have access to materials or resources at home. For example, children are invited to take home school resources if they would like to or complete t-shirts beyond the school day.

This small shift has helped educators to develop equitable and accessible opportunities in and beyond curriculum in several ways.

- *Curriculum integration*: pupils had to engage deeply with their chosen texts to represent them visually, enhancing reading comprehension, inference and expression. These are core components of the literacy and oracy curriculum provided in classrooms.

- *Equity by design*: every child receives the same materials, removing cost as a barrier and creating a level playing field where creativity, not money, defines the outcome of the project and learning.

- *Family engagement*: the initiative fosters strong home–school links, with many families enjoying the opportunity to work creatively with their children in ways that are meaningful and accessible. Parents and carers have applauded the opportunity for both the enjoyment that children get from it and the way in which school and curriculum leaders demonstrate care across it.

- *Whole-school coherence*: staff participated too, modelling creativity and belonging. The day is also linked to a shared whole-school text, the novel *Flotsam*, which allows for thematic connections in reading, writing, discussion and performance across year groups.

On average, school leaders spend just £475 in total on this opportunity. For this small amount, school and curriculum leaders are able to evolve World Book Day into a more inclusive, curriculum-rich and joyful experience for all pupils. This case study shows that curriculum equity is not only about what is taught, but also about how pupils experience and access the curriculum, both within and beyond the classroom. At Brambles Primary Academy, World Book Day became an extension of the reading curriculum, shaped by the school values and its understanding of the economic realities many families face.

Educators also demonstrate that poverty-informed curriculum thinking is not about reducing expectations or diluting content. It is about thoughtful and intentional design in such a way that the curriculum delivers rich experiences that are accessible to all, not just those who can afford them.

Confidence, one of the pupils involved in the project, says: 'It is such a fun day, and I felt like I really got to celebrate reading!'

REFLECTION 2.3

- To what extent are you currently considering poverty-related barriers explicitly in the curriculum design process? How might you ensure you do this in the future?
- Where in the teaching process do these conversations take place and who is in the room?
- How are these discussions and decisions shared with those in classrooms and other educational settings?

BEYOND CURRICULUM

As Christine Counsell (2018) writes:

> *Curriculum is all about power. Decisions about what knowledge to teach are an exercise of power and therefore a weighty ethical responsibility. What we choose to teach confers or denies power. To say that pupils should learn 'the best that has been thought and said' is never adequate. Start the conversation, and questions abound: 'Whose knowledge?'; 'Who decides on "best"?'*

Curriculum is never neutral. It is an expression of power, values and vision. It is shaped by the people and systems that design it and interpreted by those who deliver and experience it. In communities where poverty shapes the conditions of daily life, curriculum decisions take on even greater significance. They influence not only what children come to know, but what they come to believe is possible.

Throughout this chapter, we have explored how a poverty-informed approach to curriculum is not about lowering expectations or offering a diluted version of what others receive. Rather, it is about understanding the structural and systemic barriers that make access to learning inequitable – and then actively designing against them. This means creating curriculum that is ambitious, inclusive and rooted in the places it serves.

Curriculum context matters. It shapes language, identity, culture, opportunities and constraints. A curriculum that ignores the context it serves can risk rendering children invisible in their own classrooms. Conversely, a curriculum that recognises and values the richness of place can help pupils feel seen, known and capable of shaping their worlds. It can connect local context to wider narratives, validating lived experience while also expanding horizons.

But recognising place and context also comes with a responsibility. Poverty is not evenly distributed, and neither are resources, opportunities, or voices. Schools serving communities with poverty are often expected to do more with less, while contending with higher levels of need. A curriculum that is truly equitable must acknowledge this imbalance and actively work to counter it – not through deficit narratives or simplistic interventions, but through sustained, thoughtful and systemic responses.

This includes curriculum intent that refuses to pathologise poverty or simply assumes low aspiration in children or families. As Treanor reminds us, poverty restricts what feels possible, not what is hoped for. Curriculum, therefore, must be a means of expanding possibility, broadening what children can see, imagine and aim for. It should create routes to power *and* participation, offering all pupils the knowledge, skills and opportunity to navigate and shape their lives with agency and dignity. Some of these themes are explored further in other chapters across the breadth of this book.

REFLECTION 2.4

- If you are currently a practising educator, to what extent is your curriculum mapped against the poverty-related barriers pupils in your context most commonly face (e.g. food insecurity, transport access, digital exclusion)?

- Where is this well evidenced and/or seen?

- Where are the gaps?

- What cross-school or curriculum strategies might help?

FINAL THOUGHTS

A poverty-informed curriculum is an equity-focused curriculum; this work cannot happen in isolation. It must be part of a broader professional culture that values collaboration, co-production and continuous learning in schools and other educational settings. It requires listening to children and families, working with multi-agency partners, and drawing on the professional expertise of those closest to the context. It is not a single policy or curriculum plan, but a posture of humility, justice and hope.

This work is difficult. It resists shortcuts and demands long-term commitment. But it is also profoundly hopeful. When we attend to both the place we serve as educators and equity, curriculum becomes more than a vehicle for knowledge transmission, it becomes a form of care, a structure of possibility and a scaffold for belonging.

Educators and curriculum designers have the opportunity, and the responsibility, to be civil architects of such curricula; to reject false binaries between excellence or equity; to embed justice into the architecture of learning; to ensure that every child, regardless of background or postcode, can encounter a curriculum that not only teaches them about the world, but shows them they have a place in shaping it.

REFLECTION 2.5

- If you are aiming to be an education practitioner in the future, how might you gain the evidence you need to ensure you are addressing the poverty-related barriers faced by children?

- Consider a specific subject or unit of study in the curriculum. In what ways does the curriculum reflect the local place, history and community you and any learners you teach are part of, without limiting access to wider knowledge, culture and opportunities?

FURTHER READING AND RESOURCES

Evidence Based Education (EBE) (2020). *The great teaching toolkit: Evidence review*. EBE.

The book is an evidence-based review that synthesises research on teacher effectiveness to provide a *model for great teaching* built around four key dimensions that enhance student learning.

Harris, S. and Morley, K. (2025). *Tackling POVERTY AND DISADVANTAGE IN SCHOOLS*. Bloomsbury.

This book offers practical, research-based strategies for educators and school leaders to understand and combat the complex challenges of poverty and disadvantage across the whole school, the classroom and the wider community.

Mazzoli Smith, L. and Todd, L. (2016). *Poverty-proofing the school day: Evaluation and development report*. Newcastle University, Research Centre for Learning and Teaching.

The book discusses an audit process that removes obstacles to learning by identifying and changing unintentional school practices that stigmatise or financially burden students living in poverty.

Rowland, M. (2021). *Addressing educational disadvantage in schools and colleges: The Essex way*. Unity Research School and Essex County Council.

The book sets out an evidence-based strategy (the Essex Way) for school leaders and staff to improve the learning experiences and future prospects of disadvantaged students.

Harris, S. That Poverty Guy. https://thatpovertyguy.substack.com/

Offers evidence-informed, practical guidance and passionate commentary for educators and leaders on addressing social disadvantage and tackling educational inequality in schools.

Poverty Unpacked: Podcast Episode #48: Tackling poverty and disadvantage in schools. https://poverty-unpacked.org/2025/08/29/episode-48-tackling-poverty-and-disadvantage-in-schools/

The Poverty Unpacked podcast explores the hidden emotional, social and policy-related dimensions of poverty through conversations with researchers, activists and those with lived experience, challenging common misconceptions.

REFERENCES

Counsell, C. (2018). Taking curriculum seriously. *Impact*, *12*, September. Chartered College of Teaching. https://my.chartered.college/impact_article/taking-curriculum-seriously/

Gorard, S. (2016). A cautionary note on measuring the pupil premium attainment gap in England. *British Journal of Education, Society and Behavioural Science*, *14*(2), 1–9.

Jensen, E. (2009). *Teaching with poverty in mind: What being poor does to kids' brains and what schools can do about it.* ASCD.

Montacute, R. and Cullinane, C. (2021). *Learning in lockdown: Research brief.* The Sutton Trust.

Myatt, M. (2018). *The curriculum: Gallimaufry to coherence.* John Catt Educational.

Sobel, D. (2018). *Narrowing the attainment gap: A handbook for schools.* Bloomsbury.

Treanor, M. C. (2017). *Growing up in Scotland: Briefing 91.* Centre for Research on Families and Relationships.

Wiliam, D. (2013). *Principled curriculum design.* SSAT.

3
SUBJECT KNOWLEDGE AND THE ANTI-RACIST CURRICULUM

KARAN VICKERS-HULSE, MALCOLM RICHARDS, SARAH WHITEHOUSE AND JANE CARTER

THIS CHAPTER

This chapter explores the ideas that:

- challenge the myth of subject knowledge as neutral
- provide a practical framework for embedding anti-racist pedagogy across primary subjects
- promote a relational, community-centred and justice-oriented approach to subject knowledge and curriculum development.

KEY TERMS FOR THIS CHAPTER

Critical race theory (CRT): a way of thinking about racism that sees it as built into systems (laws, schools, policies), not just individual prejudice.

Funds of knowledge: the skills, knowledges, habits and practices learners bring from home and community. These are assets that educators can draw on to connect learning to learners' lives.

Equality: giving everyone the same resources or opportunities (treating all equally).

Equity: giving resources or support according to need, so that all learners can achieve comparable outcomes (i.e. fairness, not sameness).

Social justice: a goal and orientation for schooling in which opportunities, voice, recognition and power are redistributed to correct social inequalities and support all learners, especially marginalised ones.

Voice of the learner: letting learners express their views, experiences, questions and choices in decisions about their learning, rules, curriculum - centring them as active participants rather than passive recipients.

Race: socially constructed categories often based on perceived physical or phenotypical traits (e.g. skin colour) that have been used to maintain power differences.

Ethnicity: cultural identity based on shared traditions, language, heritage and ancestry.

Anti-racist pedagogy: an approach to teaching that intentionally works to identify, challenge and change racist structures and practices in settings, curriculum and school systems.

Dialogic teaching: an approach where learning is co-constructed through dialogue, questioning and discussion; learners and educators both bring ideas, challenge, reflect and build understanding together.

INTRODUCTION

In this chapter we explore the role of subject knowledge in fostering an anti-racist curriculum within primary education as well as identifying a range of practical, anti-racist pedagogies. Subject knowledge can be seen as neutral; however, critical race theory (Delgado and Stefancic, 2017) reveals how dominant knowledge hierarchies have historically marginalised the contributions and lived experiences of racially minoritised communities. By examining how racism and colonial legacies are embedded in primary curricula, we argue in this chapter for a critical re-evaluation of what is taught, how it is taught and whose knowledge is valued in education. Historically, school curricula have prioritised Eurocentric perspectives, particularly in subjects such as humanities, sciences and the arts (Apple, 2014; Moncrieffe, 2020). This reinforces racial inequalities by positioning Western knowledge as the truth while ignoring or sidelining non-Western ways of knowing (Pirbhai-Illich et al., 2022). For instance, while science is often presented as an objective discipline, Rezende et al. (2021) note a lack of 'attention to its [science curriculum's] intrinsic social, political and cultural aspects' (p. 2). Similarly, Sealey-Ruiz (2021) identified how primary history curricula frequently emphasised narratives of national pride and Britishness while ignoring the impacts of colonialism such as slavery. These omissions contribute to a racialised hierarchy of knowledge that privileges certain worldviews over others. To challenge these narratives and norms, in this chapter we build on culturally relevant (Ladson-Billings, 1995) and culturally sustaining pedagogy (Paris and Alim, 2017) to explore how anti-racist approaches can be embedded. Anti-racist subject knowledge requires not only diversifying, but also transforming pedagogical approaches. Dialogic teaching (Alexander, 2020) and enquiry-based learning can encourage critical engagement with knowledge production, enabling learners to question dominant narratives and recognise the political nature of knowledge (Freire, 1970). In this chapter we provide practical strategies for educators to integrate anti-racist pedagogy into their practice. We, as authors, believe that anti-racist education is not an optional addition, but a fundamental aspect of subject knowledge development. By critically examining the racialised nature of knowledge, educators can work towards a curriculum that fosters justice, equity and transformative learning experiences for all. In this chapter we respond to ongoing calls within education policy and practice, such as the DfE's focus on inclusive teaching and the recommendations of the Commission on Race and Ethnic Disparities (2021), to equip educators to critically re-evaluate subject knowledge and embed anti-racist pedagogies that challenge the Eurocentric and exclusionary nature of many primary curricula.

RACISM AS A SAFEGUARDING ISSUE

Racism is increasingly being recognised as a safeguarding concern within educational contexts, with growing calls for schools to adopt anti-racist approaches as part of their statutory duty to protect all learners. Boakye (2022a and b) highlights that schools are often unsafe spaces for learners from racially marginalised backgrounds unless proactive measures, such as anti-racist policies and staff training, are implemented. This perspective is supported by findings from the Learner Safeguarding Practice Review Panel (2025), which examined safeguarding reviews involving Black, Asian and mixed-heritage learners and identified a systemic failure to engage with issues of race and racism. The report called for a 'sea change' in safeguarding practice, emphasising the urgent need to address racial inequality as a matter of child protection. Together, these perspectives reinforce the imperative for schools and other education establishments to view anti-racist practice not as an optional enhancement, but as a fundamental component of safeguarding policy and practice.

CRITICAL RACE THEORY AND CULTURALLY SUSTAINING PEDAGOGY IN THE ANTI-RACIST CURRICULUM

Critical race theory (CRT) has been applied within the English education context to examine how systemic racism is embedded within laws, policies and institutions (see Cole and Maisuria, 2007; Parsons and Thompson, 2017). CRT is useful in identifying structural white supremacy. White supremacy is the political, social, economic and cultural structures and practices that often go unseen but result in disproportionate benefits to people racialised as white (McIntosh, 1989; Picower, 2009). CRT challenges the notion of teaching as a politically impartial act (Commission for Racial and Ethnic Disparity, 2021). It demonstrates that subject knowledge and curriculum are not colour-blind, arguing that racism is not merely the product of individual biases but a deeply rooted societal structure (Gillborn, 2008). Aspiring anti-racist practitioners can, by making use of critical race-informed analysis, find 'pockets of possibility' to interrogate whose and what knowledge is valued, whose histories are told and how power operates within the curriculum (Smith and Lander, 2022). In terms of subject knowledge, a CRT-informed analysis encourages us to critically reflect on the content and resources that the curriculum demands educators deliver (Glowach et al., 2023). For example, in English, it prompts a shift away from English canonical texts, which can use Eurocentric narratives to present characters who are not white in a racist, deficit-informed manner. Instead, educators can choose inclusive texts and accounts that highlight creativity, resistance, cultural value and contributions of Global Majority communities (Saleh, 2023). Alongside CRT, *culturally sustaining pedagogy* (CSP) is an educational approach that seeks to maintain and promote learners' cultural identities while simultaneously fostering academic achievement (Ladson-Billings, 2014). CSP complements CRT through advocating for the preservation and celebration of learners' cultural identities, recognising culture as a dynamic set of values, beliefs and practices that varies across learners' social identities (Paris and Alim, 2017). CSP encourages educators to reject practices which encourage all learners to act in the same ways and value the same things, and instead to embrace the diversity of learners' own cultural identities (Esteban-Guitart, 2024). For example, research by Snell and Cushing (2022) has demonstrated that Ofsted inspectors in England value 'Standard English' in spoken language in schools to the detriment of both learners and educators who speak different dialects. Educators can resist these racist and classist standards by allowing learners to speak in their own dialects and valuing these as equal to 'Standard English'. Such pedagogical approaches are particularly powerful in anti-racist settings, where learners' identities, funds of identity and the subject knowledge they bring become assets rather than obstacles (Richards et al., in press). The use of multiple, complementary tools is a feature of anti-racist teaching which moves practice from being inclusive to transformative and requires educators to encourage learners to name their realities, question injustice, recognise bias and imagine equitable futures (Freire, 1970).

UNCONSCIOUS BIAS

Moule (2009) states that biases are rooted in stereotypes and prejudices and the first step to becoming an anti-racist educator is to begin to reflect on our own biases: what are they and where did they come from? People often unwittingly act on an unconscious or hidden bias and recognising that we may have a bias for or against a group can help us to consider our responses or actions more carefully. Greenwald and Banaji (1995) define unconscious bias as the automatic, implicit stereotypes that influence our understanding and actions and cause us to act without conscious intent. These biases can be shaped by the societal and cultural norms we are exposed to as well as individual experiences; even those of us who are committed to social justice and equity have unconscious biases. Gladwell (2005) highlights that we do not deliberately choose our unconscious attitudes and that they may well conflict with our stated values, but it is worth knowing what our unconscious biases are as they are a powerful indicator of how we may act in spontaneous situations. Acknowledging biases opens doors for learning and allows people to consciously work for equity (Polite and Saenger, 2003). For us as educators, unconscious bias can impact our approaches as educators as well as learners' learning experiences. For example, educators may unconsciously hold lower academic expectations for learners based on race, gender, class, or language background (Gillborn, 2008). Research shows that Black Caribbean and Gypsy/Roma/Traveller learners face disproportionate exclusion rates in UK schools often due to biased perceptions of behaviour (DfE, 2019; Gillborn et al., 2012). Educators may prioritise dominant white, Western narratives, excluding diverse perspectives and reinforcing the Eurocentric worldview (Moncrieffe, 2020). Alongside this, unconscious bias can affect whom educators call on to respond to questions, how they respond and react to learners as well as the emotional tone of educator–learner interactions (Riviere, 2021). The impact of unconscious biases displayed in education can be significant to a learner's sense of belonging. When learners do not see their identities, languages and histories reflected in the curriculum, they can feel excluded and undervalued (Ladson-Billings, 1995). Implicit cues as to who is seen as 'able' or 'successful' can negatively impact performances, particularly among racially minoritised learners and repeated exposure to biased attitudes has been proven to limit learners' self-belief, participation and educational outcomes (DfE, 2017).

In this chapter, we will ask you to pause regularly to ask yourself a question. These questions are designed to prompt honest, critical reflection and support your own professional growth as you aim to develop as an equitable and inclusive educator.

REFLECTION 3.1

Begin by thinking about the nature of education; consider the inherent positionality and power we have as educators and the impact we have on the development of the young people we work with.

- What aspects of your own identity (race, gender, class, language, ability, religion, etc.) shape how you see the world?

- In what ways do you act as an ally to minoritised learners in your education community?

- Who or what supports you to challenge unconscious bias in your practice?

BUILDING AN ANTI-RACIST CURRICULUM

Whether you are a home educator designing a curriculum from scratch, or working within a school following a rigid national curriculum, all educators have opportunities to make choices about what and how they teach and have some agency (even when they may not feel like it). We, as educators, play a vital role in creating the curriculum for our learners, but our choices are never neutral, which puts us in a position to be agents for positive change. Education is part of the social system which upholds systemic oppression, but this also means it is a site that can contribute to the dismantling of that oppression, particularly if educators critically reflect on what is taught, how it is taught and how to nurture relationships that shape and develop learning. As educators, we can become allies by creating inclusive spaces where all learners feel heard by amplifying marginalised voices and using the curriculum to disrupt stereotypes and inequality. Brookfield (1995) asks us to look to the future and envision the role of education in shaping a more just and sustainable world and move beyond content delivery to consider designing a curriculum that prepares learners to think critically, act ethically and contribute to social transformation. For this to happen, we need collective dialogue about values and aspirations so educators can support learners towards agency, empowerment and action.

PRINCIPLE ONE: REPRESENTATION

Our identities as learners, within our family, community, school and society are formed by the information and messaging we are consciously and unconsciously receiving daily. This tells us who we are, how we are perceived by those we know and how those who we do not know might see us. A part of this messaging comes through the curriculum and pedagogic approaches. Very quickly we can identify in both the content of what we are taught and how we are taught it, who is named and who is not, who speaks and who is silent, and who acts and who is acted upon (Paul, 1998). Thomas (2022, p. 66) asks us to reflect on our childhoods and 'how many toys, books, and resources' we had 'that represented you?' While some of us will not even have considered this question before because we know, for a certainty, that we have seen ourselves in all these things as we grew up, for others, they will see themselves in only a few or none of these things. Thomas (2022, p. 62) argues that representation is essential if learners are to 'develop a positive racial identity'. Representation in curricula is how individuals, communities, cultures and experiences are used across subject areas (Archer and Francis, 2006). Curricula often present learners with a view of the world that has been validated by wider society and enshrined in law. If that world is stereotyped, does not include people that look like us (and, indeed, our society as a whole), or conflicts with or does not acknowledge home identities and values, then that curricula does not enable those learners to grow their identities positively. This can negatively impact learning, so to enable all learners to have a positive experience in the learning environment positive representations are essential.

Many argue that *representation* is not unproblematic. Gillborn (2008) argues that it can be tokenistic and used to sidestep the wider issue of addressing structural and systemic racism in the education system. Tikly et al. (2022) argue that there is a need to move beyond ideas of representation and to look more fundamentally at the construction of the curriculum and question whose knowledge and ideas of representation are included and why. Representation should therefore be seen as one part of a wider approach, but it does provide a starting point for reflection and critical questioning. Other chapters in this book explore subjects such as history, geography and sciences, and address why and how these subjects need to be decolonialised. The principles in this chapter will help you to reflect on different subjects and provide examples of actions that you as educators can take.

Literature is important when considering representation. Reading is both a foundation skill and at the heart of every area of the curriculum. The texts that children encounter in their homes, educational spaces and other areas of their lives inform their worldviews and can impact on their own identity formation (Carter, 2025). The Centre for Literacy in Primary Education (CLPE) has, since 2017, been reviewing children's books published each year with a focus on representation. Their yearly reports, titled *Reflecting realities*, are an essential read for all educators and pre-service educators. Their work was in part prompted by Bishop's (1990) seminal work, 'Mirrors, windows and sliding glass doors'. Bishop identifies how books should be mirrors for learners, enabling them to see themselves reflected. Books can also be 'windows' for learners – enabling them to see into the world and lives of others, as well as 'sliding glass doors', allowing the reader to momentarily enter the world created in the book. Of course, this principle also applies to other aspects of representation alongside race, including disability, gender, socioeconomic status, faith, sexuality and neurodiversity. Inclusion of diverse characters in texts is not sufficient for true representation and CLPE (2018) warns of the danger of 'wallpapering' – the scattering of Black and Brown characters throughout a book as part of the background illustrations, or as minor characters that appear just a few times and disappear as the plot develops. They highlight the potential for the reinforcement of racial tropes and stereotypes including the implication that the stories of the white characters are the ones that really matter. Similarly, Enriquez (2021, p. 104) warns against 'foggy mirrors' stating that 'close approximations are not good enough'. Nor are 'tiny windows', her way of suggesting that learners need to have access to more than just one type of representation of those who share a characteristic such as race, as lived experiences are diverse within cultural groups. If our shelves are full of books of Black heroes and do not show the ordinary and the day-to-day experiences, the unconscious messaging suggests, 'if you are Black, you only get to be in a book if you are a hero'. If the only representation of Black and Brown characters on our shelves are of refugees or of characters from far away, stereotyped countries, then this provides a further, single unhelpful representation. This does not mean we get rid of books that feature migration or Black heroes, but it does mean we need to make sure that these are not the only books with Black and Brown characters.

REFLECTION 3.2

If you feel comfortable to, reflect on the curriculum you experienced as a child or adult learner, and consider:

- whose stories and which authors, scientists and artists were you taught about?

- did you see yourself in the curriculum?

- can you think of an experience where you read a book that acted as a 'mirror' to your own experiences, or that you felt misrepresented them? How did that make you feel?

It has become much easier to find high-quality children's books that have positive representation and books written where the authors and illustrators represent the diversity of society. Although there is still a long way to go for positive representations in children's publishing, it has become much easier to find quality texts with diverse characters and authors. You can find sources of quality children's literature in the Further Reading section.

PRINCIPLE TWO: FUNDS OF KNOWLEDGE

In anti-racist practice, it is essential to reject negative stereotypes and ensure that children's individual cultures are not minimised or excluded (Esteban-Guitart, 2024, p. 7). This requires educators to create more equal relationships between themselves, learners, families and households, as well as wider community members, who should be seen as intellectually competent, regardless of socio-cultural, linguistic, or economic status (González et al., 2005). While the notion of *funds of knowledge* (FoK) emerged in the mid-1980s (Vélez-Ibáñez, 1989), testament to its relevance in adapting to changing perspectives in anti-racist, social justice and equity is that it remains a valid and relevant pedagogical approach for educators, learners and transformation of curricula (Hogg, 2011; Denton and Borrego, 2021). The term 'funds of knowledge' refers to the knowledge and skills that learners gain from the activities they engage in within their homes and communities (Moll et al., 1992). In the context of anti-racist practice, this principle recognises that children's experiences of race, identity and belonging are diverse and often complex. However, educators may have statutory and mandatory duties in which legislative definitions and guidance on race, ethnicity and nationhood maintain a colour-blind and race neutral approach to subject knowledge. This reductive approach reinforces 'white supremacy' as dominant and normal in the 'so-called' knowledge-rich curriculum (Neumann et al., 2020).

By contrast, educational initiatives which have been developed from the FoK framework have put into practice and shown effectiveness in several ways:

- improving the academic performances of minority, minoritised and migrant learners;

- advancing teaching innovation through the creation of culturally sensitive pedagogies and subject knowledge;

- building sustained relationships based on trust, beyond stereotypes, prejudices and deficit narratives that can often exist between educators and their learners, families and communities (Rodriguez, 2013; Subero et al., 2015).

FoK approaches demonstratively improve relationships with learners, families and households and community, establishing processes of mutual trust and helping to transform power relations. They do this through the mutual valuing, fostering and exchange of knowledge between both contexts (Chesworth, 2016; van't' Gilde and Volman, 2021). For example, Carter et al. (2022) collaborated with teachers and community-identified 'influencers' to identify relevant and appropriate examples of literature with which to engage children. The resulting introduction of oral stories, songs, poetry and rhymes from across local Somali communities into lessons, extensions to school library access and teacher engagement resulted in greater school involvement with families previously described as 'hard to reach', and improved relations between teachers, students and the community. Cultural community experiences were validated within the learning environment. For teachers this is not without challenge. To build a curriculum that is genuinely anti-racist and transformative, teachers must commit to creating spaces for children and communities to influence the development of practice in the classroom. This involves encouraging contributions to subject knowledge, and being prepared to resist demands placed on children to behave and speak in idealised, middle-class, white ways (Cushing, 2023).

REFLECTION 3.3

What steps might I take to begin adopting a funds of knowledge approach?

PRINCIPLE THREE: THE CENTRAL ROLE OF THE LEARNER'S VOICE IN ANTI-RACIST CURRICULUM DESIGN

In anti-racist curriculum design, centring the voice of the learner is not only a pedagogical imperative, but also an ethical one. It acknowledges that learners are not passive recipients of knowledge but active meaning-makers with lived experiences, insights and identities that shape their engagement with the curriculum. In the context of anti-racism, this becomes particularly vital: learners' experiences of race, identity and belonging are diverse and often complex. To build a curriculum that is genuinely inclusive and transformative, educators must create space for learners to speak, be heard and influence both what and how they learn. This principle builds upon the concepts of funds of knowledge (González et al., 2005) and culturally sustaining pedagogy which encourages educators to recognise and value the cultural, linguistic, and experiential assets that learners bring to the education setting. By foregrounding these funds, we acknowledge learners as holders of valid and valuable knowledge. In anti-racist curriculum design, this can help educators move away from tokenistic representations of diversity and instead co-construct knowledge with learners, centring their realities, questions and reflections. Creating opportunities for learners to express themselves through discussion, art, storytelling, drama, or structured dialogue allows their experiences to shape the curriculum. This approach aligns with learner rights-based education, especially Article 12 of the UN Convention on the Rights of the Child (1989), which states that every learner has the right to express their views freely in all matters affecting them. In practice, this means not just listening to learners, but also responding meaningfully to their ideas and concerns, particularly when these relate to race, injustice, or exclusion. A vital part of this process involves creating a safe and inclusive environment. Without trust and emotional safety, learners are unlikely to speak openly, especially about difficult or painful topics. Educators play a key role in modelling inclusive language, addressing microaggressions, challenging stereotypes and signalling that all voices are welcome. This environment enables the amplification of voice and the development of *agency* – a learner's belief that their thoughts and actions matter. This is discussed further in Chapter 5, which has a section on creating psychologically safe learning environments. Incidents of racism, whether experienced or observed by learners, present critical moments where voice and agency must be prioritised. Too often, learners who experience racism are silenced, disbelieved, or made to feel that their perceptions are invalid. This is where frameworks such as the RESPECT Project used arts-based methods to encourage learners to share their experiences of racism (see link in Further reading). Educators can use the resources produced from the project to guide restorative responses, validate learners' feelings and support them in naming and understanding what has happened. Amplifying child voice is not without its challenges. It requires educators to sit with discomfort, relinquish some control and genuinely listen – especially when learners question systems, policies, or behaviours. Yet this is where the deepest learning and transformation can occur. As hooks (1994) reminds us, education should be the practice of freedom, and freedom begins with listening.

REFLECTION 3.4

- How might I create space for all children to share their perspectives and experiences?
- How might I make sure these are then listened to and acted upon?

PRINCIPLE FOUR: SENSITIVE AND CONTROVERSIAL ISSUES

Curriculum design that supports anti-racism is inevitably shaped by both historical and present-day events that provoke moral, political, or social debate. Such issues, often termed 'sensitive' or 'controversial', present both challenges and opportunities for educators (Whitehouse and Jones, 2024). When managed effectively, they can deepen learners' critical thinking, foster empathy and promote meaningful engagement with democratic values. A sensitive or controversial issue is not universally defined; it is often shaped by the context in which it is taught. For example, what is considered a neutral historical event in one school might be deeply personal and painful in another, depending on the demographic make-up and lived experiences of the learners in the school. The Department for Education (DfE, 2021) (for educators in England) has provided some guidance on teaching political and sensitive issues, advising educators to maintain balance and avoid promoting partisan political views. However, this guidance has been criticised for discouraging open discussions about systemic racism, colonial legacies and protest, especially in relation to movements such as Black Lives Matter (Lander, 2023). One way to responsibly approach controversial issues is to situate them in local contexts that allow learners to connect their learning with the places and histories they know. A recent research project led by authors Carter and Whitehouse (2025) explored how educators approached the theme of tolerance in response to the toppling of the statue of Edward Colston in Bristol in 2020. While some schools may avoid this topic due to the sensitive nature, schools who took part in the research project used it as a catalyst for deep learning. The learners debated the role of statues in public spaces, considered the meaning of protest, and reflected on the legacy of transatlantic slavery in the city. This project provided a rich opportunity to explore the relationship between history, memory and justice, rooted in the lived reality of the learners' environment. The learners provided a list of significant local individuals who could take the place of Colston on the now empty plinth. Importantly, the project revealed the danger of focusing solely on 'issues' when exploring race and identity. While it is necessary to engage with histories of oppression, educators must also create space to celebrate Black and Brown culture, joy and resistance. Positive representation – through literature, local role models and cultural celebration – offers a powerful counterbalance to narratives of trauma. As Ladson-Billings (1995) argues, culturally relevant pedagogy must affirm learners' identities, not just critique systems of power. Educators therefore have a dual responsibility: to ensure learners are not shielded from difficult truths and to ensure these truths are taught in ways that are developmentally appropriate, emotionally safe and culturally affirming. Navigating this terrain requires thoughtful planning, strong subject knowledge and sensitivity to the dynamics of each learning community. Collaborating with parents, community leaders and colleagues can help ensure a shared understanding of the purpose and pedagogical value of addressing controversial topics.

REFLECTION 3.5

How can I use local events or figures to make sensitive issues more relevant and accessible?

Sensitive and controversial issues are not obstacles to teaching – they are essential components of an education that prepares young people to think critically and act ethically in a complex world. By approaching such topics with integrity, curiosity and care, educators can play a vital role in shaping inclusive, informed and socially conscious learners.

FINAL THOUGHTS

You as educators have the power to move beyond superficial diversification to genuine transformation. We have aimed to demonstrate in this chapter that building an anti-racist curriculum is not an optional enhancement to teaching, but a fundamental reimagining of subject knowledge and pedagogy. By interrogating dominant narratives and recognising how curricula have historically reinforced Eurocentric hierarchies, educators are challenged to move beyond superficial diversification towards genuine transformation. Critical race theory and culturally sustaining pedagogies are valuable frameworks for reflection and action, supporting pre-service and in-service educators to examine their own identities, positionalities and unconscious biases. Central to this work is the voice and agency of learners, whose lived experiences, funds of knowledge and cultural identities must shape what and how we teach. Representation, when thoughtfully embedded, offers powerful opportunities for affirmation and belonging, though it must be coupled with systemic change to avoid tokenism. Similarly, the role of community knowledge, and the importance of addressing sensitive and controversial issues, reminds us that anti-racist education is deeply relational and context dependent. Inevitably, educators can be caught in difficult positions in attempting to implement anti-racist responses to improving subject knowledge: where anti-racism work takes place, responsibility rests with one or two skilled and confident people, meaning this is an isolated learning experience not embedded within the structures and processes, and largely unsustainable (Arday and Mirza, 2018); there can be a lack of training and institutional support for embedding anti-racism into curriculum; and it can be absent in policies, educator standards and inspection frameworks (Picower, 2009). Also, limited access for educators to development time and resources means, on a practical level, connecting with the needs of all learners can be difficult, especially in a multi-ethnic, multi-lingual and diverse context. However, such action can be an important initiation, for any anti-racist examination of subject knowledge transformation must act to eliminate deficit narratives, therefore relying upon educators who can reflect on their practices through learning from learners, families, households and communities; embed processes of critical understanding; and anticipate the possibilities of better futures (Freire, 1970). An anti-racist curriculum is not static but an ongoing process of listening, reflection and collective action. By embracing this commitment, educators can create settings that are not only inclusive and equitable, but also sites of justice, hope and transformation.

REFLECTION 3.6

Below are some final reflective questions for you to consider as you continue your journey to becoming an anti-racist educator.

- Do my curriculum resources provide authentic, meaningful representation – or do they risk tokenism?

- When addressing sensitive or controversial issues, how do I balance care, honesty and critical engagement?

- What changes, small or systemic, am I prepared to make to embed anti-racist practice?

FURTHER READING AND RESOURCES

CHILDREN'S LITERATURE

World Kid Lit. https://worldkidlit.org/

A resource promoting children's literature translated from other languages and books by international and BAME creators.

Centre for Literacy in Primary Education (CLPE). https://clpe.org.uk/

Provides training, resources and research to support high-quality, reflective literacy teaching in primary schools.

Literacy Trust. https://literacytrust.org.uk/

A national charity dedicated to improving the reading, writing, speaking and listening skills of children and young people.

Books for Topics. www.booksfortopics.com/

A website offering curated book lists organised by age, topic and curriculum link to help teachers select quality literature.

POLICY AND PROCESS

National Education Union: Anti-Racism Charter. https://neu.org.uk/latest/library/anti-racism-charter

A formal document setting out key principles and commitments for challenging racism within schools and the education system.

CHILDREN'S VOICE

RESPECT project in Bristol. https://respectprojectbristol.org/

A project focused on researching and supporting children's voice and participation in their communities.

CURRICULUM AND RESOURCES

Friends, Families and Travellers: Working Towards Equality. www.gypsy-traveller.org/teaching-resources/

Resources providing guidance and activities to improve the education and wellbeing of Gypsy, Roma and Traveller pupils.

Learning Corner. https://learning-corner.learning.europa.eu/index_en

Educational materials for teaching about the EU, its culture, countries and peoples in the classroom.

Advance HE's Anti-racist Curriculum Project. www.advance-he.ac.uk/anti-racist-curriculum-project

A project providing resources and guidance for higher education to review and develop a truly anti-racist curriculum.

The Black Curriculum's Education Programmes. https://theblackcurriculum.com/education-programmes

Education programmes that aim to integrate Black British history into the UK school curriculum.

Resources to support learners and educators of African and African diaspora descent CARGO©. https://cargomovement.org/

Resources dedicated to supporting learning about people of African and African diaspora descent.

South Asian Heritage Trust Toolkit for Schools. https://southasianheritage.org.uk/2024-schools-toolkit/

A resource kit designed to help schools celebrate and teach about South Asian history and culture.

DARPL – Diversity and Anti-Racism Professional Learning. https://darpl.org/

Offers professional learning to promote diversity and anti-racism practice in education.

REFERENCES

Alexander, R. (2020). *A dialogic teaching companion*. Routledge.

Apple, M. W. (2014). *Official knowledge: Democratic education in a conservative age*. Routledge.

Archer, L. and Francis, B. (2006). *Understanding minority ethnic achievement: Race, gender, class and 'success'* (1st ed.). Routledge. https://doi.org/10.4324/9780203968390

Arday, J. and Mirza, H. S. (Eds.). (2018). *Dismantling race in higher education: Racism, whiteness and decolonising the academy*. Palgrave Macmillan.

Bishop, R. S. (1990). Mirrors, windows and sliding glass doors. *Perspectives: Choosing and Using Books for the Classroom*, *6*(2), ix–xi.

Boakye, J. (2022a). *I heard what you said*. Picador.

Boakye, J. (2022b). Racism in English education should be seen as safeguarding issue, says author. *The Guardian*. 5 June. www.theguardian.com/education/2022/jun/05/racism-england-schools-education-safeguarding-issue-jeffrey-boakye

Brookfield, S. (1995). *Becoming a critically reflective educator.* Jossey-Bass.

Carter, J. (Ed.). (2025). *Putting social justice and equity at the heart of reading for pleasure.* Routledge.

Carter, J. and Whitehouse, S. (2025). Teaching tolerance: Navigating complexity in the English curriculum [Manuscript submitted for publication].

Carter, J., Mohammad, H. and Aidid, F. (2022). Somali 'influencers' in and beyond a school community using funds of knowledge to influence family and children's reading engagement. *Educational Futures, 13*(2). https://uwe-repository.worktribe.com/output/10142067

Centre for Literacy in Primary Education. (2018). *Reflecting realities: Survey of ethnic representation within UK literature 2017.* https://clpe.org.uk/research/clpes-reflecting-realities-survey-ethnic-representation-within-uk-learnerss-literature-0

Chesworth, L. (2016). A funds of knowledge approach to examining play interests: Listening to children's and parents' perspectives. *International Journal of Early Years Education, 24*(3), 294–308. https://doi.org/10.1080/09669760.2016.1189815

Cole, M. and Maisuria, A. (2007). *Critical pedagogy and the crisis of capitalism: Education at a crossroads.* Peter Lang.

Commission on Race and Ethnic Disparities. (2021). *The report of the Commission on Race and Ethnic Disparities.* UK Government.

Cushing, I. (2023). The knowledge-rich project, coloniality, and the preservation of whiteness in schools: A raciolinguistic perspective. *Educational Linguistics,* 1–21. https://doi.org/10.1007/s10648-023-09694-1

Denton, M. and Borrego, M. (2021). Funds of knowledge in STEM education: A scoping review. *Studies in Engineering Education, 1*(2), 71–92. https://doi.org/10.21061/see.16

Delgado, R. and Stefancic, J. (2017). *Critical race theory: An introduction.* New York University Press. https://scholarship.law.ua.edu/fac_books/4

Department for Education (DfE). (2017). *Unlocking talent, fulfilling potential: A plan for improving social mobility through education.* https://assets.publishing.service.gov.uk/media/5a82c6cb40f0b62305b94499/Social_Mobility_Action_Plan_-_for_printing.pdf

DfE. (2019). *Permanent and fixed-period exclusions in England: 2017 to 2018.* https://assets.publishing.service.gov.uk/media/5d3967a0ed915d0d0e7a82df/Permanent_and_fixed_period_exclusions_2017_to_2018_-_main_text.pdf

DfE. (2021). *Political impartiality in schools.* www.gov.uk/government/publications/political-impartiality-in-schools

Enriquez, G. (2021). Foggy mirrors, tiny windows, and heavy doors: Beyond diverse books towards meaningful literacy instruction. *The Reading Teacher, 75*(1), 103–106.

Esteban-Guitart, M. (2024). The funds of knowledge and identity approach: Blueprints for social justice (pp. 1–16). In M. Esteban-Guitart (Ed.), *Funds of knowledge and identity pedagogies for social justice: International perspectives and praxis from communities, classroom, and curriculum.* Routledge.

Freire, P. (1970). *Pedagogy of the oppressed.* Seabury Press.

Gillborn, D. (2008). *Racism and education: Coincidence or conspiracy?* Routledge. https://doi.org/10.4324/9780203928424

Gillborn, D., Rollock, N., Vincent, C. and Ball, S. J. (2012). 'You got a pass, so what more do you want?': Race, class, and gender intersections in the educational experiences of the Black middle class. *Race Ethnicity and Education*, *15*(1), 121–139. https://doi.org/10.1080/1 3613324.2012.638869

Gladwell, M. (2005). *Blink: The power of thinking without thinking*. Little Brown.

Glowach, T., Mitchell, R., Bennett, T., Donaldson, L., Jefferson, J., Panford, L., Saleh, A., Smee, K., Wells-Dion, B. and Hemmings, E. (2023). Making spaces for collaborative action and learning: Reflections on educator-led decolonising initiatives from a professional learning network in England. *Curriculum Journal*, *34*(1), 100–117. https://doi.org/10.1002/curj.194

González, N., Moll, L. C. and Amanti, C. (2005). *Funds of knowledge: Theorizing practices in households, communities, and classrooms*. Routledge.

Greenwald, A. G. and Banaji, M. R. (1995). Implicit social cognition: Attitudes, self-esteem, and stereotypes. *Psychological Review*, *102*(1), 4–27. https://doi.org/10.1037/0033-295X.102.14

Hogg, L. (2011). Funds of knowledge: An investigation of coherence within the literature. *Teaching and Teacher Education*, *27*(3), 666–677. https://doi.org/10.1016/j.tate.2010.11.005

hooks, b. (1994). *Teaching to transgress: Education as the practice of freedom*. Routledge.

Jovés, P., Siqués, C. and Esteban-Guitart, M. (2015). The incorporation of funds of knowledge and funds of identity of learners and their families into educational practice: A case study from Catalonia, Spain. *Teaching and Teacher Education*, *49*, 68–77. https://doi.org/10.1016/j. tate.2015.03.001

Ladson-Billings, G. (1995). Toward a theory of culturally relevant pedagogy. *American Educational Research Journal*, *32*(3), 465–491. https://doi.org/10.2307/1163320

Ladson-Billings, G. (2014). Culturally relevant pedagogy 2.0: A.k.a. the remix. *Harvard Educational Review*, *84*(1), 74–84. https://doi.org/10.17763/haer.84.1.p2rj131485484751

Lander, V. (2023). *Educator professionalism and the politics of race*. Routledge.

Learner Safeguarding Practice Review Panel. (2025). *'It's silent': Race, racism, and safeguarding learners* [PDF]. Department for Education. www.gov.uk/government/publications/race-rac ism-and-safeguarding-learners

McIntosh, P. (1989). White privilege: Unpacking the invisible knapsack. Wellesley College, Center for Research on Women.

Moll, L. C., Amanti, C., Neff, D. and González, N. (1992). Funds of knowledge for teaching: Using a qualitative approach to connect homes and classrooms. *Theory into Practice*, *31*(2), 132–141. https://doi.org/10.1080/00405849209543534

Moncrieffe, M. (2020). *Decolonising the curriculum: Transnational perspectives*. Routledge.

Moule, J. (2009). Understanding unconscious bias and unintentional racism. *Phi Delta Kappan*, *90*(5), 320–326. https://doi.org/10.1177/003172170909000507

Neumann, E., Gewirtz, S., Maguire, M. and Towers, E. (2020). Neoconservative education policy and the case of the English Baccalaureate. *Journal of Curriculum Studies*, *52*(5), 702–719. https://doi.org/10.1080/00220272.2020.1759145

NSPCC. (2025). *Safeguarding learners from Black, Asian and minoritised ethnic communities*. NSPCC Learning. https://learning.nspcc.org.uk/safeguarding-learner-protection/learners-from-black-asian-minoritised-ethnic-communities

Ofsted. (2014). *Are you ready? Good practice in school readiness.* www.gov.uk/government/publications/are-you-ready-good-practice-in-school-readiness

Paris, D. and Alim, S. (2017). *Culturally sustaining pedagogies: Teaching and learning for justice in a changing world.* Teachers College Press.

Parsons, C. and Thompson, L. (2017). *The theory and practice of educational leadership* (3rd ed.). Routledge.

Paul, L. (1998). *Reading otherways.* Thimble Press.

Picower, B. (2009). The unexamined Whiteness of teaching: How White educators maintain and enact dominant racial ideologies. *Race Ethnicity and Education, 12*(2), 197–215. https://doi.org/10.1080/13613320902995475

Pirbhai-Illich, F., Martin, F., Iorga, W., Richards, M. and Mustafee, R. (2022). An inquiry into de/colonising educational relationships in higher education: Inquiry report. https://doi.org/10.13140/RG.2.2.31006.41281

Polite, L. and Saenger, E. B. (2003). A pernicious silence: Confronting race in the elementary classroom. *Phi Delta Kappan, 85,* 274–278.

Rezende, F., Ostermann, F. and Guerra, A. (2021). South epistemologies to invent post-pandemic science education. *Cultural Studies of Science Education, 16,* 981–993. https://doi.org/10.1007/s11422-021-10091-3

Richards, M., Whitehouse, S., Jones, V., Podpadec, T., Gorell Barnes, L. and Pawson, C. (in press). Exploring children's experiences of racism in school: Implications for anti-racist educator education and development. In M. Sapona, R. Willems and P. Smith (Eds.), *The Cambridge handbook of bias-based bullying.* Cambridge University Press.

Riviere, C. (2021). Unconscious bias and educator–learner interactions: A study of primary classrooms in England. *Educational Review.* https://doi.org/10.1080/00131911.2021.1876658

Rodriguez, G. M. (2013). Power and agency in education: Exploring the pedagogical dimensions of funds of knowledge. *Review of Research in Education, 37*(1), 87–120. https://doi.org/10.3102/0091732X12462686

Saleh, A. (2023). Black British literature in the secondary English classroom. *Changing English, 30*(4), 342–358. https://doi.org/10.1080/1358684X.2023.2234567

Sealey-Ruiz, Y. (2021). *Racial literacy: A policy research brief.* National Council of Teachers of English.

Smith, H. J. and Lander, V. (2022). *Competing agendas in educator education: Preparing educators for diversity and social justice.* Trentham.

Snell, J. and Cushing, I. (2022). 'A lot of them write how they speak': Policy, pedagogy, and the policing of 'nonstandard' English. *Literacy, 56*(3), 199–211. https://doi.org/10.1111/lit.12298

Subero, D., Vila, I. and Esteban-Guitart, M. (2015). Some contemporary forms of the funds of knowledge approach: Developing culturally responsive pedagogy for social justice. *International Journal of Educational Psychology, 4*(1), 33–53. https://doi.org/10.17583/ijep.2015.1389

Thomas, A. (2022). *Representation matters: Becoming an anti-racist educator.* Bloomsbury.

Tikly, L., Barrett, A., Batra, P., Bernal, A., Cameron, L., Coles, A., Juma, Z., Mitchell, R., Nunes, N., Paulson, J., Rowsell, J., Tusiime, M., Vejarano, B. and Weldemariam, N. (2022). Decolonising educator professionalism: Foregrounding the perspectives of educators in the Global South. *UNESCO Background Paper.* https://doi.org/10.5281/zenodo.7097105

United Nations (UN). (1989). *Convention on the rights of the child.* www.ohchr.org/en/instru-ments-mechanisms/instruments/convention-rights-child

UN. (2022). *2030 development agenda 'fails' on racial equality and non-discrimination. UN News – Human Rights.* https://news.un.org/en/story/2022/07/1121942

van 't Gilde, J. and Volman, M. (2021). Using culturally responsive pedagogy to enhance equity in education. *European Journal of Teacher Education, 44*(1), 44–63. https://doi.org/10.1080/02619768.2020.1847934

Vélez-Ibáñez, C. (1989). Transmission and patterning of funds of knowledge: Shaping and emergence of confianza in US Mexican learners. Paper presented at Society for Applied Anthropology Annual Meeting, Santa Fe.

Whitehouse, S. and Jones, V. (2024). Context, consciousness and caution: Educators of history in England and the exploration of sensitive and controversial issues in practice. In R. Waller, J. Andrews and T. Clark (Eds.), *Critical perspectives on educational policies and professional identities* (pp. 209–227). Emerald. https://doi.org/10.1108/978-1-83753-332-920241013

4
SUBJECT KNOWLEDGE AND SPECIAL EDUCATIONAL NEEDS AND DISABILITIES

EMMA JONES

THIS CHAPTER

This chapter explores the ideas that:

- the ways educators define, construct and interpret special educational needs and disabilities and the language used to talk about pupils' needs influence teaching practice and outcomes for children

- educators' decisions about curriculum content and pedagogy have ethical implications

- having strong subject knowledge supports educators to teach all children in an inclusive, accessible and individually relevant way.

KEY TERMS FOR THIS CHAPTER

- *Alternative and augmentative communication* (AAC): including using devices, such as tablets, to communicate.

- *Disability*: restrictions to access and participation caused by interactions between the individual and their environment.

- *Impairment*: an individual characteristic or condition.

- *Medical model*: a perspective that frames disability as the consequence of individual impairments.

- *Neurodivergent*: specific neurotypes including, but not limited to, autism, ADHD, dyslexia, dyscalculia, dyspraxia and Tourette's.

- *Neurodiverse*: an umbrella term used to refer to cognitive diversity.

- *Ordinarily available inclusive provision* (OAIP): this encompasses the environmental, pedagogical and physical provision always available to all pupils.

- *Reasonable adjustments*: as outlined in the Equality Act (2010), a legal requirement to make adjustments to avoid disadvantaging individuals.

- *SEND*: special educational needs and disabilities.

- *Social model*: a perspective that frames disability as the consequence of social and environmental barriers preventing equitable participation.

INTRODUCTION

In this chapter, I introduce key ideas and practical considerations related to *special educational needs and disabilities* (SEND). I highlight how different aspects of SEND can influence subject knowledge, as well as approaches to planning, teaching and assessing a diverse range of learners.

You might have heard SEND referred to as *additional learning needs* (ALN) or *additional support needs* (ASN). While there are subtle differences in the meaning of these phrases, the overall focus on supporting diverse learners remains.

As this book explores subject knowledge, you might wonder why a SEND-focused chapter is needed. This is because the number of pupils with complex needs attending mainstream settings is increasing (ACARA, 2024; Audit Scotland, 2025; DfE, 2025). So, all teachers are teachers of SEND and need the knowledge and skills to teach effectively.

It is important to note that definitions of SEND and available statistics differ between nations. UNESCO's (2020) *Global education monitoring report* suggests that most children with SEND attend segregated education settings, if they attend at all. In Europe, an average of 60 per cent of children with SEND attend mainstream settings. This is potentially problematic, as Article 23 in the United Nations Convention on the Rights of the Child (UNCRC) states that *all* children with SEND are entitled to: 'Education [...] in a manner conducive to the child's achieving the fullest possible social integration and individual development' (UN, 1989, p. 7).

The *Salamanca statement* (UNESCO, 1994) echoes this commitment to inclusive education and integration. Emerging from the World Conference on Special Needs Education in Salamanca, Spain, it called on all governments to legislate and facilitate inclusive education, including access to mainstream schools. The statement has shaped policy and practice internationally and remains a landmark in international efforts to promote inclusive education, reinforcing all children's right to learn. To enact this right, teachers need a sophisticated understanding of approaches to planning, teaching and assessing.

How teachers conceptualise SEND varies depending on context and perspective. This can pose challenges for educators, who may feel that they cannot do the 'right' thing in supporting their pupils. In this chapter, we will explore models of disability and identify how such perspectives might impact teaching practice. I aim to show how valuing diverse ways of knowing, alongside strong subject and pedagogical knowledge, equips teachers to plan inclusive lessons, challenge inequalities and recognise all pupils as capable learners.

CONSTRUCTIONS OF SEND

What does SEND mean to you? You might think of a medical diagnosis, a particular learner, or a legal definition. You might associate the term with a visible disability or with specific behaviours or challenges. These are all valid, yet partial, interpretations. It is important to examine the assumptions and experiences underpinning them because they affect our practice.

The House of Commons Education and Skills Committee (2006, p. 16) argues that, 'The premise on which SEN provision is based [...] is fundamentally flawed. Children exist on a broad continuum of needs and learning styles, but do not fit into neat categories [...]. The category of "SEN" is an arbitrary distinction.' Despite this statement, the term 'SEND' remained in use by the government at the time and subsequent ones in England.

No language choice is flawless, but it is important to recognise that whatever terms your nation uses to refer to children who face additional barriers to learning, these terms and ideas are not 'right' or 'wrong' and change over time with social and political shifts. For example, consider the disability and inclusivity discourses advocated by US President Donald Trump. Various media outlets accuse him of mocking disabled people, suggesting that autism is linked to vaccines (Looi, 2025) and commenting in favour of eradicating some disabilities (Shah, 2024). A political leader voicing these attitudes could influence nationwide attitudes and provision for people with SEND.

This influence is particularly evident in the conversations led by US health secretary Robert F. Kennedy Jr, who, in April 2025, declared the sharp rise in autism diagnoses an 'epidemic' and vowed to launch 'a massive testing and research effort' to identify its causes (BBC News, 2025). He issued plans to fund research identifying the factors causing what he perceived to be a life-limiting disease. Such rhetoric, combined with political action, could negatively reshape how a nation perceives autism and autistic people.

By contrast, consider the case of Oliver McGowan, who died due to medical professionals failing to understand his autism and learning disability (Oliver's Campaign, n.d.). After his death, his mother campaigned for mandatory autism and learning disability training for health and social care staff. Thousands of professionals now attend training that promotes inclusive practice and disability rights. More importantly, the training is always delivered by an autistic person and someone with a learning disability, following the disability rights principle of 'Nothing about us, without us.' What impact could Oliver's family experiences have, not just on professionals attending their training, but also on wider societal perceptions of SEND?

If SEND is not a fixed concept, then the idea of inclusive practice is also open to interpretation. I don't seek to provide a final definition in this chapter, but rather to explore constructions of SEND and inclusion.

As your career progresses, your perspective on SEND will evolve. You may begin to question familiar approaches, encounter new models of inclusion, or adapt your practice in response to the needs of the learners you meet. Through engagement with research, training and dialogue with children, families and colleagues, it is vital that you remain reflective and responsive.

MEDICAL VERSUS SOCIAL MODELS OF SEND

Common conceptions of SEND are sometimes referred to as models. While there are many models of SEND, this chapter discusses two dominant but contrasting approaches: the *medical model* and the *social model*. You can learn more about other models of SEND in the Further reading section of this chapter.

In the medical or deficit model, key ideas are:

- disability is the product of an individual's deficiency or impairment; language refers to disorders and diagnoses that outline what is 'wrong' with the individual;

- disability should, where possible, be diagnosed and treated;

- medical professionals are the primary decision-makers;

- the neurodiverse or disabled individual is a passive recipient of care;

- it is the individual's responsibility to 'fit in' with society (Shamsabadipour, 2025).

While some readers might be shocked or upset by this view, it pervaded the Global North until very recently and still permeates some professions, nations and social groups. This is partly due to a lack of understanding: disabled and neurodiverse people were often indefinitely admitted to secure hospitals because society did not know how to support them, and few medical professionals tried to listen to patients' perspectives to hear how they wanted to live (Waltz, 2023). Even now, diagnosis often forms a 'gateway' to accessing support for children with additional needs. It is easier to organise and ringfence funding when people are categorised according to medical diagnoses.

The deficit model is also prevalent in cultures where disability is viewed as a tragedy (Scavarda, 2024) or even a divine punishment for sin (Bogart, 2021). Families living in such cultures might internalise the view that they need to correct their child's needs to reduce shame (Oduyemi et al., 2021).

While the medical model pervades harmful perceptions of SEND and is widely rejected by SEND communities, it is essential to understand why people might hold these views. However, I must stress that the medical model does not provide a useful framework for educators as it implies that neurodiverse and disabled people are faulty and cannot achieve the same as non-disabled peers.

Goldacre (2014) also highlights the extent to which the medical model can create or reinforce stigma. He cites several studies suggesting that, when people believe that neurodiversity has a biological cause, they are more likely to fear or avoid neurodiverse and disabled people. He suggests that this might be because we perceive biological characteristics as uncontrollable and therefore think that we cannot help.

The medical model may seem like an outdated way of viewing SEND, but Jarrett (2020) argues that it is a relatively modern perspective. He suggests that in England before the mid-19th century people who would now be diagnosed with learning disabilities were accepted and integrated members of society. Communities were adaptive, and the only criterion for social inclusion was being human. The introduction of a medical model of disability in the mid-19th century was not grounded in human necessity, but in an increasing obsession with classification and bureaucratised state control.

By contrast, the social model shifts focus from the individual onto societal and structural barriers to participation, offering a more inclusive framework for teaching. This model distinguishes between an impairment and a disability. For instance, an individual might have a physical impairment that affects their ability to walk. Without mobility aids and environmental adaptations, society disables the individual. However, if they are provided with a mobility aid and an accessible environment in which to use it, they can participate in physical and social contexts. It is not the impairment which disables them, but the social barriers of lack of aids and a suitable environment. This distinction forms the basis of the social model.

Key aspects of the social model are:

- disability is not an individual impairment, but a consequence of social, physical and attitudinal barriers;
- inclusion, accessibility and equal rights are more important than 'fixing' differences;
- society has a responsibility to change to support participation;
- neurodiverse and disabled individuals should be the most important voice in discussions about the support they want or need (Roberston and Jaswal, 2024).

This is a more productive model for educators because the social model emphasises what educators can do to support children rather than 'fix' them, making the approach more inclusive and the impact more achievable.

— REFLECTION 4.1

Before reading this chapter, did your views, language and practice align more closely with the medical or social model? What values and experiences lead you to think in this way?

The following case studies explore how the medical and social models might influence an educator's choices.

CASE STUDY: JAMIL

Jamil is a Year 3 pupil who struggles with reading fluency and comprehension. He avoids reading aloud, becomes anxious during literacy lessons and is withdrawn when asked to work independently with texts.

According to the medical model, Jamil may have a diagnosable literacy disorder or cognitive deficit. This is an internal problem that the teacher tries to fix through corrective literacy interventions.

According to the social model, the teacher must consider the barriers in their teaching practices and the learning environment. They ask him what he finds difficult about reading and adapt teaching and resources accordingly. They seek texts that are relevant to his life and interests, offer audio versions of material and encourage paired reading to reduce anxiety.

CASE STUDY: EVIE

Evie is in Year 5 and frequently interrupts lessons, calls out answers and walks around the classroom. She often receives sanctions for not following instructions. Staff describe her as 'difficult to manage'.

From a medical perspective, the teacher blames Evie for her behaviour, arguing that she chooses to behave that way. When Evie receives an ADHD diagnosis, the teacher believes that there is nothing they can do to support her because it's 'the way she is'. They use strategies such as medication, a behaviour plan and structured sanctions to 'correct' Evie's behaviour.

From a social perspective, the teacher talks with Evie and establishes what changes could support her. They adapt the environment by considering factors such as sensory stimulation, cognitive load, reducing demands and providing regular movement breaks. They believe that Evie's behaviour communicates unmet needs that the teacher can better support with some adaptations.

In reality, approaches to supporting pupils with SEND are more complicated than this binary discussion, and there are many more models of disability to consider. Social language and mindset towards SEND vary, so what feels socially acceptable today might seem abhorrent in a few decades. Terms such as 'imbeciles' and 'the feeble-minded' used to be common, socially acceptable language that many would now recoil at. It is important to remain open to self-reflection and listen to the preferences and values of the people our language describes.

Additionally, try to avoid thinking that any model is completely 'good' or 'bad'. For example, diagnosing neurodivergence can be extremely affirming, medication can improve quality of life and literacy interventions can be very effective at improving literacy skills and long-term academic outcomes. The key is to avoid blaming and shaming children with SEND, focusing on how they want to be supported and how the environment can change to reduce barriers to learning and wellbeing.

It is also important to question the values, assumptions and prejudices that inform how we label and discuss disabilities. Rossetti and Tashie (2005) identify that all humans are different, but labelling some differences as deficiencies creates a hierarchy of desirable versus undesirable differences. Prejudice creates and is reinforced by these hierarchies. Crucially, they note that the bias and discrimination directed at disabled and neurodivergent people are often expressed as compassion. This reflects the charity or 'tragedy' model of disability, in which segregation or special treatment is framed as 'help', but is fuelled by pity, and is 'done to' the individual, sometimes against their will (Ware et al., 2022). Thus, this approach reinforces inequality. For example, learners are often placed in specialist classrooms or facilities. Specialist provision is sometimes the most suitable option, and specialist school educators are highly skilled professionals. However, people must interrogate their decisions and reflect honestly on the assumptions underpinning them. They might ask: 'Am I basing this decision on what the learner wants and is capable of, or on preconceived ideas about their disability?'

In his lecture reflecting on how the language and understanding of disabilities relate to his lived experience, Unwin (2022) urges the need for a new, more honest model. He argues,

We can help people, not by trying to change them, not by telling them to be better, not by imposing on them meaningless aspirations, not by expecting them to achieve things, but by accepting them as they are, in all their particularities.

He argues that the social model goes too far, pretending that individual differences do not exist and that all humans can achieve the same things. He suggests that people and organisations claiming to be inclusive are rarely as widely accessible as they believe. We therefore need to avoid aligning solely with one model, instead interacting with and supporting people in an individualised way. This aligns with the critical realist model of disability proposed by Bhaskar and Danermark (2006). Their seminal work is included in the Further reading section of this chapter.

VALUING DIVERSE KNOWLEDGE

Within this, it is important to value different ways of learning and knowing. Though schooling differs between global contexts, many education systems favour transactional teaching approaches, where teachers impart their knowledge to pupils by talking or providing reading materials, and assess knowledge primarily through writing activities and summative tests. Within these systems, listening and reading are valued ways of learning. Knowing facts dictated by the curriculum and expressing this knowledge through grammatically correct writing is often treated as the optimal way to demonstrate subject competence.

But learning and knowing can be more diverse. Consider the following examples.

1. A child from a Gypsy, Roma, Traveller or Indigenous background may struggle with standardised literacy tests but excel in oral storytelling, memory, or reciting family histories. Rather than insisting that the child develop their writing skills, we might value their oral traditions and assess their knowledge and understanding through spoken tasks. Educators might adapt their curriculum to ensure that content reflects the child's life experiences and funds of knowledge.

2. A child who finds it hard to sit still and concentrate during lessons engages deeply when learning through movement, hands-on tasks, or physical interaction. Rather than insisting that the child should sit still and listen, the educator might plan active learning activities and introduce movement and adaptive seating in the classroom.

3. A child may struggle with maths but thrive in drama, music, or personal development, demonstrating empathy and creative expression. The educator might shift their teaching and assessment practices to value and build upon these artistic and empathetic skills.

4. A Deaf child using British Sign Language (BSL) may not engage with spoken instruction in a mainstream classroom. Rather than teaching the hearing children and expecting a translator to integrate the child into the class, the teacher might diversify their teaching approaches, communicating via multiple modes to make learning accessible for all children.

5. A non-speaking student uses symbols on an *alternative and augmentative communication* (AAC) device to communicate. Where some teachers might feel that they cannot teach this pupil to read and write, others might recognise that reading and communicating through symbols is a valid form of literacy, and plan to develop the child's skills in this area.

These examples highlight how shifts in perspective can help educators teach more inclusively. This is more complicated than it might seem. Take the final example of the non-speaking child using an AAC device. The educator needs strong subject knowledge to adapt teaching and learning activities and ensure that the child can engage using their AAC device. They need to understand how reading and writing symbols might differ from standard text and prepare to assess the child's work while accounting for these differences.

Consider example two in the list above. Allowing children to move freely and access fidget and proprioceptive resources in the classroom is relatively easy. Planning all learning activities to be practical and physical without detracting from the core objectives is difficult.

Such adaptations require sophisticated pedagogical content knowledge so that teachers can understand the various ways of engaging with key concepts, skills and ideas.

CURRICULUM DESIGN

Key concepts, skills and ideas are usually defined according to the curriculum. However, many children's development does not align with national curricula. This misalignment is not because these children are lacking, but because curricula often reflect narrow assumptions about what 'normal' learning looks like.

Many national curricula are designed based on the experiences and needs of non-disabled, white, upper-middle-class learners (Race et al., 2022). This can result in content, pacing and teaching methods that are exclusive, marginalising pupils whose identities, backgrounds and learning styles differ.

For example, all children develop different skills at different rates (Berkshire Healthcare, 2025). Many new parents worry that their child is behind in meeting development milestones or that their child's progress in one area is weaker than in others. These variances in developmental progression are typical among all humans, yet curricula often dictate linear, age-based progression based on the assumption that all children will know and do the same things, in the same order, at the same time. This mismatch between human variance and fixed teaching is further compounded by the standardised tests common in many nations, which rely on all children expressing their understanding in the same way.

National curricula also often fail to account for cultural diversity, often favouring texts, topics and approaches associated with a politically favoured group (Maylor, 2021). Children from culturally diverse backgrounds may appear to make less progress in their learning and fall 'behind', when they are simply alienated or disengaged from a curriculum that does not feel relevant.

As educators, it is important to evaluate and challenge curriculum content. Curricula do not consist of universal facts: they are constructed frameworks that reflect certain values and priorities, typically created by political parties to suit their agendas. Educators need strong subject knowledge so that they can interrogate the curriculum and adapt it to suit their learners.

This involves asking questions like:

- who is represented in this curriculum and who is missing?

- whose knowledge, histories and ways of learning are valued?

- how accessible is this content for individual learners?

Asking these questions helps educators diversify their teaching approaches, design inclusive and flexible assessments and recognise when a curriculum choice reflects political or cultural bias rather than pedagogical value. The curriculum is not the only way to know and 'do' a subject.

MAKING THE LEAST DANGEROUS ASSUMPTION

Sometimes, children with SEND are excluded from curriculum learning not because the educator does not value their ways of learning, but because they hold the misconception that subject knowledge is irrelevant for the learner. For example, children with complex SEND might work at pre-curriculum expectations and therefore access a sensory or life-skills curriculum. While a sensory curriculum can be an excellent way to make learning accessible, it should not replace access to a balanced curriculum. All children should access all subjects in some form.

It is important to make the *least dangerous assumption* (Donnellan, 1984). This involves presuming competence, setting high expectations in all subjects and creatively supporting all learners towards personalised, relevant goals. This does not mean that all children should know the same facts and perform the same skills, but that no child should be discounted from a subject due to perceived barriers.

Consider the late Jonathon Bryan. In his memoir, *Eye can write* (Bryan, 2018), he details his frustrations while attending a specialist school. As Bryan's cerebral palsy prevented him from moving or speaking, teachers assumed that he could not access curriculum learning, instead repeating daily sensory activities and CBeebies programmes. His mother and a private tutor made the least dangerous assumption, believing that Bryan could learn with the right support. He learned to write using eye-tracking and wrote a book about believing in the capability of every child.

Bryan's story highlights the negative consequences of simplifying the curriculum for children with SEND and emphasises their potential when educators believe that they are capable. In practice, this is complicated. To effectively support children accessing the curriculum at different stages, educators need a secure understanding of curriculum progression from early childhood to post-primary education. They need a strong knowledge of children's strengths and needs, and how they might progress to their end goal.

Consider the specialist teacher who worked with Bryan. He was seven but could not yet read or write. She needed to understand how children develop early literacy skills. The physical act of writing with an implement would not be possible, so she needed to identify his other strengths, namely his eye movements, and have a strong knowledge of differing approaches to teaching writing in this way. Bryan's access to the curriculum depended on her highly specialist subject and pedagogical knowledge.

It is also important to remember that for many children, their development does not align with curriculum progression. This can make it difficult for educators to assess children's progress and identify suitable next steps. They therefore require a deep understanding of the breadth of knowledge and skills in each subject so that they can identify targets that are relevant and meaningful for individuals.

REFLECTION 4.2

How might the principle of the least dangerous assumption influence your day-to-day planning and assessment for children with diverse needs?

The following case studies exemplify how educators' assumptions and their subject knowledge impact the quality of education for individual children.

CASE STUDY: REUBEN, AGE 11

Reuben has a visual impairment and works below expected levels in literacy. His teacher is planning a science lesson about states of matter. They design a tactile experiment: Reuben handles ice, water and steam, tracking changes using thermo-sensitive materials. He uses voice notes to describe what he observes, using a scaffolded word bank with Braille labels. Reuben demonstrates understanding of physical changes and particle models through a verbal explanation recorded on a tablet.

The teacher assumes that Reuben understands the science curriculum to the same level as his peers. They use their subject and curriculum knowledge of states of matter to determine the core knowledge, and their understanding of Reuben's strengths to make this knowledge accessible for him. They demonstrate a willingness to engage with more than one way of knowing.

CASE STUDY: AISHA, AGE 9

Aisha has ADHD and struggles with sustained attention and writing. She enjoys strategy-based games and storytelling. Her teacher is planning a history lesson about the Romans. They identify that the Roman Empire's expansion offers a natural link to planning and strategy. Aisha is asked to design a Roman campaign plan using maps and symbols, focusing on why the Romans chose certain locations to conquer. She uses drawing, talk and a recording app to explain supply routes, terrain and battle tactics.

The teacher assumes that Aisha is a competent historian who will enjoy history. Their subject knowledge helps them to see links between the core history objectives and learning in other areas. This helps them plan a cross-curricular activity that supports Aisha's learning and enjoyment.

CASE STUDY: LOGAN, AGE 6

Logan uses a wheelchair. He has limited upper-body strength but enjoys competition and group activities. His teacher is planning an athletics PE lesson focusing on sprinting and throwing. Logan participates in wheelchair racing using a sports wheelchair. He trains in precision ball throws at various angles and targets, building strength and coordination. He competes in class challenges. He is encouraged to take a leadership role in analysing form and coaching others.

The teacher assumes that Logan can participate in sports with the right adaptations and equipment. They need strong subject knowledge to understand how to support pupil progress and safety in PE, irrespective of physical disabilities. They treat Logan as a competent learner, helping him develop his physical ability and understanding of sports.

In all three cases, the class teacher cannot rely on the curriculum alone because the children's interests, skills and needs do not align with this framework. Instead, the teacher adapts the learning approach to support the children's skills and interests, using wider knowledge of the subject and teaching strategies. In each case, they assume that the child is competent, with the right support.

PROFESSIONAL LANGUAGE

The language we use to discuss needs and provision reflects our assumptions and can shape how we approach teaching, learning and assessment.

Consider the following terms. Depending on your nation, you may have heard some of them used in practice. What do the terms mean, and what constructions of SEND do they denote?

- Differentiation.

- Reasonable adjustments.

- High-quality teaching.

- Quality-first teaching.

- Adaptive teaching.

- Enabling learning (including enabling adults).

- Ordinarily available inclusive provision (OAIP).

Differentiation and reasonable adjustments are examples of making changes for a specific child because the learning planned for the rest of the class is inaccessible. While such strategies can support access to learning, they work on the assumption that individual differences require individual alterations.

By contrast, adaptive teaching and enabling learning focus on flexible activities that children can access in various ways. The Welsh Government's emphasis on 'enabling adults' (HWB, 2023) is particularly key to understanding this perspective: it is not the child's responsibility to blend in with their non-disabled peers. Educators are responsible for making learning accessible.

There is also a subtle but important difference between language such as 'high-quality teaching' versus 'ordinarily available inclusive provision'. The former emphasises inclusive teaching practice, where the latter refers to provision, which also encompasses the role of the classroom environment, routines, adults and resources.

The case studies below demonstrate how a learner's wellbeing, learning and inclusion vary according to the educator's approach.

DIFFERENTIATION: ART

In a lesson on observational drawing, the educator knows that some children with dyspraxia and dysgraphia struggle to control motor movements and plan their sketches. One of these children is given a dot-to-dot to draw instead, and the others are given a simpler object to sketch.

OAIP: ART

In the same lesson, the educator provides a variety of tools (e.g. thick-handled pencils, digital drawing tablets) and allows children to choose their medium. They use visualisers and enlarge reference images. The focus is on expressing form and shade, not replicating a perfect image. Peer models are used for additional guidance.

REASONABLE ADJUSTMENTS: GEOGRAPHY

In a topic on rivers, the educator explains key terms using a PowerPoint™ and models how to label a river diagram. Children complete a worksheet matching terms to definitions and labelling features on a river cross-section. A few children struggle with working memory, literacy skills, language processing and/or use English as an additional language. For these children, the educator provides a different worksheet where half of the definitions have already been completed and the language in the labels is simplified.

OAIP: GEOGRAPHY

In the same lesson, the educator uses an animation of river processes, colour-coded diagrams and 3D models. Vocabulary is pre-taught through multilingual word banks and physical gestures. Children use tablets to record voice explanations of each river feature, working in pairs.

None of these approaches is entirely right or wrong. In the first example for each subject, the educator understands children's needs and takes steps to ensure that tasks are achievable. But, in the OAIP examples, more diverse provision and approaches mean that everyone can access the same learning in an individually relevant way, rather than being treated differently or being prevented from achieving the same as their peers. Consider the impact on these children's long-term wellbeing.

Teaching flexibly using inclusive approaches is perhaps easier in some subjects than others. Practical curriculum areas such as visual and performing arts, sports and technology often rely less on conventional literacy skills and encourage collaboration. They involve self-expression and curricula typically cover a range of skills and styles.

By contrast, the sciences, humanities, mathematics and literacy often teach defined knowledge, skills may be less flexible and learning often includes greater written and spoken language demands. In these subjects, it is even more important that educators have sufficient subject knowledge to enact inclusive provision and adaptive approaches to learning.

REFLECTION 4.3

- In which subjects do you feel most and least confident to adapt teaching to support all learners?
- How could you develop your knowledge further to support inclusive practice?

FINAL THOUGHTS

Many curricula emphasise standardised approaches and outcomes which do not meet all children's needs. However, even within highly restrictive curricula, educators have the power to make decisions which can improve educational experiences and outcomes. The content they choose to offer or omit for pupils with SEND has significant implications for social equity, inclusion and long-term life chances. This means that educators' decisions are not just a pedagogical issue, but also an ethical one.

Consider the following statistics:

- in the UK in 2024, 53 per cent of known disabled people were employed compared to 81.6 per cent of non-disabled people (DWP, 2025);

- diagnosed neurodivergent children are more likely than neurotypical peers to have poorer physical and mental health, lower educational attainment, lower employment rates and more interaction with the criminal justice system (Vo and Webb, 2024);

- in England, 8.9 per cent of pupils with an education and healthcare plan (EHCP) progressed to higher education by age 19, compared to 51.2 per cent of pupils with no identified SEN (DfE, 2024).

Reflect on the statistics you have just seen as you read:

- in 2018, a third of teachers in 43 countries reported that they did not adjust their teaching to meet students' needs (UNESCO, 2020);

- Warnes et al. (2021, p. 31) found that some teachers perceive children with SEND as 'an onerous adjunct to an already stressful "regular" teaching role'.

These statistics highlight the extent of the lifelong inequalities children with SEND face. They also suggest that educators are not always well-placed to address these inequalities due to a lack of knowledge, skill and, sometimes, negative attitudes. A combination of strong subject knowledge and skilled pedagogy is needed to address these inequalities.

Throughout this chapter, you have explored how special educational needs and disabilities are defined, constructed and interpreted, and how these constructions influence teaching practice. You have examined the medical and social models of disability and considered the importance of shifting the focus away from 'fixing' children and towards removing barriers to meaningful learning.

Strong subject knowledge allows educators to plan creatively and inclusively, valuing diverse ways of learning and knowing. Rather than assuming that all children will meet the same goals in the same way, you have considered what it means to presume competence, make the least dangerous assumption and ensure all children can access a curriculum that is relevant, challenging and affirming.

You have also reflected on the language we use to describe needs and provision, and how everyday decisions about curriculum content and pedagogy are deeply ethical. Educators' choices shape children's access to opportunity, their sense of belonging and their longer-term outcomes. This makes inclusive subject teaching both a professional responsibility and a matter of social justice.

As you finish this chapter, take a moment to reflect on your own beliefs, assumptions and areas for development. How has your perspective on SEND and subject knowledge shifted? Inclusion is every educator's responsibility. Being reflexive and investing time in continued professional development are key to ensuring that all children can access high-quality education. By developing your subject and pedagogical knowledge, you can support better outcomes for all children, helping to create a more just, inclusive society.

FURTHER READING AND RESOURCES

BBC News. (2025). *Love on the Spectrum cast questions RFK Jr's comments about autistic people.* www.bbc.co.uk/news/articles/cd6jlvq59njo

Cast members of *Love on the Spectrum* discuss and denounce RFK Jr's comments about autism, calling them harmful and inaccurate compared to the lived experiences of autistic people.

Bhaskar, R. and Danermark, B. (2006). Metatheory, interdisciplinarity and disability research: A critical realist perspective. *Scandinavian Journal of Disability Research*, 8(4), 278–297. doi: 10.1080/15017410600914329

Uses critical realism for an interdisciplinary view of disability research.

Bryan, J. (2018). *Eye can write: A memoir of a child's silent soul emerging.* Lagom.

A memoir by Jonathan Bryan, who has severe cerebral palsy and is non-speaking, detailing how he found his voice by learning to communicate with his eyes.

Erickson, K. and Koppenhaver, D. (2019). *Comprehensive literacy for all: Teaching students with significant disabilities to read and write.* Brookes.

Guide to teaching comprehensive literacy to students with significant disabilities.

Lien, V. (2025). Decolonising special educational needs and disabilities (SEND): A systems theoretical framework for global inclusivity. *Systems Research and Behaviour Science, 42*(2), 517–530. doi: 10.1002/sres.3138

Proposes a systems framework for decolonising SEND and achieving global inclusivity.

Open University. (2025). *Timeline of learning disability history.* https://university.open.ac.uk/health-and-social-care/research/shld/timeline-learning-disability-history

Provides a chronological overview of significant historical events, policy changes and shifts in societal attitudes regarding learning disability in the UK, from early institutionalisation to modern rights and inclusion.

Rolfe, S. (2019). Models of SEND: The impact of political and economic influences on policy and provision. *British Journal of Special Education*, 46(4), 423–444. doi: 10.1111/1467-8578.12284

Analyses how political and economic influences shape SEND policy and provision.

UNESCO. (1994). *The Salamanca statement and framework for action on special needs education.* UNESCO. https://unesdoc.unesco.org/ark:/48223/pf000009842

Report establishing the principle of inclusive education.

UNESCO. (2020). *Global education monitoring report: Inclusion and education: All means all.* https://unesdoc.unesco.org/ark:/48223/pf0000373718

Global report on the necessity of inclusion in education.

REFERENCES

ACARA. (2024). *School students with disability.* www.acara.edu.au/reporting/national-report-on-schooling-in-australia/school-students-with-disability

Audit Scotland. (2025). *Briefing: Additional support for learning.* https://audit.scot/uploads/2025-02/briefing_250227_additional_support_for_learning.pdf

Berkshire Healthcare. (2025). *Typical development.* https://cypf.berkshirehealthcare.nhs.uk/health-and-development/your-baby-and-you/typical-development/

Bhaskar, R. and Danermark, B. (2006). Metatheory, interdisciplinarity and disability research: A critical realist perspective. *Scandinavian Journal of Disability Research, 8*(4), 278–297. https://doi.org/10.1080/15017410600914329

Bogart, K. R. (2021). The moral model of disability is alive and well. *Psychology Today.* www.psychologytoday.com/gb/blog/disability-is-diversity/202105/the-moral-model-disability-is-alive-and-well

Bryan, J. (2018). *Eye can write: A memoir of a child's silent soul emerging.* Lagom.

Department for Education (DfE). (2024). *Labour market outcomes: Chapter 3 special educational needs.* https://assets.publishing.service.gov.uk/media/67487e8d6f60e776797239a5/Chapter_3-_Special_Educational_Needs.pdf

DfE. (2025). *Special educational needs in England.* https://explore-education-statistics.service.gov.uk/find-statistics/special-educational-needs-in-england/2024-25

Department for Work and Pensions (DWP). (2025). *The employment of disabled people 2024.* www.gov.uk/government/statistics/the-employment-of-disabled-people-2024/the-employment-of-disabled-people-2024

Donnellan, A. M. (1984). The criterion of the least dangerous assumption. *Behavioral Disorders, 9*(2), 141–150. www.jstor.org/stable/43153291

Equality Act. (2010). www.legislation.gov.uk/ukpga/2010/15

Erickson, K. and Koppenhaver, D. (2019). *Comprehensive literacy for all: Teaching students with significant disabilities to read and write.* Brookes.

Goldacre, B. (2014). *I think you'll find it's a bit more complicated than that.* Fourth Estate.

HWB. (2023). *Enabling learning.* https://hwb.gov.wales/curriculum-for-wales/designing-your-curriculum/enabling-learning

Jarrett, S. (2020). *Those they called idiots: The idea of the disabled mind from 1700 to the present day.* Reaktion.

Lien, V. (2025). Decolonising special educational needs and disabilities (SEND): A systems theoretical framework for global inclusivity. *Systems Research and Behavioral Science, 42*(2), 517–530. https://doi.org/10.1002/sres.3138

Looi, M. (2025). Trump watch: What are the US government's plans for autism? *BMJ, 389.* www.bmj.com/content/389/bmj.r820

Maylor, U. (2021). Curriculum diversity and social justice education: From New Labour to Conservative government control of education in England. In A. Ross (Ed.), *Educational research for social justice* (pp. 223–247). Springer. https://doi.org/10.1007/978-3-030-62572-6_11

Oduyemi, A. Y., Okafor, I. P., Eze, U. T., Akodu, B. A. and Roberts, A. A. (2021). Internalization of stigma among parents of children with autism spectrum disorder in Nigeria: A mixed method study. *BMC Psychology, 9*. https://doi.org/10.1186/s40359-021-00687-3

Oliver's Campaign. (n.d.). *Oliver McGowan's story.* www.olivermcgowan.org/

Race, R., Ayling, P., Chetty, D., Hassan, N., McKinney, S. J., Boath, L., Riaz, N. and Salehjee, S. (2022). Decolonising curriculum in education: Continuing proclamations and provocations. *London Review of Education, 20*(1). https://doi.org/10.14324/LRE.20.1.12

Robertson, Z. S. and Jaswal, V. K. (2024). Barriers to inclusion: Incorporating the social model in the study of children's understanding of disability. *Cognitive Development, 70.* https://doi.org/10.1016/j.cogdev.2024.101435

Rolfe, S. (2019). Models of SEND: The impact of political and economic influences on policy and provision. *British Journal of Special Education, 46*(4), 423–444. https://doi.org/10.1111/1467-8578.12284

Rossetti, Z. and Tashie, C. (2005). Outing the prejudice: Making the least dangerous assumption. www.forliving.org/inspirational-reading/least-dangerous-assumption.pdf

Scavarda, A. (2024). The shame-blame complex of parents with cognitively disabled children in Italy. *Sociology of Health and Illness, 46*(5), 966–983. https://doi.org/10.1111/1467-9566.13742

Shah, P. (2024). *Donald Trump's dangerous views on disability and the power to think differently.* www.justsecurity.org/98261/disability-think-differently-trump/

Shamsabadipour, A. (2025). Disability models: Societal impacts and policy implications. In *The Palgrave Encyclopaedia of Disability* (pp. 1–10). https://doi.org/10.1007/978-3-031-40858-8_409-1

The House of Commons Education and Skills Committee. (2006). Special educational needs: Third report of session 2005–06. *Volume I: Report, together with formal minutes.* HMSO. https://publications.parliament.uk/pa/cm200506/cmselect/cmeduski/478/478i.pdf

UNESCO. (2020). *Global education monitoring report summary, 2020: Inclusion and education: All means all.* https://unesdoc.unesco.org/ark:/48223/pf0000373721/PDF/373721eng.pdf.multi

United Nations (UN). (1989). *United Nations convention on the rights of the child.* www.ohchr.org/en/instruments-mechanisms/instruments/convention-rights-child

Unwin, S. (2022). Need not diagnosis: Towards a more realistic language and understanding. *The Michael Lewis Inaugural Lecture, LSBU.* www.stephenunwin.uk/thoughts-and-provocations/2022/7/2/need-not-diagnosis-towards-a-more-realistic-language-and-understanding

Vo, S. and Webb, L. (2024). Support for neurodivergent children and young people. *Parliamentary Office of Science and Technology (POST).* https://researchbriefings.files.parliament.uk/documents/POST-PN-0733/POST-PN-0733.pdf

Waltz, M. (2023). *Autism: A social and medical history.* Palgrave Macmillan. https://doi.org/10.1007/978-3-031-31015-7_3

Ware, S. M., Zankowicz, K. and Sims, S. (2022). The call for disability justice in museum education: Re-framing accessibility as anti-ableism. *Journal of Museum Education, 47*(2), 130–137. https://doi.org/10.1080/10598650.2022.2077079

Warnes, E., Done, E. J. and Knowler, H. (2021). Mainstream teachers' concerns about inclusive education for children with special educational needs and disability in England under pre-pandemic conditions. *Journal of Research in Special Educational Needs, 22*(1), 31–43. https://doi.org/10.1111/1471-3802.12525

5
USING REFLECTION TO DEVELOP SUBJECT KNOWLEDGE THROUGH EFFECTIVE CLASSROOM INTERACTIONS

SIMON C. RIPLEY

THIS CHAPTER

This chapter explores the ideas that:

- classroom interactions are complex learning opportunities that can benefit the development of subject knowledge in the primary classroom

- reflecting on aspects of interactions can help us improve their effectiveness

- focusing on the outcomes of an interaction can help us develop our practice and enhance opportunities to develop subject knowledge.

KEY TERMS FOR THIS CHAPTER

Interaction: two-way process of developing learning through a transactional process of communication.

Reflection: post-event consideration of key themes to generate an understanding that can be used for personal development to shape future interactions, in this particular case.

Transaction: the giving and receiving of knowledge and opinions between the participants with a view to assessing learning, developing this further and generating a shared understanding of position in relation to the content of the interaction. Please note that this informs interactions in the moment as well as over the longer term.

Support: the processes and practices that are used to ensure learning takes place as required by the individual in relation to the learning objectives.

Challenge: the processes and practices that are utilised to ensure greatest learning gains rather than just reaching an acceptable standard.

INTRODUCTION

Interactions in the classroom, or any learning environment, are such a deeply embedded part of practice that the importance of these, and their complexity, can often be overlooked. I will be honest with you right from the start of this chapter, that for too long I saw interactions as mainly one-way, uncomplicated opportunities to try inspiring the children I worked with and share my subject knowledge, which was probably because I had found that other aspects of what I was doing in the classroom were deemed a priority. After considerable time spent reflecting on my own practice, I began to research the potential of this fundamental factor. Interactions, for me, have always been a favourite part of working with children. I increasingly came to realise that these interactions, in all of their many forms, present us with very real and effective opportunities to collaboratively learn alongside the children we work with and for them to learn from each other (Beck and Kosnik, 2021). In a nutshell, interactions are supercharged vehicles that can be harnessed to enhance the acquisition, exploration, consolidation and application of subject knowledge across every aspect of the primary curriculum.

Following on from my admission above, Warren and Lessner (2014) highlight the importance of effective educator–child interactions in securing progress. However, they caution that this is not considered with the same gravitas as other aspects of successful pedagogy. So why does this chapter exist? If we can understand more about classroom interactions ourselves then we can view them alongside other aspects of classroom practice that require thought, development and practice. They no longer need to just be about subject knowledge transfer but instead can become a powerful tool in improving outcomes for children in all aspects of the curriculum. Moreover, the skills involved in interactions are transferrable and applicable in all learning environments.

This chapter is applicable across all of the subjects contained elsewhere in this book and to support the application of your learning from here in practice.

SUBJECT KNOWLEDGE

In a primary classroom it could be perceived by children that the adults 'know everything there is to know' about the subjects they are teaching (Carroll and Alexander, 2020). Obviously, this can never be the case for many reasons, not least of which the broad range of subjects covered in primary curricula around the world. What is important is that educators ensure that they have secure subject knowledge across all curriculum areas they teach, seek to develop their knowledge further and consider recent *evidence-based practice* in how to most effectively teach these (Ogier, 2022).

Cuthbert and Standish (2021) strongly suggest that the very basis of any curriculum is *knowledge* and share how developing knowledge could be seen as moving knowledge from the everyday type towards increasing specialised forms. The example they share is that 'bird' is an everyday word that conveys knowledge of a particular type of animal with shared characteristics. If we were to discuss a parrot then we are specialising our knowledge by knowing more finely tuned information about a specific type of bird. Semantically we would be sharing our understanding of the information which is knowledge of what a bird is through a more nuanced appreciation of the features of a specific type of bird. This example above relates to the idea of our subject knowledge, and that of the children we teach, acting as *building blocks* for learning of more specialised subject knowledge. This is one way of conceptualising how our role as educators enables children's subject knowledge to progress and deepen. This can apply across all subjects in a curriculum of any format and is a useful starting point for the exploration of the concept of knowledge.

Following on from the building block idea shared above, we understand that children will come to us with a set of these building blocks which may have been enhanced through high-quality teaching in the past or reduced by low levels of attendance, for example. Regardless, the subject knowledge children bring to our lessons is that we often call *prior knowledge.* Much has been written about prior knowledge and the importance of knowing this (Bell, 2021) is of obvious benefit to educators when planning and delivering subject content in ways designed to enhance subject knowledge (and how this can be applied in cross-curricular ways; Barnes, 2015).

Here it is useful for us to consider the concept of *funds of knowledge* (FoK) which sets out to contextualise the sources of knowledge that are available to any individual (Moll et al., 1992). FoK differ from prior knowledge in that they (the 'funds') have contributed to prior knowledge but also can act as current and future sources of knowledge. As an educator you are a FoK for the children you work with. Other FoK for them could include parents/carers, family, friends, access to media, cultural resources available to them, the internet (hopefully with adequate controls over content and quality of content) and so many others. Why is this important? Well, an exploration of FoK that are available to the children we work with can help us enhance their learning of subject knowledge as individuals ('your sister is a nurse so you could ask her about …' or 'I know that you like watching …', for example). In addition, children can be FoK for each other as well as for educators. Understanding FoK is a powerful tool that will support us in our interactions (and enhancing peer interactions) throughout all of the coming factors that will be discussed.

REFLECTION 5.1

- Can you think of some examples of your own FoK?
- How might these support you in developing children's subject knowledge?

INTERACTIONS AS COMPLEX, YET EFFECTIVE, LEARNING OPPORTUNITIES

The impact of effective interactions is crucial to improving outcomes and can lead to long-lasting positive self-perceptions of children, as highlighted by many academics over time, including Castle and Buckler (2018), Jamil et al. (2015) and Burnett (1999). However, interactions are complex and this chapter marks a starting point for your exploration of these. The complexity of interactions within an educational environment, termed 'interactionism' (Castle and Butler, 2018), can have a significant benefit to academic achievement, including a direct relationship to subject knowledge, as well as on holistic development.

This chapter will explore six features of effective classroom interactions, providing examples to support your development as a practitioner. Before we go any further, I think it is important to share one of the key questions that has shaped my enthusiasm for and focus on classroom interactions.

The fundamental question that underpins this chapter could be viewed as:

> *Did the child gain something positive from this interaction that s/he would not otherwise have had? (Fisher, 2016, p. 3)*

From a subject knowledge perspective, the question above could be expanded to include the specific nature of the gain, as well as the skills needed to utilise this knowledge in whatever way required by a task or learning objective.

THE POWER OF REFLECTION

Reflection is the suggested way to consider how effective interactions are within your experience, with a view to adopting a new appreciation and enhanced range of approaches to secure their successes. Time is always against us educators and there are always so many things that we could devote our attention to. However, *reflective practice* is something that is seen as a key driver to performance improvement (Pollard, 2023). I remember a time when I was a newly qualified teacher (NQT) discussing the lack of available time to reflect on practice with my mentor. They were very definitely an advocate for reflective practice and remained adamant that taking time to properly consider lessons I had just taught was crucial. Following this open conversation, I took some time to sit at my desk, looking at nothing in particular and just 'reflected' on my lessons. Within minutes someone had entered my room and asked me if I had 'run out of things to do'. Obviously, this comment was made because I probably looked like I was just daydreaming and wasting the precious commodity that is time.

Educators highly value reflective practice (Ferreira, 2021) yet do not necessarily have the skills or time to effectively utilise this process to the full extent we should. By encouraging your exploration of interactions in greater depth and utilising reflective practice, the aim of this chapter is to guide you in a series of steps that will enhance your skills in ways that will improve a range of outcomes for the children you work with.

PSYCHOLOGICAL FRAMING

This could be considered as the *classroom ethos* dimension of interactions; however, I feel that this label neglects the ways which children will respond to and perceive classroom dynamics in very different ways. Psychological framing is more about ensuring that children have a safe, yet appropriately challenging, environment in which to work; have a *growth mindset* (Dweck, 2012) (you will explore this concept further below) that will help them learn the resilience that they will, as we do, need throughout their lives; and feel a sense of belonging through secure, positive relationships with educators and their peers.

High expectations of children have been proven to be a driver for curriculum success (Busch and Watson, 2021; Carroll and Alexander, 2020) provided that support is available as and when needed (NASEN, 2020). We should endeavour to balance support and challenge to meet the learning needs of all the children we work with, resulting in greater levels of progress. Having high aspirations ensures that children recognise they will be pushed to achieve their best (both in subjects where they have higher levels of confidence and those where they may lack confidence) with the opportunity to access support when they find subject material to be 'too hard' to access or use. There is a fine balance between support and challenge, yet our approach should always be considered on an individual basis with challenge being a natural part of any lesson regardless of ability (the level and type of challenge will vary, but challenge will still exist as a natural part of the learning process). The same can be said of support, as even the most able learners may encounter aspects of learning to be something they can face difficulty with. Support should be available and accessible for all to the same degree, although the format may be different.

One way we can promote children having high aspirations for themselves and their peers is through the sparking of curiosity. Studies have demonstrated that curiosity impacts positively on children's outcomes, boosts mental wellbeing and supports a drive towards deeper engagement with curriculum content (Harvard Business Review Press, 2024). This in turn links with the concept of *psychological safety* which will be discussed next. Clark (2020) suggests that curiosity stems from a nurturing environment where relationships are strong. They argue that curiosity comes from the freedom to be able to explore learning without the fear of making mistakes, and being encouraged to take risks in their approaches and interactions. To avoid stifling this curiosity it is therefore important to create a nurturing and safe learning context. This can be achieved through open questions which challenge children to an appropriate degree (and this part is not an exact science, as learning is an even more complex concept than interactions, but that does not mean we should opt out of consistently trying) and promoting student-led practice.

We all make mistakes. I make many on a regular basis (but I genuinely make fewer if I am utilising reflection practices effectively). It is often heard that people say we 'learn from our mistakes', but how true is this for the children we work with? Do they have the skills to learn from times when they achieve less than the teacher-identified desired outcome? Do we spend time teaching them these skills? Do we really learn from our mistakes and, if we do, are we ensuring that the psychological framing in the classroom reinforces this?

Children who are ready to take risks with their learning and are comfortable to 'get it wrong' experience a feeling of psychological safety (Edmonson, 2023). A psychologically safe environment can only exist if children know they will be empowered to learn from their mistakes in a way that moves their subject knowledge as shown in Figure 5.1.

Acquisition ⟶ Exploration ⟶ Consolidation ⟶ Application

Figure 5.1   Moving subject knowledge forwards

It is vital to provide learners with the space to try all these aspects without the anxiety challenge an unsafe environment can bring (something which undoubtedly prevents children from pushing themselves out of their comfort zone). This sense of real safety brings associated benefits to learning (Staricoff, 2021). For example, you can imagine the improvement to self-esteem that comes with surprising yourself by exceeding expectations. Being able to have evidence that you have challenged yourself and succeeded can foster greater self-belief and be used to encourage children to take further risks with their learning in ways that may not happen if they do not experience these positive moments following these. There is also benefit to the relationship between the educator, who showed them that they may feel that they are unable to do something initially but actually can, and the empowered child;. Growth mindset, as set out below, suggests that this is actually illustrating that children may feel they are unable to achieve something, but the reality is that they are unable to do so *yet*. Interactions, as small-scale and less visible features of lessons, are an ideal opportunity to encourage children to take real risks with their learning. The risk is reduced by the approach of the teacher, therefore psychological safety can be established and maintained much more easily than with a whole class.

To secure the greatest outcomes, Table 5.1 shows how a combination of aspiration and feeling psychologically safe (or not) can impact on progress.

Table 5.1   Adapted from the work of Edmonson (2023)

	Low standards/aspirations	High standards/aspirations
High psychological safety	Enjoying the status quo	'Failing well' (and learning so much from it)
Low psychological safety	Checking out	Avoiding risks or covering up failure

Growth mindset is another aspect of psychological framing that can have significant impact on the perceptions children have of their ability to learn. Introduced by psychologist Carol Dweck (2012), many published works have targeted the way children talk negatively about themselves both internally and in their interactions with others. A common phrase that may be heard is 'I just can't do maths.' This example of a fixed mindset can then become a self-fulfilling prophecy. However, if an educator reflects back a more positive, growth mindset, their response to this statement can entirely shift the narrative. 'You think you can't do maths, *yet*' (Brock and Hundley, 2018). This subtle emphasis change demonstrates, firstly, that you understand that the child is saying they struggle in a subject-specific context (and this helps to build relationships much more effectively than by dismissing the child's concerns). Secondly, it provides a structure for future interactions, where the child is aware that what they feel now will not always be the case, and that you believe in their ability to overcome these hurdles. Truly one word can make a huge difference, but as children get older and their beliefs get more ingrained it may take longer for them to move towards this more positive way of thinking about themselves.

REFLECTION 5.2

How might I ensure that the children feel confident taking risks with their learning?

INITIATION METHODS

The next feature of interactions that we will consider is how interactions begin.

- Did you initiate it?

- Did the child?

- Does that matter to the outcome of the interaction?

In short, the answer to the third question is: yes it does. We shall now consider why it matters and what we can do with this understanding.

There is a vast difference between an adult initiating an interaction based on their own reasoning and when a child is seeking an interaction for their own reasons. We can use this knowledge to frame interactions in a way that develops our use and application of subject knowledge. If the adult initiates an interaction, will they be focusing on gauging subject-specific understanding, or will it be to gain confirmation that the children are secure in the task that they have been asked to do? If the child initiates the interaction, is this because they want to be supported with the task processes, seek reassurance, question their understanding, or could it even be to seek to develop their subject knowledge even further beyond the level the curriculum demands?

Initiation of interactions is predicated on a complex set of factors. For example, children's agency, and by implication, their willingness to initiate interactions, can significantly be affected by their mood and those of their peers. Canovi et al. (2019) found that mood was a significant contributor to student agency; they imply that there would be an impact from the teacher's perspective too. These authors recognise, and cite Hohti (2016), to stress the importance of emotional considerations in pedagogy in general, including interactions. So, following on from the section above on psychological framing, it is important to consider how this is linked to the level of interaction initiation by children.

It is possible to encourage children to seek support via interactions when they require it, as opposed to interactions only being offered by adults in the room (Davison et al., 2023). However, there are a variety of reasons why children will not always initiate interactions. In these instances, it is appropriate for educators to do so when they identify that there may be a reason. Van Es and Sherin (2002) highlighted the importance of recognising when an interaction with a student is beneficial and when it is unnecessary. This distinction is important; unnecessary interactions can potentially limit learning (Fisher, 2016). There may be a need to pause when working with children so as to not interfere with their learning by forcing an interaction at the wrong time (Fisher, 2016). Recognising the difference between beneficial and necessary, as well as good timing of educator initiation, is a skill which can be developed further by educators at any stage of their career through the use of reflection (Bates, 2023).

LINGUISTICS

Considering the words we use, and the way in which we sequence these to convey meaning, is a key aspect which impacts on the effectiveness of classroom interactions. Due to the importance of the actual words we use and way we use them we must consider how subject-specific words are used to support development of subject knowledge and its application (remembering that some words will be used in multiple subjects).

Linguistics has long been viewed as a core element of classroom practice including interactions (Delamont, 1976). Use of specific language has a huge impact on conveying meaning, as well as increasing the retention and use of subject knowledge (Littleton and Howe, 2010). There is much evidence to suggest that use of language should be combined with the structural and scaffolding elements that are utilised in traditional classroom discourse (Pickering and Garrod, 2021; Mercer and Hodgkinson, 2008). By carefully considering the words teachers use alongside how they are conveyed (Dix, 2017; Denton, 2007), with careful thought given to children's comprehension (Hayes and Whittaker, 2015), it should be possible to improve the effectiveness of interactions between educators and children. Further to this is recognition that language use can be effectively developed – for example, through modelling (Dempster and Robbins, 2017).

As a starting point for incorporating linguistics into our development of interactions you may wish to consider each of these examples and how they could be used:

- encourage 'classroom talk' on a regular basis and develop children's understanding of the way they use language to convey meaning (Thwaite et al., 2020);

- avoid using combinations of words that might be vague and therefore reduce clarity for the reader/listener (Groshell, 2024);

- only use well-selected metaphors that will hold meaning for the children you are working with or explore more complex, less familiar metaphors to ensure that there is clarity over exactly what is being shared and why. Welton and Telford (2004) present a structured method for providing greater clarity over metaphor meaning, including visual representation and use of examples. One example that they give is 'facing the music', which may seem easy to understand at first but without clarity of meaning this may be confusing for some children. Please refer to the Further reading section after the conclusion for this and similar published works to further your understanding of the key themes discussed throughout this chapter;

- remember that non-linguistic aspects of communication such as tone will have an impact on conveyance of meaning (Pickering and Garrod, 2021).

COMMUNICATION METHODS

Linguistics in the sense discussed so far does not take into account the importance of non-verbal communication, which is heavily stressed by Thwaite et al. (2020) and Ekman and Friesen (2003). The ways we communicate are complex, but as a starting point here are some methods we can use alongside linguistic communication:

- use of visual prompts such as pictures and symbols (see speechandlanguage.org.uk for support and resources);

- break our communication, whatever the format, into smaller parts or chunks as we would with instructions in the ways suggested by multiple authors including Reid and Green (2016);

- provide physical reference points such as visual timelines (based on the principle of visual timetables suggested by Wood (2019) and others);

- use *objects of reference*, which are physical items used to support understanding (Askew, 2016);

- allow children time to adequately process the information you are sharing. The length of time required by children to effectively process information or formulate responses can vary significantly between individuals, so it is important to get to know your learners well (Nash, 2020);

- use, and encourage the use of, signing through Makaton (see Makaton.org for resources and support);

- make sure that you scaffold the use of all the above methods so children can engage with them effectively (Ball and Fairlamb, 2025).

REFLECTION 5.3

- Why might providing time for children to adequately process information be a challenge? What can we do about this?

- How can we adapt our language use when asking questions to provide greater clarity? What might help us recognise that changes are needed?

PEER INTERACTIONS

Peer interactions, in pairs and in groups, can be very powerful ways of improving subject knowledge retention and application for children. Kerr and Hertel (2011) provide some useful features to consider when planning for peer interaction activities in order to increase their effectiveness.

When setting up peer interactions it is useful to consider the following:

- familiarity of individuals with each other (which is different to being 'friends' if the psychological framing within the classroom is positive) can have benefits;

- rotating peer combinations;

- clarity of task expectations;

- perceptions of individual contributions linked to achieving success;

- ensuring that the ability gap between peers is not too large as this can be counterproductive (remember rotations);

- effective scaffolding of skills required for the interactions.

Following this final point, Ball and Fairlamb (2025) explain in great depth the fundamental importance of scaffolding across the full range of abilities and prior experiences. Learning to talk to each other and support learning (Bosanquet et al., 2021), including through the accurate use of subject-specific vocabulary, is a developmental skill that we should scaffold and model for children. In order to ensure that peer interactions are as effective as possible, time should be taken with the children to explore the nature of interactions and the specific purposes which they are being used for (Beck and Kosnik, 2021). Educators modelling this effectively in their interactions with children will support development of these skills (Myatt, 2020).

Interactions related to the reciting of subject-specific knowledge are useful, though they require a different level and set of skills when we ask children to discuss their understanding and ideas (Ball and Fairlamb, 2025). It is not only important to ensure this understanding is developed (being very specific with task objectives and providing prompts etc., as suggested by Hayes and Whittaker (2016)); also care should be taken to foster a genuinely purposeful ethos for peer interactions where the children understand and demonstrate behaviours for learning which facilitate working as 'effective teams' (Bates, 2023). They should not only participate using these skills, but also benefit from understanding how these interactions can help develop their own subject knowledge in conjunction with their peers as well as positively impact on the learning of others (examples of which include active listening, respect for all contributions, active participation through turn-taking and questioning and peer-praise). Through effective modelling, scaffolding and monitoring of peer interactions we will see an increase in engagement and reduce off-task time.

The practices of educators here can be magnified through the effect of *contagion* as described by Harvard (2025) and explained by Hess and Fischer (2016). The latter study evidenced children being more likely to mimic positive learning behaviours if they perceived that their peers were demonstrating them. This study even went on to demonstrate that it was the perception of the way peers were behaving that had the biggest influence and not the actual behaviours; if a child sees their peers engaging effectively in subject-specific discussions then they are more likely to engage effectively themselves.

THE ENDING OF AN INTERACTION

It is my belief that any interaction between a teacher and a child should end in the same way that an interaction between professionals should, as advocated for by authors such as Owen (2022). Whether the interactions last moments or take considerably longer, it is important to finish with an agreed set of next steps, a positive mindset and clarity over next steps.

REFLECTION 5.4

- How can we assess the effectiveness of an interaction, between educator and child or peer-peer, at any point during it?

- How can we ensure any next steps at the end of an interaction and how they link to the task are understood by the children?

THE TRANSACTIONAL NATURE OF INTERACTIONS

Before we move on to consider how reflection can help us improve interactions within the classroom, it is important to remember that the nature of interactions, as well as the benefits that they can bring to the learning of subject knowledge, are transactional.

As a summation of learning interactions and their role in the acquisition, retention, understanding and application of subject knowledge, we need to acknowledge that interactions are a two-way process (Littleton and Howe, 2010). They can be used effectively to increase confidence levels of the children we work with and we, as educators, can learn much from those children (both from a subject knowledge perspective and from gaining greater understanding of the individuals we interact with). As subject knowledge increases and can be applied in increasingly challenging contexts (and out of context), a transactional approach can provide building blocks for children's future learning, help to foster positive learning relationships and provide us, as educators, with knowledge of the individual which can be used in our next interactions. This knowledge, subject and relational, will build up over time and support the improvement of outcomes in multiple ways. After we interact, we should reflect, asking ourselves what we have learned from the interaction.

REFLECTION 5.5

How can you help children understand the importance of interactions being a two-way process like this?

REFLECTION AS A DEVELOPMENTAL TOOL

Reflection is a common feature of professional practices including those in education (Johns, 2022). We can use reflection to consider interactions to understand if we are making the most of these opportunities.

Reflective practice is a well-defined concept within the education sector as a tool for analysing pedagogy through the lens of the educator, either by themselves or in conjunction with another education professional (DfE, 2024). Reflection is designed to improve future practice by considering past events to identify methods for improving future outcomes (Brookfield, 2017).

Ferreira (2021) highlights the fact that reflection occurs both *in* action (while the lesson is happening) and *on* action (following the lesson). Debate on this practice centres around the purpose of reflection: is it something that is designed to adjust practice in situ or is it a developmental process intended to have identifiable impact in the future (Hayes, 2014)? The opinion of authors is mixed on this as it will depend very much on the structure and way in which reflection is used. However, Shyman (2020) recognises the importance of both in and out active reflection, even going as far as to suggest that teachers are continually reflecting on practice as part of their professional identity.

With so much written about reflective practice I would suggest that you find a model that works best for you. There are many to choose from; some of these will suit you more than others. You will find suggested reading at the end of this chapter to support you with this alongside further discussion on the role of reflection, including analysis of a reflective model, in the concluding chapter of this book.

REFLECTION 5.6

How might reflecting on an interaction support you to develop a) a child's subject knowledge and b) your own subject knowledge?

FINAL THOUGHTS

Let us take the final part of this chapter to reflect on what you have read here about how we can use interactions to enhance the acquisition, exploration, consolidation and application of subject knowledge. Despite being told here that interactions are complex, you now have multiple tools and strategies that can support the development of your practice.

Imagine how you can piece together practices which enable increasingly effective interactions in education for no financial cost and across all aspects of the curriculum. These interactions will enhance children's learning and use of subject knowledge, as well as creating an environment where learning is contagious.

Finally, let us return to the questions which set the fundamental principle that has underpinned this chapter. I ask myself this in my work with children as well as with adults. The above chapter sets the context, shares some considerations for you to spend time with, both by reflecting outside the moment and in the moment whenever possible or as you become more familiar with the approach that best suits you. These internal conversations should not be self-critical, but should be about you genuinely reflecting on some key classroom interactions with the starting point being:

Did the child gain something positive from this interaction that s/he would not otherwise have had? (Fisher, 2016, p. 3)

Hopefully, the answer will be yes more often than not. And when the answer is yes, things can get even more exciting. This is the point when we focus our efforts and reflections on what we can do to increase those positive learning gains even further.

FURTHER READING AND RESOURCES

Ball, R. and Fairlamb, A. (2025). *The scaffolding effect* (1st ed.). Taylor & Francis.

A guide to effective, evidence-based strategies for teachers to apply scaffolding and adaptive teaching to support student learning from novice to expert.

Dawes, L. and Sams, C. (2017). *Talk box: Activities for teaching oracy with children aged 4–8* (2nd ed.). Taylor & Francis.

A practical resource offering lesson plans and activities to develop oracy (speaking and listening) and collaborative discussion skills in children aged four to eight.

Fisher, J. (2016). *Interacting or interfering? Improving interactions in the Early Years*. McGraw Hill Education.

Encourages Early Years staff to analyse if they are supporting or hindering learning, providing guidance to improve adult–child interactions.

Muncaster, K. and Clarke, S. (2020). *Growth mindset every child a learner: Teaching for success*. Hodder Education.

A handbook of practical strategies for embedding a 'growth mindset' culture in primary schools to foster the belief that every child is a capable learner.

Nash, R. (2020). *The interactive classroom: Practical strategies for involving students in the learning process* (3rd ed. [rev. ed.]). Corwin.

Provides teachers with strategies to increase student participation by transforming the classroom environment from passive observation into active, interactive learning.

REFERENCES

Askew, M. (2016). *A practical guide to transforming primary mathematics: Activities and tasks that really work* (1st ed.). Routledge. https://doi.org/10.4324/9781315817316

Ball, R. and Fairlamb, A. (2025). *The scaffolding effect: Supporting all students to succeed*. Routledge.

Barnes, J. (2015). *Cross-curricular learning 3–14* (3rd ed.). Sage.

Bates, B. (2023). *Learning theories simplified: … and how to apply them to teaching* (3rd ed.). Sage.

Beck, C. and Kosnik, C. M. (2021). *Classroom teaching in the 21st century: Directions, principles and strategies*. Open University Press.

Bell, M. (2021). *The fundamentals of teaching: A five-step model to put the research evidence into practice* (1st ed.). Routledge. https://doi.org/10.4324/9780429342318

Bosanquet, P., Radford, J. and Webster, R. (2021). *The teaching assistant's guide to effective interaction: How to maximise your practice* (2nd ed.). Routledge.

Brock, A. and Hundley, H. (2018). *In other words: Phrases for growth mindset.* Ulysses Press.

Brookfield, S. (2017). *Becoming a critically reflective teacher* (2nd ed.). Jossey-Bass.

Burnett, P. C. (1999). Children's self-talk and academic self-concepts: The impact of teachers' statements. *Educational Psychology in Practice, 15*(3), 195–200. https://doi.org/10.1080/0266736990150305

Busch, B. and Watson, E. (2021). *The science of learning: 77 studies that every teacher needs to know* (2nd ed.). Routledge.

Canovi, A. G., Kumpulainen, A. R. K. and Molinari, L. (2019). The dynamics of class mood and student agency in classroom interactions. *The Journal of Classroom Interaction, 54*(1), 4–25.

Carroll, J. and Alexander, G. (2020). *The teachers' standards in primary schools: Understanding and evidencing effective practice* (2nd ed.). Sage.

Castle, P. and Buckler, S. (2018). *Psychology for teachers.* Sage.

Clark, T. R. (2020). *The 4 stages of psychological safety: Defining the path to inclusion and innovation.* Berrett-Koehler.

Cuthbert, A. S. and Standish, A. (Eds.). (2021). *What should schools teach? Disciplines, subjects and the pursuit of truth.* UCL Press.

Davison, K., Malmberg, L. and Sylva, K. (2023). Academic help-seeking interactions in the classroom: A microlongitudinal study. *British Journal of Educational Psychology, 93*(1). https://doi.org/10.1111/bjep.12538

Delamont, S. (1976). *Interaction in the classroom.* Methuen.

Dempster, K. and Robbins, J. (2017). *How to build communication success in your school: A guide for school leaders* (1st ed.). Routledge. https://doi.org/10.4324/9781315282176

Denton, P. (2007). *The power of our words: Teacher language that helps children learn.* Northeast Foundation for Children.

Department for Education (DfE). (2024). *Initial teacher training and early career framework.* https://assets.publishing.service.gov.uk/media/661d24ac08c3be25cfbd3e61/Initial_Teacher_Training_and_Early_Career_Framework.pdf

Dix, P. (2017). *When the adults change, everything changes: Seismic shifts in school behaviour.* Independent Thinking Press.

Dweck, C. (2012). *Mindset: How you can fulfil your potential.* Constable & Robinson.

Eckman, P. and Friesen, W. V. (2003) *Unmasking the face.* Malor.

Edmondson, A. (2023). *Right kind of wrong: Why learning to fail can teach us to thrive.* Atria.

Ferreira, R. (Ed.). (2021). *Teacher identity development within a community of practice.* Nova Science.

Fisher, J. (2016). *Interacting or interfering? Improving interactions in the early years.* Open University Press.

Groshell, Z. (2024). *Just tell them: The power of explanations and explicit teaching.* John Catt.

Harvard, B. (2025). *Do I have your attention? Understanding memory constraints and maximising learning*. Routledge.

Harvard Business Review Press. (2024). *Emotional intelligence: Curiosity*. Harvard Business Press.

Hayes, C. (2014). Developing as a reflective Early Years professional: A thematic approach. *Critical*.

Hayes, R. and Whittaker, P. (2015). *Understanding and supporting pupils with moderate learning difficulties in the secondary school: A practical guide*. Taylor & Francis.

Hess, U. and Fischer, A. (Eds.). (2016). *Emotional mimicry in social context*. Cambridge University Press.

Hohti, R. (2016). Classroom matters: Research with children as entanglement (Doctoral thesis). University of Helsinki.

Jamil, F. M., Sabol, T. J., Hamre, B. K. and Planta, R. C. (2015). Assessing teachers' skills in detecting and identifying effective interactions in the classroom: Theory and measurement. *The Elementary School Journal*, *115*(3), 407–432. https://doi.org/10.1086/680353

Johns, C. (Ed.). (2022). *Becoming a reflective practitioner* (6th ed.). Wiley.

Kerr, N. and Hertel, G. (2011). The Köhler group motivation gain: How to motivate the 'weak links' in a group. *Social and Personality Psychology Compass*, *5*(1), 43–55. https://doi.org/10.1111/j.1751-9004.2010.00337.x

Littleton, J. and Howe, E. (2010). *Educational dialogues: Understanding and promoting productive interactions*. Routledge.

Makaton.org. (2025). https://makaton.org/

Mercer, N. and Hodgkinson, S. (2008). *Exploring talk in schools: Inspired by the work of Douglas Barnes* (1st ed.). Sage.

Moll, L. C., Amanti, C., Neff, D. and Gonzalez, N. (1992). Funds of knowledge for teaching: Using a qualitative approach to connect homes and classrooms. *Theory Into Practice*, *31*(2), 132–141. https://doi.org/10.1080/00405849209543534

Myatt, M. (2020). *Back on track: Fewer things, greater depth*. John Catt Educational.

NASEN. (2020). *Understanding inclusion miniguide*. https://nasen.org.uk/resources/understanding-inclusion

Nash, R. (2020). *The interactive classroom: Practical strategies for involving students in the learning process* (3rd ed.). Corwin.

Ogier, S. (Ed.). (2022). *A broad and balanced curriculum in primary schools: Educating the whole child* (2nd ed.). Learning Matters.

Owen, J. (2022). *How to lead* (6th ed.). Pearson Education.

Pickering, M. J. and Garrod, S. (2021). *Understanding dialogue: Language use and social interaction*. Cambridge University Press.

Pollard, A. (2023). *Reflective teaching in primary schools* (6th ed.). Bloomsbury.

Reid, G. and Green, S. (2016). *100 ideas for primary teachers: Supporting children with dyslexia*. Bloomsbury.

Shyman, E. (2020). *Finding the teacher self*. Rowman & Littlefield.

Speechandlanguage.org.uk. (2025). https://speechandlanguage.org.uk/educators-and-professionals/

Staricoff, M. (2021). *The joy of not knowing*. Routledge.

Thwaite, A., Jones, P. and Simpson, A. (2020). Enacting dialogic pedagogy in primary literacy classrooms: Insights from systemic functional linguistics. *The Australian Journal of Language and Literacy*, *43*(1), 33–46. https://doi.org/10.1007/BF03652042

Van Es, E. A. and Sherin, M. G. (2002). Learning to notice: Scaffolding new teachers' interpretations of classroom interactions. *Journal of Technology and Teacher Education*, *10*(4), 571–596.

Warren, C. A. and Lessner, S. (2014). 'Who has family business?' Exploring the role of empathy in student–teacher interactions. *Perspectives on Urban Education*, *11*(2).

Welton, J. and Telford, J. (2004). *What did you say? What did you mean? An illustrated guide to understanding metaphors*. Jessica Kingsley.

Wood, N. (2019). Visual timetable. In *50 fantastic ideas for children with EAL*. Bloomsbury.

PART 2

DEVELOPING SUBJECT KNOWLEDGE

6
ART AND DESIGN

TERESA SMITH

━ THIS CHAPTER ━

This chapter explores the ideas that:

- art and design is a significant and valuable subject at the heart of developing children's creativity, curiosity, confidence and understanding of themselves and the world

- art education involves complex relationships and connections: to others, to a dynamic knowledge base, to the past, to the present and to the future

- educators must provide inclusive emotional, physical and curricula safe spaces to enable and challenge children's authentic expression and artistic development.

━ KEY TERMS FOR THIS CHAPTER ━

Aesthetic: related to visual style, sometimes (but not always) linked to beauty and perceptions of 'beautiful'.

Art elements: elements that make up all art, craft and design work. They mix and match to create different effects, moods and outcomes.

Convergent: thinking, or art outcomes, that develop towards each other, similarly, in a prescribed way.

Craft: the intelligent design and skilful hand-making of objects and artefacts.

Creativity: 'The capacity to imagine, conceive, express, or make something that was not there before' (James et al., 2019, p. 2).

Divergent: thinking, or art outcomes, that develop in different directions.

Expressive: conveying thought and feeling.

Materials: the substances used to create art, craft and design works. Tools are used to manipulate the materials and create the desired effect.

Processes: the techniques and approaches that are used to apply materials to create an art, craft or design work.

INTRODUCTION

Art in schools shouldn't be sidelined … it should be right there right up in the front because I think art teaches you to deal with the world around you. It is the oxygen that makes all the other subjects breathe.

(Alan Parker, 2018)

It is not easy to think of an education system that has placed as much value on art in schools as filmmaker Alan Parker suggests we should. The reasons for that are beyond the scope of this chapter, but I love the notion of curriculum subjects as living, breathing entities. Art and design are pervasive in our lives: they can be seen all around us, and they mean so many different things to so many people. The subject has something for everyone and can take so many forms – it can be as loud as it is quiet, as bold as it is uncertain, as messy as it is organised. A quality art and design education can be whatever we need it to be – full of hope, possibility and oxygen for us all.

Eisner's philosophy was that we see art education as an adventure for the mind (2002), building on Holt's articulation of the teacher as a travel agent (1970). When we consider art education in these terms, we can begin to see how it comes alive as a subject full of exciting knowledge, skills and creativity. The journey or adventure analogy is a strong reminder that sometimes the art and design programmes we teach will need to be carefully and explicitly planned, and at other times they will benefit from embracing elements of going 'off the beaten track' and into the unknown. The adventure will look and feel different to everyone because there are a limitless number of different ways to create and think about art.

There are also infinite variations of what your art education may have been, and some of your art experiences may not always have risen to the above. Nevertheless, all educators should recognise art and design's power to transform children's ways of looking at and knowing the world. Every child is entitled to experience the benefits that creative and cultural activity brings, to enjoy and belong in that adventure.

The contribution that art and design make to the education of children, and consequently to the lives of adults, is well-articulated via research. The Art Now report published by The All-Party Parliamentary Group for Art, Craft and Design in Education (2023), is a strong example, as well as several recent Cultural Learning Alliance publications (2017, 2025a, 2025b) and campaigns by Arts Councils across the UK. The research emphasises the range of direct and indirect cognitive and emotional benefits the arts offer – they can make us cleverer, happier and healthier. In addition, the United Nations Convention on the Rights of the Child (1989) creates specific rights for children to express themselves through art and to participate in cultural life and the arts. We can support these rights by ensuring that art education is recognised for its potential as a profoundly intellectual activity, not a luxury, and not sidelined. It has an important place at the heart of developing the whole child.

THE IDENTITY OF ART AND DESIGN

The subject of art and design shares the creative process with other expressive arts such as dance, drama and music, but as a representative of the visual arts it also has its own distinct issues and discrete body of knowledge and skills. When we talk and write about 'art and design' as a discipline, we should note that craft, the act of skilfully making objects by hand, is integral too. It is for writing purposes only that omissions have sometimes been made here, but, in practice, all of 'art', 'craft' and 'design' matter.

When I mention creativity in relation to art and design, I am referring to the concept of creativity as a broader human capacity or capability. Artistic responses and processes can be considered one manifestation or development of that wider creativity. Art nurtures creativity, allowing individuals to translate their inner thoughts, feelings and experiences into tangible forms, but we must be careful not to conflate the two terms.

There are many terms that have been used to value the various types of knowledge to be found in art and design:

- 'technical knowledge, expression and appreciation of the work of others' (DfE, 2013);

- 'practical, theoretical and disciplinary' knowledge (Ofsted, 2023);

- 'productive, cultural and critical' knowledge (Eisner, 1972);

- 'creating and presenting, evaluating and appreciating' (Education Scotland, 2008);

- 'explicit, tacit, conceptual and affective' knowledge (The National Society for Education in Art and Design, 2024).

Whichever knowledge-language your curriculum employs, there should be content and space for the development of a range of art and design essentials, which I have organised here into a triad of three overarching strands:

- creating

- thinking

- being/becoming.

These should be thought of as a scaffold of holistic elements that represent the essence of the subject. They are interdependent; while creating and thinking may be able to be divided at surface level, at a deeper level they are not separable and it is not helpful to treat them in this way.

Alongside the explanation of each strand, I have suggested attitudes, skills and knowledge that are related.

There are also guiding questions, which can be used to help evaluate curriculum content and plan new art and design experiences for learners.

STRAND 1: CREATING

Creating is at the heart of art and design. Hickman (2005) expresses this as 'aesthetic significance', arguing that art-making is a basic human predisposition. Learning in art and design needs to be practical and experiential.

Attitudes, skill and knowledge related to creating may include explicit facts, but also tacit knowledge gained through exploration of materials and processes (i.e. knowledge which is practised intuitively, rooted in personal experience, difficult to articulate, like riding a bike). It will include elements of expression, communication and interpretation.

GUIDING QUESTIONS

Is there space and scope for children to:

- draw on what they already know, embracing their lived experiences, interests and aspirations?

- connect and represent points of reference that matter to them, including starting from their imagination?

- be curious, follow their natural inclinations?

- explore materials and processes in an open-ended, flexible way?

- practise, refine and perfect practical skills and techniques?

- engage playfully, without always knowing the direction of learning or what the final outcome might be?

- work individually and collaboratively where appropriate?

- make mistakes and learn through these?

- be fulfilled by making? Does it sustain them and fill them with joy?

STRAND 2: THINKING

Art and design education is also about children 'learning to think aesthetically about images and their creation … helping them advance their ability to see the world aesthetically and to describe it in artistically sensitive ways' (Eisner, 2002, p. 75). Looking and noticing are important tools for the artist – close observation is an active process to help generate thoughts and ideas. The objects and images children make can be seen as evidence of thinking and learning (Key and Stilman, 2009), and conversations before, during and after making can help us to understand children's motivations and ideas. Thinking about art helps children to see how others have made sense of complex worlds, as well as how they themselves fit into those worlds (Key and Stilman, 2009). Artist Bob and Roberta Smith advocates that all schools should be art schools – at least in attitude if not in curriculum – and this is because 'art school teaches you how to think, not what to think' (Smith, cited in Gompertz, 2015, p. 189).

Attitudes, skills and knowledge related to thinking may include critical and creative thinking, understanding your own work as well as the work of other artists, craftspeople and designers, and contextualising and connecting learning with other subject areas.

GUIDING QUESTIONS

- Do these art and design experiences challenge learners to engage cognitively, generate ideas, think imaginatively, explore meanings, interpretations and connections?

- What are learners encouraged to think about? How is this thinking enabled to be shared with and expressed to others?

- What theoretical, political, social, or historical contexts do children need to understand to help them make sense of others/their own work?

- Are learners able to make their own decisions about their artwork? How much autonomy are they given at each stage?

- Are they encouraged to think laterally rather than linearly?

- Are there opportunities to problem-solve and identify solutions?

- Are there opportunities for learners to employ a range of senses in their activity?

- Are learners given time to reflect and review their work, and that of others?

STRAND 3: BEING AND BECOMING

'The arts are about understanding, and expressing, the qualities of human experiences' wrote Ken Robinson (NAACCE, 1999, p. 79), who recognised that creating and celebrating art is a joyful practice. When we create our own art and observe the art of others, we make connections which explore and speak to our emotions and identities, giving them form and representation (NAACCE, 1999). An effective art education places children in a powerful space to think, ask questions and have their voices heard. In that artistic space they can celebrate the things that are important to them, understanding what it is to be a creative person and engaging with holistic elements that support them in living their lives well (Ogier, 2017).

Attitudes, skills and knowledge related to being and becoming are about understanding the place of art in our world and how it connects to oneself, as well as how it explores wider questions about humanity and life itself.

GUIDING QUESTIONS

- Are children encouraged to ask and answer 'big' questions about and through art?

- Are children given space to form and justify their own opinions, encouraged to think about value, assumptions, purpose and quality?

- How do these activities harness and develop children's sensibilities of memory, imagination and observation?

- Are children building self-confidence, independence and resilience?

- Is children's cultural awareness being developed?

- Does their art learning help them know themselves, and build their sense of agency and belonging?

MODELS OF KNOWLEDGE IN ART AND DESIGN

Strong subject knowledge is arguably the foundation of both *learning in* and *enjoyment of* art and design, yet debate around art and design knowledge, pedagogy and curriculum content never seems to quieten. Dominating political priorities and 'changing paradigms' in arts education have arguably muddled developments and marginalised the subject over many years (Abbs, 2003).

There is plenty of further reading you can undertake to help you better and more fully understand the histories and traditions of art in education. I encourage you to do this, but, for a start, some models of thinking that sit comfortably with excellent art and design provision include:

- *social constructivism*: theorists including Jereme Bruner, Jean Piaget, Lev Vygotsky, Howard Gardner and John Dewey were advocates of a collaborative learning model, in which children learn from each other as well as from a more competent 'other' person.

Social constructivism is a useful theory for art educators because it 'permits teachers to learn alongside children and to use questioning skills to push their personal or collective enquiries much further; often way beyond the limits imposed by more product-driven paradigms' (Ogier, 2017, p. 60);

- *process over product*: alongside social constructivism, the work of Lawrence Stenhouse (1926–1982) helps us to recognise the value in a process-driven model of art education instead of a product or objective driven model. He saw teachers as active participants, observers and facilitators, rather than deliverers of prescribed learning. Stenhouse's ideas on teaching as a vehicle for social justice, and a focus on thinking skills as opposed to knowledge-gain, are conducive to quality teaching and learning in art and design;

- *child-centred approaches*: these prioritise self-expression and creativity and place more emphasis on the child than subject-discipline. These progressive approaches became more common in the post-war period and challenged the utilitarian, authoritarian beliefs that had gone before (Fleming, 2010). Over time, *responding* to artwork was embraced as well as *creating* artwork. The works of Marion Richardson (1892–1946) and Victor Lowenfeld (1903–1960) continue to influence how we view children and their art in this way, with a focus on children's creative expression and opportunities for personal development in and through art activity. The Reggio Emilia approach, originating from Italy, which centres on the child as competent, curious and imaginative, also epitomises this philosophy. It is powerfully represented in the poem 'The hundred languages of children' (see Further reading, Malaguzzi, 1994);

- *aesthetic sensitivities*: Elliot Eisner's powerful endorsements of open-ended responses and flexibility in teaching, and his assertion that arts experiences are 'one of the most potent means for developing [children's] minds' (Eisner, 2002, p. 208) hold strong today for many art educators. He placed the senses, feelings and emotions at the core of learning experiences, advocating that there is power in learning to see the world from an aesthetic perspective.

We cannot ignore that in recent years, many curricula have been underpinned by *knowledge-rich* movements, subscribing to Hirsch's (2016) prioritisation of core knowledge that is shared and communal. This shared knowledge is also usually designed to be quantifiable, comparable and sequential. Many art educators are concerned that if this is taken as the sole perspective on knowledge, it significantly limits the breadth and depth of what art and design can offer as a discipline.

When thinking about art and design education, the concept of knowledge must include much more than quantifiable facts or retrievable certainties. Knowledge has many diverse manifestations; knowledge-rich can – and must – be interpreted in multiple ways. Kidd (2020) extends the notion of knowing to include understanding and connecting to humanity. We need to be clear that knowledge cannot only be acquired by explicit/direct instruction; specialised and powerful subject-specific knowledge also comes through making and doing.

These are simplified portrayals of some educational theories and art traditions, yet despite their over-generalisations they offer a small taste of the theoretical base within which the subject resides and within which art educators work. My experience is that there are many false dichotomies within current art and design discourse, yet art and design is not a subject that can be reduced to binary interpretations of its elements, so we must try not to do so. Many polarised elements – for example, knowledge versus skills, process versus product, appreciation of art versus participation in art, traditional versus contemporary, enquiry-based versus direct instruction – are better understood as being reciprocal rather than mutually exclusive. Each part is important, but only balanced together can they offer the learner the whole.

The important takeaway is that art and design educators should feel confident to question changing paradigms and taken-for-granted perspectives within education. If we don't engage with these debates, which Steers called 'the lifeblood of art education' (Steers, 2003, p. 21, cited in De Rijke, 2019), then it is all too easy to end up with misrepresentation or 'shoehorning' of the subject into approaches that don't 'fit'. You should be prepared to wade into the debate, find the gaps, question approaches and lean into what works for both you and your learners.

KEY CONCEPTS

It should be clear by now that art and design teaching is much more than the simple transfer of blocks of knowledge. Nonetheless, there are key skills and concepts that art and design educators need to know to teach the subject effectively. If we were to argue the notion of art as a form of communication, then these are the alphabet, sentence, grammar and text components of everyone's art language. They need to be taught explicitly to children, with time offered to consolidate and practice and become confident and comfortable with skills.

Be mindful that this is not a definitive list, and there can and should be differences in how these are experienced by children in different contexts. All of these are essential experiences which will provide provocations to children for new creating, thinking and being in relation to art and design.

ART ELEMENTS

These visual, tactile and spatial art elements are the fundamental building blocks of the world we live in, structuring every artwork, craft artefact or piece of design there is around us. They work by connecting with each other to create a particular image, effect, focus or feeling. There are seven main elements; pattern is often included as a useful eighth. Some naturally complement others; they can be taught separately or in combination together.

Furthering your own confidence in identifying, discussing and creating with these will support you in fully understanding each element's potential and how you can support children to use them within their own making.

- *Line*: comes in all sorts of shapes, sizes, weights and styles. They are used to describe objects, add detail or create expression.

- *Colour*: has a huge influence on how a piece of art or design looks. People usually respond strongly to colours and the emotions they provoke. Simple explorations might include primary colours, secondary colours, harmonious colours, tints and shades.

- *Tone* (value): how light or dark a colour or surface appears. Tones can create different moods and visual effects by using combinations of tonal values, contrasts and boundaries.

- *Shape*: two-dimensional: an image on a surface has shape. The outline can be geometric or organic, soft or hard-edged. Positive shapes often represent solid objects; negative shapes can show the surrounding space.

- *Form*: this is the shape, visual appearance or structure of three-dimensional objects. A solid object has form. Form can be represented in a two-dimensional surface using tone.

- *Space*: exists around, between and adjacent to shapes or forms. Three-dimensional work creates real space. Two-dimensional works can create implied space.

- *Texture*: this can be actual texture in a work surface, or an implied texture that suggests how something feels.

- *Pattern*: a design or motif in which any of lines, shapes, forms and colours are repeated or sequenced.

EXPERIENCE OF MATERIALS AND PROCESSES

Art and design learning needs to be experiential and practical. Children need to be given time to explore and discover the possibilities of a range of materials and processes in significant and appropriate depth.

Drawing, painting, printmaking, collage, textiles, sculpture and digital media all offer different potential in primary education. Installation, performance art, illustration and graphic design are also possibilities. Drawing is often considered a practice to develop distinctly, for its individual powers, as well as to underpin working with other materials. Drawing is also often the groundwork of mark-making experiences in early childhood.

Figure 6.1   Art elements

Knowledge and understanding of these are built through activity, reflection and evaluation. Sometimes they can be explored discretely through a unit of work or series of lessons, and sometimes they may be interlinked and connected.

Children's experiences around a different material should offer them the opportunities as listed in the Creating 'Guiding questions' section, earlier in this chapter. Those questions speak directly about children's work with these materials and processes. Alongside those creating experiences, there should also be opportunity for children:

- to make connections with works of other artists, craftspeople and designers, and the communities around them;

- to make connections with the formal art elements;

- to develop understanding of sustainability in relation to resources and processes.

INTRODUCTION TO THE WORK OF ARTISTS, CRAFTSPEOPLE AND DESIGNERS

Sharing the work of artists, craftspeople and designers with children must play a part of an effective art and design curriculum. Ogier (2017) explains that work should be carefully chosen to ensure it is relevant to the learning being undertaken, and so that children can situate their own artwork within an extensive artistic tradition. Yet which artists, craftspeople and designers are chosen for study is open to significant debate, as many disciplines, including the arts, have begun to recognise the failings of a predominantly white, male-oriented discourse of the past. Art educators should choose artworks that inspire them and connect with the children they teach, carefully considering whose knowledge is being offered, shared and prioritised through their curricula (Holdstock, 2024).

USE OF SKETCHBOOKS

Sketchbooks are wonderful things. They should be used with every age group, for the safe space they offer children to play, explore, try and struggle, all of which bring growth in essential art skills. AccessArt has been an advocate of the use of sketchbooks for many years. They have an evolving collection of resources designed to help teachers and learners navigate quality sketchbook use (see Further reading and resources).

REFLECTION 6.2

- Which art and design-based knowledge, skills and attitudes do you think will be most useful for children to have accumulated before they leave primary education?

- What can art and design offer for children's futures that other subjects may not?

MORE IMPORTANT CONCEPTS

To teach art and design effectively, the following concepts should also be considered and used to underpin the purposeful choices you make as an art educator:

- *start from the child/learner*: both child-centred starting points and knowledge-based starting points are powerful. We find knowledge-based starting points in the subject itself, in the curriculum programmes and schemes that we use as educators, and we find child-led starting points in the everyday interactions we have with children: their memories, imaginations and observations (Roberts, 2008). When we work with children it is difficult not to notice that they have a natural inclination to enjoy creating, and a willingness to have a go (Tutchell, 2014). With those observations it feels easy to argue that children's lived experience is central to learning in art, and that fixed schemes become rather pointless if children's art sensibilities are ignored;

- *the role of the adult*: recognition of child art as its own worthy entity around the 1950s resulted in a changed perception of the role of the art educator – moving from instructor to facilitator and nurturer. Educators can do much to promote enthusiasm for and learning in art and design, and an open mind and genuine respect for the subject and for their *facilitator* role are essential prerequisites. To return to the notion of art education as a journey, do not be afraid of being on the journey alongside your learners; being a few steps ahead is often advisable, but is not always the only way to journey! My advice is to always to find time to create with your learners, don't apologise for your own artwork and model your own enjoyment of the materials being used. Responses to children's art-making should be sensitive, respectful and celebratory, listening to what children say about their work and offering helpful, carefully considered feedback. Do not make assumptions about a child's purpose or intentions or be too quick to correct. Do reflect back to children positivity and correct language related to art and design and always offer generous amounts of time and attention to children as artists in their own right;

- *growth and progression*: a quality art and design education will be designed as a continual pathway, starting from early childhood experiences and children's early developmental needs. It will sequence learning to build on prior knowledge and experiences and secure confidence and progression through repeated encounters. While art subject aims and pedagogical approaches span all ages and stages, the focus and complexity will need adaptation. Younger children benefit from freer, more open-ended exploration, whereas a shift to more guidance and technical instruction can, in some scenarios, be beneficial for older children. Be assured that there is no set age or stage at which children should be introduced to a new material, process, or artist. To use printmaking as an example, a four-year-old may work with their hands, feet or found objects to decorate large rolls of paper with immediate playful prints. They might enjoy exploring the sensory elements of the printing, the rapid transference of the image and overlap of prints which occur naturally as they work. In comparison, a ten-year-old with several previous encounters with printmaking might take a more intentional route: the block to print may be carefully designed and created prior to printing, and they may be able to discuss the intended whole composition in relation to layering and colour choices. Despite the differences, and the additional skills required to make the ten-year-old's outcome successful, both children here will benefit from the haptic, sensory and immediate nature of printmaking as a process. We should approach all material experiences in a similar way.

CHALLENGES AND TENSIONS

Art education is complicated by negative attitudes, a curriculum that struggles with the non-linear creative process and ongoing issues of inclusivity and keeping the art curriculum dynamic; these challenges and tensions will be discussed here.

LEARNER AND TEACHER ATTITUDES

There is a complex relationship between achievement and self-esteem; notions of 'I can't draw' and 'I'm not creative' can quickly develop in children at an early age if we're not careful. Some of these barriers will be built up within children themselves – perhaps because of lack of confidence, or a fear of risk-taking – and some will build up because of external factors – such as lack of time in the curriculum, or failure to teach children the skills they need. Educators must recognise the frustrating liminal space or imbalance between *knowing that* or *knowing how to* and the practical application of that knowledge in terms of a learner's vision for what they want to create or achieve. A narrow curriculum and lack of exposure to a wide range of examples and experiences can also be key contributors to these feelings of despondency.

Strategies for overcoming these barriers include making it clear to learners that they all have it in them to be creative. Every art educator needs to search for each child's creativity and celebrate and nurture it. Share wide, far-reaching examples of art and design works and artists. Make sure you plan in suitable time to teach the techniques and skills children need, because feelings of success are vital. Build up an ethos of playfulness and risk-taking in your setting. Protect art time every week to build positive habits and attitudes through regular, quality exposure to the subject.

Careful consideration of your own attitudes and response to the subject is important, so that you can ensure positive attitudes to art learning are affirmed to children. It is vital to understand that art and design education is not solely about building up artists of the future; in addition it supports the development of wider life skills, ready for a multitude of careers.

NON-LINEAR TRAJECTORIES

Non-linear trajectories are regularly travelled in learning in art and design, and this can create tension if you are working within a curriculum that is more *product-led* than *process-led*. We can draw confidence from knowing that deviation from a straightforward sequential trajectory is typical of many artists' ways of working. They may follow an instinctive approach, feeling their way through ideas, moving backwards, forwards and sideways in reflection and experimentation. Making may speed up or slow down at unexpected moments. Pauses are likely to be important. Sometimes unexpected discoveries and masterful making happen in serendipitous, accidental moments. Valuing this way of working makes art and design less easy to fit into a fixed curriculum and timetable model, but learners benefit when we resist forcing it to fit the mould of other disciplines.

ART SHOULD BE INCLUSIVE OF ALL LEARNERS

With its focus on the learner at the centre of experiences, and its responsive, flexible approach to teaching, art is well-placed to be accessible and fulfilling for all. Some research has shown the subject to be 'instrumental in reaching marginalized and disadvantaged learners, offering diverse benefits such as improved communication, self-confidence, critical thinking, and social skills' (O'Sullivan et al., 2023, p.140). It is also one of the only subjects that offers space for exploring and expressing feelings, thoughts and experiences. Yet despite the alignments between art teaching and inclusive pedagogies, concerns remain about accessibility of the arts for children from poorer socioeconomic backgrounds (CLA, 2025b) and The Runnymede Trust (2024), when calling for a more diverse curriculum, highlighted the significant under-representation of systemically marginalised minority ethnic artists in art education. The exclusivity of the art world within both the education sector and wider society is clearly a challenge that educators should be engaging proactively with.

ART KNOWLEDGE IS DYNAMIC

The needs of an ever-evolving and changing society must be the starting point for what is taught in art and design, and how it is taught. Our cultures are not static and this means that the canon of knowledge for art and design is also never static nor absolute and shouldn't be considered so. The Runnymede Trust (2024) reflects 'the classroom experience has become limited by an educational system ... that favour[s] a narrow art canon. Young people are losing so much of the richness and innovation that learning and making art should offer.' The notion of developing children's *cultural capital* has also increasingly been recognised as problematic in recent years, with questions being asked of whose cultures and voices we prioritise and whose we silence. The Arts Alive report sums up that arts education curricula should 'incorporate diverse cultural perspectives, avoid tokenism, and challenge dominant mainstream views, promoting genuine intercultural understanding and appreciation' (O'Sullivan et al., 2023, p. 140). I recommend Holdstock's *Teaching a diverse primary art curriculum* (2024) for practical examples of this in action. There is much still to develop in this respect.

REFLECTION 6.3

- Which artists, craftspeople, designers, cultures and stories do you remember from your own education?
- Who and what was included, and who and what might have been missed out? Why is this important?

CREATING SPACES FOR QUALITY ART AND DESIGN LEARNING

To ensure high-quality art education, educators must consciously cultivate stimulating spaces that encourage genuine creativity and support the individual expression of every learner.

CURRICULA SPACE

An effective art and design curriculum should encourage expressive and creative activity, requiring both convergent and divergent modes of thinking. Ensure your curriculum does not exacerbate an unhelpful hierarchy of ways to communicate – all forms of visual expression using a range of materials should be prominently positioned in there. Don't be too quick to push children along the same creating and thinking pathways – we need to value diversity of thinking and outcome rather than uniformity, so be wary of any units of work that end up with all outcomes looking the same. I love the mantra 'you do you' – and this is certainly a good art mantra to help children understand that individual responses and diversity of thought are valued. Always ensure you hold high expectations for all – children are capable artists in their own right and should be challenged to progress their skills and knowledge, just as we would challenge and support children in all other disciplines.

PHYSICAL SPACE

Gormley (in Hickman, 2005, p. 10) wrote of the art room as 'a zone dedicated to the exercise of curiosity'. Educational settings should provide a stimulating environment in which imagination, originality and expression are valued. Ensure there is a wide range of tools and good-quality materials available that offer opportunities for experimentation and creative application. Try to make these materials freely available at the side of a classroom or setting so that children develop independence in choosing and using them, as well as skills in looking after and maintaining art equipment. Think too about the purpose of displays within your setting – displays which share process as well as product show children that you value the art learning journey.

PEDAGOGICAL SPACE

You should give space and time in the majority of lessons for playful and divergent exploration of materials and processes. Certainly, we should encourage children to be expressive and creative in their own work rather than copying the teacher or another artist's work. Giving children space to make their own decisions is vital – but do be cautious, as such decision-making should be carefully planned to be within their capacity. Questioning is critical in art lessons when used as a way of affirming, challenging and deepening children's thinking. Guided discovery is an effective teaching method – it may look organic and free, but will usually need careful planning. Focused teaching through modelling and direct instruction is sometimes a more appropriate way for children to learn or practise a technique, so don't be afraid of this. Utilise visualisers and demonstrate techniques practically whenever you can. Modelling of finished outcomes should be less frequent, to avoid the issue of children simply copying your own adult outcomes. Instead, offer plenty of support, suggestions and 'jumping off' points that children can use to help them along on their own journeys. Model the process of learning through mistakes. Gompertz (2015) reminds us that trial and error and 'failure' are parts of the very fabric of making. We need to support children to navigate these processes, so that they do not stop or lose confidence at every hurdle.

MENTAL SPACE

Art and design must offer feelings of safety and belonging to children, and individually and culturally responsive pedagogies play a pivotal role in this. Children also need a carefully planned balance between supportive direct instruction and a keen valuing of their creative freedom and expression. Try not to discourage or be afraid of some rule-breaking; it can be typical of art and design activity and can sometimes need a good dose of courage and creativity from educators to enable this.

EDUCATOR DEVELOPMENT SPACE

If you haven't done so already, do give some careful thought to the type of art educator you want to be, to give you confidence in moving forwards and staying true to the subject and to your principles. Develop a positive attitude to the broadening of your own art skills and creative being. When you enjoy learning and teaching art alongside the children, you will feel more confident to be flexible in your approach and happy to take risks or follow the unexpected path. Look locally and nationally for art and design continuing professional development opportunities – there are many, sometimes free, courses that can help you develop knowledge of skills and processes. Galleries often have useful educator development programmes too. Try to always explore a material or process yourself before teaching it to children. For those of us who want to develop stronger advocacy for art in education, finding an alliance with similar-thinking arts educators can be particularly empowering. Social media is great for connecting like-minded professionals, for sharing of ideas and inspiration. Be pro-active in joining organisations and groups that feed your own art educator strengths as well as the gaps.

FINAL THOUGHTS

In this chapter, we began by establishing the fundamental importance of children's right to a broad, effective and enjoyable art and design education. We affirmed that art is a significant and valuable subject, lying at the heart of developing children's creativity, curiosity, confidence and their understanding of themselves and the world around them. We then moved on to explore the critical debates about knowledge, skills and attitudes that have been central to art education for many years,

Art curricula must be richly representative of the pasts we have come from, enable meaningful conversations about the world we live in now and offer robust aspirations for the futures we are moving into. Children deserve more, not less art, craft and design, and we need to actively protect and celebrate all the hope, possibilities, joy and intellectual oxygen they bring to all of us.

FURTHER READING AND RESOURCES

AccessArt. www.accessart.org.uk/

Charity providing visual arts resources and creative learning advice.

AccessArt sketchbook resources. www.accessart.org.uk/sketchbooks/

Guidance on the purpose and best use of sketchbooks in art education.

Adams, E. (2013). Drawing to learn, learning to draw. www.nsead.org/files/f7246b7608216d52696dc3ed81256213.pdf

Explores the link between drawing for cognitive learning and learning to draw.

Art UK. The superpower of looking. https://artuk.org/learn/the-superpower-of-looking

Strategies to develop students' observational and visual literacy skills through art.

Crafts Council. Make First pedagogy. www.craftscouncil.org.uk/learning/make-first

A teaching method prioritising hands-on making and material exploration for learning.

Holdstock, K. (2024). *Teaching a diverse primary art curriculum.* Bloomsbury.

A practical guide that empowers primary teachers to build a diverse, engaging art curriculum across multiple art forms by taking inspiration from artists of various backgrounds and cultures.

National Society for Education in Art and Design (NSEAD). www.nsead.org/

The leading professional subject association for art, craft and design.

Malaguzzi, L. (1994). The hundred languages of children. www.reggiochildren.it/en/reggio-emilia-approach/100-linguaggi-en/

Foundational paper on the Reggio Emilia approach, emphasising children's *hundred languages* (modes of expression).

Tate. www.tate.org.uk/ and Tate Kids. www.tate.org.uk/kids

UK national art gallery and its site for children, offering art collections and educational resources.

Wenham, M. (2003). *Understanding art: A guide for teachers.* Sage.

A guide for teachers to enhance their understanding of art for confident and effective teaching.

REFERENCES

Abbs, P. (2003). *Against the flow: Education, the art and postmodern culture*. Routledge.

Cultural Learning Alliance (CLA). (2017). *Key research findings: The case for cultural learning*. www.culturallearningalliance.org.uk/wp-content/uploads/2024/01/CLA-key-findings-2017.pdf

CLA. (2025a). *Evidencing the value of arts subjects: A capabilities framework*. www.culturallearningalliance.org.uk/wp-content/uploads/2025/06/CLA-Capabilities-Framework-May-2025.pdf

CLA. (2025b). *Report card 2025*. www.culturallearningalliance.org.uk/wp-content/uploads/2025/03/CLA-2025-Report-Card_AW.pdf

Department for Education (DfE). (2013). *The national curriculum in England: Key stages 1 and 2 framework document*. www.gov.uk/government/publications/national-curriculum-in-england-primary-curriculum

De Rijke, V. (2019). *Art and soul: Rudolf Steiner, interdisciplinary art and education* (Vol. *25*). Springer Nature.

Education Scotland. (2008). *Curriculum for excellence 3–18 years*. www2.gov.scot/resource/doc/226155/0061245.pdf

Eisner, E. W. (1972). *Educating artistic vision*. Macmillan.

Eisner, E. W. (2002). *The arts and the creation of mind*. Yale University Press.

Fleming, M. (2010). *Arts in education and creativity: A literature review* (2nd ed.). Creativity, Culture and Education.

Gompertz, W. (2015). *Think like an artist … and lead a more creative, productive life*. Penguin.

Hickman, R. (2005). *Why we make art: And why it is taught*. Intellect.

Hirsch, E. (2016). *Why knowledge matters*. Harvard Education Press.

Holdstock, K. (2024). *Teaching a diverse primary art curriculum*. Bloomsbury.

Holt, J. (1970). *What do I do Monday?* Dell.

James, S. J., Houston, A., Newton, L., Daniels, S., Morgan, N., Coho, W., Ruck, A. and Lucas, B. (2019). *Durham Commission on Creativity and Education*. Arts Council UK and Durham University. https://durham-repository.worktribe.com/output/1634947

Key, P. and Stilman, J. (2009). *Teaching primary art and design*. Sage.

Kidd, D. (2020). *A curriculum of hope: As rich in humanity as in knowledge*. Independent Thinking Press.

NACCCE. (1999). *All our futures: Creativity, culture and education*. HMSO.

Ofsted. (2023). *Curriculum research reviews series: Art and design*. www.gov.uk/government/publications/research-review-series-art-and-design

Ogier, S. (2017). *Teaching primary art and design*. Sage.

O'Sullivan, C., Clotworthy, E., Nugent, M., Colleary, S., Keane, E., Piazzoli, E., Gubbins, E., Krakaur, L., Kerin, M., McCormick, S. and Heeran Flynn, L. (2023). *Arts Alive: A literature review to support curriculum specification development for the area of arts education*. NCCA. https://ncca.ie/media/6543/literature-review-for-arts-education.pdf

Parker, A. (2018). Why study art [Video]. Tate. www.tate.org.uk/art/talking-point/why-study-art

Roberts, I. (2008). Art and design: Teaching the curriculum. In R. Boys and E. Spink (Eds.), *Teaching the foundation subjects* (pp. 1–16). Bloomsbury.

The All-Party Parliamentary Group for Art, Craft and Design in Education. (2023). *Art now inquiry*. www.nsead.org/files/13a555d0c7a3c66da64bfb8049a4dae1.pdf

The National Society for Education in Art and Design. (2024). *The big landscape curriculum toolkit*. https://biglandscape.nsead.org/

The Runnymede Trust. (2024). *Visualise: Race and inclusion in secondary school art education*. www.runnymedetrust.org/visualise

Tutchell, S. (2014). *Young children as artists: Art and design in the early years and Key Stage 1*. Routledge.

United Nations (UN). (1989). *Convention on the rights of the child* (1577 UNTS, pp. 3–178). https://treaties.un.org/doc/Treaties/1990/09/19900902%2003-14%20AM/Ch_IV_11p.pdf

7

CITIZENSHIP AND ETHICS

RACHEL SIDOLI

— THIS CHAPTER —

This chapter explores the ideas that:

- creating ethical citizens is a key purpose of education both in the UK and across the globe
- there is a wide range of potential models, strategies and materials to support the teaching of ethics and citizenship to primary-aged pupils
- pupils need to engage in practical and meaningful experiences to develop their ethical and political awareness.

— KEY TERMS FOR THIS CHAPTER —

Ethics: the moral principles that guide a person's behaviour.

Citizenship: a legal status and relation between an individual and a state that entails specific legal rights and duties.

Agency: the ability to take action or consciously choose what action to take.

Participatory pedagogy: an educational approach where students are active co-creators of their knowledge and learning rather than passive recipients.

Sociology of childhood: explores how childhood is understood and experienced within a society, recognising it as a social construct rather than a fixed biological stage.

INTRODUCTION

Since the earliest examples of educational systems across the world, formal learning has been associated not only with the acquisition of knowledge and skills, but also with the development of moral and social characteristics and behaviours. While universal education is by no means to be taken for granted in the modern world, over the centuries access to schooling for primary-aged children has become increasingly widespread across the globe. Although different nations often prioritise varying academic subjects, the underlying purpose of education as a vehicle through which young people can explore the concepts of ethics (the moral principles that guide our behaviour) and citizenship (belonging to a nation and its political community) have progressively become intertwined with educational theory, policy and practice (OECD, 2023). Preparing our youngest members of society to prosper in an ever-changing world is increasingly becoming focused on the importance of enabling them to become ethical citizens both now and in the future (Gottschalk and Borhan, 2023).

AN INTERNATIONAL CONTEXT

We will begin by looking at *why* the teaching of citizenship and ethics has become so significant on the global educational stage (OECD, 2019) and also how the two ideas are intrinsically linked. UNESCO (n.d.) has universalised the principle of citizenship through its promotion of *global citizenship education* (GCED). Rather than defining the concept simply in relation to special rights, privileges and responsibilities belonging to a given country, the organisation is keen to promote a vision that transcends national borders. UNESCO perceives that in an increasingly connected and interdependent world learners of all ages should be inspired to positively contribute not only to their own local communities, but also to global society. The organisation aims to enable young people to flourish in a rapidly developing and technological world while also aspiring to cultivate tolerance and respect for others. In order to do this, UNESCO believes that learners need to have knowledge of the international social, economic, political and environmental contexts within which they live. The primary means for achieving this is through developing educational provision which should include knowledge of:

- the causes and consequences of key historical events;

- global geography and sustainability issues;

- awareness of systems of inequalities;

- a deep understanding of human rights.

UNESCO stipulates the further need to develop social, emotional, cognitive and critical thinking skills which enable learners to work in teams and interact with people from different backgrounds while gaining a positive appreciation of diverse cultural contexts, perspectives and beliefs.

UNESCO's global citizenship mission is underpinned by the goal to realise commonly shared ethical values such as respect, empathy, open mindedness, justice and fairness. It aims at promoting worldwide peace and understanding between peoples and cultures who have a shared sense of belonging to a global community. Its objectives are upheld by other international organisations such as Oxfam who also work towards the realisation of the principles of global social justice. Within the vision of these organisations, GCED is not perceived as a discrete subject area but rather designed to extend across all spheres of life, informing national policy before being realised within and beyond classroom environments. If you want to explore the work of these organisations further, you may wish to visit the Oxfam and UNESCO websites, where you can view high-quality teacher resources and classroom guides. You can find the relevant links in the further reading list below.

GCED is identified as an area that all countries should promote within the United Nation's (n.d.) *Sustainable Development Goals* (SDGs). These seventeen goals were developed to help achieve the 2030 Agenda for Sustainable Development. The programme is directed towards reducing global poverty and inequalities and advancing healthcare, education and economic growth while tackling issues of sustainability and climate change. In order to inspire young people to engage with the purposes of the SDGs, an online educational platform, *The world's largest lesson* (n.d.), has been developed in partnership with UNESCO and UNICEF. The website contains a wealth of practical resources, in multiple languages, aimed towards enabling learners across the globe to become active and informed citizens. It focuses on promoting student knowledge of the viewpoints and actions that are needed to create a peaceful, prosperous and sustainable global community. Additionally, *The world's largest lesson* inherently connects these global goals with children's rights.

Indeed, a discussion on the international context of citizenship and ethics would not be complete without acknowledging the fundamental role that the *United Nations convention of the rights of the child* (UNCRC) (UN, 1989) plays in the contemporary global educational landscape. The convention, which has been signed by 196 countries worldwide (2022), has 54 articles that cover all aspects of a child's life, including their civic, social, cultural, educational and political rights. A few examples of how it relates to the principles of ethical citizenship are recorded in Table 7.1.

Table 7.1   Relating UNCRC to principles of ethical citizenship

UNCRC Article(s)	Relationship to ethical citizenship principles
Article 12 states the need for children's views to be taken into account in all matters that concern them, thus facilitating self-expression and decision-making powers	As with UNESCO's global citizenship approach, realisation of this article entails the active involvement and participation of young people themselves (OECD, 2023; Lyle, 2014)
Articles 14, 15 and 30 refer to the freedom for children choose and practice their own religious and cultural beliefs	These articles relate to children as individuals capable of personal conviction and ethical agency
Article 42 stipulates that children must be taught about their own rights and accordingly about the rights of others	Gaining an understanding of their inalienable rights enables children to realise their own positionality as present as well as future citizens

Ensuring that even young children have a clear understanding of the rights afforded to them is increasingly becoming a hallmark of ethics and citizenship education across international communities (Gottschalk and Borhan, 2023). As well as tackling interrelated issues such as child protection, poverty and healthcare, UNICEF works to promote the realisation of children's rights across the globe, supporting the SDGs and running educational initiatives such as the Rights Respecting Schools Award and annual events including World Children's Day.

Together, these international projects aim to develop young people's thinking and perspectives about the global community in which they live. They also indicate the way in which the concepts of ethics and citizenship are inherently connected. In all discussions on global citizenship the underlying questions are: 'What do we value?' 'How should we behave?' 'What should we do?' 'Why is should we do this?' One of the key pathways in achieving thoughtful responses to these questions is through effective education on an international scale. Throughout this chapter we will see how the principles described here have increasingly become embedded within the UK's own education systems.

REFLECTION 7.1

What practical steps could you take to ensure that your students not only learn about their rights and responsibilities, but also experience them in meaningful ways within your setting?

APPROACHES TO ETHICS AND CITIZENSHIP

Enabling children to become ethical, informed and responsible citizens is one of the key underlying purposes shared across the UK's education systems. To achieve this, developing core knowledge of key concepts such as justice, equality, fairness and responsibility is essential. Pupils should learn about the different factors involved in ethical decision-making and be able to distinguish the difference between what they *could* do and what they *should* do in a range of different situations or scenarios, exploring underlying questions such as 'what does it mean to be good?' and 'why does it matter?' Within a primary context, pupils' ethical perceptions should be extended to incorporate knowledge of the moral, cultural and social beliefs of others. Ethics and citizenship content ought also to be designed to incorporate teaching about diversity, identity and rights, including those specified within the UNCRC framework. Furthermore, pupils should develop their own political literacy by exploring different systems of governance, including democracy, and should be given the opportunity to engage in practical experiences of democratic action and community involvement. Finally, ethics and citizenship education needs to take place within a broader context of pupil awareness of their own historical and geographical positionality and should consider current local, national and global issues, including those relating to sustainability.

While the subjects of ethics and citizenship are sometimes approached discretely in the UK, they are often also taught in interdisciplinary ways and through cross-cutting themes. However, as we will see, their principles also feature particularly prominently in some subject areas.

PERSONAL, SOCIAL, HEALTH AND ECONOMIC EDUCATION (PSHE) OR HEALTH AND WELLBEING

In personal, social, health and economic education (PSHE) pupils are encouraged to explore factors that influence their ethical decision-making processes and engage in developing an understanding of how their behaviour and actions may affect others both now and in the future. In this context, teaching may focus specifically on particular values (Doring et al., 2024) or the need to recognise and form positive personal and social relationships with others. Some of this learning might be achieved through discussion or circle time activities which have either been pre-planned or are a spontaneous response to issues that arise during the school day (playtimes included!). As pupils develop their own ethical understanding the intention is for them to become increasingly responsible and informed in the choices that they make. They are encouraged to advance their own critical thinking in relation to how they might respond pro-socially individually as well as collectively when encountering varying behaviours and viewpoints.

As children enter educational settings, they also rapidly develop their awareness of various rules, social norms and attitudes including those embedded within close, familiar environments; they thereby begin to advance their understandings of both ethical and political values. Through experiencing an ethos of *child-led learning*, which is a common pedagogical strategy within the UK's youngest classes, pupils should quickly come to realise the impact that their own behaviour and contributions have upon their immediate surroundings. As children progress through PSHE their sense of what it means to be a member of different educational and wider communities should become further informed. I recently taught a lesson focused upon the different roles within our school and what it means to be a 'good school citizen'. The pupils themselves formulated their own thoughts on this and their responses ('always really making sure that others feel included', 'looking after our class and school environment well', 'caring for others and making sure they have the help they need') demonstrated their own perceptions of effective citizenship within this context as an outward-looking and relentlessly active role. Throughout the primary year groups, PSHE practitioners intend to continuously facilitate pupils' experiences of ethical citizenship, through enabling consistent exploration of children's roles, rights and responsibilities which increasingly extend beyond local and national boundaries.

RELIGIOUS EDUCATION

This extension further relates to developing pupils' understanding of different spiritual and cultural beliefs. Religious education (RE) is one of the subject areas through which pupils are given opportunities to study different systems of traditional world religions, including Christianity. This involves investigation of core ethical values and how these relate to believers' societal norms and expectations as well as religious practices. At primary level, stories can be used to effectively express the influence of historical figures as well as to reflect spiritual beliefs and values such as fairness, equality and love. Developing a knowledge of celebrations, customs, rites of passage and the underlying belief systems that these represent is also a significant aspect of this area. Many schools invite visitors from different faith groups to speak to pupils firsthand about their personal beliefs and practices; there are some wonderful local organisations that can support pupils' access to different religious voices.

Furthermore, RE content is often designed to extend pupils' appreciation of the natural world – for example, through exploring different creation narratives – and considers people's agentic responsibilities in caring for our planet. Such learning may include effective provision of outdoor learning opportunities – for instance, gardening projects, intended to inspire a curiosity and wonder in the living environment. Within such contexts, practitioners work to develop attributes of compassion, empathy and respect for the beliefs of others while also enabling pupils to explore their own spiritual development, thus further supporting pupils' understanding of their own values and capacity for moral reflection and judgement. Increasingly, RE is being remodelled in the UK to include non-religious philosophical convictions (for example, humanism, secularism and atheism) and links to European Court of Human Rights legislation by acknowledging that teaching of this subject area should be objective, critical and pluralistic. This highlights the intertwining connections between an understanding of worldviews and social rights and responsibilities. As we have seen, increasing young people's understanding of different global viewpoints, as well as potentially their similarities and differences, is a fundamental aspect of international GCED programmes.

HUMANITIES

Increasing pupil knowledge of the diverse societal contexts in which they live is also considered to help develop pupils' own sense of identity within the various communities to which they belong (BERA, 2024). Within the UK's humanities' curricular frameworks, schools are given varying levels of autonomy to design and plan topics relevant to pupils' experiences. In accordance with the principles of GCED, historical themes typically aim to develop understanding of change and continuity, progressing an understanding of the interrelationships that exist within and between nations which have shaped our societies both in the past and in the present. Geography schemes, meanwhile, intend to provoke interest in the physical world, its natural resources and the diverse peoples who inhabit it.

In their discovery of places and spaces, pupils are taught about different environmental factors and the impact that people can have on natural landscapes. This leads to an increased awareness of issues linked with ecological concerns and sustainability and thematically links with the SDGs.

Within the humanities, *social studies* further focus on issues surrounding cultural heritage, political governance and social identity. Pupils are required to develop their understanding of principles of democracy and citizenship. From the earliest year groups, children must be taught about their UNCRC rights and how these might be actively expressed and enacted (see below). Pupils may be explicitly taught about how political processes work at school, local, national and international levels, broadening their scope in accordance with their maturity. Older pupils may participate in activities relating to economic priorities and privileges and how these impact on society, effectively linking with issues such as those outlined in the SDGs. Settings may engage local politicians and authorities to explain to children their decision-making structures and capacities – often through visits, letters or email exchanges. Such interactions facilitate pupils' familiarity with the concepts of citizenship, authority and governance, leading to questions relating to interconnectedness, justice and equality. Through their learning pupils should realise that the choices they make as active, informed and responsible persons can have major impacts on society and can actively shape the future of the communities in which they live.

A PARTICIPATORY APPROACH

As any experience from within education will tell you, it is not just the *what* of teaching, but the *how* that matters. As well as providing explicit lesson content that develops pupils' specific knowledge and understanding, educators themselves play an active role in implicitly promoting and transmitting values of citizenship and ethics (OECD, 2019) through their own role modelling, behaviour management and social interactions (Boekaerts et al., 2006). Practitioners are responsible for consistently promoting positive behaviour in their lessons and in wider, less formal learning situations – for example, by facilitating the enactment of school values at breaktimes or during extracurricular activities. In this respect, the development of a whole-school approach (WSA) which promotes and reflects desirable attitudes and beliefs has also been identified as playing a powerful role in transmitting pro-social values to pupils (Gottschalk and Borhan, 2023). Assemblies, cultural celebration days and visiting speakers further enhance understanding of ethical citizenship by inclusively relating to a range of diverse contexts (Doring et al., 2024).

In relation to the realisation of the UK's educational goals for pupils to become ethical, informed and contributing citizens, one of the key features that each of the curricula share is their expressions regarding a participatory approach to learning. This involves pupils playing an active decision-making role in initiating, constructing and enacting their own learning experiences. This approach, supported by the OECD Learning Compass 2030 (n.d.), is one of the key values found in international agreements on education (Ketovuori et al., 2020) and has significant consequences for pedagogical practice. The idea may be traced back to the educational philosopher John Dewey. Dewey perceived knowledge to be socially constructed with meaningful and continuous experiences being our way of making sense of the world. In his cumulative work *Education and experience* (1938), Dewey argues that for effective learning to occur there must be an 'organic connection between education and personal experience' (Dewey, 1938, p. 25). Significantly, Dewey argued that educational experiences must consider the currently existing interests and capacities of 'particular individuals at a particular time' (Dewey, 1938, p. 46). This means that educators' knowledge of, and interaction with, learners is essential. The educator should understand what activities will engage all learners within their present situation and should involve 'the active co-operation of the pupil in construction of the purposes involved in his studying' (Dewey, 1938, p. 67). For this to occur, Dewey perceived that the child must necessarily be a freely acting participant with an acknowledged voice and independent agency within a democratically structured educational process.

Increasingly, this participatory educational theory, sometimes referred to in Early Years as *child-led learning*, has been translated into practice both internationally and in the UK (OECD, 2023). Participatory pedagogy has also been perceived as an inherent requirement in enacting the rights of the child (Gottschalk and Borhan, 2023). As we have seen, active pupil participation is promoted by the principles of the UNCRC, including in Article 12. This states that children have the right to express their opinions on matters that affect them and that their views should be considered and given due weight in decision-making processes. Within this context, educational researchers have encouraged practitioners to consider pupils not as 'empty vessels' ready to be passively filled with the knowledge of an authoritative adult, but rather as competent social agents with their own political powers and human rights (Freire, 1970). Stemming from the thought of Qvortrup (1991) and developed by Uprichard (2008), this sociology of childhood perspective enables practitioners to see pupils as both *becoming* capable of future maturity, growth and learning while simultaneously *being* ethical citizens with a current capacity to cooperatively construct knowledge and elicit social action and change (Quennerstedt and Quennerstedt, 2014). Accordingly, educators are encouraged not only to teach children about their rights, but also to teach through engagement with these democratic principles of human respect, dignity and non-discrimination. Finally, pupils ought also to learn how to purposely use and defend their rights, thereby empowering them to be active global citizens (UNICEF, n.d.a. and b.).

EMPOWERING THE PUPIL VOICE

Thus, as educators we are tasked with providing pupils with authentic opportunities to be agentic participants in the learning process. This increasingly includes within educational policy and curriculum design, with practices aimed towards enabling pupils to be 'maximally self-determining' (Hart, 2008, p. 25). Hart's (1992) ladder of participation outlines different degrees of child involvement in the learning process. He argues that we should provide children with consistent opportunities, as well as the necessary skills and confidence, to operate at each of the levels. Examples of how practitioners may begin to achieve this are given in Table 7.2.

Table 7.2 Examples of participation in practice

Hart's degrees of participation	Example(s) of what this might look like in practice	What it achieves
Assigned but informed	You share the learning intentions of your activity with your pupils, perhaps identifying specific success criteria to which they may contribute	Children have a clear knowledge and understanding of the purpose of the task and of their own involvement for the completion of their activity
Consulted and informed	You regularly engage children in the planning of their own learning, asking them to suggest areas of exploration within a given topic as well as possible tasks they might like to carry out	Children feel a sense of ownership in the learning process and engagement increases as they recognise that their views and particular interests have been considered
Adult initiated, shared decisions with adults	You encourage pupils to develop their own class rules and responsibilities by creating a class charter to which they all contribute. Or you allow pupils to run a project you have initiated such as a fundraising activity or creating a school newspaper	Children feel actively involved in decision-making processes which directly affect them and gain confidence in expressing their opinions. They experience a greater sense of autonomy within their learning environment
Child initiated and directed	Pupils initiate and carry out independent learning opportunities without adult interference. These could involve play-based or role-play activities or self-created and -directed enquiry projects	Children develop the confidence and initiative to develop their skills independently, including those relating to cooperation and social interaction. They feel in control of their learning
Child initiated, shared decisions with adults	Pupils set their own agendas for class/school committees. Children meet with an adult to discuss their proposed ideas and may be charged with reporting decisions back to the wider student community	Children perceive themselves as fully involved and contributing members of the setting's community. They are able to express their views with confidence and understand democratic processes of interaction

Developing this idea of participation or agency is sometimes referred to within schools as *pupil power* or *pupil voice*. This further reflects the position that children must *have their say* in issues which affect themselves (UNCRC).

The UK governments are increasingly putting into place guidance which fosters child-centred approaches. Each nation has its own children's commissioner who, as well as being tasked with ensuring the legislative protection of children's rights, has a website containing further useful information. In nurturing their role as citizens of a democratic society, as an educator you might encourage pupils to make links with local councillors or MPs when learning about issues relating to local or national governance. Each of the UK's parliaments and Assemblies also offers free school visits during which pupils can engage in a range of hands-on experiences. These include tours of the houses or the holding of their own debate in one of the political chambers. Such activities aim to enhance understanding of democratic processes and are facilitated by initiatives such as UK Parliament Week which takes place in November each year.

To increase the strength of pupil engagement, some UK schools have established further democratic pupil bodies with particular remit over certain interest or priority areas. For instance, many settings have pupil-led eco-committees, which are supported by national organisations such as Keep Britain Tidy which runs a comprehensive Eco Schools programme. Schools can earn green flags for pupil-led activities following their own school sustainability reviews and action plans. Projects may involve recycling goals, local litter picks or biodiversity development of school or community grounds. The Eco Schools aims are explicitly linked to the SDGs and pupils must evidence their awareness of global citizenship issues to gain the award. In relation to this, the WWF provides a further array of resources on global wildlife and environmental concerns, including a range of free live lessons throughout the year. They also run a Green Ambassadors scheme which again encourages pupils to take ownership of sustainability issues within their school settings.

Another way in which you might inspire pupils to become actively involved in citizenship and ethics education is through contributing to national or community projects which may link with a current class or school topic or theme. Opportunities can be found, for instance, on Oxfam's Schools Speak Out website where pupils can take part in the charity's latest social action initiatives. Many organisations have educational support services for schools which contain information on how you might raise awareness or participate in planned campaigns. Such direct 'real-life' experiences help enable pupils to realise that their own actions can make a genuine difference. They may also facilitate empathy towards different members of society and highlight the inclusive nature of our collective social responsibilities. On an international level, OECD (2023) case studies further refer to community involvement programmes, as well as participatory budgeting and media literacy initiatives, as examples of how pupils might be empowered to develop the skills and knowledge needed to participate meaningfully in society.

REFLECTION 7.2

What do you perceive to be the opportunities and challenges of adopting a participatory pedagogical approach within the primary classroom?

PHILOSOPHY FOR CHILDREN

Another pedagogical strategy for encouraging and developing pupils' knowledge and understanding of ethical and political issues is engagement in organised philosophical discussion or debate. This approach is often referred to as *philosophy for children* (sometimes abbreviated to P4C) or *philosophy with children*. This contemporary movement has been associated with American educationalist Matthew Lipman. P4C is also supported as a method by UNESCO, with the process perceived as effective in building democratic values and promoting intercultural dialogue. P4C aims to enable pupils to construct, analyse, compare and evidence different conceptual ideas. It seeks to develop democratic *communities of enquiry* (COE) whereby children are invited to co-construct a learning environment wherein their views are listened to and valued thereby strengthening their participation in classroom life (Lyle, 2014).

A wide array of international P4C programmes with supporting materials is available. While the specific pedagogical strategies recommended can vary, the shared purpose of each of the schemes is to engage pupils in 'big concepts' and to enable them to ask deeper-level questions about their own beliefs while respecting the beliefs of others. P4C is about pupils discovering a sense of wonder in the world of ideas around them, being able to 'disagree agreeably' with their peers and developing a sense of rationality and logic when formulating, expressing and justifying their own points of view about a range of political, ethical and world issues. The UK organisation SAPERE refers to the approach as developing the 4Cs of *caring, collaborative, critical* and *creative* thinking (SAPERE, 2022). Recommended stimuli for discussion points can be stories, pictures, video clips, games, quotations or prepared argument summaries. Depending upon the technique chosen, the number of children involved in discussions can vary from pairs to whole class. Classroom organisation may take the form of children sitting in a circle or across from each other on different sides of the debate. The pedagogical role of the teacher is that of *facilitator*, encouraging pupil participation and respectful interactions. The teacher may also potentially support the extension of ideas by asking subsidiary questions such as 'can you explain why you think that?' or introduce additional complexities by asking pupils to consider 'what if ...' scenarios. For children in Early Years, role-play activities and either/or questions can be used effectively for introducing philosophical thinking skills. For example, asking 'would you rather ... have lots of money or lots of friends?' can stimulate a simple conversation around ethical ideas.

Indeed, in my own teaching experience, even very young primary school pupils have the propensity to be able to engage in quite complex argument and moral debate. A few years ago, when teaching a Year 1 class and coming to the end of a topic focused around fairy tales, my superb teaching assistant drew out an enormous castle and the pupils were tasked with placing soft toys representing different story characters either in the castle itself (if they were good) or in the adjoining dungeon (if they were bad). The activity led to a wonderful discussion about good and evil, which actions were right and wrong, and which might be forgiven, as well as thoughts about whether imprisoning someone was the right thing to do (Goldilocks was the subject of some debate I can tell you!). However, perhaps the most interesting reflection point came when the pupils came to a baby fox. Was the fox born bad? Would it learn to be bad? What if it learned to be good? The ethical questions posed resembled the more sophisticated ideas expressed several years later when one of my Year 4 pupils announced during a history session that they had discovered that many Victorians thought children were born evil. Again, the idea was hotly debated, with more balance than you might imagine, giving a beautiful insight into how these young people viewed their own ethical positionality. In this instance, such was the interest generated, that the pupils went on to explore different religious beliefs associated with the idea of inherent good and evil, thus increasing their understanding of varying worldviews and cultures as well as their own sense of place and identity as an ethical and informed global citizen.

ETHICS AND CITIZENSHIP IN ACTION

You will now explore a single case of how principles of ethics and citizenship education can work in practice.

REFLECTION 7.3

As you read, reflect on the ways in which the pupils may have developed their skills and understanding of ethics and citizenship through their participation in the project.

A CURRICULUM FOR WALES CASE STUDY APPROACH

In line with an enquiry-based approach, my Year 4 class had recently begun a topic entitled How did the Victorians transform childhood? The question was aimed at allowing pupils to explore what life was like for children from varying social backgrounds in Britain (as well as their own locality in Wales) in the 19th century. It was within this context that each class within the school was additionally tasked with setting up their own company for an upcoming Christmas fayre with the promise that whatever profits the children made, they could keep. The project was greeted with enthusiasm by the pupils and, in order to maintain a clear connection with our enquiry, it was agreed that our company would adopt a Victorian theme. Then began a series of activities and discussions whereby the pupils eventually came to develop their own clear vision for the event itself. Having voted on their company name, pupils' initial ideas for products and activities were recorded onto paired mind maps which were then displayed as a whole-class 'wall of ideas'. As part of the decision-making process pupils had the opportunity to research prices. Then through a combination of peer negotiations and further voting, the class agreed on six final ideas; three activities (including a Christmas wish tree) and three products (including gingerbread biscuits). Finally, the pupils carried out the task of completing an activity of listing and costing materials needed. The conclusion was drawn that if each pupil contributed £1, as a class they should have sufficient funds to pay for the resources they needed.

Following their budgetary decision, some children immediately volunteered that they could bring in more money to help towards the project, leading to a great P4C debate about whether it was 'fairer' for everyone to bring in the same amount or whether people should bring in what they wished to contribute. This was extended into a wonderful wider discussion 'should those who have more, give more?' which eventually led to the introduction of, and reflections upon, the idea of taxation. If I were to tell you that we may have had some budding politicians in the class, it might give you an idea of the passion with which some thoughts were expressed! The discussion raised some interesting moral questions about wealth and led to the children's consideration of how they could ensure that their own company was ethical. Within our enquiry context we had learned about Dr Thomas Barnardo and had researched his charity. A pupil's suggestion that we could make 'Barnardos bracelets' was well received. It was strongly agreed that all the profits made on this stall would be donated to the charity's Christmas appeal.

As a final step in our planning, the class moved into their pupil committees of which each child in our school in Years 3–6 is a member in order to discuss issues based on the priorities of their committee. Each group subsequently decided on their own project target:

* our *Eco-Committee* wanted to ensure that we used environmentally friendly and donated materials in order to reduce waste;

* our *Community Cadets* thought that friends and family should be formally invited to the fayre and made the suggestion of writing letters home explaining the details of our company and kindly requesting donations and materials;

* the *Pupil Caretakers* wanted to ensure that donations and resources once received were kept and stored neatly and helpfully tasked themselves with the job!

* the *Digital Champions* proposed that the class complete some digital advertising of the products and activities by creating posters and video clips to display on the class social media page;

* our *Criw Cymraeg* (Welsh Crew) wanted to pledge that customers would be greeted in Welsh and that the company signs included Welsh words and phrases.

These objectives were shared with the rest of the class, and the committees (supported by myself) took responsibility for ensuring their completion.

Plans agreed and materials bought, the time to create our products and games finally arrived and pupils rotated around the different activities in turn. In advance of the fayre the children created a plan for where the various stalls were to be placed and later rearranged the classroom accordingly. They voluntarily signed up to a rota to run the different stall sections at different times. After much preparation, the day of the fayre arrived and, following three busy hours, Christorean Creations finished trading with a profit of almost £200 as well as a £96 donation for Barnardos. Next ensued some lively research about what to purchase. It will come as no surprise that the winning idea was to buy a class pet and, after further debate relating to which animals might be best suited to our busy class environment, Year 4 became the proud owners of five fish with the remaining funds being spent on class games, including two highly coveted chess boards.

This case study is by no means a perfect example of ethics and citizenship in action and it is worth sharing with you that as a teacher, the role of facilitator, but not controller or director, is not an easy one to attempt to fulfil. Additionally, it is important to remember that children (or adults for that matter) cannot experience autonomy without the necessary supports being in place. Undoubtedly, however, the project did provide pupils with opportunities to make authentic and ethical choices and become involved in meaningful, democratic decision-making processes. From the outset pupils displayed a strong sense of ownership (and pride!) in the project and they became increasingly pro-active in taking organisational control and initiative. They developed their skills of 'real-life' problem-solving and negotiation including within a financial context. They also experienced firsthand the value of positive social interactions and cooperation and the importance of showing consideration and respect to the views and ideas of their peers including within engagement in political and ethical debate.

FINAL THOUGHTS

In a world in which interconnection and interdependence are becoming an increasingly powerful global force, successfully teaching the theory and practices of citizenship and ethics is arguably the most vital role that educators play in the development of our young people today. Throughout this chapter you have seen how the concepts are inherently intertwined as they work in tandem to extend children's awareness of the value of the democratic communities in which they live. Through promoting an understanding of international principles and the successful adoption of participatory pedagogical methods, such as those explored here, you as an educator can make a real impact – not only to the experiences of your students in the present, but also to their future capacity to create a more peaceable world. Through the teaching of citizenship and ethics, pupils may come to realise the potential of their own agency to make a difference and may learn to actively contribute to the accomplishment of a fairer and more inclusive universal society. Realisation of such goals ultimately lies at the very heart of the UK's education system which aims to enable its young people to continuously flourish as self-aware, informed and ethical global citizens, both now and in the future.

━━ **REFLECTION 7.4** ━━━

How far do you agree/disagree with the following statement? *Within the context of primary education nothing is more important than teaching our pupils how to become responsible and informed ethical citizens both in the present moment and in their future lives.*

FURTHER READING AND RESOURCES

Crowley, A., Larkins, C. and Pinto, L. (2020). *Listen–act–change: Council of Europe handbook on children's participation*. https://edoc.coe.int/en/children-s-rights/9288-listen-act-change-council-of-europe-handbook-on-childrens-participation.html

A Council of Europe handbook providing practical guidance for professionals on implementing children's right to participate in decisions (UNCRC Article 12).

Dorrian, J. and Glover, A. (2023). *Open University mind your policy language*. www.policywise.org.uk/policy-language

A comparative guide to policy language and terminology used in primary and secondary school education across the four UK nations.

Lundy, L. (2018). In defence of tokenism? Implementing children's right to participate in collective decision-making. *Childhood, 25*(3), 340–354.

An academic article that revisits the concept of tokenism in child participation.

Oxfam. (n.d.). *What is global citizenship?* www.oxfam.org.uk/education/who-we-are/what-is-global-citizenship/

Online resource explaining the concept of global citizenship.

UNESCO. (n.d.). *Global citizenship and peace education*. www.unesco.org/en/global-citizenship-peace-education

Website detailing UNESCO's approach to promoting global citizenship education (GCED) and peace education.

United Nations (UN). (n.d.). *The 17 goals: Sustainable development*. https://sdgs.un.org/goals

Official source for the 17 Sustainable Development Goals (SDGs).

UNICEF UK. (n.d.a.). *How we protect children's rights with the UN convention on the rights of the child* (UNCRC). www.unicef.org.uk/what-we-do/un-convention-child-rights

Official source detailing the 42 articles of the UN Convention on the Rights of the Child.

UNICEF UK. (n.d.b.). *Teaching and learning toolbox: Rights Respecting Schools Award.* www.unicef.org.uk/rights-respecting-schools/resources/teaching-resources/teaching-learning-toolbox/

Practical teaching resources for schools to embed the UNCRC principles and achieve the Rights Respecting Schools Award.

WWF UK. (n.d.). School resources and activities. www.wwf.org.uk/get-involved/schools/resources

Educational resources and activities for schools focused on environmental action and sustainability.

REFERENCES

BERA. (2024). *Doing Cynefin: Exploring ideas on belonging, connectedness and community in the Curriculum for Wales.* www.bera.ac.uk/blog-special-issues/doing-cynefin-exploring-ideas-on-belonging-connectedness-and-community-in-the-curriculum-for-wales

Boekaerts, M., de Koning, E. and Vedder, P. (2006). Goal-directed behavior and contextual factors in the classroom: An innovative approach to the study of multiple goals. *Educational Psychologist, 41*(1), 33–51. https://doi.org/10.1207/s15326985ep4101_5

Dewey, J. (1938). *Education and experience.* Free Press.

Doring, K., Jones, E., Oeschger, T. and Makarova, E. (2024). Giving voice to educators: Primary school teachers explain how they promote values to their pupils. *European Journal of Psychology, 39*, 3609–3631. https://doi.org/10.1027/1016-9040/a000123

Freire, P. (1970). *Pedagogy of the oppressed.* Seabury Press.

Gottschalk, F. and Borhan, H. (2023). *Child participation in decision making: Implications for education and beyond.* OECD.

Hart, R. (1992). *Children's participation: The theory and practice of involving young citizens in community development and environmental care.* UNICEF.

Hart, R. (2008). Stepping back from 'The ladder': Reflections on a model of participatory work with children. In R. Jensen (Ed.), *Participation and learning: Developing perspectives on education and the environment, health and sustainability* (pp. 19–31). Sage.

Ketovuori, H., Hirvensalo, S., Pihlaja, P. and Laakkonen, E. (2020). Pupils' experience of social participation in Finnish primary schools. *Nordic Studies in Education, 40*(4), 323–342. https://doi.org/10.23865/nse.v40.2396

Lyle, S. (2014). Embracing the UNCRC in Wales (UK): Policy, pedagogy and prejudices. *Educational Studies, 40*(2), 215–232. https://doi.org/10.1080/03055698.2014.889597

OECD. (2019). *OECD future of education and skills 2030: Conceptual learning framework.* www.oecd.org/en/about/projects/future-of-education-and-skills-2030.html

OECD. (2023). *Engaging young citizens: Civic education practices in the classroom and beyond.* www.oecd.org/en/publications/engaging-young-citizens_2166378c-en.html

OECD. (n.d.). OECD Learning Compass 2030. www.oecd.org/en/data/tools/oecd-learning-compass-2030.html

Quennerstedt, A. and Quennerstedt, M. (2014). Researching children's rights in education: Sociology of childhood encountering educational theory. *British Journal of Sociology of Education, 35*(1), 115–132. https://doi.org/10.1080/01425692.2013.783962

Qvortrup, J. (1991). *Childhood as a special phenomenon: An introduction to a series of national reports.* European Centre.

SAPERE. (2022). *P4C: A philosophical approach to teaching and learning that enables students to think with others and to think for themselves.* www.sapere.org.uk

United Nations (UN). (1989). *Convention on the rights of the child* (1577 UNTS, pp. 3–178). https://treaties.un.org/doc/Treaties/1990/09/19900902%2003-14%20AM/Ch_IV_11p.pdf

Uprichard, E. (2008). Children as 'being and becomings': Children, childhood and temporality. *Children and Society, 22,* 303–313. https://doi.org/10.1111/j.1099-0860.2007.00110.x

World's Largest Lesson. (n.d.). *The world's largest lesson.* https://worldslargestlesson.global-goals.org

8

DANCE

KATHRINA FARRUGIA-KRIEL AND EILIDH SLATTERY

┌── THIS CHAPTER ──────────────────────────────

This chapter explores the ideas that:

- dance in primary education can nurture creative and critical thinking, collaboration and communication

- interdisciplinary learning can be brought to life through dance, offering a child-centred and curiosity-driven pedagogy

- exploring the simple building blocks of creative dance through a problem-solving approach can empower both educators and learners.

┌── KEY TERMS FOR THIS CHAPTER ──────────────────

Body actions: the actions that describe the various ways the body moves, often categorised as *locomotor* (moving through space) or *non-locomotor* (staying in one place):

- *non-locomotor movements*: movements performed in one place (e.g. bending, stretching, reaching);

- *travel*: movements that cover space (e.g. walk, run, skip, galop);

- *turn*: rotation of the body (e.g. spin, twirl);

- *gesture*: isolated movements of different parts of the body (e.g. clap, kick);

- *jump*: movements leaving the floor (e.g. tuck jump, star jump);

- *stillness*: the intentional pause or cessation of movement (e.g. freeze, pause, balance).

Qualities of movement: the characteristics that describe how the body action is performed (the feeling, intention, or energy):

(Continued)

- *time*: the speed or tempo of movements (e.g. fast, slow, changes in speed);
- *dynamics*: the energy, force, or effort used in the movement (e.g. strong, relaxed, heavy, free).

Space: describing how movements fill the surrounding environment:

size of movements: the scale of the movement (e.g. big, small, wide, narrow);

levels: the height of the movement relative to the floor (e.g. low, medium, high);

direction in space and pathways: the orientation and pattern of travel (e.g. forward, backwards, diagonal, following a floor pattern).

Interactions: the element of dance that describes the relationship between dancers:

formations: the spatial arrangements of dancers relative to one another (e.g. alone, partner, group, in a circle, semi-circle).

Adapted from Smith-Autard (2002, 2010).

INTRODUCTION

As the music plays, pairs of children are purposefully engaged in learning. They have been given a problem to solve. As you walk round the space you see and hear the children's explorations and discussion as they work together to find a solution, seeking and sharing feedback. You notice they are not simply looking for an answer; they are collaborating to create possibilities. They are focused on generating multiple solutions, evolving those solutions and reaching a decision they are pleased with. You observe both verbal and non-verbal communications between the children. The teacher is moving among the pairs observing and interacting, skilfully using questions to further the children's thinking. You can hear from the interactions that the children are confidently reflecting on their creative process, and they can proudly justify their decision-making. You see the children leading and understanding the process of learning, the process of problem-solving, the process of creativity. These are skills that will transfer to all areas of learning and life.

This is a dance lesson in a primary school.

Article 31 of the *United Nations convention on the rights of the child* (UNCRC) (UNICEF, 1989) tells us that children have a right to cultural and arts experiences and that there is a responsibility to provide equitable and inclusive access to these experiences. Some children may have access to arts experiences outside school, but it is when we bring the arts into the heart of the primary school that we can provide that equitable and inclusive access for all children and realise the powerful potential of the arts. However, in both national and international research, the most underrepresented area of the arts in primary education is dance (Rolfe, 2001; Gilbert, 2005; Russell-Bowie, 2013; Snook and Buck, 2014; Cheesman, 2016; Slattery and Rae, 2022). We hope that this chapter will support educators to feel more confident to teach primary dance, facilitating more children to experience the multiple benefits of dance education. We will share knowledge and insight into dance for creativity in primary education (Craft, 2000). We explore dance-specific subject knowledge stemming from the *elements of dance* – the building blocks of creative dance (Smith-Autard, 2002, 2010). We discuss how this subject knowledge, interwoven with a problem-solving approach, can link with general pedagogical and context knowledge to allow educators to create immersive, embodied, experiential and inclusive learning experiences for all learners. We explore putting theory into practice for different stages of the primary school, with Kathrina sharing her experiences in the Early Years (Examples 1 and 2) and Eilidh discussing further activities for middle/upper stages. We advocate the benefits of interdisciplinary learning, including connections to numeracy and literacy, as well as subject-specific material such as history topics. We bring together our knowledge and experience of dance pedagogy and teacher education, to focus not only on dance development, but also the transferable skills which can be nurtured through dance.

CONNECTING AND CONSTRUCTING PEDAGOGICAL CONTENT KNOWLEDGE FOR DANCE IN PRIMARY EDUCATION

Considering how to begin exploring dance in primary education may feel daunting. However, it is important to recognise the existing knowledge, skills and beliefs that every educator brings with them when they encounter unfamiliar territory. The diagram below illustrates the value of this interconnection and facilitates reflection to strengthen feelings of self-efficacy.

REFLECTION 8.1

- What were your initial thoughts when you read the opening vignette? Was this your experience or imaginings of how dance can look in primary education?

- Referring to Figure 8.1, look first at 'Knowledge of context'. What connections might you draw upon to support the teaching of a dance lesson with a group of learners? Now, do the same for 'General pedagogical knowledge'.

These connections are the superpowers for educators.

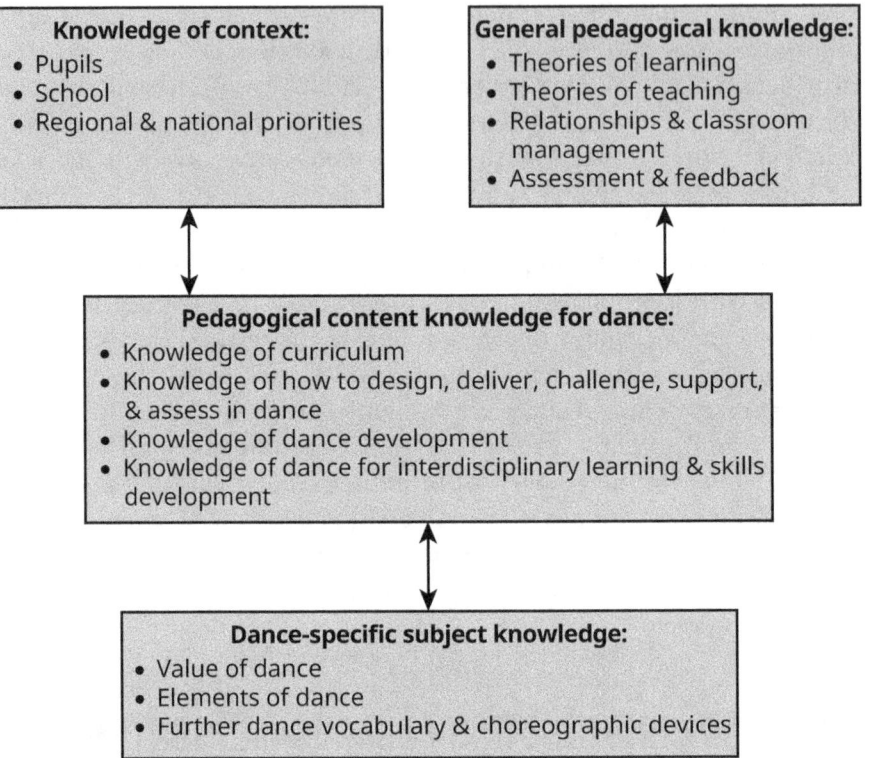

Figure 8.1   Pedagogical content knowledge for dance inspired by Shulman (1986) and Grossman (1990)

EXPLORING DANCE-SPECIFIC SUBJECT KNOWLEDGE

In this section, we will focus on *dance-specific subject knowledge* from Figure 8.1 by introducing key vocabulary forming the building blocks of creative dance. In primary education all creative movements are dance.

▬ REFLECTION 8.2 ▬▬▬▬▬▬▬▬▬▬▬▬▬▬▬▬▬▬▬▬▬▬▬

Referring to the Key Terms for this Chapter on page 117, consider the example of body actions.

Can you think of when you last enjoyed moving about to music or saw someone else (maybe a child) moving about to music?

You will regularly perform body actions in your own natural movements. For example, walking/wheeling around a space (travel), stretching to reach something (non-locomotor movement), turning round to speak to someone (turn), clapping your hands to get attention (gesture), or shouting the infamous 'Macaroni cheese, everybody freeze' and looking to make sure everyone has stopped still (stillness). Imagine a child jumping up and down desperate to tell you what they know (jump). These are all examples of body actions.

The vocabulary in the Key terms table can be used by both educators and learners to explore, create and perform movements, and also to scaffold discussion of live dance performance or recorded dance. Body actions are a great place to start. Following on from this, exploration of movement can deepen through consideration of how these body actions are performed by discussing qualities of movement, space and interactions.

CREATIVITY: A PROBLEM-SOLVING APPROACH

Foster (2019) advocates the value of dance, considering dance as a gift. Within education, dance encourages children to develop a sense of 'knowing oneself and knowing the world around us' (Koff, 2021, p. 48). We will now discuss an approach using dance-specific subject knowledge to develop curiosity, exploring play (Davies, 2003; Bruce, 2011), as well as creativity and creative thinking as facilitated through communication, collaboration and connection inspired by Craft (2000) and Chappell (2007). As Eisner states 'the arts teach children that problems can have more than one solution and that questions can have more than one answer' (2002, p. 9). Using a problem-solving or solution-focused (Craft and Chappell, 2016) approach invites the educator to guide the curiosity and creativity of the children as they build and expand their dance-specific knowledge through exploring, creating and performing. Discussion and the concept of dance appreciation (Smith-Autard, 2002) is interwoven throughout the whole process, thus the process itself becomes an extremely valuable learning opportunity as exemplified in the opening vignette. Teaching in this way creates opportunities for children to develop their creative and critical thinking and collaborative working as well as build their resilience (Snook and Buck, 2020).

While still providing space throughout the process for reflection, discussion and dance appreciation, Smith-Autard (2002) advocates for a problem-solving approach to dance. This can be considered through the lenses of exploring, creating and performing. The exploring phase allows a sense of curiosity, freedom and play, and is such an important part of the creative process, aligning with UNCRC Article 31 (UNICEF, 1989). Being able to explore a problem, generate multiple solutions, evolve those solutions and ultimately decide upon the best or most creative solution are excellent skills to develop. Fraser et al. (2009) describe this development of ideas as a stage where 'possibilities are considered, explored, tested, rejected, resurrected, and pushed in directions that are not wholly determined at the outset' (p. 108). This continues into the creating phase where children are invited to take the building blocks of their exploration phrase and begin the construction process. Acknowledging that the creative process is rarely linear, children may find themselves re-engaging with the exploration phase at any point. The performing phase can also be a way of engaging with feedback to help further develop ideas, thus aiding the creative process. A performance could simply be sharing a movement with another, performing for the class, or could grow into a much bigger performance.

The following example prompts can be used by educators to facilitate a problem-solving approach to dance. These have been grouped into the categories of exploring, creating and performing. The example prompts can be broken down further and scaffolded in any way to best support learners. They can also be edited to create 'I can'-style statements to assist with assessment and progression.

EXPLORING: EXAMPLE PROMPTS

- In pairs, how many ways can you find to travel round the room?

- With your partner, explore using different levels for your travelling movements.

- Explore how you think the character from the story may have travelled around.

- For your travelling movements, can you explore time by moving quickly, slowly, speeding up and slowing down? Be ready to share your exploration and discuss your thoughts.

- Watch this dance clip. What words would you use to discuss the dynamics of the dancers?

- With your group, explore different pathways for your movement sequence.

CREATING: EXAMPLE PROMPTS

- Create a movement sequence which involves, in any combination, one way to travel, two ways to jump, three gestures with different parts of the body and an ending pose. Now teach this to a partner.

- Watching the dance clip, identify three key features of the dance that you'd like to explore. Use this inspiration to create your own movement sequence.

- In your group choreography, ensure everyone feels comfortable to share their ideas verbally or through movement.

- In your group choreography, use your movement or your voice to communicate your ideas.

- When solving the movement problem show patience and perseverance. Afterwards, reflect on what strategies you used.

- When creating your sequence, make sure you follow all the instructions. Be ready to discuss your decision-making.

PERFORMING: EXAMPLE PROMPTS

- Focusing on the qualities of movement, can you rehearse and improve the precision of your performance?

- While watching other groups perform, can you share two strengths of their performance and make one suggestion for further exploration?

- Watch back the recording of your group performance. Discuss with your group ways you could work together to refine and improve your performance.

- In your group, think about how best to communicate your message to the audience. Be ready to discuss your thinking.

- Use the feedback and suggestions you've been given to refine and evolve your performance.

- Can you tell me about the other ideas you had for the turn in this sequence and why you decided on this way of turning?

PUTTING THEORY INTO PRACTICE IN THE PRIMARY SCHOOL

Engaging 'dance' in the curriculum in the lower primary school years offers enriching opportunities for children and young people as they 'develop a growing respect for and confidence in their body' (Randall, 2021, p. 121). Through an exploration of creativity and skill development, dance within the curriculum offers more than just movement, steps and patterns. It enhances several aspects of Early Years child development, including physical development, communication and language, and personal social and emotional development (PSED) (Palaiogolou, 2024). The curriculum in this case study is underpinned by a composite of pedagogical insights, including child-centred and curiosity-driven theories by John Dewey and Maxine Greene (notably through the legacy of Teachers' College, Columbia University), child-focused dance and movement practitioners such as Molly Davies and Tina Bruce, and creativity through the legacy of Anna Craft. These different strands offer a unique insight into learning and teaching within the context of Early Years and childhood.

The inclusion of dance within the Early Years can enrich literacy, numeracy, understanding the world and expressive arts and design. The development of a six-week dance provision emerged from experience as a professional (dance teacher education) and parent volunteer. The curriculum encourages students to explore physical communication through dance: significantly, gross/fine motor skill development and experiencing numeracy within the body. The children navigate language and communication through dance: listening, interacting and demonstrating their understanding and application of the somatic tasks. The curriculum develops incrementally through each weekly session and across the six-week delivery; the dance curriculum for Primary 1/Reception students supports various aspects of PSED, through managing themselves in class and building relationships (e.g. through creatively working with peers), class/group etiquette, listening and respecting boundaries and engaging with new opportunities. It is common to see attitudes which reflect ideas such as 'little girls go to ballet, modern, or tap' but 'boys don't dance'. These attitudes require challenging through an equitable, diverse and inclusive movement curriculum.

EXAMPLE 1: SOWING A SENSE OF CURIOSITY IN PRIMARY 1/RECEPTION

Each class can be structured with typical features of a dance class – a warm-up exercise, technical exercises and skill development for fine/gross motor skills, travelling sequences to develop spatial awareness, a creative exploration and, finally, a cool-down exercise with moments of echoing 'human' and 'holistic', child-centred teaching (Dewey, in Koff, 2021, p. 41). The areas of the class develop incrementally, as seen in Table 8.1.

Table 8.1   Summary chart for the dance curriculum (Primary 1/Reception)

	Technical skill development	Creative development
Session 1	Balancing on one leg, leaping Listening and marking rhythm 1	**Focus on *fireworks* (bonfire night)** Aim: to create a simple diagonal running phrase which culminates in a leap that represents a firework (literacy development in movement – e.g. big, loud, angry, sparks, etc.)
Session 2	Hopping two-to-one leg, alternating Listening and marking rhythm 2	**Focus on *Poppies* (BBC, n.d.)** Aim: to create a short movement-based retelling of the poppies narrative using key components of the animation's narrative and music composition, including a range of qualities, animals and structure
Session 3	Marching and balancing two-to-one leg and one to two legs Listening and marking rhythm 3	**Focus on nursery rhyme 'Hey diddle diddle'** Aim: to create a short movement-based retelling of the cat and the fiddle, drawing upon characters and features of the nursery rhyme (cat, moon, dish and spoon)
Session 4	Sideways galops with a friend, with combination of simple steps Rhythm marking: counting to four	**Focus on hibernation** Aim: to create a short dance that explores concepts related to autumnal life (e.g. leaves fall, gathering and preparing for winter)
Session 5	Forwards skipping with a friend, then solo	**Focus on preparing for winter (Raymond Briggs' *The Snowman*)** Aim: to create a short group dance on preparing for winter (e.g. ice-skating, snowball throwing etc.)

	Technical skill development	Creative development
Session 6	Combination of skips, sideways galops Counting to four	**Focus on preparing for christmas (popular tunes)** Aim: to create a short group dance on choices and arrangement of key steps they've explored in the sessions, utilising the frame of 'four' counts, spatial patterns etc. and set to popular Christmas tunes

Note: Raymond Briggs (1980) *The Snowman*. Puffin; WocomoKIDS (2020).

This curriculum offers developments across recall and enhancements for warm-ups, increased sophistication of movement patterns in the technical and skill development and a gradual development in the creative sections of the class. While in Session 1 the creative element is restricted to an exploration of fireworks (which may be driven by key words, feelings, or experiences), there is much growth and development in the exploration and possibilities surrounding being 'hedgehogs' (moving closely to the ground) in Session 4. By Session 6, students are encouraged to shape their own *movement sentence* with components that they have explored in their dance classes, fostering a healthy sense of curiosity in movement language ideas, within the context of a broad range of participants – including those who do 'once-a-week' recreational (dance) ballet classes, those who do occasional workshops and those who have had no dance experience in their young lives.

Sowing a sense of curiosity can be connected to various curriculum areas. The technical skill development fosters a greater awareness of embodied connections, facilitating what Maxine Greene describes as 'active engagement' with ideas and concepts (Koff, 2021, p. 41). Through encouraging students to be 'open [to] awareness, sensitivity and perception in the learner' (Koff, 2021, p. 41), dance supports an exploration of numeracy as explicit experiences in the body; the students work towards demonstrating phrases of four counts, while waiting or listening for the next four counts of the phrase. This is just one of the many areas of interest in this curriculum against the curiosity of explorations of feelings, being and becoming. For example, in 'Autumn leaves', we explore moving through, or shuffling or tossing, the fallen leaves. Some of the explorations are teacher-led, while other playful experiences (such as 'Hibernating animals') allow students to take the lead (or for those less assertive, follow their friends). These exercises encourage the development of a greater sense of autonomy through play with movement (Bruce, 2011), as well as re-affirm their presence and sense of *self* as they discover their own qualities of movement (Davies, 2003).

Progressing through the teaching block, I always find Session 5 a pivotal moment in the delivery of the curriculum. For four weeks, we have laid the foundations of our class etiquette, explored some basic dance conventions and ignited possibilities in creating our own movement (Davies, 2003). The next phase feels very 'grown up' for the children. We connect literacy to a multisensory exploration by focusing our creative session on Raymond

Briggs' *The Snowman* (1980), which brings much excitement to the session. Some students have seen the animated film, others have read the book and the occasional student has been to the Peacock Theatre in London. Our session focuses on the 'Snow people' in Act 2; we watch an extract from the production (from 45'39), noting how the choreography and music compositions support our development of skipping with friends using the Snow people music. The approach to learning evolves into the many dimensions and connections that dance has to literacy, numeracy and making sense of the world through arts and culture, celebrating their achievements within their dance experience. These are important reminders of the creative connections and foundations of learning in the children's first year at primary school.

EXAMPLE 2: LEARNING 'HIDE PARK' (1651)

Dance in Primary 2/Year 1 can also be explored within the context of making connections between history, music and physical education (dance) for students, aged five and six, in their second year of formal education. Through learning 'Hide Park' from John Playford's *The English Dancing Master* (1651), students are able to grasp concrete ideas of rhythm in space and time through the organisation of movement patterns, as well as the complex principles of conforming with a group of class participants (Playford Dances, 2024). The biggest challenge for the students is remembering to move when the *head/side* couples are cued to move – for example, learning to lead as heads, or wait their turn as sides, in their square set. Learning this dance also fosters a deeper sense of spatial awareness as they move within, and beyond, the configuration of the group.

'Hide Park' is learned as part of the Kings, queens and castles unit of study at a local school in southwest Surrey. As part of their broader curriculum, the students visit a local castle and also learn simple tunes on musical instruments (such as the recorder). Dance comes as an enriching addition to their curriculum. Across four weeks of study, we explore Playford's 'Hide Park' within the context of developing the students' skills and technique in dance, but also find the connections to physical education, music education and history studies. Numeracy, literacy and making sense of the world (through history and culture) continues beyond the remit of their earlier experiences outlined in Example 1. I draw upon the manuscript of 'Hide Park' in Playford's book. The music is a recording from *Picking of Sticks* (2004), performed by the Orchestra of the Age of Enlightenment and produced by Nicola Gaines Armitage (1954–2024).

Within the four weeks of teaching, each class is themed across *skill and technical development, learning Hide Park* and *connections with histories*. Like in Example 1, the 40-minute class commences with students standing in a circle, where we acknowledge every participant located at the perimeter of the circle and proceed to perform an engaging *warm-up* with useful connections to the expectations in fine/gross motor skills. We continue to build on skips and galops. Vocabularies, qualities of movement and a range of different tempi are used to support further development; in the earlier stages of the four weeks, slower-paced music is used to support the students practising their skips or galops; the pace is increased by Session 4. We also develop the complexity of the patterns (e.g. four galops followed by four skips) across a phrase of eight counts throughout the weeks. Different tracks from *Picking of Sticks* are used: 'Kettle drum' as a slower-paced track for skips and 'Black nag' to increase the pace.

Table 8.2 *Summary chart for the curriculum for Primary 2/Year 1*

	Technical skill development	**Pattern development in 'Hide Park' and connections with history**
Session 1	Remembering skips	The double step
Session 2	Galops without changing feet ('peg legs')	Moving in the square formation: head couples lead, side couples follow
Session 3	Showing the difference between galops and skips	Learning to cast away and return
Session 4	Combination of four galops and four skips in a phrase of eight	Performing 'Hide Park'

The *eight-count* phrase is central to the students' experience at this level. This aspect of numeracy becomes a connector to the expectations of learning music, as well as understanding the basic components of 'Hide Park'. We learn the *double step*, including how we must be historically 'proper' by commencing the double step with our left leg. Like a sentence, the double step has its own grammar and punctuation. We step forwards on our left foot, passing through our right foot, then left passes again and we close on two feet. The reverse double, taking the right foot first, brings us back to our starting place and also ends the eight-count phrase in its entirety.

Throughout each session, we build on how this double step is central to the choreography of 'Hide Park'. By Session 2, the students learn about *head couples* and *side couples*, why the dance emerged as a *set dance* within a square formation and how they could imagine the Tudors performing this dance within the great halls of palaces like Hampton Court. In Session 3, the students continue to learn about the trials and tribulations of working with their partner (moving side-by-side together, counting together, etc.), and we also find time to experience being a head couple (leadership skills are very evident already) and a side couple (we can't always rely on observation, so I do like to shake things up by assigning different couples to heads and sides). In Session 4, we attempt to move around the couples by casting around with eight skips, waiting for the next couples to cast for another eight counts and then the couples return to the original formation. To support the range of learners in the class, I use floor plans to represent the visual patterns in the dance. Simple arrows for head/side couples moving into the middle and returning to the outer formation, and circular patterns for the shift of the head/side couples swapping places, and their subsequent return. Other resources support the students' interest in the histories of the period. We also look at the language in Playford's book; the students are quick to pick up the differences in spellings, then and now!

Such approach to connecting various subjects and skills, including numeracy and its relationship to music and dance education, the development of curiosity within the study of history and its connection to music and dance within a primary school context moves beyond the expectations from physical education in the curriculum. These transitions through dance in the primary school offer connections to a broader range of knowledge, understanding and application of historical movement, ahead of the forthcoming goals and challenges in their next phase of learning.

EXAMPLES FROM MIDDLE/UPPER PRIMARY

There are often concerns about introducing dance in middle/upper primary, particularly in relation to those learners who appear reluctant to engage (Russell-Bowie, 2013; Slattery and Rae, 2022). Therefore, it can be useful for educators to be flexible and creative in their approaches to introducing dance. As Chappell (2007) highlights, when teaching for creativity with dance, it is important to begin by meeting the children where they are. For example, when you begin working with learners, if you feel the word 'dance' will create a barrier, initially it is perfectly fine not to use the word. Once the learners are hooked, you will find them happily requesting dance.

The following examples have been hand-picked with all of this in mind, beginning with a short introductory activity which is then extended using the problem-solving approach and the framework of exploring, creating and performing. We will then discuss examples of using recorded dance to engage in dance appreciation, enhance the learners' movement vocabularies and deepen their thinking. Finally, we explore examples of interdisciplinary learning. It is hoped these examples will give you an accessible way in to working with dance with learners.

INTRODUCTIONS AND EXTENSIONS

Dance tag is a simple and engaging game that works well as an introduction to dance. Working like most tag games, this game can be played indoors or outdoors, with or without music. Everyone runs (travel) about the space and when a child is tagged, they stand still in an agreed pose (stillness). To free someone and get them back in the game, another child will run up to them and mirror the pose. Then together they perform an agreed *freeing sequence* and the game continues.

The freeing sequence could be a high five (gesture) followed by a spin (turn). As the children become more familiar with this game you can set further criteria for the freeing sequence making use of more of the body actions. As a further extension the children could be organised into teams, with each team having their own unique pose and freeing sequence.

To further extend this game and fully embrace a problem-solving approach making use of the exploring, creating and performing framework, it is possible to create a full lesson or series of lessons which can still link back to playing the game.

- *Exploring*: in pairs, explore different ways of posing, gesturing, jumping and turning, then make a decision on your favourite way to perform each body action.

- *Creating*: next, create your pose and freeing sequence using any combination of your chosen body actions. When you're ready to share you should be able to face your partner and mirror the pose and the freeing sequence.

- *Performing*: when we're watching each pair perform their pose and freeing sequence, let's identify the body actions we can see. Afterwards let's highlight a strong part of their creation.

Within this extended activity there is opportunity to bring in feedback and to revisit the exploring phase to continually evolve the children's creations. The problem-solving approach allows opportunity to maximise the potential of the creative process. As the educator you can observe, support and formatively assess the development of the children's creative and critical thinking, skills of collaboration and their developing understanding of dance vocabulary. With the children, we can be discussing the transferrable skills they are building as they develop their ideas and explore more than one solution (Eisner, 2002; Fraser et al., 2009).

In literacy learning we often work with children to enhance a simple sentence by adding more descriptive vocabulary. The same can happen with dance. With the activity above the children could write and perform their movement sentence.

We are travelling, posing, then turning and jumping with a friend.

Using the Key terms table through a series of further movement prompts, we can invite the children to evolve their movement sentence.

We are running fast, freezing still, then turning slowly and jumping with an explosion of energy.

We are running fast round the room, freezing still in a low-level pose, then turning slowly at a low-level and jumping with an explosion of energy to free our friend and get them back in the game.

RECORDED DANCE AND DEEPENING THINKING

There are many YouTube™ channels which have movement breaks and short dances that children can follow along with. This can be a good way of helping children become comfortable with dancing. Watching live or recorded dance can be a useful stimulus to facilitate further idea development for the activity above. For example: in pairs, note down three ways you saw the dancers travelling/turning/gesturing.

If you feel these identified body actions would be safe for the children to try, the next stage would be to try them out for themselves. They can share these with each other and create further movements themselves inspired by the movements other pairs have shared.

Engaging with live or recorded dance can generate interesting discussion, supporting literacy development and oracy skills. This is an opportunity for the educator to make use of their questioning skills to deepen the children's thinking while also delving into the concept of dance appreciation (Smith-Autard, 2002). Questions/prompts could be:

- can you list three different body actions?

- let's compare and contrast the performance in these two clips – make a list of similarities and differences (you may choose to scaffold this with specific criteria regarding body actions, qualities of movement, space, interactions, music, number of dancers, costume, production etc. – start simply);

- identify two ways the dancers travelled. Can you discuss the different qualities of movement you could see between these two examples?

- choose one example of a jump and suggest a different way to perform this body action;

- what do you think the message of this dance might be? What clues led you to that conclusion?

- identify three gestures. In pairs, can you create a little sequence of movements that you can perform sitting in your seat? Add in another gesture of your choice and a finishing pose;

- what did you think about that performance? Can you tell me more about that? Can you appreciate why someone else may have a different opinion?

REFLECTION 8.3

Craft and Chappell (2016) discuss the suggested prompt 'what if?' when considering possibility thinking. Using the Key terms table and the exploring, creating and presenting prompts, can you create prompts to use with children to deepen their thinking?

INTERDISCIPLINARY LEARNING

Let's introduce a specific example of a block of dance lessons for a class of eight- to nine-year-olds. The focus of the dance lessons came as a result of watching the children work on a design activity in the classroom. The children were given paper and pencils and asked to design a robot to meet a specific criteria. I could see the children worked independently without interaction. They drew only one idea, struggled to discuss their thinking and wanted to know if they had the correct answer.

The block of dance lessons was developed to strengthen their creative problem-solving skills across all areas of learning. This series of dance lessons aimed to provide meaningful embodied experiences of the following transferable skills:

- creating multiple solutions;

- giving and receiving positive and constructive feedback;

- improvement of initial and subsequent solutions;

- learning from each other and working together;

- methodological approach to the problem;

- justification of decisions;

- risk taking;

- confidence and positive determination.

Throughout the block, each lesson would focus on and openly discuss two skills with the learners. It was important to discuss and revisit these transferable skills with the children when they were then in other learning situations too. The strong dance/movement memory from the dance sessions allowed the children to easily recall the skills they had explored in the dance sessions. Following this block of dance lessons, the next time the children were given a design problem it was fantastic to see them putting these transferable skills into action unprompted. The children were also able to discuss the improvements in their creative problem-solving approaches.

Another example was with a group of ten– to 11-year-olds where the language of numeracy and maths was woven through the dance lessons with movement problem prompts such as:

- explore the shapes you can make on your own and with a partner which show acute, obtuse and right angles. Start with just your arms. How will we know which of the angles we are demonstrating?

- there are 30 in our class, how can I calculate if groups of four, five, or six will give us equal amounts of children in each group? What type of calculation did you use?

- in your groups of three, I'd like you to imagine someone has drawn an equilateral triangle on the floor. Can you make your movements travel along the perimeter of this shape in a clockwise direction? First, who can tell me some facts about equilateral triangles before we get started?

- estimate how far your movements have travelled. Now, measure and compare your findings. Can you now reduce the distance you travel by 50 per cent?

- in your group, start standing in a circle. Your circle should have a diameter of 3 metres. You will have a trundle wheel to help you. What other facts about the circle can we work out when we know the diameter? How can we use these facts in our dance?

When planning for interdisciplinary learning (IDL) over a single lesson or a block of lessons, children should have opportunities to learn and achieve in each of the subject areas involved. As Koff (2021, p. 65) states, 'dance should not sit on the periphery of education'. Dance should be seen as a key core component of children's educational experience. Sometimes we do use one subject area as a vehicle for learning in another subject area. It is a real strength for an educator to be able to draw on all areas of their expertise to design creative, memorable and engaging learning experiences. Dance is brilliant for this – for example, dancing the water cycle or the innerworkings of a power station. Chappell (2007) encourages and challenges us to consider the ways children can show us their knowledge and understanding through an embodied approach such as dance.

REFLECTION 8.4

Can you think of IDL opportunities where you could use dance to explore a concept from another subject area to enhance the children's knowledge and understanding? What would you expect to see from the children to inform your formative assessment?

FINAL THOUGHTS

It is our hope that the opening vignette has sparked your curiosity about dance in primary education, demonstrating how it can effectively nurture creative and critical thinking, collaboration and communication in children. We trust that the key concepts, discussions of the elements of dance and practical exemplifications shared in this chapter have inspired a desire to develop your own creativity as an educator and, crucially, to nurture the expressive potential of your learners.

By deliberately embracing dance, you will soon see the profound strength in the connections you are forging across children's learning, empowering both educators and learners.

FURTHER READING AND RESOURCES

Bruce, T. (2011). *Learning through play: For babies, toddlers and young children*. Hodder Education.

Foundational text on the importance of learning through play for the Early Years (babies, toddlers and young children).

Davies, M. (2003). *Movement and dance in early childhood (0–8 years)*. Paul Chapman.

Practical resource for teaching movement and dance to early childhood pupils (0–8 years).

Smith-Autard, J. (2002). The art of dance in education (2nd ed.). Methuen Drama.

A key textbook on the theory and practice of teaching dance in education, covering pedagogy and curriculum.

Smith-Autard, J. (2010). *Dance composition* (6th ed.). Methuen Drama.

Detailed guide focusing specifically on the processes and elements of dance composition.

Randall, V. (2021). Dance: The art of movement. In S. Ogier and S. Tutchell (Eds.) (2021). *Teaching the arts in the primary curriculum*. Learning Matters, pp. 120-133.

A textbook chapter offering content and pedagogical guidance for teaching dance to primary-aged pupils.

REFERENCES

BBC. (n.d.). *Poppies*. www.bbc.co.uk/cbeebies/watch/poppies
Briggs, R. (1980). *The snowman*. Puffin.
Bruce, T. (2011). *Learning through play: For babies, toddlers and young children*. Hodder Education.
Chappell, K. (2007). Creativity in primary level dance education: Moving beyond assumption. *Research in Dance Education*, 8(1), 27–52. https://doi.org/10.1080/14647890701272795
Cheesman, S. (2016). Empowerment through risk. *Journal of Dance Education*, 16(1), 12–19. https://doi.org/10.1080/15290824.2015.1051623
Craft, A. (2000). *Creativity across the primary curriculum: Framing and developing practice*. Routledge.
Craft, A. and Chappell, K. (2016). Possibility thinking and social change in primary schools. *Education 3–13*, 44(4), 407–425. https://doi.org/10.1080/03004279.2014.961947
Davies, M. (2003). *Movement and dance in early childhood (0–8 years)*. Paul Chapman.
Eisner, E. W. (2002). *The arts and the creation of mind*. Yale University Press.
Foster, S. L. (2019). *Valuing dance: Commodities and gifts in motion*. Oxford University Press.
Fraser, D., Henderson, C., Price, G., Aitken, V., Cheesman, S., Bevege, F., Klemick, A., Rose, L. and Tyson, S. (2009). Examining and disrupting rituals of practice in the primary classroom. *Education 3–18*, 37(2), 105–199. https://doi.org/10.1080/03004270802012657

Gilbert, A. G. (2005). Dance education in the 21st century: A global perspective. *Journal of Physical Education, Recreation and Dance, 76*(5), 26–35. https://doi.org/10.1080/07303084.2005.10608250

Grossman, P. L. (1990). *The making of a teacher: Teacher knowledge and teacher education.* Teachers College Press.

Koff, S. R. (2021). *Dance education: A redefinition.* Methuen Drama.

Palaiologou, I. (Ed.). (2024). *The Early Years foundation stage: Theory and practice* (5th ed.). Sage.

Playford Dances. (2024). https://playforddances.com/

Randall, V. (2021). Dance: The art of movement. In S. Ogier and S. Tutchell (Eds.) (2021). *Teaching the arts in the primary curriculum* (pp. 120–133). Learning Matters.

Rolfe, L. (2001). The factors which influence primary student teachers' confidence to teach dance. *European Physical Education Review, 7*(2), 157–175. https://doi.org/10.1177/1356336X010072005

Russell-Bowie, D. E. (2013). What? Me? Teach dance? Background and confidence of primary preservice teachers in dance education across five countries. *Research in Dance Education, 14*(3), 216–232. https://doi.org/10.1080/14647893.2012.722614

Shulman, L. (1986). Those who understand: Knowledge growth in teaching. *Educational Researcher, 15*(2), 4–14. https://doi.org/10.3102/0013189X015002004

Slattery, E. and Rae, A. (2022). Dance education in the primary school in Scotland. Royal Conservatoire of Scotland. https://pure.rcs.ac.uk/files/17063011/Dance_Education_in_the_Primary_School_in_Scotland_Slattery_Rae_2022_RCS.pdf

Smith-Autard, J. (2002). *The art of dance in education* (2nd Ed.). Methuen Drama.

Smith-Autard, J. (2010). *Dance composition* (6th Ed.). Methuen Drama.

Snook, B. and Buck, R. (2014). Policy and practice within arts education: Rhetoric and reality. *Research in Dance Education, 15*(3), 219–238. https://doi.org/10.1080/14647893.2014.910184

Snook, B. and Buck, R. (2020). How might creative learning through dance support resilience? *Journal of Human Behavior in the Social Environment, 30*(3), 289–305. https://doi.org/10.1080/10911359.2019.1680474

UNICEF. (1989). *United Nations convention on the rights of the child.* www.unicef.org.uk/what-we-do/un-convention-child-rights

WocomoKIDS. (2020). *The Snowman: A boy and his magical snowman's wonderland adventure* [video]. YouTube. www.youtube.com/watch?v=FZJfe9YZeEY&t=2703s

9

DIGITAL TECHNOLOGIES: UNDERSTANDING THE TECHNOLOGY THAT DRIVES OUR WORLD

CLAIRE HAWKINS AND GAVIN DAVENPORT

THIS CHAPTER

This chapter explores the ideas that:

- technology is everywhere around us, but we may not stop to think about the underlying rules that govern how it works. Similarly, children don't automatically understand technology just because they are immersed in it

- all computers share common principles: taking input, storing and processing data and producing some kind of output

- most computing and technology curricula contain different elements including computer science, information technology and digital citizenship.

KEY TERMS FOR THIS CHAPTER

Algorithm: step-by-step set of instructions to solve a problem or complete a task.

Artificial intelligence (AI): training computers to perform tasks that usually require human intelligence, such as recognising images or generating text.

Computational thinking: a way of solving problems using skills like breaking tasks down (decomposition), spotting patterns, removing unnecessary details (abstraction), writing instruction (algorithms) and using logic.

Input/output: input is data received by a computer (e.g. pressing a button); output is the result shown or acted upon (e.g. a light turning on).

(Continued)

Repetition: a programming concept where instructions are repeated. This can be done a set number of times or until a condition is met.

Selection: a decision-making process in programming where the computer chooses between different actions based on a condition (e.g. IF it's raining THEN take a coat ELSE leave it).

Sequence: the order in which instructions are carried out in a program. Changing the sequence can change the outcome.

Variable: a placeholder for data that can change while a program runs (e.g. a score in a game).

INTRODUCTION

Across the teaching profession, confidence in teaching digital technologies is low (Royal Society, 2017; Chikomba 2024). The myth of digital natives persists, suggesting that children know more than teachers, but familiarity is not understanding (Prensky, 2001). All technology – from the wheel to the flush toilet – seeks to make tasks simpler, more efficient or allow humans more time for other things. Digital technologies are an evolution of this principle. This chapter explores digital technologies that surround us and how to teach the underlying concepts and empower children to be more than passive consumers.

ANYTIME, ANYPLACE: TECHNOLOGY IS EVERYWHERE

Pause and consider the digital technologies you use daily. You might think of smartphones and apps, games consoles, tablets, smart TVs. Spend a little longer and you might remember automation: street lighting, supermarket checkouts, targeted adverts and music or video recommendations. We take these technologies for granted often without thinking how they work.

Ofcom (2025) reported that 85 per cent of three- to five-year-olds go online, with 19 per cent owning a mobile phone. While much of this is passive (TV/films (76 per cent); video sharing (91 per cent); live streaming (49 per cent)), other use is potentially interactive (56 per cent messaging; 60 per cent have their own social media profiles). These percentages increase with children's ages. Despite age restrictions, 63 per cent of parents of young children believed benefits outweighed the risks in children's (mainly) supervised use (Ofcom, 2025). Children imitate the technological behaviours they see and are already immersed in this world.

The Children's Commissioner's report (2024) suggests children who feel safe online feel more positively about other areas of their lives; those who feel unsafe online tend to feel negatively about safety in their local area, their body image, their own agency and their opportunities. There are both positives and negatives to children's technological engagement. We need children to become empowered, proactive users of technology.

STOP SCROLLING, START CREATING

The World Economic Forum (2025) predicts continued growth in digital technologies employment. Children we teach now will have jobs we cannot imagine. Analytical and creative thinking, resilience, curiosity and technological literacy are vital skills for the future. Education, though, is about more than preparation for employment; it should inspire, nurture our passions and prepare us as citizens of a global community.

Turning to your technology use: what's your balance between passive scrolling and creativity? Passive use accounts for 70 per cent of children's time online; only 29 per cent post or share online and 16 per cent live stream (Ofcom, 2025). There are dangers for children sharing online, but this shows many children are consumers, not creators of content.

The media industries use creative and innovative digital technologies: music, film, gaming, art, light shows, theatre. Technology solves real-world problems: medicine, deep sea and space exploration, environmental. Technologies enhance education: immersive simulations, personalising learning. Digital technology is valuable across all aspects of life, and children should be analytical, resilient, creative and ethical users – many of the essential future skills!

DEVELOPING KNOWLEDGE AND SKILLS

Around the early 2010s, many countries developed appropriate technology-focused curricula. Though labelled slightly differently – computing, computer science, ICT, informatics, digital citizenship – and with slightly different emphases, they tend to foreground the importance of computer science and digital citizenship. Here we will not look at one curriculum specifically, but take a broad approach to consider what's important for children to learn, using *computing* as a umbrella term (Royal Society, 2012).

We suggest these domains of knowledge for primary teachers:

- *computer fundamentals*: what computers are and how they work;

- *networks and the internet*: sending data, internet and Web, searching;

- *systems analysis and design*: problem-solving;

- *programming*: instructing computers;

- *robotics/physical computing*: interacting with the world;

- *applications*: apps and technologies for creative purposes;

- *digital citizenship*: safe and ethical use.

These can be grouped into children's understanding:

- how technologies work;

- skills and knowledge to harness technology;

- responsible, safe use.

Emerging technologies like artificial intelligence (AI) and machine learning (ML) can fit within existing domains – fundamentals and applications – which should be reassuring. While technologies change and innovate, the fundamentals are still largely the same.

Sometimes beginning teachers question teaching children about technology. Prensky (2001), an educational games designer, coined the term 'digital natives'. He wrote an opinion piece suggesting post-1980 children should be taught through gaming because they are immersed in technology and therefore should find it easier to use technology than those who didn't grow up with it. This caught the popular imagination. There are many research papers dispelling this sticky myth, but we can apply our own critical thinking: you might own a smartphone and spend several hours a day on the internet and a host of applications – does it mean you inherently know all about the technology itself?

REFLECTION 9.1

- At home what technologies do children use and what gaps might result in their under-standing?

- Why is it problematic to uncritically accept the digital natives concept?

- How might socioeconomic status impact on developing technological knowledge?

YOU ALREADY KNOW MORE THAN YOU THINK

Often primary teachers worry about their technical knowledge. Let's revisit those three aspects children need to know:

- how technologies work;

- skills and knowledge to harness technology;

- responsible, safe use.

You can probably think of many examples of technology that you are able to use effectively, safely and responsibly, and you're likely to have some knowledge of how technologies work, just from your daily technology use. For instance, you keep passwords and usernames safe (3); you use apps daily for productivity and creativity (2); and you use your smartphone to send and receive data (1). What's missing is the terminology which pulls it together.

Let's use an example of sending a message via a fictional app to explain simply what the smartphone (or computer) is doing.

1. *You type and send a message*

   Data is *input* through an *input device* (keyboard/screen). The data is *stored* and *processed*.

2. *The message is secured so others can't read it*

   The message is *encrypted* (it's unreadable without a key) using a *cypher*. You may be familiar with substitution cyphers, e.g. A=Z, B=Y, C=X. Children enjoy decoding secret messages with cyphers. Digital encryption is more sophisticated than substitution cyphers, but it explains the principle.

3. *The message is sent over a wireless network, across the internet to your friend*

   The message is split into *data packets* to make it the right size. The *packets* travel through a wireless network to a *router*. A router does what you might expect – it routes data (e.g. our message) to its destination. The internet is a network of networks and your message travels through many routers. A *domain name server* (like an address book) labels the *data packets* with the destination address. This is an *Internet Protocol (IP) address*. Each device on a network has its own unique IP address (just like your home address).

4. *Your friend's phone receives the message*

   Software checks the message hasn't been damaged and all the *data packets* have arrived. The packets are *stored* on the phone and *processed* so it can be displayed correctly.

5. *Message is unlocked and opened*

   The message is *decrypted* with a *key* (the cypher). The message is *output* to the screen.

Possible ways to bring this to life for children include:

- children acting out sending and receiving data over a network taking on different network roles;

- encrypting and decrypting secret messages using a cypher, and even creating their own cyphers;

- identifying different technologies used to send data including input and output devices and network technologies.

There are excellent lesson plans and resources you can use for teaching this available from support organisations (see the Further reading section for details).

REFLECTION 9.2

- How did using a familiar context support your developing understanding?

- Can you apply this to other familiar technology use (e.g. how might you teach photography)?

LEARNING OUT LOUD: ROLE MODELLING DIGITAL CURIOSITY

Innovative and creative uses of technology are fascinating: 3D printing onboard the International Space Station, robots for dangerous situations, exoskeletons helping people walk, drone light displays and the potential applications for AI. You could call our fascination and curiosity child-like! If you can find the same fascination with any aspect of technology, then you can harness it to inspire and enthuse children. Technological evolution can seem scary yet exciting when teaching, so stay curious and willing to learn with the children.

What happens when children ask questions and we don't know the answer? It can feel very exposing, particularly if you think you must know everything (honestly, who does?). Teachers should model how to learn, thinking about learning and adjusting strategies to learn better. This is metacognition; it's thinking about how we learn and being purposeful about learning strategies. The Education Endowment Foundation's (EEF's) excellent toolkit (EEF, n.d.) draws on research evidence on the benefits of applying metacognitive strategies in your classroom. This can be a useful strategy to manage those little gaps in our knowledge. Instead of hiding the process of finding answers to questions, use it as a learning opportunity for metacognition. For example:

Jess: What is an IP address?

Teacher: That's a great question and I'm not sure of the answer. Let's find out together! Class, Jess has asked an excellent question – what is an IP address? Let's figure this out together. Who can tell me what we should try first? Yes, Naveed?

Naveed: We could ask our friends.

Teacher: That's a good place to start. Does anyone know?

Alma: It's something to do with the internet.

Teacher: I agree, Alma, so we know a little bit more now. What should we do next?

Jess: We could search online.

Teacher: Great idea! Do we remember the SMART rules?

Children reiterate the SMART rules (keep personal information safe, careful if meeting or accepting online pop-ups, etc., check information is reliable, tell trusted adults), then the teacher displays a search engine and constructs a search with the children's help. Together they discover that IP means Internet Protocol and the purpose.

A question can become a shared learning moment demonstrating lifelong learning, identifying strategies and encouraging greater autonomy in learning.

Becoming a curious learner of technology helps harness children's skills and knowledge. Celebrate their fascination and learning so children can experience real agency. Children will show you technological accomplishments you don't understand, so as a curious learner, ask them about it! Children enjoy talking about and demonstrating what they have learned. Simply saying, *'That's fantastic! How did you do that?'* celebrates children's accomplishments and means you learn from each other.

PEDAGOGICAL FOUNDATIONS

Computing pedagogy draws upon *constructivist* and *constructionist* learning theories. It is worth briefly considering these foundations. Piaget theorised that children actively construct their knowledge and mental models through interaction with their environment and meaning-making experiences, such as play (Aubrey and Riley, 2022). Building upon Piaget's theories, Papert (1993) investigated how children learn through curiosity and problem-solving, interacting with their world and receiving facilitative support. He believed computers and robotics could stimulate children's love of learning. Papert's *constructionism* theory (rooted in learning through making) was foundational for Resnick when developing the Scratch™ block-based programming environment (see scratch.mit.edu). Resnick wants Scratch to have 'low floors, wide walls and high ceilings', meaning children get started easily, explore freely and grow their capabilities. Scratch encourages autonomy and interaction with the environment.

Socioconstructivist theory emphasises interaction, communication and dialogue to make meaning – for example, Vygotsky's zone of proximal development (ZPD) suggests a learner makes more progress through dialogue with a more knowledgeable facilitator. Collaboration and dialogue is woven through much computing pedagogy – for instance, paired programming requires two children working together; collaboration is a key aspect of the pedagogical approach (Denner et al., 2014); or PRIMM (predict–run–investigate–modify–make) pedagogy teaches programming drawing on socioconstructivist principles, making meaning through dialogue (Sentance et al., 2019). These approaches also distribute cognitive load between children, enabling them to develop expertise. *Cognitive load* theory (Sweller, 1994) suggests working memory has a finite capacity – a more complex task takes more space, making learning more difficult. Skilful teachers plan and adapt activities to manage cognitive load.

Other strategies include using analogies, real-world examples and drawing on elements already culturally familiar to children, like using games such as 'Simon says' or 'Guess who', to demonstrate the logical rules behind conditions, or use physical activities like dancing to explore *algorithms* (following a set sequence of steps). Young children's engagement with computing has improved through their own digital storytelling using Scratch Jr™, allowing them to personalise stories (Horwell et al., 2021). Facilitating children's agency over learning through their aesthetic choices (characters, backgrounds, even the context of a game design) is a simple way to increase involvement and ownership. Digital technologies teaching can also draw on culturally responsive pedagogies (Gay, 2018). These approaches take account of the diversity in your classroom, encouraging children to choose projects which are meaningful to them and their experiences, and providing multiple perspectives providing rich and meaningful learning (Raspberry Pi Foundation, 2023).

DEMYSTIFYING COMPUTING: DEVELOPING TECH POWERS

We've explored how adopting a curious learner mindset supports teaching computing, alongside pedagogical principles. Now, let's consider how to bring these ideas together when teaching common computing topics.

WHAT IS A COMPUTER?

Let's think about what a computer fundamentally does: it allows you to *input* information, it *stores* and *processes* it and then *outputs* it in an appropriate form. You've already encountered this terminology when exploring how messages are sent. We will use simple examples to explain further.

At dusk streetlights come on, even though the time of dusk shifts throughout the year. How do they know when to come on? A little computer called a *microprocessor* controls each streetlight. A light *sensor* (*input* device) detects the light level and *stores* the level in the computer, a program *processes* it and when the light level reaches a predetermined low level (dusk) the light is switched on (*output*). This happens with automatic doors: movement sensors (*input*) – data is *stored* and *processed* – motor to open doors (*output*); doorbell cameras: movement sensors (*input*) – data is *stored* and *processed* – image live-streamed (*output*).

Using examples from children's daily lives helps them understand the technology around them. Physical computing or robotics extends this through hands-on experiences of real-world applications. In primary schools you may encounter:

- *microcontrollers* – for example, BBC Micro:Bits, Crumble controllers;

- *robots* – BeeBots, Ozobots, Spheros, Picohs;

- *customisable kits* – OhBots, Lego robotics (all trademarked).

Microcontrollers are generally the most affordable option, with built-in functionality through LEDs and buttons. They are extendable via crocodile clips to include motors or sensors, or can be attached to a robotic kit, such as a drone. Decisions about which resources to use may come down to both budget and perceptions about how much staff knowledge is needed to use the technology.

All these devices have input (sensors, buttons) and output (lights, motors). The children program the device to process the instructions and the program and incoming data are held in *storage*. Children see that when an *input* is provided (e.g. button is pressed), the microcontroller *stores* the instruction, *processes* their program, then *outputs* a response (e.g. turning on an LED). There are many sample projects and tutorials available – for instance, BBC Micro:Bit (https://makecode.microbit.org/) has block-based programming projects for scrolling name badges, or simple games.

COMPUTATIONAL THINKING

Computational thinking is a problem-solving approach in computing. There are five main components: algorithms, decomposition, pattern recognition, abstraction and logical thinking. Let's explore these through another example.

- You are planning a holiday. Break this big task down into smaller parts: where are we going? How long will we stay? What kind of accommodation? Who is going? This is *decomposition* – breaking down a problem into its different parts.

- You've planned a holiday before and know a travel site can help with planning. This is *pattern recognition* – spotting a pattern and then looking to repeat the actions.

- You know that your friends have different shift patterns, holiday allocations and budgets, but you realise the first thing is to identify some possibilities at different prices. This is *abstraction* – removing any unnecessary information.

- Some things are fixed and impact other elements. You can only go on certain dates and have a fixed budget. Other things might be essential: *my hotel must have a pool*. Therefore, you exclude anything that does not fit these rules. This is *logical thinking*.

- You gather information from your friends, possible dates, destinations and identify the essential criteria (rules) and repeat the same search on a number of sites. This is an *algorithm* – a set of rules or instructions which allows you (or a computer) to perform a task.

Put together this is *computational thinking*.

We can teach computational thinking explicitly to younger children through unplugged activities (meaning away from any technology), while with older age groups it can be integrated into learning activities, for instance designing a game by decomposing the different parts they need to create and planning an algorithm for their programs before going on the computer. There are many classroom unplugged activities available through support organi-sations (see Further reading). An example could be:

> a 'human robot' needs to walk across a space, pick up a ball, and return. Children write their algorithms to achieve this, then it is acted out. Children can only read what is on their algo-rithm and the human robot must enact the instructions exactly as given. Children debug their algorithms (debugging is identifying and correcting errors).

Once children understand computational thinking, it can become integrated into their normal computing activities. The teacher includes planning opportunities, which are appropriately scaffolded, to ensure children plan purposefully for computing, rather than going straight onto the computers.

PROGRAMMING

Alongside computational thinking children need to know the *four key concepts* of program-ming: *sequence, repetition, selection* and *variables*. Using these four concepts children will be able to create fun games and interactive animations. These concepts build on and reflect some of our learning from computational thinking.

Once children have written an algorithm (a set of instructions) they then need to put this into the computer as a program. We use block-based programming with primary-aged children as this removes much of the complexity of learning to program. Scratch and Scratch Jr are popular in primary schools and there are many resources, examples and tutorials available.

A *sequence* is simply a group of commands, placed together in an order which will enable the computer to perform a task. In Scratch this could be using the movement blocks to program the cat sprite (this is a character in Scratch you can program) to walk across the stage (screen) and spin around. Sequences are closely related to algorithms. With younger children you can use a visual timetable as a model – the blocks/activities are ordered on the timeline of the day and we progress through the sequence. Changing a sequence changes the outcome.

Repetition relies on pattern recognition. Consider the tasks which need to be repeated endlessly. Earlier we considered streetlights turning on and off, but there are also traf-fic crossings, automatic doors and voice recognition systems waiting to hear the trigger word – 'Siri', 'Alexa', or 'Hey Google'. These systems are using repetition. Automatic doors are endlessly checking 'Is someone there?'; voice recognition is constantly asking 'Has someone mentioned my name?' These are examples of a *forever* loop; it will keep asking the question forever. There are other types of repetition too – for instance, you might want a particular action repeated a certain number of times, perhaps a celebra-tion on screen when someone gets the answer right in your quiz (e.g. cheer three times);

this is a *count-controlled loop*. Or you might want to *repeat until* another event stops it (e.g. repeat until a particular score is reached). The concept of repetition can be taught through unplugged pedagogies, so children perform dance moves five times (count-controlled loop), or dance until the music stops (repeat until ...).

Selection is when we get the computer to make a choice based on the conditions in the program. This sounds complicated but isn't when you have some examples. So, when a voice recognition system hears its name it responds, so let's think about this as selection:

IF you hear 'Siri'

THEN say 'How can I help you?'

ELSE wait

The computer is selecting what to do (wait or ask 'How can I help you?') depending on whether it hears 'Siri' (the condition). An unplugged version you could use with children might be:

IF it is raining outside

THEN take your coat

ELSE leave your coat

Notice the use of IF–THEN–ELSE which is a block we use for selection in Scratch. Selection allows us to do more interesting things with games, or animations. If a sprite is clicked, or interacts with another sprite, it means the game can respond to this (e.g. a shark eating smaller fish which disappear as the shark eats them, then the smaller fish reappear a few seconds later):

IF small fish is touching shark

THEN hide

ELSE wait five seconds and show

Variables are placeholders for data which can change while the program is running. Consider the data a game automatically changes while you are playing: the score, your health, a timer. This data is held in a placeholder in the system. Variables change dynamically in response to things which are happening in the program. This is different to the numbers or text you see in a coding block in Scratch which, once you've changed that number or text, it stays like that; these are constants. Constants don't change dynamically while the program is running. If you are not sure whether something is a variable or a constant, think about whether you have to change that in the programming blocks (constant), or if it changes while the program is running through interactions on the stage (variable).

Variables work with selection to make games more interesting:

Set SCORE to 0

IF small fish is touching shark

THEN hide, Change SCORE by 1

ELSE wait five seconds and show

This builds on the shark game to award a point for every fish caught. When the shark catches a fish the score will increment by one point. Variables can also store text and a good example are *Ask* and *Answer* blocks in Scratch. The *Ask* block provides text input to appear at the bottom of the screen and this is linked to the *Answer* variable. The *Ask* text might be 'What is the capital of France?' The player's answer is stored in the *Answer* variable. Then you use selection to determine if the answer is right or wrong:

Ask 'What is the capital of France?'

IF Answer = Paris

THEN say 'That's right!'

ELSE say 'That's not right.'

A variable could be used to allocate a point to a correct answer and this would sit in the line:

THEN say 'That's right!', Change SCORE by 1

Children can make interactive quizzes with points system on recent curriculum topics. This cross-curricular approach integrates consolidation of another curriculum area and new learning for computing knowledge.

NETWORKS AND THE INTERNET

Networks are fundamental to technological tasks we take for granted every day. Every time you use search, send messages, upload a document, print your work, log on to an account at university or work, you send data across a network. We are connected by cables that run through walls, ceilings, underground and under the sea. They circle the world allowing us all to communicate seamlessly. Wireless connections are short distance and eventually connect to physical cables too. This physical infrastructure is the internet, this includes the computers, the routers, domain name servers, cables, switches – physical stuff you can trip over! Very little internet traffic is carried by satellites (a common misconception).

Although we tend to use the terms interchangeably, the World Wide Web (www or web) is not the internet – it is the documents and resources we use within the physical infrastructure. If the internet were a network of roads, the web would be the traffic on it.

While interconnectedness has brought many benefits, it has also brought challenges. Children need to be aware of how technologies work, so they can make informed decisions about how their data is used, how they use different services and to understand the technologies' limits and capabilities; they need to be critical and informed users. For example, we use search engines every day without considering how the results are returned, yet using a different search engine, different terms, using advanced search, changing location or sharing only limited data about yourself will change the results. Social media, streaming services and other technologies build a profile of you based on multiple data points and matching this to the likes and dislikes of profiles which have similar data points. This data is used to influence the results shown to you based upon your identified or presumed profile. The information we see is curated and pushed to us by technology companies based on these data points and their algorithms. Technologies we use are not neutral, nor are they always a power for good. Children need to make informed choices about the data they share and how they engage with technologies in a meaningful way.

DIGITAL LITERACY AND ONLINE SAFETY

Children must be equipped to navigate a digital landscape. It is a vital part of safeguarding that they learn how to identify risky content, report unwanted contact or materials and take responsibility for their digital lives and digital footprint. While specific apps change, the underlying principles of critical and analytical thinking help to maintain stability in an ever-changing digital world.

In the previous section we thought about how technology companies may use our data in unanticipated ways, which links to children's online safety and digital literacy. As well as hidden risks, there are more obvious risks for children online: grooming, cyberbullying, viewing inappropriate material, gambling, inadvertent shopping, radicalisation. This is where a computing curriculum may intersect with a citizenship curriculum and safeguarding requirements.

Schools typically have guardrails around children's IT use which prevent them from accessing known risky sites, but children must be able to navigate the online world safely when they are outside the school gates. Educators play a key role in modelling safe digital behaviour during lessons, and schools should work in partnership with families. There are many resources for teaching online safety to children such as the Safer Internet Centre (see Further reading).

CREATING DIGITAL CONTENT

Computing in all its forms is fundamentally creative. Problem-solving, making, designing and realising ideas that only existed in our heads are all tasks at which technology excels.

For many, consuming content is the first way that we interact with the digital world, but a progression to becoming makers is key for critical understanding.

Technology can be used for fun, creative and inspiring projects which are meaningful to children. The scope is only limited by teachers' imaginations. Harnessing their own creativity, children can engage in projects which are collaborative and relevant to their own lives.

Many devices integrate digital cameras to capture still images and video. Powerful free software allows children to create their own movie trailers for field trips, use desktop publishing apps to make posters for a school event or design objects for 3D printing. Linking these enjoyable classroom activities to how adults create content in the real world gives children insight into how the media around them was created and helps them critically judge its quality and purpose.

What you can do will be defined by the technology available to you. Tablet computers contain many useful in-built or free applications. School networked application suites like Microsoft 365™ or Google Classroom™ can enable pupils (and staff) to collaborate on documents and publish content internally.

Ideas to consider:

- creating an audio or video podcast about a class topic with each group selecting, for instance, a different Greek god to talk about in their episode;

- creating a stop-frame animation (linking individual photographs to create the illusion of movement) using Lego figures. The same technique could be used to make a time-lapse video of an apple decomposing!

- 3D modelling the design for a new playground trail;

- use Google™ sites to create a virtual yearbook for your class.

GENERATIVE AI AND MACHINE LEARNING

Generative AI (GAI) and ML are still in infancy, yet are having a significant impact on social, commercial, governmental and learning environments. Traditionally, when computers performed a task they followed an algorithm, a set of instructions which told the machine what to do; an example would be automating factory production lines. For ML, computers are trained on a typically narrow set of data, such as differentiating cancerous and non-cancerous cells in scans. The computer can spot these differences at an earlier stage and more consistently than humans. ML is a form of AI which has been used for many years. ML/AI works extremely well in a narrow context such as medical diagnosis, streaming service recommendations, or interactions of a non-player character in a game.

GAI is different to the narrow form discussed above. In 2019, OpenAI released ChatGPT™, it's large language model (LLM), and we were all amazed at its capabilities. LLMs are trained on

Web-based textual data; there is debate about the ethics of using Web-based material without permission or compensating the creators. As a simplification, LLMs are trained on text, then a statistical probability model is applied which relates words to each other; this allows the LLM to predict a next likely word in a sentence. Therefore, if your prompt asks 'What are the causes of climate change?' the LLM will look for words related to climate change – like fossil fuels and carbon emissions – and generate a response with those related words. This does not mean it is telling the truth, indeed *hallucinations* (or making stuff up) have been a significant problem for LLMs. This technology is evolving constantly, and newer technologies enable it to search and then generate a response based on the search results, but it can be wrong!

Children need to become critical users and effective users. Although we use natural language with AI, many of the rules of instructing a computer (logic, sequencing) are relevant to effective prompt writing. They should understand GAI is trained on a wide range of data, some of which is unreliable, untrustworthy and can contain bias, so should be checked with other reliable sources. Images are particularly useful for demonstrating bias, as image generators tend to perpetuate Western aesthetic ideals. There are other ethical issues when using GAI: creators are upset their materials are used without acknowledgement or payment; and GAI consumes massive amounts of energy and water, contributing to the climate crisis. Adverts are now using AI-generated models which has negative implications for unattainable beauty standards and impact on body image – a mental health issue for children. Teachers should be aware of the safeguarding risk posed by AI social companions who act as sycophantic AI friends, always agreeing with your decisions and encouraging you to act however you wish (Common Sense Media, 2025).

REFLECTION 9.3

- What are the key learning points for young children about ML/AI?
- How can cross-curricular opportunities be exploited when teaching ML/AI?
- What are the safeguarding issues and how should parents be involved?

HOW TECHNOLOGY IMPACTS SOCIETY AND THE ENVIRONMENT

Although GAI has brought the resource and environmental costs to the fore, technology use has always consumed resources and added to the environmental crisis. You might investigate the energy needs of the technologies we use, mining the rare minerals for microchips and the water needed to cool data centres.

Our interconnected world can have many benefits – easy communication and access to a world-wide community (particularly helpful for children struggling with aspects of their identity who find a supportive and knowledgeable community online (Gee, 2018)), and new pathways for independent learning – however, there can also be problems.

Children's digital footprints often start before they are born as parents share photographs and milestones; they begin as collaborators before becoming owners (Berg et al., 2024). Identity formation is associated with the turbulence of adolescence, yet experiences throughout our lives contribute to our identity (Erikson, 1968). Parents' sharing habits online will influence children's view of digital sharing. There are mixed reports about the impact of online activity and care needs to be taken when interpreting studies conducted with adolescents and applying the findings to the primary context. Some identify high use of social media negatively impacting wellbeing and mental health, including problematic eating and exercise regimes (Jarman et al., 2023); other studies suggest a more complex picture where children report higher life satisfaction when spending time online, where family and schooling connections are supportive (Milosevic et al., 2024). There are no easy answers, but a balanced approach, taking into account children's needs in their own context, is sensible. It is easy to suggest a ban for children online – indeed, internationally some governments are choosing this approach – but children tend to disengage when messaging is negative or authoritarian (Stoilova et al., 2021). Education has a key role in helping children – and their parents – to navigate this space. Modelling and discussing healthy balance, with outdoor activities, exercise and play as part of a daily routine, helps children to reflect on an appropriate balance for themselves.

BRINGING IT ALL TOGETHER

So much in computing requires a context for teaching. Using this productively for cross-curricular or thematic work can enrich children's learning: an animation, a game, a photography project, a presentation – all need to be about something, so use contexts from other topics or subjects to bring computing to life. Vitally, your learning objectives must reflect your computing or technology curriculum, as well as any other subject curricula.

Earlier we highlighted the value of a culturally relevant pedagogy; the topics and themes you choose to contextualise computing can enact this. Allowing children to voice their interests, concerns and questions about the world and choosing from these topics can enrich learning. Barnes (2018) advocates for sustainability themes grounded in current events which may interest or trouble children. Consider the value of themes such as:

- climate crisis and our technological lives;
- plastic pollution and marine life;
- citizenship and democracy in modern societies;
- green spaces for wellbeing.

Many schools purchase pre-written schemes and teach from these. Reviewing and altering them to suit the children's local context and interests can help to increase engagement. Awareness of the concerns and interests of your class and foregrounding opportunities to explore these through computing will capture children's curiosity and imagination.

FINAL THOUGHTS

We are all immersed in a technological world and it's important that children understand how those technologies work and influence their choices so they can engage critically and ethically with them. You already have many of the skills and knowledge you will need through your own use of technology, and you can use freely available support to develop further. Computing is a subject which demands active experimentation, collaboration and critical thought, and we should model our own learning, child-like curiosity and enthusiasm as part of the learning process.

FURTHER READING AND RESOURCES

Computing at School. www.computingatschool.org.uk/

Grassroots network supporting the teaching of computing through community and CPD.

Barefoot Computing. www.barefootcomputing.org/

Provides free, high-quality resources to build teacher confidence in teaching computational thinking.

Safer Internet Centre. https://saferinternet.org.uk/

Offers advice and resources for children, parents and educators on online safety and digital wellbeing.

CS Unplugged. www.csunplugged.org/en/

Collection of free, non-computer activities (puzzles/games) to teach computer science principles offline.

Hello World magazine. www.raspberrypi.org/hello-world

Computing and digital making magazine for educators, published by the Raspberry Pi Foundation.

National Centre for Computing Education. https://teachcomputing.org/

Government initiative providing free, complete curriculum and high-quality training/resources for computing teachers.

Raspberry Pi Foundation. www.raspberrypi.org/

Charity providing low-cost computers and free educational resources for computing and coding.

REFERENCES

Aubrey, K. and Riley, A. (2022). *Understanding and using educational theories* (3rd ed.). Sage.

Barnes, J. (2018). *Applying cross-curricular approaches creatively*. Routledge. https://public. ebookcentral.proquest.com/choice/publicfullrecord.aspx?p=5391361

Berg, V., Arabiat, D., Morelius, E., Kervin, L., Zgambo, M., Robinson, S., Jenkins, M. and Whitehead, L. (2024). Young children and the creation of a digital identity on social networking sites: Scoping review. *JMIR Pediatrics and Parenting*, *7*, e54414. https://doi. org/10.2196/54414

Chikomba, T. (2024). What are the challenges faced by primary school teachers to teach the new computing curriculum in a multi academy trust? (Doctoral thesis). Anglia Ruskin University. Anglia Ruskin Research Online (ARRO). https://hdl.handle.net/10779/aru.25549903.v1

Children's Commissioner. (2024). *'I've seen horrible things': Children's experiences of the online world* (pp. 1–59). www.childrenscommissioner.gov.uk/resource/ive-seen-horrible-things-childrens-experiences-of-the-online-world/

Common Sense Media. (2025). *Social AI companions*. www.commonsensemedia.org/ai-ratings/social-ai-companions

Denner, J., Werner, L., Campe, S. and Ortiz, E. (2014). Pair programming: Under what conditions is it advantageous for middle school students? *Journal of Research on Technology in Education*, *46*(3), 277–296. https://doi.org/10.1080/15391523.2014.888272

Education Endowment Foundation (EEF). (n.d.). *Teaching and learning toolkit*. https://educationendowmentfoundation.org.uk/education-evidence/teaching-learning-toolkit

Erikson, E. H. (1968). *Identity: Youth and crisis*. Norton & Co.

Gay, G. (2018). *Culturally responsive teaching: Theory, research, and practice*. Teachers College Press.

Gee, J. P. (2018). Affinity spaces: How young people live and learn online and out of school. *Phi Delta Kappan*, *99*(6), 8–13. https://doi.org/10.1177/0031721718762416

Horwell, B., Shrestha, P., Hardy, T., Bisserbe, C. and Holt, M. (2021). *Gender balance in computing: Evaluation of intervention 1b: Storytelling approach*. The Behavioural Insights Team. https://computingeducationresearch.org/projects/gbic-storytelling/

Jarman, H. K., Fuller-Tyszkiewicz, M., McLean, S. A., Rodgers, R. F., Slater, A., Gordon, C. S. and Paxton, S. J. (2023). Who's most at risk of poor body image? Identifying subgroups of adolescent social media users over the course of a year. *Computers in Human Behavior*, *147*, 107823. https://doi.org/10.1016/j.chb.2023.107823

Milosevic, T., Bhroin, N. N., Ólafsson, K., Staksrud, E. and Wachs, S. (2024). Time spent online and children's self-reported life satisfaction in Norway: The socio-ecological perspective. *New Media and Society*, *26*(5), 2407–2428. https://doi.org/10.1177/14614448221082651

Ofcom. (2025). *Children and parents: Media use and attitudes report* (pp. 1–67). www.ofcom.org. uk/media-use-and-attitudes/media-habits-children/children-and-parents-media-use-and-attitudes-report-2025

Papert, S. (1993). *Mindstorms: Children, computers, and powerful ideas*. Basic Books.

Prensky, M. (2001). Digital natives, digital immigrants part 1. *On the Horizon, 9*(5), 1–6. https://doi.org/10.1108/10748120110424816

Raspberry Pi Foundation. (2023). *Culturally relevant pedagogy for computing education*. www. raspberrypi.org/culturally-responsive-pedagogy-for-computing-education/

Royal Society. (2012). *Shut down or restart? The way forward for computing in UK schools* (pp. 1–121). https://royalsociety.org/news-resources/projects/computing-in-schools/report/

Sentance, S., Waite, J. and Kallia, M. (2019). Teaching computer programming with PRIMM: A sociocultural perspective. *Computer Science Education, 29*(2–3), 136–176. https://doi.org/10.1080/08993408.2019.1608781

Stoilova, M., Livingstone, S. and Khazbak, R. (2021). Investigating risks and opportunities for children in a digital world: A rapid review of the evidence on children's internet use and outcomes. *Innocenti Discussion Paper* 2020-03. UNICEF Office of Research.

Sweller, J. (1994). Cognitive load theory, learning difficulty, and instructional design. *Learning and Instruction, 4*(4), 295–312. https://doi.org/10.1016/0959-4752(94)90003-5

World Economic Forum. (2025). *Future of jobs report 2025: Insight report* (pp. 1–289). www. weforum.org/publications/the-future-of-jobs-report-2025/

10
DRAMA

REECE SOHDI

---— **THIS CHAPTER** —————————————————————

This chapter explores the ideas that:

- show how drama can nurture creativity, empathy and communication, helping children to explore complex ideas, emotions and social realities through imaginative and embodied learning

- demonstrate how drama can be embedded across the curriculum, not just as an isolated subject but as a pedagogical approach that enriches literacy, history, PSHE, science and beyond through experiential, playful methods

- promote drama as a space for inclusion, joy and empowerment, where all learners, regardless of background, ability, or confidence, can see themselves represented, develop relational trust and find their voice within a supportive classroom community.

---— **KEY TERMS FOR THIS CHAPTER** —————————————————

Imaginative play: a form of symbolic or pretend play where children use roles, narratives and objects to represent meanings beyond their immediate reality. In drama, imaginative play fosters creativity, problem-solving and the ability to explore alternative perspectives.

Embodied learning: a way of learning that involves the whole body as well as the mind. In drama, knowledge is built not only through language, but also through movement, gesture and physical expression, making abstract ideas more tangible and memorable.

Perspective-taking: the cognitive and emotional ability to imagine the world from another person's point of view. Drama encourages perspective-taking by allowing pupils to step into characters, historical figures, or social roles, supporting empathy and critical thinking.

Relational trust: the sense of mutual respect, care and reliability that develops between learners (and between learners and teachers) through collaborative activity. Drama fosters relational trust as pupils listen, take risks and build shared meaning together.

Narrative understanding: the ability to grasp and interpret the deeper layers of a story, including characters' motivations, underlying themes and alternative endings. In drama, narrative understanding is strengthened when children actively inhabit stories through performance.

Self-efficacy: a learner's belief in their own ability to succeed in tasks and overcome challenges. Drama helps to build self-efficacy by giving pupils opportunities to take risks, experiment with roles and experience success in supportive, collaborative settings.

Culturally responsive pedagogy: an approach to teaching that acknowledges, respects and incorporates pupils' cultural identities, languages and experiences into learning. In drama, this can involve exploring diverse stories, traditions and voices so all pupils feel represented and valued.

INTRODUCTION

Drama has a special place in primary education. It gives children opportunities to imagine, explore, collaborate and express themselves in ways that go far beyond pen-and-paper learning. Yet despite growing recognition of its educational value, drama is often side-lined in curriculum planning, squeezed out by the pressure to prioritise literacy and numeracy outcomes (Burnard, 2006; Fleming, 2012). Many teachers and trainees may even feel uncertain about using drama, assuming it requires specialist training or performance skills. This chapter reassures you that drama is not an 'extra' or an add-on, but a flexible and powerful approach to learning that is accessible to all educators.

Drama can be thought of as both a subject in its own right and a way of teaching across the curriculum. It helps children grow cognitively, emotionally and socially by creating spaces where knowledge is experienced through the body, the imagination and dialogue. In practice, this might mean taking on the role of a character from a story, working together to re-enact a scientific process, or exploring historical dilemmas through dramatic conventions such as role-play or conscience alley. Scholars such as Nicholson (2015) and O'Toole and Dunn (2020) show how drama allows learners to inhabit experiences and navigate complex situations, helping them to reflect on social realities through symbolic action. Other scholarly work reminds us that these benefits are especially valuable in a diverse and fast-changing world: drama can support empathy, resilience and curiosity by giving children safe ways to experiment with perspective-taking and meaning-making (Chappell et al., 2016; Baldwin, 2019; Stephenson, 2023).

Throughout this chapter, I will draw on both foundational theories (for example, Vygotsky's (1978) emphasis on play in learning, or Heathcote and Bolton's (1995) process drama) and more recent research (Kucharczyk and Kucharczyk, 2021; Cremin, 2023) to show how drama supports inclusive, creative and socially just education. Throughout, examples and principles that apply across different subjects will be used, but the focus will always remain practical and grounded in classroom contexts.

To help navigate the chapter, here's a short outline of what's ahead. I will begin by looking at drama and imagination, thinking about how children use role-play and symbolic action to develop their ideas. From there, I'll explore how drama builds communication, confidence and inclusion, particularly important for learners with special educational needs and disabilities (SEND) or English as an additional language (EAL). The next section considers drama across the curriculum, showing how storytelling, improvisation and dramatic techniques enrich subjects like literacy, history, PSHE and even science. Practice-based strategies that any teacher can use, regardless of their background in drama follows this. Finally, I will reflect on bigger issues of equity, access and representation, asking how drama can ensure all pupils see themselves (and others) represented in their learning.

Along the way, you will find key terms explained in simple language, reflective questions to prompt your own thinking and suggestions for further reading and resources. My hope is that this chapter not only develops your subject knowledge in drama, but also sparks ideas for how you might bring more imagination, voice and creativity into your classroom practice. Drama, after all, is about more than what children know; it is about how they feel, connect, create and become.

DRAMA AS A TOOL FOR LEARNING AND IMAGINATION

At the heart of drama lies the capacity to imagine otherwise. Through imaginative play, children can step into different roles, explore unfamiliar scenarios and invent new possibilities – skills that are vital for creative expression as well as the development of critical and flexible thinking. In educational terms, imaginative play refers to a form of symbolic or pretend play where children use role, narrative and objects to represent meanings beyond their immediate reality. When harnessed in the classroom through drama, this form of play creates a rich and dynamic space for intellectual, emotional and social growth.

This perspective is grounded in the work of Vygotsky (1978), who theorised that play allows children to function at the highest level of their *zone of proximal development* (ZPD) – the cognitive space just beyond their current ability, where learning occurs through social interaction. In drama, children regularly operate in this zone: negotiating meaning, solving problems and using language in ways that challenge and extend their understanding. These experiences foster embodied learning, whereby knowledge is constructed not only through verbal communication, but also through physical action, movement and gesture.

For example, Cremin and Chappell (2019) found that imaginative engagement in drama is a key driver of cognitive flexibility, enabling children to shift perspectives, explore multiple meanings and think divergently. This is particularly evident in approaches such as process drama, where learners co-construct narratives with the educator, often addressing moral dilemmas, historical conflicts, or community issues. These shared experiences create opportunities for ethical reasoning, empathy and the rehearsal of real-life situations in a safe and playful context (O'Connor and Anderson, 2015).

Drama also allows children to explore abstract concepts through metaphor and symbolic action, supporting deep engagement across the curriculum. For example, a Year 3 class exploring the water cycle might create a group movement piece in which each child embodies a water droplet, journeying through evaporation, condensation and precipitation. Through this enactment, learners develop not only content knowledge, but also a felt sense of processes that might otherwise remain abstract. Studies from cognitive science have shown that this type of embodied cognition enhances memory retention, concept development and emotional engagement (Glenberg, 2010).

Importantly, drama creates space for uncertainty, experimentation and playfulness – conditions that support curiosity, agency and learner voice. These opportunities are especially necessary in education systems that heavily emphasise targets and assessments which reflect the priorities of governments, rather than those of learners. By positioning drama as a valid and vital mode of learning, educators can challenge reductive models of education and instead celebrate the rich, creative capacities of all learners.

REFLECTION 10.1

Reflecting on what you have read so far in this chapter and your own experiences of drama and education, what do you think the value of drama education is?

DRAMA AS A SPACE FOR JOY, VOICE AND EMPOWERMENT

Drama, as explored throughout this chapter, is far more than a performative tool – it is a transformative educational space where pupils can develop confidence, creativity and critical thinking. When embedded meaningfully into primary education, drama supports not only academic attainment, but also the cultivation of empathy, self-expression and collective belonging. In a policy environment often focused on measurement and outcomes, drama invites us to return to the core purpose of education: to support the flourishing of the whole child.

One of the most powerful aspects of drama is the way it creates a safe space for authentic voice. Whether through role-play, improvisation, or devised performance, pupils are given the opportunity to articulate their thoughts, feelings and ideas in imaginative and embodied ways. This process strengthens self-efficacy, especially among children who may feel marginalised in more traditional classroom settings. In this way, drama becomes a vehicle for empowerment, offering children a sense of agency in both their learning and identity formation (Nicholson, 2015).

The collaborative nature of drama also fosters social cohesion. Working in groups to explore characters, narratives and dilemmas encourages pupils to listen deeply to one another, negotiate meaning and take creative risks. This process builds relational trust and also models democratic values of respect, shared responsibility and inclusivity (Boal, 2002; Winston, 2010). These are skills that extend far beyond the classroom, equipping pupils to navigate an increasingly complex, multicultural world.

For educators, drama offers a unique opportunity to centre joy, curiosity and learner-led exploration within the curriculum. It reminds us that playfulness and pedagogy are not mutually exclusive, and that meaningful learning often arises through spontaneity, dialogue and creative freedom (Craft, 2002; Pinchover, 2017; Aartun et al., 2023). Drama can reignite professional passion and offer space to respond more humanely and holistically to learners' needs.

As educators reflect on their own relationship to drama – whether as specialists or novices – they are invited to consider how this subject might serve as a foundation for more inclusive, just and joyful classrooms. In centring the affective, the imaginative and the collaborative, drama fosters educational environments in which every child's voice matters.

REFLECTION 10.2

How can you create more space for joy, self-expression and learner voice through drama in your own practice?

DRAMA FOR COMMUNICATION, CONFIDENCE AND INCLUSION

Drama is a deeply social art form that inherently requires children to collaborate, listen, express and respond. These qualities make it a powerful vehicle for developing interpersonal (communication between two or more people, encompassing interactions, relationships and exchanges of information) and intrapersonal (communication with oneself, encompassing internal thoughts, feelings and self-talk) skills, ranging from confidence and emotional regulation to empathy, turn-taking and active listening. For many learners, particularly those who may struggle with traditional forms of verbal or written communication, drama offers a multimodal, embodied way to connect with others and communicate meaningfully.

The development of communication skills through drama is widely documented. Research by Gill (2023) demonstrates how structured drama interventions can enhance speech, language and communication needs (SLCN), particularly in children with language delays or social communication challenges. Strategies such as storytelling, improvisation and role-play provide contextualised, emotionally engaging opportunities to use language for real purposes. As children inhabit roles and co-construct narratives, they expand their vocabulary, negotiate meaning and practise expressive language in a low-stakes, playful environment.

For children with EAL, drama supports linguistic immersion through authentic and culturally responsive experiences. Through gesture, facial expression and physical action, children can participate in meaning-making even when their verbal skills are still developing. This aligns with Cummins' (1996) theory of context-embedded learning, which highlights the importance of social interaction and visual cues in supporting language acquisition. Drama thus becomes a site of inclusion, where learners with varying linguistic abilities can participate equitably and confidently. Mercer and Dawes (2018) also note that drama and oracy share mutual affordances, with both supporting dialogic engagement and inclusive talk-rich environments for EAL and neurodiverse learners. Findings from McDonnell and O'Boyle (2021), Allder (2023) and Faitaki et al. (2025) further support the role of drama in developing dialogic competence in multilingual classrooms, showing that drama-based pedagogy significantly improves expressive language among pupils EAL learners.

Beyond communication, drama promotes self-confidence and emotional wellbeing. Taking on a role allows children to experiment with identity in a supported and imaginative space. Felsman et al. (2019) argue this can be especially empowering for those who experience anxiety or low self-esteem, as performing enables them to 'try on' confidence through role rather than direct self-exposure. Repeated opportunities to rehearse, perform and reflect also support the development of resilience and self-regulation, helping children manage nerves, navigate feedback and persist in collaborative tasks. Research by Stephenson (2023) has demonstrated how participation in drama supports wellbeing and positive self-image, especially in under-represented or marginalised communities (Vettraino et al., 2017).

Drama is also particularly impactful for learners with SEND. As Chapman and O'Gorman (2022) note, learning environments that allow for symbolic expression (such as movement, puppetry and role-play) can offer more inclusive and equitable access to curriculum content. Drama offers these learners routes to success that do not rely solely on print literacy or standardised assessment formats, helping to reframe ability and achievement in a more holistic and strengths-based way. Both Kempe and Tissot (2012) and Stratou et al. (2023) observed that children with autism spectrum conditions (ASC) demonstrated increased classroom participation and emotional expression during structured drama sessions.

When embedded meaningfully, drama fosters a dialogic learning classroom culture – one where knowledge is co-constructed through interaction, and every child's contribution matters (for more on interactions, you may wish to read Chapter 5). It encourages children to see themselves not only as learners, but also as valued communicators, storytellers and collaborators.

REFLECTION 10.3

How might your own assumptions about what counts as 'communication' influence the ways you use drama to support learners who express themselves differently?

PRACTICE-BASED APPROACHES TO TEACHING DRAMA

You do not need to be a drama specialist to integrate drama into your teaching practice. Drama strategies can be powerful, low-resource and adaptable across subjects. When used intentionally, they offer children a multimodal, emotionally engaging way to explore ideas and deepen subject knowledge. This section introduces five key drama techniques, alongside practical examples and their implications for both educators and pupils.

FREEZE-FRAME

Freeze-frame (also called tableau) is a still image created by individuals or groups using their bodies to represent a specific moment, emotion or idea. It invites interpretation, critical thinking and physical engagement with abstract or concrete concepts.

Example: In a Year 2 history lesson on the Great Fire of London, pupils form freeze-frames to represent moments such as the bakery fire, people evacuating their homes and bucket lines of firefighters. The educator then uses *thought-tracking* – inviting pupils to step out of their frame and say what their character might be thinking or feeling.

Implications: Pupils are physically and emotionally immersed in the learning. This supports embodied cognition, historical empathy and oral language development (Neelands and Goode, 2015). It also gives quieter pupils a non-verbal entry point into the topic.

The educator is supported to approach history in a more inclusive and dynamic way. Freeze-frames enable formative assessment of pupils' understanding and vocabulary without formal writing, making curriculum content more accessible.

HOT-SEATING

In *hot-seating*, one pupil assumes the role of a character and is interviewed by others in the class. The goal is to explore character motivations, narrative depth, or emotional responses.

Example: Following reading the wordless comic *The Arrival* by Shaun Tan in Year 5 English, one pupil takes on the role of the migrant protagonist. Classmates ask questions like: 'What was the hardest part of your journey?' or 'How did you feel when you arrived in the new country?'

Implications: This fosters empathy, inferential reasoning and oracy. It is particularly helpful for developing listening and questioning skills, and for pupils learning English as an additional language (Alexander, 2020).

The educator is able to observe comprehension and social-emotional engagement in a performative context. It also offers an authentic, low-pressure context for children to practise extended spoken responses.

ROLE-PLAY

Role-play allows children to take on roles to explore real or imagined situations. It fosters collaboration, negotiation and perspective-taking, and can link powerfully to PSHE, science, or the humanities.

Example: During a Year 4 geography unit on urban development, the class stages a town council meeting to debate a proposal to build a supermarket on green space. Pupils take on roles such as local residents, wildlife campaigners, shop owners and developers. They present their perspectives and try to reach consensus.

Implications: Pupils develop critical thinking, speaking and listening, and civic reasoning. They learn to articulate diverse viewpoints and develop democratic participation (Winston, 2010).

Role-play offers a creative vehicle for curriculum integration, allowing the educator to assess both subject knowledge and communication skills. It promotes inclusive participation, especially for pupils who may struggle with traditional classroom dialogue.

CONSCIENCE ALLEY

In *conscience alley*, a pupil walks between two lines of classmates who whisper or shout different viewpoints on a dilemma. The person walking down the alley must listen to the arguments and then make a decision.

Example: In a Year 3 RE lesson, pupils debate whether a character should forgive a friend who betrayed their trust. The child in role walks through the alley as one side offers arguments for forgiveness and the other against it.

Implications: This promotes ethical thinking, emotional regulation and decision-making. It enables children to hear and weigh multiple perspectives, building confidence in forming and justifying their views (Nicholson, 2015).

The educator can use conscience alley as a diagnostic tool for understanding children's values and reasoning. It can also serve as a pre-writing strategy in literacy, helping children articulate internal monologue or dialogue before writing narratives.

PROCESS DRAMA

Process drama is a co-created, improvised approach in which educators and learners explore a theme or problem together through extended dramatic action. The goal is exploration, not performance.

Example: In a Year 6 cross-curricular project, a mysterious box is 'discovered' on the school grounds. Over several lessons, pupils investigate its origin, create newspaper reports and debate what to do with it. The educator adopts a role as a museum curator, facilitating enquiry and imagination.

Implications: Pupils engage in sustained enquiry, creative problem-solving and multi-perspective thinking. The integrated approach supports literacy, science and geography in a context of narrative and discovery (O'Toole and Dunn, 2022).

This approach allows the educator to scaffold learning in an open-ended way, promoting child-led exploration and flexible curriculum mapping. It builds confidence in improvisation and encourages a dialogic, enquiry-based pedagogy.

In sum, these practical drama strategies – *freeze-frame, hot-seating, role-play, conscience alley* and *process drama* – demonstrate how accessible, low-resource techniques can powerfully enrich teaching and learning across the primary curriculum. Each offers unique opportunities for children to develop emotionally, socially and cognitively, while supporting curriculum content in meaningful, embodied ways. For educators, these approaches foster confidence in facilitating creative learning without needing to be drama specialists, offering flexible entry points into inclusive and dialogic pedagogy. Most importantly, when drama is embedded in everyday practice, it nurtures classrooms where curiosity, empathy and learner voice thrive, cultivating spaces where all children can engage, belong and express themselves fully.

REFLECTION 10.4

Which of these drama strategies could you integrate into a non-drama subject and how could it enhance the learning?

DRAMA ACROSS THE CURRICULUM

Drama holds rich potential as a pedagogical tool within an integrated curriculum, offering meaningful connections between subject areas while nurturing learners' cognitive, emotional and social development. Rather than being siloed as an 'arts-based' activity, drama can act as an intellectual and imaginative bridge between disciplines.

In literacy, dramatic conventions such as hot-seating and role-play support deeper narrative understanding – the ability to move beyond surface-level recall of a text and instead grasp the complexities of character, motivation and plot (Neelands and Goode, 2015). By stepping into character perspectives, learners are encouraged to infer motivations, predict consequences and even experiment with alternative endings. This kind of embodied storytelling enables children to engage with texts not only through traditional comprehension exercises, but also through re-living, re-telling and reimagining them in emotionally resonant ways that anchor meaning more securely.

In history education, drama can support perspective-taking, which refers to the cognitive and emotional process of imagining the world from another's point of view. This is particularly significant in exploring historical events through multiple standpoints, especially those traditionally marginalised in mainstream narratives (Cleeve Gerkens et al., 2023). Through activities like conscience alley, pupils are able to walk through moral dilemmas, power relations and ethical questions that require them to inhabit historical subjectivities, critically reflecting on whose voices are heard and whose are silenced in dominant accounts. This encourages a move away from rote memorisation towards reflective, relational learning that values complexity and ambiguity.

In PSHE and citizenship education, drama fosters affective engagement, allowing pupils to grapple with sensitive and complex social issues such as conflict, inclusion, justice, or identity in a safe, exploratory space (Stephenson et al., 2023). Techniques such as freeze-frames can be used to externalise internal states, helping children articulate emotional responses and consider multiple pathways in decision-making processes.

These embodied encounters with real-world scenarios provide learners with opportunities to build emotional literacy, moral reasoning and sociopolitical awareness.

Furthermore, drama can powerfully support transformative pedagogy, particularly when applied to themes related to identity, culture and social justice. As Heathcote and Bolton (1995) and Nicholson (2015) have argued, drama education is not solely about rehearsing for performance; it is about rehearsing for life. This in essence is an opportunity for pupils to imagine alternatives, question systems and take action through thought and expression. This approach aligns with critical and inclusive teaching philosophies, positioning drama as a means for children to challenge dominant narratives and engage in democratic dialogue within the classroom (Storsve et al., 2021).

Importantly, these outcomes are not confined to traditional 'arts' subjects. In science or mathematics, drama can animate abstract content through storytelling and role-based enquiry (such as re-enacting life-cycles, mimicking energy transfer, or embodying mathematical patterns), thus making learning more tangible and memorable (Fleming, 2012). This is because drama situates knowledge in embodied, sensory experiences, allowing learners to physically enact concepts rather than engage with them solely in symbolic or abstract form. By appealing to multiple modalities (movement, speech, gesture and emotion) drama deepens cognitive processing and strengthens memory encoding through experiential learning (Kolb, 2015). When used creatively, drama is not only an artistic practice, but also a methodology that underpins interdisciplinary and human-centred learning.

By leveraging drama across the curriculum, educators enrich subject knowledge and support the holistic development of the learner. It allows space for joy, connection and criticality, situating children as active meaning-makers capable of reshaping how knowledge is experienced and understood.

CRITICAL CONSIDERATIONS: EQUITY, CURRICULUM AND ACCESS

While the benefits of drama in education are widely documented, its provision and visibility across primary curricula remain uneven and often under threat. In many school systems, increasing emphasis on high-stakes testing, literacy and numeracy targets and standardised attainment measures has resulted in the marginalisation of arts-based subjects, including drama (Thompson, 2025). This narrowing of the curriculum poses serious questions around educational equity, especially when the expressive, collaborative and inclusive nature of drama can play such a vital role in supporting diverse learners.

Drama has the potential to act as a tool for disrupting educational inequalities, offering accessible modes of expression that transcend linguistic, cognitive, or socioemotional barriers. For learners with SEND or EAL, the multimodal nature of drama provides alternative pathways into learning, allowing participation through gesture, movement and expression even where traditional literacy may present challenges (Kempe and Tissot, 2012). Similarly, drama supports pupils who may struggle with self-confidence or emotional regulation, offering safe, imaginative spaces to practise interaction, negotiation and reflection (White, 2011). These benefits are not supplementary; they are foundational to an inclusive curriculum that is responsive to learners' needs, as you have read earlier in the chapter.

Despite this, access to high-quality drama education often depends on school priorities, educator confidence and policy context. The Durham Commission on Creativity in Education (Durham Commission, 2019) emphasised the disparity in access to the arts across UK schools, citing socioeconomic disadvantage as a key barrier to equitable arts engagement. When creative subjects are framed as enrichment rather than core, pupils in under-resourced schools are less likely to benefit. This leads to what Gadsden (2008) terms a 'cultural opportunity gap' in which pupils' access to expressive and identity-affirming curricula becomes unevenly distributed.

Drama also has a vital role to play in responding to increasingly diverse classrooms. Culturally responsive pedagogy in drama supports children to see their identities, languages and communities reflected in their learning. As Ladson-Billings (1995) argues, effective teaching draws from learners' cultural knowledge, enabling students to connect content to their lived experience. Drama makes this possible through storytelling, characterisation and the reimagining of narrative – inviting pupils to author and interpret their own realities. This is particularly powerful in exploring themes of identity, migration, belonging and justice (Gallagher and Booth, 2003).

A decolonial lens further enriches our understanding of culturally responsive pedagogy by challenging the Eurocentric knowledge hierarchies often embedded in school curricula (Andreotti, 2011; Mignolo and Walsh, 2018). From this perspective, drama becomes a pedagogical space not only for inclusion, but also for resistance – where dominant narratives can be interrogated and alternative worldviews centred. Performing arts, and drama in particular, allow children to engage with multiple ways of knowing, being and expressing beyond those typically validated in mainstream education. For example, storytelling traditions, oral histories and communal modes of performance, common to many global majority cultures, can be celebrated and integrated into classroom practice. This enables educators to move beyond tokenistic inclusion towards epistemic justice, where children's cultural backgrounds are not simply 'added in', but used to reshape the content and methods of teaching itself (Dei, 1996; Smith, 2021). When approached with criticality and care, drama offers opportunities for pupils to reimagine history, language and identity through dialogic, relational and affective learning – centred on equity, creativity and voice (for more information on anti-racism pedagogy, please see Chapter 3).

At the same time, educators face real challenges in embedding drama amid competing curriculum demands. Time constraints, lack of training, or a perceived lack of expertise can prevent even the most committed educators from using drama meaningfully (Taylor, 2024). There is a pressing need for school leaders and policy frameworks to recognise drama not as an extra, but as integral to a curriculum that fosters whole-child development. This includes creating time, professional development and cultural value around drama, particularly for schools serving marginalised communities.

REFLECTION 10.6

How might drama be used to reflect and affirm the identities and experiences of all learners?

FINAL THOUGHTS

In conclusion, embracing drama not as an *extra* but as the vibrant heart of your teaching practice reflects its proven capacity to nourish the whole child. We've seen that drama fundamentally nurtures creativity, empathy and communication, helping children to explore complex ideas, emotions and social realities through engaging imaginative play. Drama can serve as an experiential and playful methodology to enrich core subjects like literacy, history, PSHE and science. Most importantly, drama is an invaluable space for inclusion, joy and empowerment. By providing diverse learners with alternative, multimodal pathways to success, it ensures that all children, regardless of background or ability, can see themselves represented, develop essential relational trust and find their unique voice within a supportive and collaborative classroom community.

FURTHER READING AND RESOURCES

Dawson, K. and Lee, B.K. (2018). *Drama-based pedagogy: Activating learning across the curriculum*. Intellect.

Examines the mutually beneficial relationship between drama and education, bridging the gap between theory and classroom practice. It champions the versatility of drama-based teaching for use across various curricula.

Kucharczyk, S. and Kucharczyk, M. (2021). Teaching Shakespeare in primary schools: All the world's a stage. Routledge.

Offers practical strategies for introducing Shakespeare (e.g. *The Tempest, Macbeth*) to younger learners (Key Stages 1 and 2). The book shows how to make Shakespeare accessible through immersive, playful approaches that connect to drama, writing and cross-curricular learning.

Neelands, J. and Goode, T. (2015). *Structuring drama work: 100 key conventions for theatre and drama*. Cambridge University Press.

A foundational text providing 100 drama conventions – such as still image, hot-seating and thought-tracking – with clear pedagogical rationale. This resource is excellent for new practitioners looking to embed purposeful drama work that encourages critical thinking and active participation across the curriculum.

O'Toole, J. and Dunn, J. (2022). *Pretending to learn: Helping children learn through drama* (2nd ed.). Springer.

A research-informed book presenting a compelling case for drama as a pedagogical tool, offering both theory and application. It explores how role-play and storytelling deepen learning, develop metacognitive awareness and support inclusive practice for diverse learners.

BBC Bitesize. (n.d.). Video resources: Primary drama workshop. www.bbc.co.uk/teach/school-radio/articles/z6bw2fr

A series of three CPD films and resources providing practical guidance for non-specialist teachers on using simple drama strategies. The accompanying teacher notes offer a comprehensive toolkit for applying the demonstrated drama frameworks to various cross-curricular topics (e.g. traditional stories, ancient Egypt).

REFERENCES

Aartun, I., Lambert, K. and Walseth, K. (2023). How pupils' playfulness creates possibilities for pleasure and learning in physical education. *Physical Education and Sport Pedagogy*, *30*(4), 462–479. https://doi.org/10.1080/17408989.2023.2235372

Alexander, R. (2020). *A dialogic teaching companion*. Routledge.

Allder, L. (2023). *Oral fluency and drama: The effect of drama-based pedagogy on English oral fluency in Key Stage 2 EAL learners in UK primary schools* (Doctoral dissertation). University of Kent. https://doi.org/10.22024/UniKent/01.02.100356

Andreotti, V. (2011). *Actionable postcolonial theory in education.* Palgrave Macmillan.

Baldwin, P. (2019). Using drama for learning: how and why it works. *Impact.* https://my.chartered.college/impact_article/using-drama-for-learning-how-and-why-it-works/

Boal, A. (2002). *Games for actors and non-actors* (2nd ed.). Routledge.

Burnard, P. (2006). Reflecting on the creativity agenda in education. *Cambridge Journal of Education, 36*(3), 313–332. https://doi.org/10.1080/03057640600865801

Chapman, S. N. and O'Gorman, L. (2022). Transforming learning environments in early childhood contexts through the arts: Responding to the United Nations Sustainable Development Goals. *International Journal of Early Childhood, 54*, 33–50. https://doi.org/10.1007/s13158-022-00320-3

Chappell, K. A., Pender, T., Swinford, E. and Ford, K. (2016). Making and being made: Wise humanising creativity in interdisciplinary early years arts education. *International Journal of Early Years Education, 24*(3), 254–278. https://doi.org/10.1080/09669760.2016.1162704

Cleeve Gerkens, R., Sallis, R. and O'Brien, A. (2023). Reflecting on embodied experience through an expert lens: Drama as a pedagogic tool for developing academic language proficiency in the middle-primary school. *Research in Drama Education: The Journal of Applied Theatre and Performance, 29*(4), 600–619. https://doi.org/10.1080/13569783.2023.2288647

Craft, A. (2002). *Creativity and early years education.* Continuum.

Cremin, T. (2023). *Developing creativity through drama* (3rd ed.). Routledge.

Cremin, T. and Chappell, K. (2019). Creative pedagogies: A systematic review. *Research Papers in Education, 36*(3), 299–331. https://doi.org/10.1080/02671522.2019.1677757

Cummins, J. (1996). *Negotiating identities: Education for empowerment.* California Association for Bilingual Education.

Dei, G. J. S. (1996). *Anti-racism education: Theory and practice.* Fernwood.

Durham Commission. (2019). *Durham Commission on creativity in education: Final report.* Arts Council England.

Faitaki, F., Liggins, S. and Murphy, V. A. (2025). Piloting a drama-based oral language intervention. *First Language, 45*(3), 282–302. https://doi.org/10.1177/01427237251326982

Felsman, P., Seifert, C. M. and Himle, J. A. (2019). The use of improvisational theater training to reduce social anxiety in adolescents. *The Arts in Psychotherapy, 63*, 111–117. https://doi.org/10.1016/j.aip.2018.12.001

Fleming, M. (2012). *The arts in education: An introduction to aesthetics, theory and pedagogy.* Routledge.

Gadsden, V. L. (2008). The arts and education: Knowledge generation, pedagogy, and the discourse of learning. *Review of Research in Education, 32*(1), 29–61. https://doi.org/10.3102/0091732X07309691

Gallagher, K. and Booth, D. (2003). *How theatre educates: Convergences and counterpoints with artists, scholars, and advocates.* University of Toronto Press.

Gill, A. K. (2023). Drama approaches to enhance communication skills in children with special educational needs (SEN). *Asia Pacific Journal of Developmental Differences, 10*(1), 311–326. https://doi.org/10.3850/S234573412300120X

Glenberg, A. M. (2010). Embodiment as a unifying perspective for psychology. *Wiley Interdisciplinary Reviews: Cognitive Science*, *1*(4), 586–596. https://doi.org/10.1002/wcs.55

Heathcote, D. and Bolton, G. (1995). *Drama for learning: Dorothy Heathcote's mantle of the expert approach to education*. Heinemann.

Kempe, A. and Tissot, C. (2012). The use of drama to teach social skills in a special school setting for students with autism. *Support for Learning*, *27*(3), 97–102. https://doi.org/10.1111/j.1467-9604.2012.01526.x

Kolb, D. A. (2015). *Experiential learning: Experience as the source of learning and development* (2nd ed.). Pearson Education.

Kucharczyk, S. and Kucharczyk, M. (2021). *Teaching Shakespeare in primary schools: All the world's a stage*. Routledge.

Ladson-Billings, G. (1995). Toward a theory of culturally relevant pedagogy. *American Educational Research Journal*, *32*(3), 465–491. https://doi.org/10.3102/00028312032003465

McDonnell, D. and O'Boyle, A. (2021). Process drama in the classroom: A case study of developing participation for advanced EAL learners in an international school. *Scenario: A Journal for Performative Teaching, Learning, Research*, *15*(1), 56–75. https://doi.org/10.33178/scenario.15.1.3

Mercer, N. and Dawes, L. (2018). *The development of oracy skills in school-aged learners*. Cambridge University Press.

Mignolo, W. and Walsh, C. (2018). *On decoloniality: Concepts, analytics, praxis*. Duke University Press.

Neelands, J. and Goode, T. (2015). *Structuring drama work: 100 key conventions for theatre and drama*. Cambridge University Press.

Nicholson, H. (2015). *Applied drama: The gift of theatre* (2nd ed.). Bloomsbury.

O'Connor, P. and Anderson, M. (2015). *Applied theatre: Research, radical departures*. Bloomsbury.

O'Toole, J. and Dunn, J. (2020). *Pretending to learn: Helping children learn through drama* (3rd ed.). Springer.

Pinchover, S. (2017). The relation between teachers' and children's playfulness: A pilot study. *Frontiers in Psychology*, *8*, 2214. https://doi.org/10.3389/fpsyg.2017.02214

Smith, L. T. (2021). *Decolonizing methodologies: Research and indigenous peoples* (3rd ed.). Zed.

Stephenson, L. (2023). Collective creativity and wellbeing dispositions: Children's perceptions of learning through drama. *Thinking Skills and Creativity*, *47*, 101188. https://doi.org/10.1016/j.tsc.2022.101188

Stephenson, L., Sanches, A., Dobson, T. and Ali, J. (2023). Story making in brave spaces of wilful belonging: Co-creating a novel with British-Pakistani girls in primary school. *Research in Drama Education: The Journal of Applied Theatre and Performance*, *29*(1), 95–116. https://doi.org/10.1080/13569783.2023.2211512

Storsve, K., Gjærum, R. G. and Rasmussen, B. (2021). Drama as democratic and inclusive practice. *Youth Theatre Journal*, *35*(1–2), 65–78. https://doi.org/10.1080/08929092.2021.1891164

Stratou, E., Aristotelis, K., Gamvroula, A., Antonopoulos, S. and Saridi, M. (2023). The effect of drama in education on social skills development of children with autism spectrum disorders (ASD). *International Journal of Caring Sciences*, *16*(1), 464–473.

Taylor, S. (2024). *Creativity in the early years: Engaging children aged 0–5.* Routledge.

Thomson, P. (2025). Why bother with arts education in schools? *Australian Educational Researcher, 52,* 781–801. https://doi.org/10.1007/s13384-024-00741-0

Vettraino, E., Linds, W. and Jindal-Snape, D. (2017). Embodied voices: Using applied theatre for co-creation with marginalised youth. *Emotional and Behavioural Difficulties, 22*(1), 79–95. https://doi.org/10.1080/13632752.2017.1287348

Vygotsky, L. S. (1978). *Mind in society: The development of higher psychological processes.* Harvard University Press.

White, J. (2011). *Exploring well-being in schools: A guide to making children's lives more fulfilling.* Routledge.

Winston, J. (2010). *Beauty and education.* Routledge.

11
GEOGRAPHY

SARAH WHITEHOUSE AND EMMA THOMAS

THIS CHAPTER

This chapter explores the ideas that:

- enquiry-led learning enables students to develop critical thinking and investigative skills by posing questions, gathering evidence and constructing their own understanding of geographical concepts

- fieldwork provides experiential learning opportunities that connect classroom theory to real-world contexts, deepening students' sense of place and geographical understanding

- personal geographies and distant places help learners relate their own experiences to global contexts, fostering empathy, curiosity and a broader appreciation of interconnectedness in the world.

KEY TERMS FOR THIS CHAPTER

Place: a location with special features, people, or meaning.

Enquiry: asking questions and finding out answers about people, places, or the environment.

Children's geographies: how children see, explore and experience the world around them.

Fieldwork: going outside the classroom to look, measure and find out about real places.

Pedagogies of hope: ways of teaching that inspire children to care about the world and believe they can make a difference.

INTRODUCTION

As geography educators, we have the professional choice and responsibility to shape not only what we teach, but also how we teach it. Curricula provide a framework, but it is educators who decide which places to explore, which stories to tell and which approaches will inspire curiosity and critical thinking in children.

This chapter invites you to consider geography as more than facts about the world; it is about the ways we and our children experience, question and connect with places. We begin with personal geographies, recognising that every child brings their own lived experience of place into the classroom. We then turn to pedagogies of hope, which position geography as a subject that can empower children to imagine fairer, more sustainable futures. Through enquiry and fieldwork, we explore how geography develops not only knowledge, but also the investigative skills and dispositions that enable children to think geographically. Finally, we consider the challenges and opportunities of teaching distant places, ensuring that children encounter the world in ways that are authentic, inclusive and connected to their own lives.

Above all, this chapter emphasises educator agency. Geography thrives when educators make deliberate, creative choices about content, pedagogy and perspective. Your professional voice is central to how children come to understand the world and how they imagine their place within it.

WHAT IS GEOGRAPHY?

To develop an understanding of what geography is and what it looks like in the context of primary education it is necessary to consider the geographical concepts and skills that underpin this fascinating subject. For educators, a solid grasp of geographical concepts and skills is essential to effectively guide children in exploring and understanding the world around them. Geographical concepts are fundamental ideas that provide structure to geographical thinking and enquiry. These include:

- *place*: recognising that locations hold unique meanings and significance for individuals and communities;

- *space*: examining how and why physical and human features are arranged on the earth's surface;

- *scale*: considering geographical issues across different spatial levels, from local communities to global contexts;

- *interdependence*: understanding the relationships and connections between different places and communities;

- *environment*: exploring interactions between people and their natural surroundings;

- *sustainability*: ensuring resources and environments are managed responsibly for present and future generations;

- *change*: investigating how environments and places evolve over time;

- *systems*: recognising that geographical elements are interconnected parts of larger, complex structures, such as ecosystems or urban systems.

To investigate and apply these geographical concepts effectively, children need to be supported to develop a range of key geographical skills. These skills empower children not only to explore and understand the world, but also to actively engage with its complexities. Children first need to be able to understand their place in the world before they can begin to understand other places and spaces. By developing a range of geographical skills, children will be able to become active geographers capable of navigating the intricate processes involved in geographical enquiry and applying their knowledge meaningfully to real-world contexts.

Geographical skills include:

- *mapping skills*: interpreting and creating maps, understanding symbols, scale and coordinates;

- *fieldwork and data collection*: observing, surveying and gathering both qualitative (e.g. interviews) and quantitative data (e.g. measurements);

- *data analysis and interpretation*: to interpret a range of data to understand patterns and processes;

- *critical thinking and problem-solving*: evaluating evidence, identifying biases and making informed decisions;

- *communication and presentation*: effectively sharing findings through writing, visual representations and oral presentations.

CURRICULUM-MAKING

Curriculum-making is about bringing geography to life. It involves creating meaningful and challenging learning experiences by combining:

- the rich knowledge and resources of geography as a subject;

- your own professional skills and understanding as an educator;

- the backgrounds, interests and experiences of the children you are teaching.

The aim is to find the right balance between these elements so that what you teach feels purposeful, relevant and engaging. Curriculum-making is about more than following a scheme of work or delivering content from an exam specification – it's about *enacting* geography so that children can make sense of the world and their place within it.

Educators are central to this process. While you may use existing curriculum plans, it is your professional choices – the examples you choose, the questions you ask, the connections you make – that turn those plans into powerful learning opportunities. In this sense, curriculum-making is different from curriculum design, development, or planning, which can be done by people outside the classroom. Curriculum-making is what happens when an educator actively shapes learning in response to both the subject and their students.

One helpful way to think about it is to imagine three overlapping circles: the subject, the educator and the children. The most effective curriculum-making happens in the middle, where all three meet. This means engaging deeply with your subject, knowing your children well and being thoughtful about *why* and *how* you teach particular topics (Bustin et al., 2017).

PRINCIPLE ONE: PERSONAL GEOGRAPHY

An important starting point in developing children's geographical understanding is starting with what they already know. Accessing this information is important if educators are to understand how children see themselves in the world. If children are to understand the wider world they must have a secure understanding of their immediate world.

A useful starting point is to develop activities that explore children's connections to places and spaces. One way to do this is through map making where children map their connections to local places. From these maps you can see favourite places, where they spend their leisure time and who is important to them.

Catling (2005, p. 285) suggests that children construct their personal geographies through experience, imagination and interaction. He states that, 'children's geographies are personal, partial and imaginative. They should be a valid starting point for curriculum geography.'

REFLECTION 11.1

Figure 11.1 shows a map from Felix (age seven). Look at his map and consider the following questions.

- How might his map change over the next few years?
- How does his map relate to geographical concepts of location, scale and space?

(Continued)

- What do you know about Felix from looking at the map?

- How might Felix feel about the places he has drawn?

- How has Felix communicated geographical skills and concepts?

- If you were to use his map, how would you use it to develop children's personal geographies?

- What does his map not show you about his personal geography and what questions do you now have?

Figure 11.1   Felix's map, aged seven

Felix has been able to name significant places in Bristol that he is familiar with, the Clifton Suspension Bridge is somewhere he recently visited with his school on a history topic about Brunel. He has also added details about where he shops and the location of his friend's house.

The drawing and mapping of children's personal geographies is an ethnographic approach of human geography that explores how different cultural or ethnic groups understand, use, name and relate to space and place. Educators may have children who are new to the UK, so accessing their personal geographies is important. However, it is necessary to recognise that some newly arrived children may have experienced trauma; this needs to be considered. Some suggestions for how to do this are outlined below:

- *mapping activities*: allow children to share where they have come from through creative mapping (drawing places, routes, important landmarks);

- *storytelling*: invite them, when ready, to tell stories about places meaningful to them – without pressure;

- *cultural artefacts*: encourage sharing songs, foods, or traditions if they wish, showing that their histories enrich the classroom community.

Furthermore, their personal geography might be from a global place; this is often referred to as *glocal*. The term 'glocal' (an amalgamation of *global* and *local*) is used widely in geography to describe the interconnectedness of global and local places.

Biddulph et al. (2015) state that the term is often used in curriculum and pedagogy to help children:

- understand global issues through local lenses (e.g. climate change, migration, food systems);

- develop place-based thinking that connects personal experiences to global contexts.

An ethnographic approach recognises that spaces and places are culturally constructed; places are not just physical locations, they also carry social, spiritual, historical, cultural and linguistic meanings.

REFLECTION 11.2

- What do you think a map of your personal geography would look like?
- How does reflecting on this make you think differently about geography as a subject?

PRINCIPLE TWO: DEVELOPING GEOGRAPHICAL QUESTIONS AND ENQUIRY-LED LEARNING

Geographical enquiry serves as a foundational approach within geography education, integrating concepts and skills into a structured investigative process. It begins with formulating clear and meaningful geographical questions grounded in geographical concepts. Once the enquiry questions have been established, the enquiry can then progress through the collection and analysis of data. The data then is interpreted to provide deeper insights into what is being investigated. This is followed by the communication of findings, which can be done using a variety of written, visual and oral formats. Geographical enquiry requires children to engage in reflective practice, critically evaluating their methods, interpretations and conclusions. Geographical enquiry enables children to become curious, critical and informed learners interested in the world around them and beyond.

Enquiry learning enables children to understand how geographical knowledge is created and revised, enabling children to think and act *as* geographers. Catling (2014) argues that teachers play a key role in supporting geographical enquiry by equipping children with the skills and confidence to engage in geographical thinking. To do this successfully, Catling (2014) offers a three-stage framework for enquiry that is child-centred and progressive. The framework is constructed around three principles – enabling, enhancing and empowering.

- A teacher's role is as an *enabler* or *facilitator* to help children develop enquiry questions.

- *Enhancing*: a teacher's role is to challenge children's questions.

- *Empowering*: a teacher's role is to support children in refining their enquiries.

This framework can support children by offering a structure that places them at the centre of the enquiry, by establishing the conditions for successful learning. These conditions include:

- creating a safe and inclusive classroom culture;

- providing stimuli (images, stories, maps, fieldwork opportunities);

- helping children develop vocabulary, concepts and tools needed to enquire;

- modelling how to ask geographical questions.

Geographical enquiry can foster curiosity and wonder about the world by asking questions such as: 'What's it like there?' or 'Why is that happening?' This natural curiosity is a powerful driver of learning for children. Catling and Willy (2009) argue that enquiry in geography enables children to move from seeing to thinking, from noticing to analysing. These are important skills for children to become geographers. Enquiry allows for a range of learning styles and gives children a voice in their learning. Children can investigate using drawings, maps, role-play, storytelling, photos and discussion and have agency in constructing their own enquiries (Barlow and Whitehouse, 2019).

THE IMPORTANCE OF GEOGRAPHICAL QUESTIONS

Geographical enquiry will only be successful if supported by purposeful geographical questions. Therefore, asking authentic geographical questions is essential before an enquiry starts. You may want to consider questions that are:

- not too broad;

- look at causal relationships (interconnectedness);

- invite investigation rather than a single answer;

- promote critical thinking;

- connect with children's own experiences and interests;

- age- and stage-appropriate;

- encourage a sense of place and scale;

- values-led/respond to current social contexts.

The use of questions stems can be helpful too. In geography, educators can frame enquiry learning through the 5Ws (and 1H) which are:

- who?

- what?

- where?

- why?

- when?

- how?

DIFFERENT MODELS OF GEOGRAPHICAL ENQUIRY

There are many models of enquiry which educators may find useful to support children's geographical knowledge, skills and understanding. When educators choose a model to follow, it is important to consider the needs of your children and select a model which best suits your context. Here are some points to consider:

- make sure your enquiry questions fit the context of the enquiry and consider the starting points of the children in your class so they can make connections;

- consider different methods of data collection that suit the age and stage of the children;

- analyse the data collected in relation to the enquiry question;

- draw conclusions and identify futures questions, acknowledging that a purposeful enquiry question leads to further questions.

Below are some other models of enquiry which educators may find useful when considering the type of geographical enquiry learning for their children.

1. The *5-Step Enquiry model* (plan–do–review) by the Geographical Association (GA).

    Steps:

    - *ask*: pose a geographical question (e.g. 'what is it like in this place?');

    - *collect*: gather information (fieldwork, maps, images);

    - *analyse*: sort and interpret findings;

    - *conclude*: make sense of what has been found;

    - *evaluate*: reflect on learning and enquiry process.

2. The GA's *Plan, Enquire, Reflect* model

    - *Plan*: identify what is being investigated and why.

    - *Enquire*: use methods (mapping, fieldwork, discussion).

    - *Reflect*: review findings and how they change thinking.

3. The *Investigative Cycle* (Bale, 1994)

    An early model still relevant for enquiry-based learning.

    Cycle: stimulus → questioning → data collection → analysis → conclusion → evaluation

4. The *Creative Enquiry model* (Catling and Willy, 2009)

    This model involves more open-ended questions.

    Features:

    - begins with stimulus or curiosity;

    - encourages big questions, such as 'what would it be like to live here?';

    - allows for diverse forms of expression (drawing, drama, storytelling).

    Children need opportunities to explore their own ideas about place, not simply answer questions set for them (Catling and Willy, 2009).

REFLECTION 11.3

Which of the above models do you find most interesting and why?

PRINCIPLE THREE: TEACHING DISTANT PLACES

Teaching distant places is an important part of geography teaching as it can enable children to learn about the world beyond our own doorstep. Through teaching distant places, children can develop their understanding of how other people live and notice patterns in how humans and the environment connect. It also shows us how the world is linked together – for example, the food people eat, the clothes people wear, even the weather we feel can be connected to distant places. By learning about them, it can support children to think critically about global problems and potential solutions. To develop a robust enquiry for teaching about distant places, there are several issues which need to be considered.

DEVELOPING AN APPROPRIATE PEDAGOGY

The choice of pedagogical approach is an essential component that needs to be considered. As a general guide younger children may learn best through concrete, sensory and imaginative experiences, while older primary children can begin to understand more abstract ideas like climate, culture, economy and environmental change. A useful starting place could be through the choice of resources that you may want to use to support children's geographical understanding. While there are many resources available online, it is important to consider what resources you will use and what they represent in terms of place. While we encourage the use of stories, picture books, images, artefacts and film clips, each resource will need to be thoughtfully weighed up in terms of its suitability. Some considerations for assessing suitability are outlined below.

- Are people shown in varied roles (e.g. workers, leaders, families, students)?

- Do the images/texts present people with dignity and agency, not only as victims?

- Is there a balance of challenges and achievements in the place studied?

- Is the information up to date and based on reliable sources?

- Does it show change over time, not just a 'frozen' picture?

- Are local voices/perspectives included?

- Is respectful, neutral language used (e.g. 'low-income country' not 'Third World')?

- Does it explain why inequalities exist, rather than implying they are natural?

- Is difference presented as part of diversity, not as 'exotic' or 'strange'?

- Do photos show a range of daily life (schools, celebrations, work, technology)?

- Are children shown with varied emotions (happy, curious, serious, playful)?

- Are multiple landscapes shown (urban, rural, industrial, natural)?

- Does the resource avoid reinforcing a 'single story' about a place or people?

- Will children leave with a sense of diversity and complexity, not stereotypes?

- Does it foster empathy, curiosity and respect?

Encourage the use of maps, globes, atlases at a range of scales, and aim to use photographs taken by people who live in the place under study. There is much documented research (Budke et al., 2019; Ofsted, 2023; Decolonise Geography, 2021) that demonstrates how the use of resources can reinforce stereotypes, misinformation and deficit thinking. Therefore, to avoid perpetuating stereotypes and the exoticism (when distant places or people are shown or imagined as mysterious, unusual, or romantic just because they're far away or different from what we know) of people, places and cultures it is essential that we adopt the use of real, nuanced representations.

STARTING WITH SIMILARITIES OR DIFFERENCES?

Throughout your enquiry you need to scaffold learning so that children focus on similarities and differences. Starting with similarities may promote empathy and connections which can help children see that people everywhere have similar needs – food, family, shelter, learning, play. This approach may reduce *othering* and avoids positioning distant places as strange or inferior, which is a form of *deficit theorising* (which focuses on what people and places don't have rather than what they do). Avoid deficit-based comparisons (e.g. 'They are poor' vs 'Their way of life is different and adapted to their environment'). Starting with similarities can also help children build a sense of global citizenship, emphasising shared humanity and responsibility for the planet. This approach can support children as they can consider familiar experiences (e.g. school, clothes, homes), providing a strong foundation for comparison. However, it is important to not oversimplify complex contexts as this can result in tokenism, which is when people, places, or cultures are included in lessons only in a very shallow or symbolic way, instead of being explored in depth with explanation of cultural and environmental differences. In this case, children may not develop a deep understanding of geographical diversity if similarities dominate.

Starting with differences can encourage curiosity and questioning. Children will be exposed to unusual landscapes, customs, or housing styles that will often intrigue them and encourage the use of geographical questions. This can highlight the richness of diversity of distant places which can encourage exploration of how geography shapes culture and lifestyle. Starting with differences can also support children's critical thinking by helping them examine why places vary and how environments influence daily life. However, this approach risks reinforcing stereotypes or exoticism if not handled carefully. Furthermore, it can create a sense of distance or disconnect if children can't relate the differences to their own lives. Younger children may struggle to make meaning from too many unfamiliar concepts without anchoring them in known experiences.

We suggest starting with similarities to build connections, then explore differences to deepen understanding. Catling and Willy (2018), argue that starting from the familiar helps children relate to distant places, but exploring difference is essential to develop true intercultural understanding. This is important as it develops children's value and understanding of different cultures, helping them to set places in context through shared human experiences. Do consider how you connect this 'distant' place with children in a meaningful way. A useful starting point is to make connections to children's own everyday experiences; you can do this by asking geographical questions such as:

- where does your food come from?

- have you ever seen a mountain or river?

- what do you wear in different weather?

- where do your clothes come from?

Educators can avoid over simplifying contrasting places by asking children:

- how are these places different?

- why are these places different?

It is important for educators to contrast places that are similar in size and settlement type to enable *place to place* contrasts. For example, contrasting places of a similar geographical size, such as a village to village or city to city, enables children to develop their understanding of physical and human differences like economy, land use and culture rather than differences driven by size or scale. Educators can consider:

- are you exploring how people live differently in the same country (e.g. contrasting rural and urban areas)?

- are you exploring global differences in similar settings (e.g. place to place contrasts)?

USING IMAGES AND ARTEFACTS

Images can be used to foster creativity and curiosity within a geographical enquiry focusing on the study of distant places. Lambert and Morgan (2010) stress that visual materials provide powerful access to place knowledge and can frame how children conceptualise other parts of the world. To borrow an analogy from Bishop (1990), who was writing about the power of children's literature, images and artefacts can help develop geographical understanding by providing windows into the lives of others. This encourages children to negotiate, interpret and construct meaning from images. We advocate that a range of images are useful in geography; these can include reading maps, photographs, satellite images, diagrams and globes (Barlow and Whitehouse, 2019). To use images as a pedagogical approach, it may be useful to think of them as individual jigsaw pieces that children can put together to create a 'picture' of a place. This will need explicit modelling and scaffolding so children can critically analyse the images.

DANGER OF STEREOTYPES

When teaching distant places in primary geography, it's important to consider the danger of the single story. Presenting only one perspective – for example, showing an African country solely through poverty, or the Amazon only through the rainforest – can reinforce stereotypes and give children an incomplete understanding. By providing multiple stories and perspectives, teachers help pupils see places as complex, diverse and connected. This approach develops empathy, challenges stereotypes and supports children in becoming open-minded global citizens.

It is important for educators to reflect on their own perceptions of places and where their perceptions have come from, as an educators' culture, education and personal experiences can influence how they introduce distant places to children. These perceptions can unintentionally bias how places are represented if subject knowledge is limited. Catling and Martin (2011) argue that teachers' subject knowledge and place-based experiences inform both what is taught and how it is framed in the classroom. Therefore, educators need to reflect on their own geographical assumptions to avoid reinforcing narrow or biased views. Some questions you can ask before you begin teaching about a distant place could be:

- what are my perceptions and views of this place?

- where and how have I developed my understanding of distant places?

- how has the media represented this place?

CRITICALLY ENGAGING WITH IMAGES

There is need to challenge stereotypes and consider the multiple perspectives of any place, so we must be aware that photos can reinforce stereotypes and misinformation. Teaching children to be critical about images helps children go beyond the surface and tokenistic understanding. Look for images that raise questions to challenge assumptions about people and places – images that offer a juxtaposing perspective and a range of perspectives to challenge assumptions, stereotypes and disrupt a dominant single narrative about a place. Children need to be taught that images are constructed for a purpose, they are not neutral and they capture something specific. We encourage children to consider:

- why was this image taken?

- who took the image?

- what was the purpose?

- what does it show?

- what doesn't it show?

- whose story is being told?

- who isn't being represented?

- how are they being represented?

- what is the purpose and the intended audience?

THE IMPORTANCE OF LANGUAGE

Language is crucial when teaching about distant places because it shapes how children understand, relate to and interpret the world beyond their immediate experience. Children's views of the wider world are constructed through the language they hear and use at home, school and in the wider community. Therefore, the words that teachers use in their classrooms can either build empathy and curiosity – or reinforce stereotypes and distance. It is important to use language that avoids exoticising or creating deficit narratives of places, which can reinforce stereotypes and limit children's understanding of people and places.

It is necessary to model and encourage children to use specific geographical vocabulary when describing places, environments and people. This needs careful planning and the explicit modelling of vocabulary that supports an enquiry into distant places. As places, especially distant places, may be unfamiliar to children's personal geography, this modelling will help them describe these places using appropriate geographical terms. This will help avoid the use of pejorative language like: Third World, slum conditions, us and them, Africa is a country, native and exotic (Anderson et al., 2021)

TEACHER CHOICE AND AGENCY

The recent research review series into geography by Ofsted (2021; 2023) echoed the importance of teacher agency in selecting distant places to study. Providing educators with agency enables them to plan a carefully balanced sequence of work that supports children's knowledge of distant places in a coherent way. Many curricula allow for freedom for educators to choose places that can enhance the learning of the children in their class. This can create a bespoke learning experience for the children in their context.

If children are curious about a place this will drive engagement, understanding and learning beyond the classroom. Lambert and Morgan (2010) argue that curiosity lies at the heart of geographical learning; it is through curiosity that children engage with the world and begin to ask meaningful questions about it. Children who are curious about a place ask geographical questions which develop their understanding of the world and their place in it.

There are many ways educators can spark children's curiosity about a place:

- stories

- imagery

- sounds

- questions

- links with children's personal geography.

A question educators might like to ask before teaching distant places could be: *is the starting point of enquiry framed through wonder?*

PRINCIPLE FOUR: PEDAGOGIES OF HOPE

Pedagogies of hope is an approach to education developed by Brazilian educator Paulo Freire (1970) that is grounded in transformation, optimism and social justice. This type of pedagogy aims to empower children through centring possibilities of change on an individual, community and global level.

Here are some of the key concepts of pedagogies of hope:

- a *belief in children's capacity for change*: children are agents of change with hope as an act of resistance against inequality and injustice;

- *learning should be related to real-life contexts*: this pedagogy recognises injustices and inequality while viewing this as something that can be changed where hope is a cycle of reflection and action;

- *critical consciousness*: children explore these issues with a view to reimagining and imagining better and preferred futures.

WHY DEVELOPING CHILDREN'S AGENCY IS IMPORTANT?

Children need to be empowered by geography teaching to see themselves as agents of change. Educators can do this in several ways:

- providing real-life role models;

- teaching stories of children as agents of change;

- providing children with opportunities to be agents of change, in school and the local community.

There are resources that utilise the concept of pedagogy of hope. One example is the *DRY: Diary of a water superhero* primary book (McEwen et al., 2019), which is a picture book that can be used by educators as a story of children as agents of change. You can access an electronic copy of the book, alongside teaching resources, here: https://dryutility.info/learning/

Educators can bring stories into their classroom which centre children as agents of change, providing examples of *joyful geographies* (an approach to teaching geography which inspires happiness, connection and curiosity) for children to learn from. Some examples of stories you might like to use include:

- the two school children who successfully led a campaign to ban single-use plastic bags in Bali. www.youtube.com/watch?v=P8GCjrDWWUM

- environmentalist and campaigner Vanessa Nakate. www.bsg.ox.ac.uk/people/vanessa-nakate

- climate activist Greta Thunberg. www.bbc.co.uk/news/world-europe-49918719

Joyful geographies can also be taught by framing the learning through key questions such as:

- who is telling the story?

- where does the story begin?

- who is asking the questions?

The next section gives an example of how such questions can be used to drive a joyful geographical enquiry about recycling.

DIFFERENT RECYCLING PRACTICES

Who is telling the story?

Explore examples of different recycling practices for food waste:

1. personal stories (share and discuss): *My future my voice ambassador stories*, Earth Day. www.earthday.org/stories-mfmv/

2. local stories. https://bristolgoodfood.org/stories/

3. national stories: *5 countries leading the fight to end food waste*. www.foodhero.com/en/blogs/countries-fighting-food-waste

PRINCIPLE FIVE: FIELDWORK

Fieldwork is the process of children observing, recording and analysing geographical information which develops their geographical understanding. We support Clarke and Witt's (2017, 2022) concept of field visiting as an approach where educators can go beyond extractive fieldwork and enable children to develop relationships with field sites that offer opportunities for creative insights. Such creativity invites new and different perspectives which more formal methods may miss. Engaging with field sites in this way could contribute towards children building a sense of place and ecological respect.

Fieldwork is:

- a purposeful investigation of the local or wider area;

- an investigation of any geographical area from the classroom windowsill to the entire school grounds and beyond;

- enquiring about the world geographically, asking questions, collecting data, analysing results and drawing conclusions;

- relational – about *being with* the field space.

Fieldwork is not:

- only part of a school trip;

- something that has been done outside school;

- just observing an area;

- something you are *doing* to the field.

FIELD VISITING

We support the work of Clarke and Witt (2017, 2022); they suggest that fieldwork is beyond merely doing 'work' *to* field sites and is instead a relational, creative engagement *with* places. They offer a few key principles for the process of field visiting:

- *entanglement*: the context of field visiting is a co-created, interdependent encounter where all participants (human and non-human – plants, water, animals, soil etc.) are entangled together rather than observing nature as something which is separate;

- *journalling practice*: an artistic and deeply attentive journalling method which may involve sketches, words and collage where attention is paid to the curious, fleeting and small. This practice is a generative act and provides an opportunity for curiosity, noticing and care;

- *open-ended encounters*: providing space for the children's encounters with a place to be open-ended allows for surprising, unplanned and playful moments which can be generative;

- *sensory*: mixing sensory experiences such as reflection, sketching and walking with both graphic and poetic methods enables embodied knowledge-making. Such knowledge is lived, felt and imaginative.

WHAT MAKES FIELD WORK EFFECTIVE?

A strong geography provision has effective fieldwork at the core. Purposeful fieldwork provides children with real, contextual experiences to develop their geographical skills, knowledge and understanding in meaningful ways. Careful planning of fieldwork should allow for engaging, rich, inclusive and memorable experiences for geographical knowledge to be both created and revised by children.

Some key points to consider are:

- *is it purposeful*? Effective fieldwork should offer rigour in its geographical question(s) and purpose. Not simply a day out, it should offer opportunities for children to study aspects of a subject that particularly interest them (Roberts, 2013);

- *have you considered age and stage*? Effective fieldwork needs to be aligned with children's cognitive development to allow for some autonomy in their exploration. Young children need support to notice, record and interpret their surroundings in ways that are meaningful to them (Catling and Willy, 2009);

- *is it locationally progressive*? Begin with the familiar and the local; you can build up towards unknown places and distant places. Think local, national then global as children progress through the primary curriculum. This is also an opportunity for children to develop new fieldwork skills in a familiar context. 'Primary fieldwork should develop children's spatial awareness and understanding of place by building up from the local' (GA, 2012, page unknown).

DIFFERENT TYPES OF FIELDWORK

There are different forms of fieldwork which relate to the location of study, the enquiry focus and the methods used. Here are the forms of fieldwork often used as part of primary geography:

- *testing a hypothesis*: this is a structured process where children explore a geographical predication or question through firsthand observation, data collection and analysis;

- *teacher-led*: for this type of fieldwork the teacher has planned the questions, methods and locations under study;

- *enquiry-led*: this form of fieldwork is question-led, with children investigating a big geographical question to draw their own conclusions.

How does field work support the development of geographical concepts and skills?

Fieldwork is *how* geographers create and revise geographical knowledge. By crafting geography teaching that enables the children to *be* geographers, educators can provide opportunities for children to develop their geographical knowledge as geographers in the way geographers do, through fieldwork. For example, children can't know of the impact rivers have on settlement type until they know how to observe, map read, analyse data and ask questions etc.

Fieldwork supports the understanding of some of the key geographical concepts (introduced in the first section of this chapter) in the following ways:

- *place*: via experiential connections with real places;
- *space*: through the exploration of spatial relationships and patterns;
- *scale*: by drawing connections in local, national and global contexts;
- *interdependence*: via investigation of the human–environment interaction.

WHERE TO VISIT, AGE, STAGE AND SCALE

Scale is important in fieldwork as it introduces children to new and real places, enabling them to:

- develop their understanding of how locations connect with each other;
- explore distance, size and extent;
- understand how to make links between local observations and wider patterns/systems.

Fieldwork provides the lived experience through which children can develop an understanding of geographical scale–from the personal to the global (Catling and Willy, 2009).

A progression of scale in fieldwork could be:

1. personal and local scale;
2. comparing local and wider environments;
3. understanding multiple scales (e.g. how a local issue links to regional and/or global issues).

FIELDWORK SKILLS

It is important to provide children with opportunities to develop the knowledge they need to carry out fieldwork. This can be done by allowing children to practise the following procedural elements of fieldwork individually; not all of these will be needed in every study.

- *Data collection*: methods for observing and recording.

- *Data presentation*: methods for organising findings.

- *Data analysis*: methods for interpreting data.

RISK ASSESSMENT: TO SUPPORT YOU GOING, NOT STOP YOU GOING

Risk assessments are an important part of fieldwork as they are there to support educators to provide children with opportunities to explore different environments. Risk assessments enable educators to identify the different types of potential risks and plan steps to mitigate the risk so the children can safely engage in effective fieldwork.

REFLECTION 11.4

How does the concept of field visiting change your ideas about the nature and practice of geography?

FINAL THOUGHTS

Geography teaching and learning is more than maps and memorising facts; it is the lens through which children can develop their understanding of the world and their place within it. As educators, we have the privilege and responsibility to cultivate global citizens who are informed, compassionate and curious. Ultimately, high-quality geography teaching creates opportunities for children to ask better questions, make richer connections and develop a sense of belonging in, and responsibility for, the world. By positioning children as active participants in their geographical learning, educators not only equip them with concepts and skills, but also nurture dispositions of curiosity, criticality and care that can last a lifetime.

FURTHER READING AND RESOURCES

Blewitt, J. (2021). *Teaching geography creatively* (3rd ed.). Routledge.

A guide focused on creative teaching methods for delivering the primary geography curriculum.

Catling, S. and Willy, T. (2018). *Understanding and teaching primary geography*. Sage.

A foundational text on understanding and teaching primary geography, covering subject knowledge and pedagogy.

Catling, S. and Willy, T. (2022). Learning primary geography: Ideas and inspiration from classrooms. Routledge.

Offers practical classroom ideas and inspiration for learning and teaching primary geography.

Catling, S. (2018). *Bloomsbury curriculum basics: Teaching primary geography*. Bloomsbury Education.

A concise book focused on the curriculum basics and core teaching principles for primary geography.

Enser, M. (2021). *Powerful geography: A curriculum with purpose in practice*. Crown House.

Discusses the concept of *powerful geography*, focusing on building a curriculum with purpose and rigorous content.

Lennard, E. (2025). *How to lead it: Primary geography*. Bloomsbury Education.

A guide providing practical advice on leadership and management for the primary geography subject leader.

Scoffham, S. (2023). *Teaching primary geography* (2nd ed.). Sage.

A comprehensive textbook on the theory and practice of teaching primary geography.

REFERENCES

Anderson, E., Das, S. and Whittal, J. (2021). Decolonising the geography curriculum: Reflections from higher education. *Area, 53*(2), 381–389.

Bale, J. (1994). *Primary geography: A reader for teachers*. Routledge.

Barlow, A. and Whitehouse, S. (2019). *Mastering primary geography*. Bloomsbury.

Biddulph, M., Lambert, D. and Balderstone, D. (2015). *Learning to teach geography in the secondary school* (3rd ed.). Routledge.

Biddulph, M., Mitchell, D. and Somerville, M. (2021). *The really useful primary geography book* (3rd ed.). Routledge.

Bishop, A. J. (1990). *Cultural transitions in mathematics education*. Kluwer Academic.

Budke, A., Kuckuck, M., Meyer, M., Schäbitz, F., Schlüter, K. and Weiss, G. (2019) *Fachdidaktik Geographie*. Springer Spektrum.

Bustin, R., Butler, D. and Hawley, D. (2017). GeoCapabilities: Educators as curriculum leaders. *Teaching Geography, 42*(1), 61–63.

Catling, S. (2005). Children's personal geographies and the primary geography curriculum. *International Research in Geographical and Environmental Education, 14*(4), 284–289.

Catling, S. (2014). *Research and debate in primary geography*. Geographical Association.

Catling, S. and Martin, F. (2011). Contesting powerful knowledge: The primary geography curriculum as an articulation between academic and children's geographies. *Curriculum Journal, 22*(3), 317–335.

Catling, S. and Willy, T. (2009). *Teaching primary geography*. Sage.

Catling, S. and Willy, T. (2018). *Understanding and teaching primary geography*. Sage.

Clarke, H. and Witt, S. (2017). A pedagogy of attention: A new signature pedagogy for educators. British Educational Research Association Conference, University of Brighton, 5–7 September.

Clarke, H. and Witt, S. (2022). Field-visiting: Paying attention to a more-than-human world. In M. Biddulph, S. Catling, L. Hammond and J. McKendrick (Eds.), *Children, education, and geography: Rethinking intersections* (pp. 132–144). Routledge.

Decolonise Geography. (2021). Teaching about a place? *Stop and think first!* https://decolonisegeography.com/blog/2021/04/teaching-about-a-place-stop-and-think-first/

Freire, P. (1970). *Pedagogy of the oppressed*. Seabury Press.

Geographical Association (GA). (2012). *The GA primary geography handbook*. Geographical Association.

Lambert, D. and Morgan, J. (2010). *Teaching geography 11–18: A conceptual approach*. Open University Press.

McEwen, L., Gorell Barnes, L., Jones, V., Whitehouse, S. and Williams, S. (2019). *DRY: Diary of a water superhero*. https://issuu.com/uwebristol/docs/dry_the_diary_of_a_water_superhero

Ofsted. (2021). *Research review series: Geography*. www.gov.uk/government/publications/research-review-series-geography

Ofsted. (2023). *Getting our bearings: Geography subject report*. Office for Standards in Education. www.gov.uk/government/publications/subject-report-series-geography/getting-our-bearings-geography-subject-report

Roberts, M. (2013). *Geography through enquiry: Approaches to teaching and learning in the secondary school*. Geographical Association.

Scoffham, S. (2023). *Teaching primary geography* (2nd ed.). Sage.

12

HEALTH AND WELLBEING

JANE CALCUTT

THIS CHAPTER

This chapter explores the ideas that:

- health and wellbeing are fundamental components of education and are crucial for the holistic development of young learners

- wellbeing is a multifaceted concept that encompasses physical and mental health, and it can be promoted through a holistic educational approach

- effective health and wellbeing education involves integrating these topics across the statutory curriculum, applying safe and inclusive pedagogical strategies, and responding to current social and emotional needs.

KEY TERMS FOR THIS CHAPTER

Mental health: not simply the absence of mental illness; it exists on a continuum and represents a distinct state of emotional, psychological and social wellbeing.

Wellbeing: a broader holistic concept that includes mental health, but also encompasses physical health, social connectedness and overall life satisfaction.

Resilience: the ability to adapt well and recover from challenges, stress, adversity, or trauma. It involves emotional strength, problem-solving skills and the capacity to maintain or regain wellbeing in difficult situations.

Trauma-informed practice: an approach that prioritises emotional safety and recognises how trauma affects learning, behaviour and relationships, responding with empathy and support to avoid re-traumatisation.

Positive psychology: the scientific study of strengths, values and factors that contribute to human flourishing, focusing on wellbeing, resilience, optimism and personal growth rather than solely on mental illness or dysfunction.

INTRODUCTION

Health and wellbeing are fundamental components of education, playing a crucial role in the holistic development of young learners. In the UK, persistent concerns about both mental and physical health continue to influence the priorities of policy-makers, educators and school communities. According to UNICEF (2025), there has been a sustained decline in child wellbeing across developed nations, with the UK facing particularly significant challenges. Drawing on my experience as both a primary school teacher and a university lecturer, I have developed a deep appreciation for the importance of teaching health and wellbeing. I believe that nurturing these areas is essential not only for supporting children's overall development, but also for empowering them to achieve their full potential. In this chapter, I examine how different dimensions of health are understood within the broader context of wellbeing. I introduce key factors that shape children's holistic development and consider the role of formal education in promoting healthy, purposeful and fulfilling lives. I discuss the integration of health and wellbeing within statutory curricula, highlighting approaches through individual subjects, cross-curricular initiatives and the development of a setting-wide ethos that reinforces these principles. I also present strategies for teaching these topics in ways that are safe, effective and creative. Finally, I examine specific initiatives designed to address contemporary challenges. Collectively, these discussions underscore the importance of nurturing all aspects of wellbeing from an early age.

REFLECTION 12.1

What is one thing you do every day that helps you feel happy and healthy and why is it important to you?

DEFINING PHYSICAL AND MENTAL HEALTH WITHIN THE BROADER CONCEPT OF WELLBEING

Everyone experiences both physical and mental health, which are closely linked and can fluctuate over time. Physical health ranges from optimal functioning to illness, influenced by lifestyle, genetics and access to healthcare. Education and public health campaigns play a vital role in promoting positive behaviours such as balanced diets, regular exercise, vaccinations and avoiding harmful substances. Mental health is increasingly recognised as central to quality of life through education and advocacy, yet misconceptions may still persist, with some individuals wrongly equating it with illness or personal weakness. Educators need a well-rounded understanding of health to effectively teach curriculum content, support pupils facing challenges and maintain their own wellbeing. The terms 'mental health' and 'wellbeing' are frequently used together but often without clear distinctions (Ereaut and Whitling, 2008). Keyes' (2002) model distinguishes different states of mental health and wellbeing. Keyes proposed that mental health is not simply the absence of mental illness, but a distinct state that includes emotional, psychological and social wellbeing. *Flourishing* describes a state of high wellbeing and positive mental health. Importantly, individuals living with mental health challenges can still find meaning, satisfaction and personal growth in their lives. With the right support and treatment, they too can achieve a flourishing state, showing that mental illness does not prevent someone from thriving. In contrast, *languishing* refers to low levels of wellbeing without a clinical diagnosis of mental illness. This state is characterised by diminished emotional responsiveness, reduced motivation and a sense of detachment from one's surroundings. If left unaddressed, languishing can increase the risk of developing mental health issues over time. Swarbrick's (2023) *dimensions of wellness* (shown in Figure 12.1) is a useful framework that illustrates a holistic view through outlining eight interconnected areas for the support and promotion of flourishing. While some aspects naturally evolve as children grow, and others may be shaped significantly by external influences, these areas can be acknowledged, nurtured and developed over time. When used as a guiding framework, this model highlights how a broad, balanced and creative curriculum can actively support and promote all aspects of wellbeing.

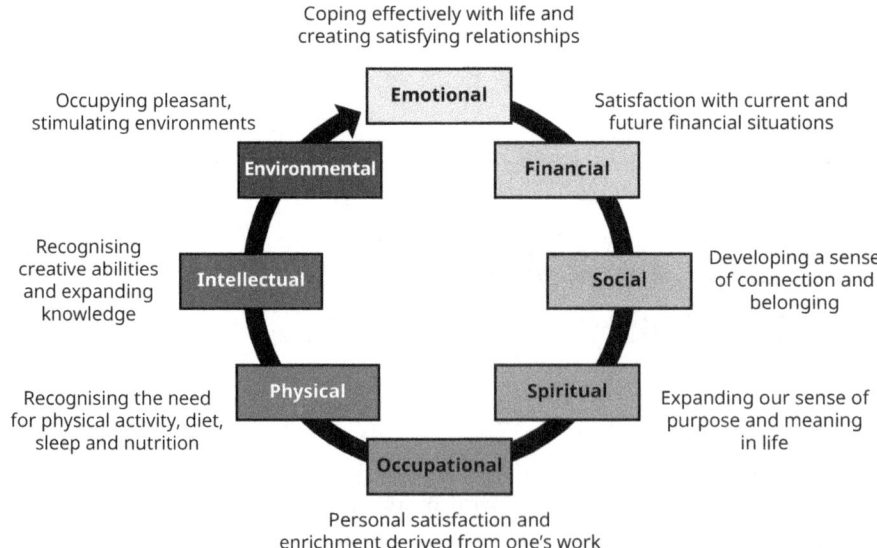

Figure 12.1   Dimensions of wellness (adapted from Swarbrick, 2023)

REFLECTION 12.2

Consider activities or habits that contribute to your sense of wellbeing and personal growth.

- How do these fit within this framework?

- Are there specific areas that you have influence over and could intentionally develop further?

Taking time to explore these dimensions can help identify strengths, recognise gaps and make choices that support your own personal wellbeing.

Wellbeing is a rich and multifaceted concept that encompasses more than just mental, emotional, social and physical health. Recognising the connections between these areas is especially important when promoting a broad and balanced curriculum that supports child development throughout their primary years.

CHILD DEVELOPMENT AND THEORETICAL MODELS

During the primary years, children experience significant changes across cognitive, emotional, social, physical and moral domains. They develop more advanced thinking and problem-solving skills, improve emotional regulation and develop deeper, more stable relationships with peers. Physically, they gain coordination and strength, while also becoming more aware of their bodies. At the same time, they begin to form a clearer sense of identity, values and independence, laying the foundation for lifelong learning and wellbeing. It is important to understand factors that affect children's health and wellbeing as they grow. As you examine the models presented here, consider what they mean for educators and how they might influence approaches to health and wellbeing education.

REFLECTION 12.3

Consider current social issues, such as poverty, digital safety and family dynamics.

How might these contextual factors affect children's wellbeing, and in what ways could educators respond to these challenges?

Bronfenbrenner's (1992) *bioecological* model of five external influences is widely used in education to understand the complex interplay between a child and their surroundings. The *microsystem* relates to influences that are close to the child including:

- family
- friends
- educational settings.

The *mesosystem* involves interactions between people within the microsystem including:

- parent–teacher relationships through meetings, parents' evenings and attending events;
- interactions between home and educational settings such as parents helping with homework or newsletters keeping families informed and involved;
- friendships between children's families – for example, playdates or family gatherings.

The *exosystem* is the layer of external environments that indirectly influence the child such as:

- parent employment status affecting family income, routines and stress levels;
- policies, including homework, behaviour or inclusion;
- local government decisions – for example, funding for parks, libraries or community events.

The *macrosystem* encompasses the broader external factors that shape a child's development, even though the child may not be directly aware of them. These influences may include:

- religion or philosophical worldviews;
- cultural norms and traditions such as language, customs and heritage;
- societal structures – for example, laws, economic systems and political climate.

Finally, the *chronosystem* concerns transition over the life–course that may affect a child such as:

- parental separation;
- moving house;
- pandemics;
- technological shifts.

Specific circumstances within each of these layers could have either positive or negative influences on dimensions of a child's wellbeing.

Engel's (1977) *biopsychosocial* model can also be applied to education and wellbeing by integrating biological, psychological and social factors. In terms of biology, cognitive development, neurological conditions and physical health impact a pupil's ability to learn and thrive. Psychologically, emotional resilience, motivation and mental health conditions affect engagement and academic success. Social factors include family support, peer relationships, socioeconomic status and cultural influences. Educators can use this model to create inclusive learning environments, support children with diverse needs and promote holistic wellbeing.

Humanistic psychology emphasises the whole person, including thoughts, feelings and potential for growth. Maslow's (1943) *hierarchy of needs* is often visualised as a pyramid with five levels, moving from most basic at the bottom to the most advanced at the top. If a lower level is weakened, subsequent levels are negatively affected. This model illustrates the importance of health and wellbeing for child development and can also be applied to educational settings. The first level includes physiological needs such as food, water, warmth, rest and shelter. In an educational environment this would include access to meals, a comfortable classroom temperature and rest breaks. If a child's basic needs are not met, they may struggle to focus and learn. The second level involves feelings of security, safety and stability. Children in education should have emotional security, clear routines and feel safe from bullying. The third level recognises the importance of love and belonging. Positive peer relationships, an inclusive classroom culture and supportive teachers would promote these feelings. The next level identifies self-esteem needs such as recognition and achievement. Opportunities to succeed, praise, encouragement and pupil voice will all enhance this area of development. Self-actualisation lies at the top of this pyramid. This is where an individual fulfils their true potential. Engaging learning opportunities for problem-solving, creativity and independence can be found here. Health and wellbeing help meet needs at every level, from teaching about nutrition and hygiene to fostering resilience and self-confidence.

Together, these three frameworks emphasise the value of a holistic approach to education, encouraging educators to consider the wider environment, individual needs and social contexts that shape a child's learning and development. However, like all theoretical models, they are subject to ongoing critique due to limitations in their generalisability and practical application. For instance, Maslow's hierarchy of needs has been widely questioned for its rigid, linear structure and cultural assumptions, which may not reflect the diverse realities of individuals (Wahba and Bridwell, 1976). In the context of disability, it can be particularly problematic to suggest that a child with physical impairments cannot reach self-actualisation simply because their health needs are affected. While theories provide valuable tools for guiding educational practice, they must be applied with care, always considering the specific context and the unique circumstances of those involved.

EDUCATIONAL PHILOSOPHIES AND PERSPECTIVES ON WELLBEING IN EDUCATION

Critically engaging with a range of educational philosophies and perspectives is vital when making decisions about wellbeing education. This approach enables educators to reflect on current practices, uncover underlying issues and understand the reasons behind shifting priorities. By exploring diverse viewpoints, educators can more clearly identify both systemic changes that are needed and the specific areas within their own influence where they can make a difference. This reflective process supports the adoption of more inclusive and effective strategies, ensuring that wellbeing education is genuinely responsive to the needs and circumstances of children in their local communities.

Research indicates that students who are physically and emotionally healthy are more likely to engage in learning, demonstrate positive behaviours and achieve meaningful academic progress (Steinmayr et al., 2018). However, it is worth questioning whether academic achievement should be the sole focus of education. Tierney (2020) challenges the prevailing emphasis on data, outcomes and performance metrics, advocating instead for a renewed focus on meaning and purpose. He outlines four educational philosophies which can be linked to enhancing specific elements of health and wellbeing.

- *Personal empowerment* supports wellbeing by helping children build autonomy, confidence and self-awareness. Empowered learners make informed health choices, set goals and seek support. Activities that develop self-reflection, emotional regulation and decision-making directly enhance wellbeing.

- *Cultural transmission* strengthens wellbeing by connecting children to their heritage, traditions and shared values. Celebrating cultural identity fosters belonging and self-esteem, while learning about diverse cultures promotes empathy, respect and social harmony.

- *Preparation for work* contributes to wellbeing by equipping children with practical skills, resilience and purpose. Learning to manage stress, communicate effectively and balance life and work supports long-term mental and physical health. Career education also helps pupils align future paths with their strengths, interests and future financial needs.

- *Citizenship education* enhances wellbeing by encouraging civic responsibility, ethical awareness and community engagement. When children feel connected to society and understand their role in it, they gain a stronger sense of purpose and belonging. Activities like community service and social justice discussions support both individual and collective wellbeing.

While each philosophy offers a distinct perspective, they can be thoughtfully integrated within a well-designed curriculum. Drawing on Swarbrick's model (2023), each philosophy can be seen to support particular dimensions of wellness, further enriching a variety of purposeful educational experiences.

ASPECTS OF EDUCATING FOR HEALTH AND WELLBEING

Health and wellbeing are supported through a combination of direct teaching, community involvement, themed events and the influence of an organisation's ethos. Beyond formal lessons, the hidden curriculum is reflected in values, relationships and daily routines which play key roles in shaping attitudes and behaviours. Children develop respect, resilience and empathy not only through structured learning, but also through everyday interactions and modelled priorities.

Themed events such as Anti-Bullying Week, Mental Health Awareness Week, charity initiatives and sports days are designed to raise awareness, promote inclusion and encourage healthy habits. These special occasions complement a curriculum that is adapted to the unique needs of the local community, ensuring that learning is relevant and meaningful for every child.

At the heart of this approach is the statutory curriculum, which identifies essential learning, guaranteeing that every child receives a consistent foundation in health and wellbeing, regardless of background or setting. While the statutory curriculum provides structure and accountability, it should also allow educators flexibility to address specific needs in their communities.

EXAMPLES OF NATIONAL CURRICULA

UK national frameworks have shared principles, but are also tailored to meet local needs and challenges (DfE, 2025; DE NI, 2021; Education Scotland, 2025; Welsh Government, 2021).

All curriculum documentation highlights the importance of:

- *physical health*: children learn about healthy eating, exercise, personal hygiene and how their bodies change as they grow;

- *mental and emotional wellbeing*: children are taught to recognise and manage emotions, build resilience and understand the importance of mental health;

- *relationships and social skills*: curricula cover making friends, showing respect and empathy and dealing with issues like bullying;

- *safety and risk*: children are taught how to stay safe online and offline, manage risks and know when and how to seek help;

- *citizenship and community*: children explore belonging, diversity, rights and responsibilities and caring for their environment;

- *growing and changing*: lessons address puberty, making healthy choices and setting personal goals for the future.

Although requirements, structures and terminology vary, all UK curricula prioritise pupil voice, encouraging children to express themselves and feel valued, with the shared goal of helping every child become a confident, healthy and capable learner. While some topics lack statutory status, this flexibility allows settings to design curricula that best meet the specific needs of their pupils and communities.

HEALTH AND WELLBEING IN SUBJECT-SPECIFIC AND CROSS-CURRICULAR CONTEXTS

Health and wellbeing topics can be meaningfully addressed across the curriculum. Subjects such as personal, social, health and economic education (PSHE) and personal and social education (PSE) serve as central platforms for developing emotional literacy, fostering healthy relationships and promoting both mental and physical wellbeing, but think back to Swarbrick's (2023) dimensions of wellness. Consider subjects within the primary curriculum and how they can develop each area of wellbeing. Some examples are highlighted below.

- *Science* engages with topics such as the human body, nutrition, hygiene, and the physiological benefits of exercise.

- *Physical education* (PE) supports physical health while also nurturing teamwork, resilience and self-confidence.

- *First aid* could be incorporated within any of these lessons.

- *Literacy* provides opportunities for children to explore emotions, empathy and social dynamics through stories and discussion.

- *Art and music* offer creative outlets that enhance emotional expression, regulation and imaginative thinking.

- *Geography* topics cover citizenship, communities, careers, sustainability and safety around roads, railways and water.

- *History* includes stories from different cultures helping children to explore diversity, identity and inclusion in the modern world. Influential figures can inspire qualities such as perseverance and courage, showing how people have fought for rights and freedoms over time.

- *Design and technology* incorporates healthy eating and economic enterprise.

- *Computing* includes online safety and making informed choices when using the internet.

- *Religious education* involves exploring personal values, celebrations, life events, morality and ethical choices, promoting understanding and respect for religions and traditions.

Embedding health and wellbeing within other subjects helps children engage with key concepts in real-life contexts, enhancing understanding and promoting inclusive learning. However, this approach could lack depth, with important topics only briefly covered. It may also be inconsistently delivered, depending on an educator's confidence and curriculum priorities. Without specific training, educators may struggle to address sensitive issues effectively; wellbeing risks becoming a tokenistic add-on. Assessment could be more challenging when wellbeing is not taught directly and might be overlooked during planning. Teaching topics as a standalone subject allows for deeper exploration, structured progression and a recognised safe space for emotional development. Combining both approaches ensures health and wellbeing are consistently reinforced and given the focused attention they deserve.

SAFE AND INCLUSIVE PEDAGOGICAL PRACTICE

This section explores a range of evidence-based strategies for teaching health and wellbeing safely and meaningfully. These approaches are grounded in research and best practice (PSHE Association, 2025), ensuring that children not only gain essential knowledge for making informed choices, but also develop the practical skills, core values and real-life applications needed to lead healthy, balanced lives. Safe practice is essential in health and wellbeing education for several important reasons.

1. *Physical safety*

   Activities that include physical movement, role-play, or outdoor learning can carry risks. Safe practice ensures that children are physically protected through proper supervision, appropriate equipment and clear boundaries.

2. *Emotional safety*

   Health and wellbeing topics often touch on sensitive issues such as emotions, relationships or personal experiences. Safe practices create a supportive and respectful environment where pupils feel comfortable expressing themselves without fear of judgement or embarrassment.

3. *Social safety*

   Ground rules and safe spaces help pupils engage in discussions about personal and social issues in a way that is respectful and inclusive. This promotes empathy, active listening skills and mutual respect.

4. *Safeguarding and inclusion*

   Health and wellbeing lessons should encourage children to act responsibly and make thoughtful, informed decisions. By modelling safe practices, educators help children understand how to make healthy, respectful choices, while reinforcing key principles such as personal boundaries, consent and self-care. Given the sensitive nature of topics, pupils may sometimes share personal concerns. It is therefore essential that educators follow safeguarding procedures and clearly communicate the limits of confidentiality, fostering a safe and trusting environment.

Schools and other educational settings have both a legal and moral duty to safeguard pupils' wellbeing. Implementing safe practices ensures compliance with safeguarding policies, health and safety regulations and professional standards. Inclusive practice means creating a learning environment where all children, regardless of background or ability, can participate fully and succeed. It involves recognising diversity, removing barriers to learning and adapting teaching to meet individual needs, promoting equity, belonging and respect. Health, emotions and relationship discussions must be inclusive of pupils from LGBTQ+ families, varied ethnic backgrounds and those with specific learning needs. Content should be adapted using visual aids, simplified language and alternative communication methods when required. Lessons should challenge stereotypes and promote critical thinking about media, gender roles and societal norms. Pupils should be encouraged to reflect on fairness, respect and equality in their lives and communities. Staff must engage in ongoing training and self-reflection to address unconscious bias. Inclusive language, strong safeguarding awareness and cultural sensitivity are essential for creating a respectful, supportive learning environment for all.

RESOURCES AND EXAMPLES USED IN LESSONS

These should reflect a diversity of lived experience and identities, including:

- cultures

- family structures

- disabilities

- genders.

Alongside explicit discussion on diverse characteristics, using resources where these traits appear incidentally, rather than being the focus, helps present them as a normal part of everyday life. When materials only reflect a narrow range of identities and experiences, it can unintentionally suggest that these are the norm, while different characteristics are seen as *other*.

TEACHING SENSITIVE SUBJECTS

While we may all encounter topics that feel uncomfortable or challenging to discuss in any subject, my experience in developing and coordinating a primary health and wellbeing curriculum revealed that relationship and sex education (RSE) was the area that generated the most concern among the school community. Relationships education and lessons on puberty are now statutory in all UK primary schools and in the following case study, you will explore how some principles related to sensitive subjects can be put into practice.

REFLECTION 12.4

Which topics might be considered particularly sensitive or challenging to teach?

LEADERSHIP, MANAGEMENT AND CURRICULUM ORGANISATION

The PSHE Association (2021) emphasises the importance of subject leads, designated governors and senior leaders having a clear understanding of statutory requirements and the confidence to deliver high-quality, evidence-based PSHE. As Health and Wellbeing Lead, I worked closely with governors and senior staff to shape policy and select age-appropriate resources. We used a spiral curriculum approach (Bruner, 1976), where key concepts are revisited and deepened over time, particularly vital in RSE to ensure sensitive, age-appropriate learning that develops as children mature.

PARENT INVOLVEMENT

Parents in England, Scotland and Northern Ireland may request to withdraw their child from sex education outside the science curriculum, but schools must still consider whether additional content is needed to meet pupils' developmental needs. Before the final year of primary, schools are required to consult with parents about specific RSE content and offer guidance to support aligned conversations at home. Once materials were agreed, my school held sessions for parents to review the policy, explore lesson content and provide feedback. These sessions also examined national and local data, emphasised RSE's safeguarding role and shared evidence linking PSHE to improved health outcomes. Pupil feedback, gathered via the school council, further informed these discussions by highlighting current needs.

STAFF TRAINING

Teaching RSE must be inclusive, accurate and follow safe practice. Educators need subject knowledge, confidence and skills to manage sensitive topics, create safe spaces, and assess progress. At my school, staff received tailored training using modelled lessons, team teaching and peer observation. This supported a safe, inclusive environment, alongside strategies for managing embarrassment, cultural sensitivities, challenging questions and disclosures. Staff also had opportunities to learn and refine effective teaching techniques, which will now be explored further.

HEALTH AND WELLBEING PEDAGOGIES

Planning effective health and wellbeing education requires a thoughtful approach to both curriculum content and the specific learning outcomes it seeks to achieve. Holistic personal development includes the promotion of physical health, the support of mental and emotional wellbeing, the development of social skills and relationships, the fostering of personal safety and the encouragement of lifelong healthy habits (Mäkelä et al., 2025). On a broader societal level, individuals who are well-rounded in these areas contribute positively to future communities through their social responsibility, emotional intelligence and overall wellbeing (Corbin et al., 2021). However, meaningful learning here must go beyond the acquisition of knowledge. It also involves nurturing essential skills, attitudes and beliefs that enable children to reflect, engage and make informed choices. To facilitate this, content must be delivered within a safe and supportive environment where pupils feel confident to share their feelings, explore values, express opinions and consider the views of others without fear of judgement. Purposefully selected activities are essential for creating and maintaining such an inclusive and effective learning space.

GROUND RULES

It is essential that educators work with children to establish ground rules on how they behave towards each other both within and outside the classroom. The creation and constant reference to agreed ground rules promotes emotional safety, respectful dialogue, builds trust, manages sensitive content and empowers pupils. Examples of ground rules include listening respectfully to others, keeping personal information private, using kind and inclusive language, allowing everyone a chance to speak and respecting differing opinions.

BASELINE ASSESSMENTS

All children have existing knowledge and beliefs shaped by influences such as family, peers, school, media and the wider community. Understanding these prior experiences is essential for appropriately pitching learning and addressing any misconceptions. Initial assessments also help track progress and inform future planning.

Examples include:

- *floor books*: large scrapbooks where pupils record learning through drawings, writing and photographs providing a shared reference for future lessons;

- *mind-maps*: created individually, in groups, or as a class to help organise ideas around a theme, capture initial understanding and show progress when updated;

- *graffiti sheets* for children to freely write or draw responses to prompts, encouraging open, creative expression;

- *quizzes* at the start or end of lessons assess understanding and help correct misconceptions;

- *storyboards* using drawings or sequences explore concepts or scenarios;

- *draw-and-write tasks* in response to questions like 'What does a good friend look like?' or 'How do you feel when you're worried?' help express ideas that a child might struggle to articulate verbally.

DISTANCING TECHNIQUES

These activities offer children a secure and objective way to engage with sensitive topics without the need to share personal experiences. Approaches such as using fictional characters or scenarios, through storybooks, cartoons, films, puppets, or invented personas, help create emotional distance, allowing pupils to explore issues from a more detached perspective. Drama-based methods like role-play, hot-seating and conscience corridors encourage children to consider different viewpoints in a depersonalised context; Chapter 10 offers a detailed explanation of these techniques. Circle time discussions using talking objects promote inclusive sharing, while giving children the option to pass or speak through a symbolic item. Third-person questioning, such as 'What might someone do if ...?' helps reduce pressure and maintains emotional safety. Likewise, case studies and dilemmas support group analysis and critical thinking without requiring personal disclosure.

CHALLENGING QUESTIONS

Establishing an environment where children feel confident to ask questions is fundamental to their learning, but educators must feel prepared to respond to a wide range of queries. Resources such as a question box, worry monster, question wall, or 'ask it basket' offer children safe and accessible ways to share their thoughts before, during and after lessons. If any questions raise concerns, children should be invited to speak privately with a member of staff. When faced with a challenging or inappropriate question, it is important to remain calm and acknowledge the child's curiosity. If the question is not suitable for group discussion, it should be gently redirected for a private conversation. These systems help manage sensitive topics, but any concerns must always be addressed in accordance with safeguarding procedures. Lessons should also include information about sources of support available both within and beyond the educational setting. Children need opportunities to develop the skills to seek advice, express concerns and understand what to expect when accessing help from different services.

REFLECTION 12.5

Consider a challenging topic you have taught (e.g. conflict resolution, body image, or healthy relationships).

Even if you did not know the specific terminology, did you use any of the tools described here, such as ground rules, a specific type of baseline assessment (like a graffiti sheet or mind-map), or a distancing technique (like role-play or case studies)? Which ones?

How might you combine some of these techniques to aid you in future?

RESPONDING TO CURRENT NEEDS WITH SOCIAL AND EMOTIONAL LEARNING

We are living through times of profound uncertainty and complexity, shaped by global conflict, economic disruption, rising inequality, hunger and poverty. Additional pressures, such as climate change, online adversity and isolation, concerns about artificial intelligence and disinformation, refugee crises, political polarisation, sedentary lifestyles and consumer-driven ideals of happiness contribute to an increasingly challenging world. In this context, it is understandable that many children and young people feel anxious and vulnerable as they face an unpredictable future. While primary curricula are beginning to reflect these priorities, limited access to specialist services places greater responsibility on educators to identify and support pupils (Lowry et al., 2022), while also promoting healthy lifestyles (Norwich et al., 2022). A range of initiatives now aim to enhance curriculum content and culture, but, given the time and resource constraints educators face, adopting evidence-based approaches is essential to ensure meaningful impact and efficient use of resources.

Social and emotional learning (SEL) is recognised by key organisations, including the Early Intervention Foundation (EIF) (2017), Education Endowment Foundation (EEF) (2025) and The Royal Foundation Centre for Early Childhood (2025), as essential to children's wellbeing. SEL develops core skills such as emotional regulation, empathy, resilience, communication and decision-making, which are increasingly vital in a fast-paced, digital world. Reduced face-to-face interaction and the lasting effects of pandemic-related disruption have limited opportunities for collaborative play and peer connection, leaving some children without key developmental experiences. Many pupils also face adversity or trauma; SEL helps them build resilience, coping strategies and healthier relationships. For neurodivergent learners inclusive, tailored approaches can aid emotional regulation, social communication and positive self-image. Collaboration for Academic, Social and Emotional Learning (CASEL, 2023) identifies five core competencies of SEL:

- self-awareness;

- self-management;

- social awareness;

- relationship skills;

- responsible decision-making.

While there is not space to go into detail here, you can find more information from the EEF (2019, and see Further reading), which outlines strategies for implementation, including explicit teaching, modelling and curriculum integration. Effective SEL should be sequential, focused and reinforced through whole-organisational ethos and activities. Successful delivery also requires careful planning, ongoing support and regular monitoring. A wide range of resources, including frameworks, lesson plans and evidence-based interventions, are available from organisations such as Mentally Healthy Schools (2025).While resilience-focused programmes are among the initiatives that support the development of SEL, they have also generated complex academic debate. Resilience itself is a multifaceted concept, which Southwick et al. (2014) describe as potentially a trait, a process, an outcome, or a combination of these. In educational settings, resilience is nurtured through positive relationships, inclusive environments that promote belonging, opportunities for autonomy and skills such as self-awareness, emotional regulation and coping strategies. However, the concept is not without criticism. One concern is that resilience may place undue emphasis on individual responsibility, potentially normalising adversity (Mahdiani and Ungar, 2021). When framed primarily as a personal trait or skill, resilience can divert attention from broader systemic issues such as poverty, inequality and lack of support. This framing can risk placing the burden on children to 'bounce back' from hardship without addressing underlying causes. Promoting resilience without sufficient support may lead children to endure difficult circumstances rather than seeking help or advocating for change.

Educators can address these potential issues by adopting a whole-setting approach that goes beyond individual traits. This includes creating safe, inclusive environments, embedding trauma-informed practices (see Further reading) and fostering strong relationships among staff, students and families. Resilience should be taught as a developmental process, tailored to diverse cultural and personal contexts and supported by adequate resources and mental health services. Crucially, educators must avoid placing the burden solely on children to cope and instead work to address the systemic factors that contribute to adversity.

There is also concern that SEL could be viewed solely as a targeted intervention, rather than a universal approach supporting the long-term wellbeing of all children. This perception can shift by adopting a *positive psychology* lens, which emphasises flourishing over reactive problem-solving. The *PERMA* model (Seligman, 2011), outlines five core elements of wellbeing, beginning with the promotion of positive emotion, which involves recognising and experiencing joy and gratitude. Engagement encourages being fully absorbed in meaningful activities while relationships highlight the importance of social connections. Meaning intends to foster a sense of purpose and accomplishment includes goal setting, feeling capable and celebrating success. Several organisations champion resilience through strength-based, holistic approaches, including BoingBoing (2024), ReachOut Schools (2025) and Teachappy (Bethune, 2023).

CURRENT CONCERNS FOR HEALTH AND WELLBEING

While mental health is increasingly prioritised in educational policy, equal attention should also be given to physical health. Despite strong evidence linking regular physical activity to improved health outcomes (WHO, 2019), sedentary behaviours continue to rise globally (Guthold et al., 2018). Although school-based interventions show some success (WHO, 2021), over 80 per cent of school-aged children still do not meet the recommended 60 minutes of daily moderate-to-vigorous activity (WHO, 2022). This shortfall is influenced by a decline in outdoor play, increased screen time (Palmer, 2015) and personal barriers such as low confidence, peer pressure and body image concerns (Youth Sport Trust, 2025). While children are aware of the benefits of physical activity, digital distractions and self-esteem issues often hinder participation. These findings underscore the urgent need for more curriculum time, greater investment and enhanced staff training to create school environments that promote and enhance physical activity. You can find more detail about supporting physical health in Chapter 16.

Evidence also highlights ongoing challenges around healthy eating for children within the UK. Barnardo's (2025) reports that nearly one in five parents regularly choose less nutritious food due to financial pressures, with many teachers personally covering the cost of meals for hungry pupils. The Food Foundation (2025) links rising food costs and restricted school budgets to difficulties in providing nutritious meals, which for many pupils are their only hot meals of the day. Lidl GB (2025) found that 73 per cent of teachers are unable to teach diet diversity, often due to limited time, resources and training, leaving many children unfamiliar with even basic vegetables. Collectively, these findings point to the need for increased funding, more curriculum time and better staff training to help educators create environments where healthy eating is accessible, prioritised and effectively taught. Although the curriculum emphasises the importance of healthy eating and regular physical activity, educators must consistently reinforce these messages to ensure all aspects of wellbeing are clearly understood, genuinely valued and actively supported.

FINAL THOUGHTS

In this chapter, I have examined health as a multi-dimensional concept, situated within the broader framework of wellbeing. Drawing on key influences that shape children's holistic development, I have emphasised the critical role education plays in nurturing healthy, purposeful and fulfilling lives. With many years of experience as a primary school teacher, I recognise the importance of embedding health and wellbeing meaningfully across the curriculum. I have explored both discrete subject teaching and cross-curricular approaches, while considering strategies that support safe, creative and effective delivery. I have also reflected on how a responsive, well-structured curriculum, underpinned by a nurturing and inclusive school ethos, serves as an essential component for integrating mental and physical wellbeing into everyday practice. Furthermore, initiatives designed to address current mental health challenges have been discussed, with particular emphasis on the role of social and emotional learning as a foundation for positive mental health. Ultimately, I believe that promoting all dimensions of health and wellbeing from an early age is vital in preparing children with the knowledge, skills and values they need to thrive in an increasingly complex and demanding world.

FURTHER READING AND RESOURCES

Boingboing. (2024). https://boingboing.org.uk

A Resilience Revolution organisation that promotes a 'seriously different' approach to resilience in communities and services, emphasising social justice and co-production.

Education Endowment Foundation (EEF). Primary SEL Guidance. Available at: http://educationendowmentfoundation.org.uk/education-evidence/guidance-reports/primary-sel

The EEF's guidance report on effective evidence-based approaches to primary social and emotional learning (SEL).

Mentally Healthy Schools. www.mentallyhealthyschools.org.uk

A free, evidence-based website providing resources, toolkits and practical advice for primary school staff to support children's mental health and wellbeing.

ReachOut Schools: Resilience. (2025). https://schools.au.reachout.com/resilience

Provides practical information and resources for schools to help young people build resilience and support their mental health.

Little Book of Trauma Informed Practice. http://traumainformedlancashire.co.uk/wp-content/uploads/2023/05/Little-Book-of-Trauma-Informed-A5-Final-print-2023.pdf

A concise guide offering key principles and strategies for adopting a trauma-informed approach in schools and services.

Bethune, A. (2023). *Wellbeing in the primary classroom*. Bloomsbury.

A practical guide for teachers on embedding wellbeing in the primary classroom, covering how to teach happiness and positive mental health.

Cowley, A. (2021). *The wellbeing curriculum.* Bloomsbury.

A resource detailing a wellbeing curriculum model for primary schools, focused on embedding children's wellbeing across school life and policy.

REFERENCES

Barnardo's. (2025). *Nourishing the future.* Barnardo's. www.barnardos.org.uk/research/nourishing-future

Bethune, A. (2023). *Wellbeing in the primary classroom.* Bloomsbury.

Bronfenbrenner, U. (1992). Ecological systems theory. In R. Vasta (Ed.), *Six theories of child development: Revised formulations and current issues* (pp. 187–249). Jessica Kingsley.

Bruner, J. (1976). *The process of education: Revised edition.* Harvard University Press.

Collaboration for Academic, Social and Emotional Learning (CASEL). (2023). *What is the CASEL framework?* CASEL. https://casel.org/fundamentals-of-sel/what-is-the-casel-framework/

Corbin, J. H., Abdelaziz, F. B., Sørensen, K., Kökény, M. and Krech, R. (2021). Wellbeing as a policy framework for health promotion and sustainable development. *Health Promotion International, 36*(Suppl_1), i64–i69. https://doi.org/10.1093/heapro/daab066

Department for Education (DfE). (2025). *Physical health and mental wellbeing (primary and secondary).* www.gov.uk/government/publications/relationships-education-relationships-and-sex-education-rse-and-health-education/physical-health-and-mental-wellbeing-primary-and-secondary

Department of Education Northern Ireland (DE NI). (2021). *Children and young people's emotional health and wellbeing in education framework.* www.education-ni.gov.uk/publications/children-young-peoples-emotional-health-and-wellbeing-education-framework-final-version

Early Intervention Foundation (EIF). (2017). *Social and emotional learning: Supporting children and young people's mental health.* Foundations What Works Centre for Children and Families. https://foundations.org.uk/our-work/publications/social-emotional-learning-supporting-children-and-young-peoples-mental-health/

Education Endowment Foundation (EEF). (2019). *Improving social and emotional learning in primary schools.* https://educationendowmentfoundation.org.uk/education-evidence/guidance-reports/primary-sel

EEF. (2025). *Social and emotional learning.* https://educationendowmentfoundation.org.uk/education-evidence/teaching-learning-toolkit/social-and-emotional-learning

Education Scotland. (2025). *Health and wellbeing.* https://education.gov.scot/curriculum-for-excellence/curriculum-areas/health-and-wellbeing/

Engel, G. L. (1977). The need for a new medical model: A challenge for biomedicine. *Science, 196*(4286), 129–136. https://doi.org/10.1126/science.847460

Ereaut, G. and Whiting, R. (2008). *What do we mean by 'wellbeing'? And why might it matter?* Linguistic Landscapes Research Report DCSF-RW073. https://dera.ioe.ac.uk/id/eprint/8572/1/dcsf-rw073%20v2.pdf

Guthold, R., Stevens, G. A., Riley, L. M. and Bull, F. C. (2018). Worldwide trends in insufficient physical activity from 2001 to 2016: A pooled analysis of 358 population-based surveys with 1.9 million participants. *The Lancet Global Health*, *6*(10). https://doi.org/10.1016/s2214-109x(18)30357-7

Keyes, C. L. (2002). The mental health continuum: From languishing to flourishing in life. *Journal of Health and Social Behavior*, *43*(2), 207. https://doi.org/10.2307/3090197

Lidl GB. (2025). *Teachers admit to learning gaps in healthy eating lessons as Lidl invests £500k in schools programme*. https://corporate.lidl.co.uk/media-centre/pressreleases/2025/lidl-invests-500k-in-healthy-eating-schools-programme

Lowry, C., Leonard-Kane, R. and Jani, A. (2022). Teachers: The forgotten health workforce. *Journal of the Royal Society of Medicine*, *115*(4), 133–137. https://doi.org/10.1177/01410768221085692

Mahdiani, H. and Ungar, M. (2021). The dark side of resilience. *Adversity and Resilience Science*, *2*(3), 147–155. https://doi.org/10.1007/s42844-021-00031-z

Mäkelä, T., Sinnemäki, J., Kankaanranta, M. H., Fenyvesi, K., Meyers, C. and Kreis, Y. (2025). Towards a framework for conceptualising holistic wellbeing in schools. *International Journal of Wellbeing*, *15*(2), 1–21. https://doi.org/10.5502/ijw.v15i2.4473

Maslow, A. H. (1943). A theory of human motivation. *Psychological Review*, *50*(4), 370–396. https://doi.org/10.1037/h0054346

Mentally Healthy Schools. (2025). *Social and emotional learning: Targeted support*. www.mentallyhealthyschools.org.uk/targeted-support/targeted-support-tool/social-and-emotional-learning/

Norwich, B., Moore, D., Strentiford, L. and Hall, D. (2022). A critical consideration of 'mental health and wellbeing' in education: Thinking about school aims in terms of wellbeing. *British Educational Research Journal*, *48*(4), 803–820. https://doi.org/10.1002/berj.3795

Palmer, S. (2015). *Toxic childhood: How the modern world is damaging our children and what we can do about it*. Orion.

PSHE Association. (2021). *Statutory RSHE*. https://pshe-association.org.uk/guidance/ks1-4/statutory-rshe

PSHE Association. (2025). *Guidance and tools to help you teach safe and effective PSHE education*. https://pshe-association.org.uk/guidance/ks1-5/teaching-pshe-education

Public Health England (PHE). (2021). *Promoting children and young people's mental health and wellbeing: A whole school or college approach*. www.gov.uk/government/publications/promoting-children-and-young-peoples-emotional-health-and-wellbeing

Seligman, M. (2011). *Flourish: A new understanding of happiness and well-being*. Nicholas Brealey.

Southwick, S. M., Bonanno, G. A., Masten, A. S., Panter-Brick, C. and Yehuda, R. (2014). Resilience definitions, theory, and challenges: Interdisciplinary perspectives. *European Journal of Psychotraumatology*, *5*(1). https://doi.org/10.3402/ejpt.v5.25338

Steinmayr, R., Heyder, A., Naumburg, C., Michels, J. and Wirthwein, L. (2018). School-related and individual predictors of subjective well-being and academic achievement. *Frontiers in Psychology*, *9*. https://doi.org/10.3389/fpsyg.2018.02631

Swarbrick, M. (2023). *The evolution of the wellness model*. Collaborative Support Programs of New Jersey. https://cspnj.org/wp-content/uploads/2024/02/Wellness-Model-Evolution-2023-1.pdf

The Food Foundation. (2025). *The broken plate report.* https://foodfoundation.org.uk/publication/broken-plate-2025

The Royal Foundation Centre for Early Childhood. (2025). *The shaping US framework.* https://centreforearlychildhood.org/our-work/research/the-shaping-us-framework/

Tierney, S. (2020). *Educating with purpose: The heart of what matters.* John Catt Educational.

UNICEF. (2025). *Child well-being in an unpredictable world.* www.unicef.org/innocenti/media/11111/file/UNICEF-Innocenti-Report-Card-19-Child-Wellbeing-Unpredictable-World-2025.pdf

Wahba, M. A. and Bridwell, L. G. (1976). Maslow reconsidered: A review of research on the need hierarchy theory. *Organizational Behavior and Human Performance, 15*(2), 212–240. https://doi.org/10.1016/0030-5073(76)90038-6

Welsh Government. (2021). *Curriculum for Wales: Statutory guidance.* www.gov.wales/curriculum-wales-statutory-guidance

World Health Organization (WHO). (2019). *Motion for your mind: Physical activity for mental health promotion, protection and care.* https://apps.who.int/iris/handle/10665/346405

WHO. (2021). *Promoting physical activity through schools: A toolkit.* WHO.

WHO. (2022). *Promoting physical activity through schools: Policy brief.* WHO.

Youth Sport Trust and University of Manchester. (2025). *The role of PE, school sport and physical activity in supporting young people's mental wellbeing: Summary report.* www.youthsporttrust.org/media/1u5lua0q/yst-uom-role-of-pesspa-summary.pdf

13
HISTORY

HELEN CRAWFORD, AILSA FIDLER AND REBECCA HARRIS

THIS CHAPTER

This chapter explores the ideas that:

- knowledge within history is constructed and is therefore provisional
- there are different types of historical knowledge
- considerations of why we teach history can impact upon knowledge selection and curriculum organisation.

KEY TERMS FOR THIS CHAPTER

Historical sources: traces of the human past.

Historical evidence: sources and interpretations that are used to support an historical claim in response to an historical enquiry.

Historical claims: knowledge claims about the past rooted in the discipline of history.

Historical interpretations: constructed claims about the past, produced 'subsequently' or after the event, which use historical sources as historical evidence. They take the form of historical scholarship, documentaries, websites, paintings, films, personal reflections.

Historical enquiry: the process of asking questions, selecting and evaluating evidence and making judgements about the past.

Substantive (first order) concepts: abstract terms (e.g. trade, monarchy) which frame specific phenomena.

Disciplinary (second order) concepts: organising concepts that shape how we make sense of the past and communicate that understanding.

INTRODUCTION

History is a beautifully complicated and fascinating subject. It is the story of people, which can spark our curiosity, raising questions about how they lived and, of course, how we know.

This chapter examines different conceptions of subject knowledge in history, the purpose of history education and how knowledge should be deployed and sequenced within a curriculum.

REFLECTION 13.1

How would you explain what history is to a child?

When people are asked to explain what history is, they often say that it is a study of the past, of those people and events that have shaped the world into what it is today. They may speak about the history they have studied, the Romans, the ancient Greeks, world wars or key people who were important in shaping aspects of life in their locality, nation or wider world. All of this may suggest that the past is a fixed thing that is waiting to be told, learned or discovered: names, dates, who did what, when and why. Sometimes school experiences of history can support this if children are asked to memorise long lists of names, dates and events.

WHAT IS HISTORY?

There can be no doubt that history is a study of the human past. Historians consider historical sources, the things that have been left behind from previous times: documents, photographs, objects, buildings. They use these historical sources, alongside the work of other historians or the archaeological record, to attempt to answer questions that they have about the past. Those questions are shaped by their worldview. For example, historians in Victorian Britain, when history was a relatively new academic area of study, were interested in 'great' people and empires. However, modern historians are more likely to be interested in issues surrounding gender or environmental history. Historians may ask questions relating to where the silences are – whose voices have not been recorded and remembered, why that silence is there and what it may tell us. These silences also remind us that our knowledge of the past is incomplete. Even if we know a great deal about a key event or person, we cannot ever know everything. We must interpret the past using the historical sources that we have as historical evidence when we make historical claims. Of course, this historical interpretation may alter as more sources are discovered, or different questions are asked. This is reflected in school history, as Hawkey (2023, p. 3) highlights, a curriculum is never static, it 'reflects the priorities and concerns of the present'. The past did happen, but history is not fixed; it is a continuously evolving discipline.

SUBSTANTIVE KNOWLEDGE: THE INGREDIENTS FOR WHAT IS TAUGHT

Some aspects of the past have been substantiated; there is enough evidence to tell us, for example, that the American President John F. Kennedy was assassinated on 22 November 1963. This *substantive knowledge* – the part of the past that we are relatively sure of – gives us the ingredients for what is taught in history: dates, names, places, key events. This 'knowledge about the past' (Ofsted, 2023) supports children in developing their understanding of the context they are learning about and gives them the ingredients to be able to begin to build an answer to historical questions. Substantive knowledge is the *what* of the past and as such is crucial when we study history.

CHRONOLOGICAL KNOWLEDGE: AN ORGANISING FRAMEWORK

Children need to be able to put the people and events that they learn about, the substantive knowledge, or substance of history, into some sort of historical order. Developing *chronological knowledge* and understanding supports them in making links within and across periods. Chronology and time are difficult concepts and giving children a structure to support their cognition is vital; the use of sequencing and timelines can help (Hodkinson and Smith, 2018). Chronology also allows children to develop a sense of period: how did people live, what was life like?

Without chronological knowledge it would be difficult for children to understand why things happened or how things changed. Stow and Haydn (2000, p. 87) suggest that chronology gives a 'mental framework to make sense of the past'. Chronological knowledge offers an organising framework for the history that children learn; without it their mental image of the past would have no structure and therefore make no sense. Chronology is a key and unique aspect of history and, in many ways, distinguishes it from other subjects (Stow and Haydn, 2000).

DISCIPLINARY APPROACHES: SHAPING HOW WE EXPLAIN THE PAST

Chronological knowledge supports children in understanding change including the reasons for it and the speed at which it happened (Cooper, 2018). Change is a *disciplinary concept*; these concepts are sometimes referred to as second order or procedural. They relate to the *how* of history: how it is argued and communicated. They allow history to be debated, giving it further form to support sense-making, shaping the way history is done (Lee and Ashby, 2000). The range of disciplinary concepts includes:

- *change and continuity*: how things changed and stayed the same;

- *cause and consequence*: why things happened and their impact;

- *similarity and difference*: the experiences of different groups in a time period or within one group; what was the same and how did they differ?

- *significance*: is something that is applied; it is not inherent. Questions therefore need to be asked about why significance is claimed and by whom to support meaning-making;

- *historical interpretations*: consider the existence of different accounts of the past and how and why they are constructed.

(HA, 2025)

SUBSTANTIVE CONCEPTS (E.G. POWER, AUTHORITY ETC.)

Substantive concepts, sometimes referred to as first order or abstract concepts, are another way of organising the past that relate to the substance of history. Substantive concepts may appear in a range of contexts and children's understanding of them will grow over time. For example, the concept of 'monarchy' may be introduced to children in Early Years through fairy tales and kings and queens. Later, children may learn about Egyptian pharaohs or obas in the Kingdom of Benin and so build their understanding of the concept of monarchy. There are a vast number of broad substantive concepts, including power, trade, migration, which cross over periods of time, and more specific concepts, which apply to a moment in time, such as the Suffragette movement. Like substantive knowledge, these concepts give further meaning to the past, as children encounter them in different, specific contexts.

THE PROCESS OF HISTORICAL ENQUIRY

Any content that children learn needs to be investigated through historical enquiry (Cooper, 2018). Effective history teaching must include asking (and answering) historical questions, using sources as evidence to answer them and so developing an understanding of how (and why) different historical interpretations are created; this cannot be done effectively without drawing upon both substantive and disciplinary knowledge and concepts. Cooper (2018, p. 15) suggests this means children need to learn to 'integrate content with process' to understand why there are different interpretations and how they are constructed.

Historical enquiry is also sometimes seen as a way of organising a curriculum through the use of an overarching enquiry question which pupils respond to at the end of a unit of learning (Sullivan, 2018). The question may be rooted in a disciplinary concept or perhaps focus on something that genuinely puzzles a historian and so ensure, through careful selection of substantive knowledge, that all aspects of history are integrated into effective teaching.

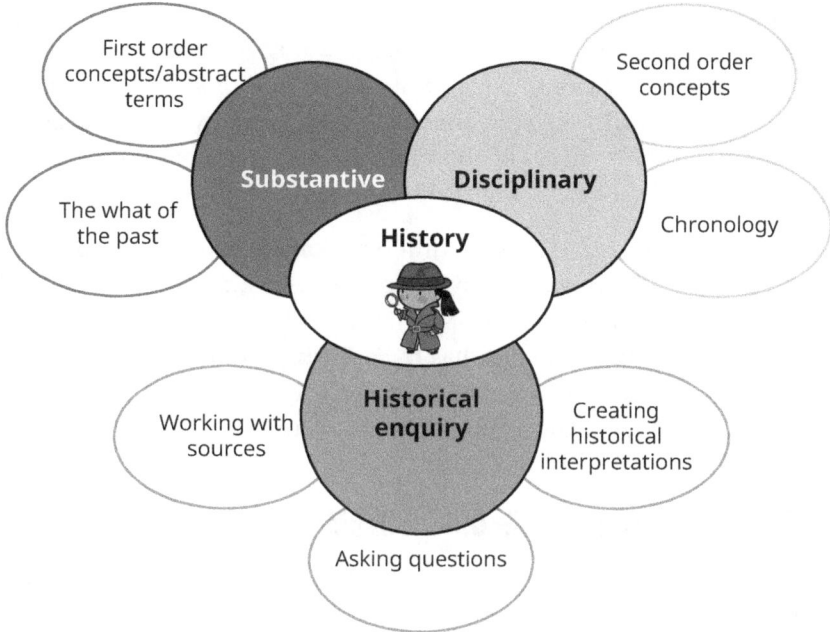

Figure 13.1 What is history?

TYPES OF KNOWLEDGE IN HISTORY EDUCATION

This section introduces other ways we can conceptualise historical knowledge. This matters because our conceptualisation of knowledge shapes what we feel is valuable for pupils to know.

REFLECTION 13.2

How is historical knowledge different from other subject knowledge?

THE PROVISIONAL NATURE OF HISTORICAL KNOWLEDGE

As noted above, our knowledge of what happened is based upon what has survived from our predecessors. Therefore, we cannot fully know what the past was like; instead we have to make deductions and inferences from what has been left, meaning the conclusions we draw are necessarily tentative and provisional – and are therefore open to change. Our understanding of the past is thus a *construct*.

One way to understand this process is to consider whether history is more like a jigsaw puzzle or Lego. The analogy of a jigsaw puzzle is appealing, as it suggests a careful piecing together of the evidence from the past can yield a complete picture of what it was like. However, this assumes there is an agreed single picture of the past. In many ways, the Lego analogy is more helpful. If we say that the traces of the past are like Lego bricks, then we can put them together in a myriad of different ways and create different versions of the past.

This means it is perfectly possible to have different constructions or accounts of the past (or historical interpretations). However, this does not mean that any account of the past is admissible, otherwise things like Holocaust denial would be deemed a valid interpretation of history. Our understanding of the past has to conform to notions of truth. This does not mean there has to be a single 'true' version of the past, but accounts of the past have to be based on the full facts of what is known; historians' accounts are scrutinised and debated.

CORE CONTENT AND KNOWLEDGE-RICH CURRICULUM

One of the basic questions in a history curriculum is what knowledge should be taught. This is particularly pertinent when considering what substantive knowledge to include. This is complex, given the vast scope of history that could be taught.

The American educationalist, E. D. Hirsch's idea of *core knowledge* has been influential in recent debates. His book, *Cultural literacy: What every American needs to know*, published in 1987, listed around 5,000 names, phrases, dates and concepts that were deemed essential for someone to be considered 'culturally literate'. For Hirsch, core knowledge was a social justice issue, as he found that students from disadvantaged backgrounds, often failed to understand texts they were reading because they lacked knowledge of common reference points.

In some educational systems, this focus on core knowledge has morphed into *knowledge-rich* curricula, where schools identify the knowledge they want pupils to know, which is sequenced and taught in such a way that pupils develop memorable networks of knowledge (Quigley, 2019). Yet calls for core knowledge and knowledge- richness raises questions about what knowledge is deemed essential and who decides; in many cases it seems that such decisions rest with teachers, which places a huge responsibility on them and presupposes they have the necessary knowledge to make carefully informed decisions. This matters because the exclusion of topics or different voices can send out powerful messages about what is not deemed important.

POWERFUL KNOWLEDGE

Another influential idea, proposed by Michael Young and Joe Muller (2010), is the notion of *powerful knowledge*. They acknowledge that knowledge is crucial, but draw a distinction between different forms of knowledge, which then inform curricula. They term these curricula as 'futures':

- *Future 1* is very much the Hirschian model of core knowledge, which Young and Muller critique as 'knowledge of the powerful' – that is, what some member of a political elite has decided others ought to know. The concern is that such knowledge is seen as uncontested and incontestable;

- *Future 2* positions subject knowledge as less important than learning how to learn and engagement with generic skills. The lack of substantive knowledge means that learners are often confined to the limits of their existing knowledge;

- *Future 3* is based in subject disciplines; rather than a knowledge of the powerful Young and Muller position this curricula as developing powerful knowledge. For the teaching of history, this reflects how history operates as a subject in terms of a process of enquiry, where our understanding of the past is organised by disciplinary concepts. Central to powerful knowledge is the emphasis on how we come to know about the past, how claims about what we believe happen are made and that any understanding of the past is provisional. However, like core knowledge, it does not provide guidance about what substantive knowledge pupils should know.

HINTERLAND KNOWLEDGE

The term *'hinterland knowledge'*, coined by Christine Counsell (2018), is defined by Ofsted (2023) as 'background information that helps to make core knowledge meaningful by placing it within a rich context'. Counsell argues hinterland knowledge is as important as core knowledge as it helps pupils make sense of something, brings it to life and enables connections between areas of the curriculum. It is not simply a case of providing definitions or glossaries of terms for pupils, they need to have a meaningful, tangible insight into the ideas and mentalities of a period. For example, understanding the impetus behind the Renaissance is made easier by telling the story of the humanist Poggio Bracciolini – a book hunter – searching for ancient manuscripts to gain 'new' insights, and his joy at his discoveries. This sort of story provides meaningful context to draw upon. It adds colour and texture to the past. It needs to be considered in the planning stages, as its use often precedes a focus on the core knowledge of the lesson.

It is therefore important for teachers to construct means to help children create their own imagined construct of the past. Hill (2020) has argued that resources such as stories, images and maps can all help learners begin to envisage the past. He also advocates for both 'inside-out' and 'outside-in' approaches to knowledge selection: in the former the teacher begins with the small and specific and moves outward; in the latter, the teacher begins with the bigger historical picture and then zooms in with a focus on the particular.

HISTORICAL EMPATHY

A heavily contested area of historical knowledge is the idea of *historical empathy*, which does divide the history teaching community. For some, it is an essential part of history and a key reason for their initial attraction to the subject, trying to understand how people in the past felt and thought. For others, it is something that is impossible to know and therefore pointless.

In part, the issue is to do with defining the act of empathising with others. Is empathising a cognitive act, an affective one or something entirely different? The role of imagination is also an issue – to what extent are we supposed to draw on our imagination when trying to empathise? How do we stop pupils looking at the past through their own eyes and help them to look at it from the perspective of the people at the time? There is also the question whether people in the past had the same emotional reactions to life events as people today.

For example, if we wished pupils to empathise with Queen Elizabeth I and her dilemma as to whether she should sanction the execution of her cousin, Mary, Queen of Scots, whose presence in England became the focus of Catholic plots against Elizabeth, we would need to consider various issues. First, we are asking pupils to engage with a mindset nearly 500 years old. Second, we are asking pupils to engage with an adult mindset and someone who wields immense political power. Third, we want pupils to put themselves in a position where they have the power of life and death over others. This makes empathising highly complex.

For Endacott and Brooks (2013), historical empathy is possible. They see it as a combination of historical contextualisation, perspective-taking and affective connection. To achieve this, they suggest various activities and questions that, for example, get pupils to recognise differences between the past and present, exploring perspectives from different source material and reflecting on the contexts in which perspectives existed.

THE PURPOSE OF HISTORY

Understanding why a subject is included in a curriculum, and then why specific topics are included, is an essential issue for teachers to grasp (especially if we are to avoid teachers simply regurgitating their own experience of being taught history). This matters, particularly in a subject like history, because the way history is used (and/or abused) matters; it shapes the way we see ourselves and others. For example, the way divided societies such as Cyprus teach history can easily reflect partisan perspectives of the different communities, serving to perpetuate division. Yet there are diverse rationales for teaching history; indeed Chapman et al.'s (2018) study of trainee history teachers identified 13 potential reasons among this group of subject specialists.

REFLECTION 13.3

What do you think is the purpose of teaching history to primary school children?

Knowing why history is being taught does shape what is taught, as well as potentially how it is taught. For example, if history teaching is to promote a strong sense of national identity, then key moments in a nation's history, which highlight positive developments, as well as moments of coming together in adversity could be a focal point. As will be explained in this section, there are different positions that history teachers can adopt – none are 'correct', but it is important that teachers are aware of their views and look to ensure they are internally coherent.

INTRINSIC PURPOSES

A crude distinction between the reasons for studying history is between *intrinsic* and *extrinsic* purposes. The intrinsic purpose of studying history is to get better at history. For Peter Lee, certain purposes, such as developing a sense of patriotism, are not contingent on learning history, as it is perfectly possible to become more (or even less) patriotic without ever studying history. Such aims have no necessary connection to a study of the past and are therefore pointless ambitions.

Instead, Lee argues that the value of learning history is in its transformative powers, as 'it changes pupils; it changes what they see in the world, and how they see it' (Lee, 1992, p. 23). For history to do this, pupils need to understand how the past is constructed, how claims to knowledge are made and how history is understood and conceptualised. In short, such ideas are based in the nature of the subject and in notions of powerful knowledge.

Other potentially intrinsic purposes link to Chapman et al.'s (2018) categories of helping pupils understand the present and the world in which they live, as well as contributing to an understanding of the human condition, by looking beyond their own experiences. As such, a study of history allows pupils to see the world differently.

EXTRINSIC PURPOSES

Others argue that history fulfils wider educational goals. Barton and Levstik (2004) argue that history has a clear role to play in fostering democratic citizenship. For pupils to learn to participate and contribute effectively in a democratic society they need to develop ways of thinking and acquire knowledge that examines the range of human experiences.

In such a model, history also has a role in helping pupils understand their relationship to others. This could be at a personal, group and/or national level. As part of this, the intention could be to generate pride in belonging to a group, or it could focus more on understanding. For example, there is clear value in knowing the history of the country in which a pupil resides, but should this focus predominately on stories to generate a positive sense of belonging, or should it include events which resulted in harm to others? Clearly a mixed position could be adopted, but it does raise questions about the relationship between what teaching history is trying to achieve and what content would support that aim.

Another issue is whether teaching history has any moral purpose or value. Various studies (e.g. Husbands et al., 2003) have highlighted that history teachers view the subject as having a clear moral agenda in creating empathetic, tolerant, responsible citizens through an exploration of diversity in the past.

HISTORICAL CONSCIOUSNESS

The idea of *historical consciousness* originated in the work of Jörn Rüsen (2006). As a concept, it provides an understanding of how history can be used and is therefore linked to issues around both purpose and pedagogy.

Historical consciousness is about the vast array of cultural resources that feed into someone's sense of the past, and how that shapes the way people see the past, present and potential future actions. Rüsen (2006) has developed a typology to explain how pupils may draw on the past. These include:

- *traditional*: where current actions are derived from traditional ways of doing things; provides a sense of communal belonging;

- *exemplary*: inspiration is drawn from role models in the past or rules/ways of being to justify actions in the present;

- *critical*: we use our understanding of the past to offer a counter-narrative, to justify that previous ways of doing things do not necessarily apply;

- *genetic*: where the focus is on how things change and evolve through time.

Although Rüsen's typology offers a useful insight into how the past might be used, it does raise questions about how pupils actually see the past and whether they actively draw on it as a useful resource to make sense of the present and future.

TRANSFORMATIONAL KNOWLEDGE

Deng's work has sought to address some of the unanswered questions and tensions in debates around what knowledge to teach. For Deng (2021), a key issue is the transformations that knowledge can generate. Drawing upon *Bildung*-centred *Didaktik*, he argues the focus is 'on the cultivation of human powers by means of knowledge' (p. 1658). Part of the focus of Bildung is to develop an individual's intellectual and moral capabilities in order to understand how the self is linked to the wider world; content is chosen that supports this development. In many ways, Deng's argument is linked to how students learn to think historically and the power that provides for students – for example, giving new ways of seeing the world, providing ways of analysing, explaining and understanding the past, looking at how knowledge of the past informs how we see the present and future. Deng's argument looks beyond notions of powerful knowledge and emphasises that education is about the commitment to human wellbeing and agency, and the development of human capabilities.

SELECTING WHAT AND WHOSE HISTORY TO TEACH

Selecting which topics or periods of the past to include on the curriculum does, of course, link back to debates regarding the place, value and purpose of the subject at school level (Lee, 1992). Substantive content knowledge in history is, by its very nature, context-dependent and reflects particular worldviews or societal norms. What is included on the curriculum also involves decision-making about what is not to be included.

REFLECTION 13.4

Think about the history you learned at primary school: what topics did you study and whose voices did you hear?

Educators may want to consider the balance between global, national and local history units and/or the different weighting given to political, social, cultural, economic or military dimensions. A history curriculum for primary pupils should also involve consideration of child maturation: decisions about whether certain topics might be too sensitive, complex or controversial for younger children.

DIVERSIFYING THE CURRICULUM

Diversity links to the disciplinary concept of similarity and difference, acknowledging the importance of including a range of voices from the past, and moving beyond a 'dead, white, male' content focus. A diverse history curriculum is important for both intrinsic purposes (seeing the past as multi-dimensional) and also extrinsic purposes (allowing all children to see themselves in the curriculum and to challenge prejudice and discrimination). As such it may also be associated with pupil identity construction and citizenship formation.

The most recent Historical Association (HA) survey of primary teachers in England (HA, 2025) suggests that, while primary schools have become more aware of the importance of a diverse history curriculum, the focus tends to reside mainly with gender and/or ethnicity, with less attention given to other under-represented groups. A broad curriculum, however, should encompass a range of other intersectional dimensions such as age, social class, LGBTQ+ and Gypsy, Roma and Traveller (GRT) history. The challenge for curriculum-makers is providing a balanced curriculum without resorting to tokenism or focusing solely upon individuals who were perhaps atypical for their time.

DECOLONISING THE CURRICULUM

In recent years, there have been calls to go beyond diversifying the curriculum, with a focus on *decolonising* the curriculum. This can refer to the process of examining not just whose stories we might choose to teach, but also who has told these stories, in what ways and for what purposes or ends. It therefore involves (re)consideration of both the selection of particular substantive knowledge and also (re)engagement with disciplinary processes – for example, giving greater weight to indigenous knowledge bases such as oral traditions of storytelling (Allen et al., 2024). Decolonising the curriculum aims therefore to decentre Eurocentric history by looking at topics from non-Western perspectives.

CURRICULUM AS MIRROR AND WINDOW

Another area to consider is the extent to which the curriculum content should act as a *mirror* of children's experiences or as a *window* opening up new vistas (Style, 1988).

Waldron (2003) found that primary-aged children's understanding of history as a subject and their emerging sense of time draws upon both the personal and the everyday. Familiar contexts therefore help pupils to develop their ability to think historically, drawing on their present to make sense of the past. A curriculum mirror might lend itself to a rationale for including a content focus on places known to children or to topics such as 'schools' or 'houses and homes'.

However, recent focus on powerful knowledge as a subject rationale seems to be more aligned with a theme of curriculum as window, moving pupils beyond their own, potentially narrow, everyday experiences. This raises the question of the extent to which curriculum content should expose children to new people, new places and new phenomena beyond the familiar and the vernacular. A balanced and developmentally appropriate primary curriculum is perhaps one where teachers are cognisant of both the child and the subject and, in doing so, consider the value of both the mirror and the window.

CURRICULA DESIGN

Curriculum-making in history not only involves decisions about what to teach, but also how to organise and sequence the curriculum. For example, should periods of history be taught in chronological order? Should the curriculum be centred around particular themes or an overarching framework? Another key debate, especially in the primary phase, is the extent to which history should be blended or integrated with other subjects or areas of the curriculum.

A CHRONOLOGICAL CURRICULUM STRUCTURE

One approach is to sequence the curriculum in broadly chronological order. However, adopting such an approach to curriculum design means that pupils may only encounter a period once and that younger children tend to be faced with earlier periods of history. This may not be developmentally appropriate due to their emerging sense of time and also means that pupils will potentially have a less mature understanding of earlier periods. It may also limit younger learners' engagement with a fuller range of both diverse voices (e.g. LGBTQ+ history) and types of historical sources (e.g. photographic and digital footage).

A *chronological approach* to content delivery is also not feasible in a formal school environment where the history curriculum is based upon a cyclical or rolling programme. This is often the curriculum structure used by schools which have mixed-aged classes. Although traditionally associated with small schools in rural areas, mixed-aged classes are becoming more widespread in areas with falling pupil rolls (e.g. due to the 'hollowing out' of families from some urban centres). In schools with a multi-year cyclical curriculum, teachers need to carefully consider the entry points of different pupil cohorts to the history curriculum, being mindful of which topics they have yet to encounter.

A THEMATIC CURRICULUM STRUCTURE

You can also select a *thematic approach* to curriculum organisation. For example, you might use a substantive concept such as monarchy, settlement or trade as the basis for curriculum planning. The curriculum is thus designed for children to deliberately encounter the concept in an increasingly complex range of contexts, over time and place, as they move through the school. The substantive concept, in this instance, serves as an organising curriculum thread (Ofsted, 2023). One challenge for educators, however, is to ensure that substantive content is not selected simply to serve the overarching concept. A bigger challenge rests on deciding which concepts should be chosen to be foregrounded and for what reasons.

Increasingly, educators are interested in environmental history and, as a result, it is sometimes being used as a curriculum theme by making light touch but purposeful changes. Kitson and Riley (2024) suggest, as one example, including lessons about how people relate to the environment in each period covered. Such a focus is rooted in current concerns with the planetary crisis and indicative of the evolving nature of the subject. Again, this links back to decisions about the value, purpose or vision for the subject at school level.

AN INTEGRATED CURRICULUM STRUCTURE

A final approach to consider is whether history should be taught discretely with cross-curricular links made to other subjects or fully integrated within broader curriculum areas.

Many countries do not teach primary history as a standalone subject. Instead, it is subsumed into curriculum areas such as *social studies* (Scotland), *humanities* (Wales) or *the world around us* (Northern Ireland). Integrated approaches to curriculum planning are often premised on the assumption that primary learners benefit from a holistic curriculum. This is a view that has its basis in constructivist theories of learning which seek to avoid, 'artificial barriers in the minds of young children' (Hayes, 2010, p. 383). Integrating historical study within other fields may also provide a more authentic real-world context for learning, preparing children to meet the challenges of our times (Barton and Ho, 2021).

Arguments in favour of subject-specific approaches to curriculum design tend to be premised upon theoretical rather than empirical knowledge bases – for example, Young and Muller's (2010) argument, outlined earlier in this chapter, that subject teaching should be based on the specialised knowledge that is drawn from the traditions of distinct disciplinary communities. Weak or tenuous cross-subject connections can result in a lack of disciplinary rigour and may not therefore provide the necessary structure for pupils to develop key features of learning in history, such as chronological understanding (de Groot-Reuvekamp et al., 2014). However, case study research, conducted by Percival (2018) in three English primary schools, found that cross-subject links do not necessarily challenge disciplinary integrity. His research found that strong subject leadership, meaningful subject connections and learning outcomes based explicitly upon historical concepts were the most important variables in successful curriculum enactment. Secure knowledge of the subject therefore results in effective teaching and learning of the subject.

REFLECTION 13.5

What do you think might be the advantages or disadvantages of different types of curricula models?

How might your purpose for teaching history and inclusion of different voices shape your curricula?

COMMON MISCONCEPTIONS

Identifying and planning to address misconceptions is a key way teachers can reduce barriers to learning and enable all learners to fully access the curriculum.

One key misconception is children displaying confused chronology and showing anachronisms (attributing something to a period to which it does not belong). For example, pupils may conflate periods a long time ago with more recent ones; they may fail to understand that some periods had a very long duration (e.g. ancient Egypt) and some a much shorter one (e.g. World War II); they may find it difficult to understand that different periods of the past coexisted: that the Aztecs in Mexico, the Mughals in India and the Tudors in England were all 16th century CE. Frequent use of timelines, both within periods and across periods, can help support children to develop their mental map of the past. Dating conventions (terms such as BC/BCE and AD/CE) also need to be clearly and systematically explained to pupils on a regular basis.

Children may also dismiss a historical source (for example, a wartime propaganda poster) as *biased* and therefore less reliable, rather than understanding that this bias gives us valuable insight into the views, motives or norms of its creator. Children can also find the nature of historical interpretation challenging, believing that only one interpretation can be valid and therefore 'true'. This leads back to one of the key principles introduced at the start of this chapter: the importance of introducing children to the disciplinary nature of the subject, so that they see history as a construct rather than as a direct facsimile of the past.

FINAL THOUGHTS

This chapter set out to establish what history as a subject is and what knowledge means within it.

History is:

- a study of the human past;

- organised around a chronological framework to support the development of a mental timeline;

- a discipline with its own way of thinking which shapes how we make sense of the past;

- constructed through the process of historical enquiry, asking and answering questions using historical sources as historical evidence to make historical claims;

- more like Lego than a jigsaw, as there can be many historical interpretations of the past.

Knowledge within history is provisional and evolves because history is a construct. Deciding what historical knowledge to teach is rooted in considerations of what the subject and its purpose is. This will also impact upon decisions about how a curriculum should be organised as well as what should be taught.

History, as we established at the beginning of this chapter, is beautifully complicated and as such is potentially challenging. However, the study of history is also enjoyable. Cooper (2018, p. 57) suggests that the reason both children and teachers enjoy history so much is because it connects us to people in the past, sharing 'our common humanity. We are part of the continuum of past, present and future.' We all enjoy a good story, and the study of history allows us access to an infinite number of fascinating ones.

FURTHER READING AND RESOURCES

Allen, A., Kavanagh, A. M. and Cassaithe, C. N. (2024). *Beyond single stories: Changing narratives for a changing world* (1st ed.). Information Age.

Providing a framework for educators to move beyond singular, narrow narratives in the curriculum and explore multiple, diverse perspectives to reflect a changing world.

Cooper, H. (2018). *History 5–11: A guide for teachers* (3rd ed.). Routledge.

A comprehensive guide for teachers on understanding the history curriculum for primary ages (five to 11) and the pedagogy for effective teaching and learning in history.

Historical Association. www.history.org.uk/primary/categories/336/module/8821/guidance-for-trainee-and-early-career-teachers

A resource from the leading subject association offering specific guidance and support for trainee and early career teachers of primary history.

The Historical Thinking Project. https://historicalthinking.ca/

A Canadian-based project providing resources and a model focused on six core concepts of historical thinking to help students think like historians.

Tiffany, S. (2023). *Mr T does primary history*. Corwin.

A practical resource for primary teachers, offering ideas, strategies and resources for teaching the primary history curriculum.

REFERENCES

Allen, A., Kavanagh, A. M. and Cassaithe, C. N. (2024). *Beyond single stories: Changing narratives for a changing world* (1st ed.). Information Age.

Barton, K. C. and Ho, L.-C. (2021). *Curriculum for justice and harmony: Deliberation, knowledge, and action in social and civic education* (1st ed.). Routledge.

Barton, K. and Levstik, L. (2004). *Teaching history for the common good*. Lawrence Erlbaum Associates.

Chapman, A., Burn, K. and Kitson, A. (2018). What is school history for? British student-teachers' perspectives. *Arbor*, *194*(788), a443. https://doi.org/10.3989/arbor.2018.788n2003

Cooper, H. (2018). *History 5–11: A guide for teachers* (3rd ed.). Routledge.

Counsell, C. (2018, April 7). Senior curriculum leadership 1: The indirect manifestation of knowledge: (A) curriculum as narrative. *The dignity of the thing*. https://thedignityofthethingblog.wordpress.com/2018/04/07/senior-curriculum-leadership-1-the-indirect-manifestation-of-knowledge-a-curriculum-as-narrative/

de Groot-Reuvekamp, M., Van Boxtel, C., Ros, A. and Harnett, P. (2014). The understanding of historical time in the primary history curriculum in England and the Netherlands. *Journal of Curriculum Studies, 46*(4), 487–514. https://doi.org/10.1080/00220272.2013.869837

Deng, Z. (2021). Powerful knowledge, transformations and Didaktik/curriculum thinking. *British Educational Research Journal, 47*(6), 1652–1674. https://doi.org/10.1002/berj.3750

Endacott, J. and Brooks, S. (2013). An updated theoretical and practical model for promoting historical empathy. *Social Studies Research and Practice, 8*(1), 41–58.

Hawkey, K. (2023). *History and the climate crisis: Environmental history in the classroom.* UCL Press. https://discovery.ucl.ac.uk/id/eprint/10174668/

Hill, M. (2020). Curating the imagined past: World building in the history curriculum. *Teaching History, 180*, 10–20.

Historical Association (HA). (2025). *Primary history survey 2024.* www.history.org.uk/primary/categories/709/news/4381/primary-history-survey-2024-the-results

Hodkinson, A. and Smith, C. (2018). Chronology and the new National Curriculum for history: Is it time to refocus the debate? *Education 3–13, 46*(6), 700–711. https://doi.org/10.1080/03004279.2018.1483804

Husbands, C., Kitson, A. and Pendry, A. (2003). *Understanding history teaching.* Open University Press.

Kitson, A. and Riley, M. (2024). The potential of primary history. *Primary History, 96*, 6–10.

Lee, P. (1992). History in schools: Aims, purposes and approaches. A reply to John White. In P. Lee, J. Slater, P. Walsh and J. White (Eds.), *The aims of school history: The National Curriculum and beyond* (pp. 20–34). Tufnell Press.

Lee, P. and Ashby, R. (2000). Progression in historical understanding among students ages 7–14. In P. Stearns, P. Seixas and S. Wineburg (Eds.), *Knowing, teaching and learning history: National and international perspectives* (pp. 199–222). New York University Press.

Ofsted. (2023). *Rich encounters with the past: History subject report.* www.gov.uk/government/publications/subject-report-series-history/rich-encounters-with-the-past-history-subject-report

Percival, J. (2018). History and its links across the curriculum. *Education 3–13, 46*(6), 712–727. https://doi.org/10.1080/03004279.2018.1483805

Quigley, A. (2019). EEF blog: What do we mean by 'knowledge rich' anyway? Education Endowment Foundation. https://educationendowmentfoundation.org.uk/news/eef-blog-what-do-we-mean-by-knowledge-rich-anyway

Rüsen, J. (2006). Historical consciousness: Narrative structure, moral function and onto-genetic development. In P. Seixas (Ed.), *Theorizing historical consciousness* (pp. 70–78). University of Toronto Press.

Sullivan, R. (2018). DfE clarifies reference to enquiry-based learning. *Historical Association.* www.history.org.uk/ha-news/categories/455/news/3613/dfe-clarifies-reference-to-enquiry-based-learning

Stow, W. and Haydn, T. (2000). Issues in the teaching of chronology. In J. Arthur and R. Phillips (Eds.), *Issues in history teaching* (pp. 83–97). Routledge.

Style, E. (1988). Curriculum as window and mirror. In *Listening for all voices.* Oak Knoll School Monograph.

Waldron, F. (2003). Irish primary children's perceptions of history. *Irish Educational Studies*, *22*(2), 63–89. https://doi.org/10.1080/0332331030220209

Young, M. and Muller, J. (2010). Three educational scenarios for the future: Lessons from the sociology of knowledge. *European Journal of Education*, *45*(1), 11–27. https://doi.org/10.1111/j.1465-3435.2009.01413.x

14
LANGUAGES

ELIZABETH MALONE

┌─ THIS CHAPTER ─────────────────────────────────

This chapter explores the ideas that:

- examine the historical, political and pedagogical dimensions of primary language education across the UK and beyond

- provides practical, inclusive strategies that can be implemented straight away in your classroom

- introduces the term 'intercultural understanding' and considers how this can be used in a meaningful way with young learners.

┌─ KEY TERMS FOR THIS CHAPTER ─────────────────────

Home nation: refers to the individual countries within the UK (England, Scotland, Wales, Northern Ireland) and their distinct educational policies.

Multilingualism: the ability to speak and understand more than one language.

Grammar: the system and structure of a language, including syntax, morphology and punctuation.

Vocabulary: the body of words used in a particular language or by a particular person or group.

Case study: a real-world example used to illustrate educational practices or concepts.

Target language: the language being taught or learned, as opposed to the learner's native language.

Language transfer: when learners apply rules from their first language to a second language, which can lead to errors or insights.

(Continued)

Metacognition: awareness and understanding of one's own thought processes; in education, it refers to teaching students how to learn.

Four modalities: the four core language skills: speaking, listening, reading and writing.

Language acquisition: the process of learning a language.

Echo reading: a technique where students repeat after the teacher to practise pronunciation and rhythm.

Listening station: a classroom setup where students can listen to audio recordings to improve comprehension.

Story sequencing: an activity where students arrange story elements in order to reinforce understanding.

Phonics: a method of teaching reading by correlating sounds with letters or groups of letters.

Sound wall: a visual display showing phonetic sounds and corresponding words/images to support pronunciation.

Sound buttons: interactive tools that play recorded sounds or words to aid language learning.

Scaffolding: providing structured support to help learners gradually achieve independence in tasks.

Intercultural understanding (ICU): the ability to appreciate, respect and engage with cultural diversity and perspectives.

Dialogic teaching: an approach that encourages open-ended discussion and dialogue to deepen understanding.

Intersectionality: the interconnected nature of social categorisations such as race, class and gender, which can affect experiences and identities.

INTRODUCTION

Language education in the UK has evolved significantly over the past century, shaped by shifting political priorities, cultural contexts and educational reforms across the four home nations. In this chapter, you will start by exploring the historical development of primary language teaching, highlighting how national strategies, local initiatives and global influences have impacted the way languages are introduced to young learners.

Alongside this historical and policy overview, the chapter aims to exemplify practice by offering educators concrete, practical ideas they can try out in their classrooms. Through case studies, it illuminates how inclusive, creative and context-sensitive approaches to language teaching can be implemented. These examples are designed to inspire and support educators in making language learning meaningful, engaging and responsive to the diverse needs of their pupils.

By combining policy analysis with grounded classroom practice, this chapter provides a rich foundation for understanding both the *why* and the *how* of primary language education today.

SECTION 1: POLICIES AND PURPOSES FOR LANGUAGES EDUCATION

To understand how languages are taught in schools today, it helps to look at how language education has developed over time, especially in the UK, as each home nation has been shaped by a different history.

Historically, learning foreign languages was mostly something older children did in grammar or private schools. Younger children in primary schools didn't usually learn languages, and when they did, it was often Latin or ancient Greek rather than modern languages like French or Spanish. Things began to change in the 1960s when England introduced the Primary French Project, one of the first efforts to teach a modern language to younger children (Malone, 2015). It showed that children were enthusiastic about learning languages, but also revealed a major challenge: teachers didn't have enough training or support. This issue continues to affect language education today.

In Scotland, Wales and Northern Ireland, language learning in primary schools was even less common. Each country had its own priorities. For example, Scotland chose not to focus on foreign language learning but instead on basic literacy and numeracy (Johnstone et al., 2000). Wales worked to revive the Welsh language after years of suppression (Ellis and McCartney, 2011) and Northern Ireland's complex political and cultural landscape made schools cautious about introducing foreign languages.

During the 1980s and 1990s, there wasn't a clear national plan for teaching languages in primary schools. Instead, different regions developed their own projects. In England, programmes like PRISM and PILOTE aimed to train teachers and create structured lessons. Scotland launched the Modern Languages in the Primary School (MLPS) initiative (Murray, 2017), which introduced languages like French and Spanish to children aged seven to 11 (Martin, 2008; Sharpe, 2001). These efforts were promising, but often depended on individual teachers and lacked consistent support. In Wales, the focus remained on Welsh–English bilingualism; foreign languages were rarely taught in primary schools. Northern Ireland introduced a pilot programme in the early 2000s, but it wasn't part of the official curriculum and didn't last long.

In the early 2000s, the UK began to take language learning more seriously. England introduced the Languages for All: Languages for Life strategy, encouraging schools to start teaching languages earlier (DfES, 2002). This led to languages becoming a required subject for children aged seven to 11 in 2014. However, younger children were still left out and many teachers felt unprepared to teach languages confidently. Scotland's earlier enthusiasm began to fade; Wales continued to focus mainly on Welsh. Northern Ireland's pilot programme continued for a while, but was eventually stopped due to funding cuts.

Since 2010, the UK's four nations have taken different paths:

- England made languages compulsory for older primary children (from Key Stage 2) (DfE, 2013), but focused heavily on phonics, grammar and vocabulary. Some experts worry this makes language learning feel too mechanical and less about real communication (Porter et al., 2022). Furthermore, the English National Curriculum (DfE, 2013) mandates languages should be taught for the purpose of language progression.

- Scotland launched the 1+2 Language Policy, aiming for every child to learn two additional languages. Many schools have adopted the policy, but challenges remain, especially around teacher training and fitting languages into a busy curriculum.

- Wales introduced the Curriculum for Wales (2022), which brings Welsh, English and international languages together under one framework. This helps children see language learning as part of a bigger picture. However, schools in rural or disadvantaged areas may struggle to fully implement this vision.

- Northern Ireland ended its primary languages programme in 2015 and hasn't replaced it. Without a national plan, language learning now depends on individual schools and outside organisations.

Across Europe, many countries are introducing foreign languages to children at a younger age. By 2023, 15 EU countries were starting language lessons before the age of seven, and most others by age eight or nine (European Commission, 2024). This shows a strong belief that early exposure to languages helps children develop better skills and attitudes towards learning them.

Why is this happening? Many parents and governments see language learning as a way to help children succeed in a global world. Learning any language can improve communication skills, help people understand different cultures and even boost job opportunities later in life. Research also shows that younger children are often more flexible in their thinking, which can make it easier for them to pick up new languages.

The Council of Europe has said that learning languages is important for building tolerance, understanding and cooperation between countries. This is especially important in parts of Europe where there have been political tensions or conflict. Language learning is seen as a way to bring people together and help overcome divisions (Council of Europe, 2022).

However, not all countries are moving in the same direction. In some places, political changes have led to less support for foreign language programmes. Some governments are focusing more on national identity and less on multicultural education, which can make it harder to promote multilingualism.

Even with these challenges, the European Union still strongly supports the idea of learning multiple languages. But events like Brexit, the Covid-19 pandemic and rising political tensions have made the situation more complicated. As a result, the picture of language learning across Europe is now more mixed, with some countries pushing forward and others pulling back.

As an educator, understanding your local context (as well as the historical one) can help you make language learning more meaningful. You might explore the languages spoken in your community, use children's home languages in the classroom, or connect language learning to local culture and identity. Even simple activities like greetings in different languages or songs can help children feel included and excited about learning. Let's explore a case study of how one educator, Mr Thompson, has achieved this in his class.

CASE STUDY: MR THOMPSON

Mr Thompson teaches Year 3 at a primary school in Manchester, where the classroom reflects the city's vibrant cultural and linguistic diversity. With over 40 per cent of his children speaking a language other than English at home, he recognised the importance of making language learning not only accessible, but also meaningful and inclusive. This means teaching the National Curriculum objectives (for language progression) in French, but also simultaneously integrating children's home languages and cultural identities into everyday classroom practice, using simple but powerful tools such as sound buttons, labels and internet-based resources.

To begin, Mr Thompson introduced sound buttons into his classroom as a way to celebrate the languages spoken by his children. He invited families to record greetings in their home languages, including Urdu, Polish, Somali and Arabic. Each button was labelled with the name of the language and a small flag/icon. Every morning, children would take turns pressing a button to hear a greeting, which the class would then repeat together. This simple ritual quickly became a part of the school day. Children were excited to hear their own languages represented, and those unfamiliar with the languages were curious and eager to learn. The activity fostered a sense of pride and belonging, especially among multilingual learners, and helped build a classroom culture of respect and celebration.

Alongside this, Mr Thompson transformed his classroom into a multilingual environment by using dual-language labels. Everyday objects such as the door, window and whiteboard were labelled in English and one other language, which rotated weekly to ensure all children's languages were included. He also created a *Language of the Week* board, featuring key vocabulary and simple phrases. Children were actively involved in creating the labels and teaching their classmates how to pronounce the words. This not only reinforced vocabulary learning, but also gave children ownership of the classroom space and their learning.

━━ **REFLECTION 14.1** ━━━━━━━━━━━━━━━━━━━━━━━━━━━━━━━━━━━━━

Primary languages history shows that language education is shaped by local culture, politics and priorities. In your setting, it's important to think about what you want children to gain from learning languages. Consider:

- is it about communication, cultural understanding, or building confidence?

- how do local factors like community languages or values influence us as educators and children as learners?

- what is your understanding of the statutory requirements for teaching primary languages in your setting?

- how else could you supplement language learning?

- what language resources do you have (don't overlook children or staff members here!)?

SECTION 2: LEARNING CONTEXTS

Language learning can vary widely depending on the setting, the children and the educators. Some children learn languages every day in immersive environments, while others only have short lessons once a week. Some grow up speaking more than one language, while others only hear a foreign language at school. Educators also differ in how confident and enthusiastic they feel about teaching languages. All these factors affect how well children learn and enjoy languages (Holmes and Myles, 2019).

IMMERSIVE VS SPORADIC LEARNING: TIME AND ITS IMPACT

In immersive settings, such as Welsh-medium or Irish-medium schools, children hear and use the target language throughout the day. This helps them learn naturally and develop fluency. In contrast, sporadic learning, where children have one or two short lessons a week, can lead to slower progress and limited language use (Curtain, 2000; Liddicoat et al., 2007).

Research shows that children need enough time with a language to make real progress, and younger children need more time than older ones (Nikolov and Djigunović, 2006; Martin, 2000a). If lessons are too short or infrequent, children may only learn basic words and phrases. Teachers can help by using the language in other parts of the day, such as during songs, routines, or games. This increases exposure and helps children remember what they've learned.

Bruner's spiral curriculum (1960) offers a useful framework for language teaching because it encourages teachers to revisit familiar topics throughout the year, each time introducing greater complexity. This approach supports natural language acquisition by allowing children to build on what they already know, reinforcing vocabulary and structures while gradually expanding their linguistic repertoire.

To apply this in practice, as an educator, you could begin by selecting core themes that are relevant and engaging for children. These themes, such as weather, food, family, animals, daily routines, school life and emotions, can be explored repeatedly across different stages of development.

Each time the theme is revisited, the language used becomes more sophisticated, helping children move from simple words to full sentences and eventually to more complex grammatical structures.

CASE STUDY: WEATHER

For example, the theme of weather can be introduced with basic vocabulary like 'sunny' and 'rainy', supported by songs, flashcards and visual charts. As children progress, they can begin forming descriptive phrases such as 'It is sunny today' or 'It was rainy yesterday', using sentence-building games and role-play activities. Later, with older children, they could write weather forecasts, compare climates and use future and past tenses to express ideas like 'It will be cloudy tomorrow' or 'Last week it was stormy.'

Table 14.1   Thematic (weather) progressive language example

Focus	Activities	Language targets
Basic vocabulary	Flashcards, songs (e.g. 'What's the weather like today?'), weather chart	Words: sunny, rainy, cloudy, snowy
Descriptive phrases	Sentence-building games, role-play weather reports	Phrases: 'It is sunny today.' 'It was rainy yesterday'
Complex sentences and grammar	Write weather forecasts, compare climates, use past/future tense	'It will be cloudy tomorrow.' 'Last week it was stormy'

To support this progression, you could draw on a wide range of resources. Songs offer catchy and repetitive language that reinforces vocabulary and bilingual picture books provide visual and contextual support. Don't worry if your school doesn't have bilingual books; you can create your own using sticky notes as flaps displaying the target language over the English word. Embedding themes across the wider curriculum further strengthens language learning. In maths, children might count weather symbols or measure rainfall. In science, they can explore seasons and climate. Art lessons can involve creating weather collages with labelled vocabulary, and role-play activities might include setting up a weather station or presenting a news broadcast in the target language.

MONOLINGUAL AND BILINGUAL LEARNERS: DIFFERENT NEEDS IN THE CLASSROOM

Many classrooms include both *monolingual* and *multilingual* learners. Multilingual children, those who speak more than one language, may find it easier to learn new languages because they are used to switching between languages. Monolingual children, those who speak only one language, may need more support to understand how languages work (Nikolov, 2009; Martin, 2000b).

Teachers should plan lessons that help both groups. Multilingual children can be encouraged to share their language skills, while monolingual children may benefit from extra practice and clear explanations. Including community and heritage languages, such as Arabic, Polish, or Mandarin, can make learning more meaningful and help all children feel included (Byram, 1997).

Some children may not wish to share their language skills, not wishing to 'other' themselves. This can sometimes happen in largely monolingual, monocultural settings where the child is the only one with these abilities, and their desire not to share should be respected. Potentially, if the learning environment culture changes over time, these children may then wish to share.

It's also important to recognise that learners often bring habits and ideas from their first language into the second. This can be helpful – for example, when grammar rules are similar – but it can also lead to mistakes. A child might apply sentence patterns or pronunciation from their home language that don't fit the new one. These kinds of *transfers* (Martin, 2000a; Murphy et al., 2014) are a normal part of learning and can be used as teaching moments. By helping children notice these patterns, teachers can support deeper understanding and encourage learners to think about how languages are similar and different.

CASE STUDY: LANGUAGE TRANSFER

Child: Amira, age seven

Home Language: Arabic

School Language: English

Amira recently moved to the UK and speaks Arabic at home. She's confident in conversation and enjoys learning English, but her teacher notices a recurring mistake: Amira often says 'He go to school' instead of 'He goes to school.'

This mistake is a classic example of language transfer. In Arabic, verbs don't change in the same way for third-person singular subjects (there are other languages which also follow a similar format, e.g. Mandarin Chinese), so Amira is applying the rules she knows from her first language to English. She's not being careless; she's using logic based on her existing knowledge.

REFLECTION 14.2

- As an educator, how can you use Amira's language transfer as a learning opportunity?

- Could you use this language transfer as a teaching moment for all children and not just Amira?

- Would this teaching be located in the languages lesson, an English lesson, or elsewhere in the school day?

- Have you noticed any other patterns in any of the ways in which the other children use language? Have you explored why they do this?

THE ROLE OF THE EDUCATOR: PASSION, CONFIDENCE AND TRAINING

I've come to a frightening conclusion that I am the decisive element in the classroom. It's my personal approach that creates the climate. It's my daily mood that makes the weather. As a teacher, I possess a tremendous power to make a child's life miserable or joyous. I can be a tool of torture or an instrument of inspiration. I can humiliate or heal. In all situations, it is my response that decides whether a crisis will be escalated or de-escalated and a child humanized or dehumanized.

(Ginott, 1972, Preface)

Educators play a key role in how children feel about learning languages. When teachers are excited and confident, children are more likely to enjoy lessons. Even if a teacher isn't fluent in the language, their enthusiasm can make a big difference (Nikolov, 1999).

Many educators say they don't feel confident teaching languages because they don't speak a foreign language themselves (Collen and Duff, 2024), but this can be a positive position as a role model for children also learning a foreign language for the first time. Some children assume that educators just 'know everything' and were created that way(!). This provides space to model for the children how to learn – *metacognition* – and discuss internal strategies for learning. It's a chance to model how to learn and how to make mistakes. These skills will support children with language learning and are transferable across the curriculum.

CASE STUDY: MODELLING METACOGNITION IN YEAR 3 SPANISH

Teacher: Mrs Patel

Class: Year 3 Spanish

Helping children reflect on how they learn new vocabulary, Mrs Patel begins a lesson on Spanish words for animals. Before introducing the vocabulary, she says:

> Today we're learning some new Spanish words. But before we start, let's think about how we remember new words. I like to link the word to something I already know or a vivid image in my head. For example, gato means cat, and it sounds a little like 'GATsby'. So I imagine a fancy cat wearing an old-fashioned Gatsby-style hat strutting around at a glamorous party!

Mrs Patel then shows an AI graphic of the cat wearing a Gatsby style hat, dancing on the board and the children laugh. She asks them to repeat the word again and again. She writes the word 'gato' on the board and asks, 'What helps you remember new words? Do you like drawing, acting them out, or saying them with a friend?' Children share their ideas, and Mrs Patel encourages them to try different strategies during the lesson. As they practise words like *perro* (dog), *pájaro* (bird), and *pez* (fish), she reminds them: 'Think about what's working for you. Are you remembering better when you say the word out loud, act it out, or think of a vivid image?'

At the end of the lesson, children reflect in their learning journals. By modelling her own thinking and encouraging children to reflect on theirs, Mrs Patel helps them develop meta-cognitive skills, learning how to learn. This supports all learners, especially those new to language learning, by giving them tools to become more independent and confident.

REFLECTION 14.3

- Have you ever spoken aloud what you are thinking for learners? If not, what has stopped you?
- Consider, what are your metacognitive strategies when learning a new language?
- Which could you model for the children?

SECTION 3: PEDAGOGICAL APPROACHES TO DEVELOPING FL LANGUAGE KNOWLEDGE AND SKILLS.

When teaching foreign languages to children aged three to 12, it's important to think carefully about how we help them develop the key skills of speaking, listening, reading and writing – often referred to as the *four modalities* (Ofsted, 2021). These skills don't grow in isolation; they are shaped by how much time children spend with the language, how it's taught and the opportunities they have to use it in real-life contexts, as well as the interplay between them. In many learning environments, language lessons are short and infrequent, so making the most of every moment is key.

One effective principle is to embed language learning across the school day. This means using the target language not only in dedicated lessons, but also during everyday routines, such as taking the register, giving instructions, or transitioning between activities. For example, in French, a teacher might say 'Bonjour!' instead of 'Good morning', or use simple commands. Greetings like '你好' (nǐ hǎo – hello) or instructions such as '请坐' (qǐng zuò – please sit) can be used to build familiarity and confidence.

Another helpful approach is to make learning playful and interactive. Young children learn best when they're having fun (Nikolov, 1999) and games are a great way to practise language skills without pressure. One basic example is 'Run and Touch', whereby, as a warmer for a PE lesson, flashcards are distributed across the playground. The English word (or the target language) is called out, and children run to touch the correct card. To build on this, children could play 'Pass the parcel: Vocabulary edition'. Children sit in a circle and pass around a parcel while music plays. When the music stops, the child holding the parcel unwraps a layer to reveal a picture or word in the target language. In German, the word might be *Apfel* (apple), and the child could say '*Ich mag den Apfel*' (I like the apple). This game encourages speaking, listening and memory recall, and can be adapted for different age groups and topics, developing with complexity.

LISTENING

Listening is the foundation of language learning. Children need to hear the language often and in different ways to get used to its sounds and rhythms (Renukadevi, 2014). In many classrooms, listening activities are limited to educator talk or recordings, which can be repetitive and dependent on the educator. To make listening more engaging and readily available, educators can play songs, rhymes and short cartoons in the target language, or set up individual stations where students can hear the language. Reading familiar stories aloud, especially those with strong visual support, can help children connect sounds with meaning. Exposure to different accents and voices is also important, as it prepares children for real-world communication. The more varied and frequent the listening input, the better children will understand and respond.

It's also important to give children chances to show they understand without worrying about producing language (Xu, 2015). They can do this by physically responding or touching flashcards, which helps build confidence before speaking.

SPEAKING

Speaking is often the most visible part of language learning, but it can also be the slowest to develop. In many primary schools, children only get one or two short lessons a week, meaning they often rely on memorised phrases rather than speaking freely (Ofsted, 2021). To help children become more confident speakers, it's useful to create regular chances for them to use the language in everyday situations and with each other, rather than always answering educator questions. Simple routines like greetings, classroom instructions, or asking for help can be done in the target language. Role-play and drama are also great tools, allowing children to practise speaking in a fun and relaxed way.

CASE STUDY: LISTENING AND SPEAKING

Miss Sacks teaches a class of English-speaking children who are beginning to learn Italian. Recognising that listening is a key component of language acquisition, she designs a learning experience around the familiar story of Little Red Riding Hood (*Cappuccetto Rosso* in Italian). She chose this story because it was familiar to the children, the language is repetitive and the story is supported by visuals. This means children are relaxed, not worried about not understanding and can enjoy listening and joining in.

- Miss Sacks begins by introducing key vocabulary from the story using flashcards and props: *la nonna* (grandmother), *il lupo* (wolf), *il cestino* (basket) and *il bosco* (forest). On another day, she might read the story and elicit from children the words they have heard.

- She pronounces each word slowly and clearly, encouraging repetition with accompanying gestures.

- She then reads a simplified version of *Cappuccetto Rosso* in Italian. She made this book herself using a 'big book' version in English and covering up the words with sticky notes, which can be lifted like flaps to reveal the English word.

- Miss Sacks uses expressive intonation and points to illustrations to support comprehension. Children listen attentively, and she pauses at key moments to ask simple questions in Italian, such as *'Chi è questo?'* ('Who is this?') and *'Dove va Cappuccetto Rosso?'* ('Where is Little Red Riding Hood going?').

Children participate in *echo reading*, repeating key phrases like *'Che occhi grandi hai!'* ('What big eyes you have!') to practise pronunciation and rhythm. To reinforce listening, she plays an audio version of the story read by a native speaker. Children are encouraged to close their eyes and imagine the scenes. Later, they hear the story read by a different voice to become familiar with varied accents and intonations. Miss Sacks also sets up a *listening station* in the classroom corner where children can use headphones and listen to the recording.

By using a familiar narrative with strong visual and emotional cues, Miss Sacks creates a listening-rich environment that supports vocabulary acquisition, pronunciation and comprehension. The varied listening inputs (teacher voice, audio recordings, peer repetition) help children become more confident in recognising and responding to spoken Italian.

In the next class, Story Sequencing is used. Pupils arrange picture cards in the correct order based on what they heard, using Italian words to describe each scene. The following week,

Miss Sacks recaps the story by reading it aloud again, inviting children to join in. Afterward, they move on to role-play in small groups, acting out the story using simple Italian dialogue. Sentence starters and prompts are provided as support.

READING AND WRITING

Reading and writing in a foreign language should be introduced gradually (Arunthawatchai et al., 2025). In the Early Years, the focus is usually on listening and speaking, with some simple reading and writing activities. As children progress through primary school, they can begin to explore grammar and sentence structure. Revisiting key ideas regularly, as in Bruner's (1960) spiral curriculum, helps children deepen their understanding over time and makes learning stick. Using stories, pictures and hands-on activities makes reading and writing purposeful and enjoyable.

To support reading and writing, especially in early stages, phonics can be a powerful tool. Children benefit from learning how sounds and letters work in the target language, particularly when they differ from English. A sound wall is a visual display showing the sounds of the target language alongside example words and images. In French, the wall might include /ʃ/ with a picture of chat (cat), or /u/ with fou (crazy). In Mandarin, it could show pinyin sounds like 'zh' with '猪' (zhū – pig), or 'x' with '小' (xiǎo – small), alongside tone marks. Educators can refer to the wall during lessons, and children can use it to decode new words when reading or writing. Interactive elements, like flaps, magnets, or sound buttons, make it even more engaging.

By combining these strategies – embedding language throughout the day, using playful games and supporting literacy with phonics and sound walls – educators can create a rich and supportive environment for language learning, even when time is limited.

WRITING STRATEGIES

When teaching young children to write in a foreign language, educators can use several supportive strategies:

- *writing frames*: templates providing basic structures for children to follow, allowing focus on content rather than grammar or spelling. For example, when writing about family: 'My name is ___,' 'I live with ___' and 'My favourite person is ___ because ___.' This kind of support helps children to express themselves while practising key sentence patterns in the target language; it also builds their confidence;

- *scaffolding*: breaking tasks into smaller, manageable parts and offering support at each stage. Educators might use modelled writing, where they write a short text in front of the class and explain their choices aloud using metacognitive techniques;

- *visual aids*: picture dictionaries, word walls and labelled classroom objects help children connect words with meanings. Before writing about animals, children might learn key words like 'tail', 'claws', or 'fur' and practise saying them aloud, then complete a simple sentence like 'A tiger has ___', before writing their own descriptions using a writing frame.

By combining writing frames, scaffolded activities, visual supports and creative tasks, educators can create an environment where children feel encouraged to write in a foreign language. These strategies help develop writing skills and foster enjoyment and engagement.

SECTION 4: DEVELOPING INTERCULTURAL UNDERSTANDING

Helping children develop *intercultural understanding* (ICU) in language lessons means going beyond surface-level exposure to food, festivals, or folklore and facts (Kramsch, 1991). It involves fostering early critical awareness of cultural perspectives, values and practices, encouraging children to reflect on their own assumptions and engage meaningfully with diverse worldviews. ICU develops skills such as empathy, curiosity and openness, and can create opportunities for authentic intercultural dialogue that go beyond stereotypes or tokenistic representations. Foreign language education is an excellent vehicle for this learning, though it is not the only location for it.

One effective method is *dialogic teaching*, where children are encouraged to talk openly about different cultural perspectives, values and traditions. These conversations help pupils reflect on their own views and challenge stereotypes. It also helps children understand that everyone has a culture; it is not something only others possess. As Woodgate-Jones and Grenfell (2012) explain, children in the early and primary years are still forming their cultural identities and are especially receptive to exploring how others live, think and communicate; intersectionality is an important part of this.

Storytelling and literature are powerful tools for ICU. When children read traditional tales or culturally diverse stories in the target language, they begin to understand different worldviews. Stories supported by illustrations and repeated language patterns make these experiences more accessible and enjoyable. Doye (1996) argues that intercultural learning should be part of everyday classroom experiences, not an occasional activity. These experiences can take place throughout the day, even outside dedicated language sessions.

Another approach is cross-curricular integration, where ICU is explored through subjects like geography, history and art. For example, learning where French is spoken – such as Senegal, Haiti and France – helps children understand that cultures are diverse and not defined by a single story. As Byram (1997) notes, language learning is inseparable from cultural learning because language reflects the social contexts in which it is used.

Children themselves may be the greatest resource for ICU. Recognising and celebrating community and heritage languages is essential. Including languages like Arabic, Mandarin, or Swahili in the curriculum helps children feel seen and valued. Martin (2000b) highlights that valuing home languages boosts self-esteem and strengthens identity. However, care should be taken so children are not 'forced to share' – participation should be voluntary.

CASE STUDY: CRITICALLY ENGAGING WITH CULTURAL CONTENT

Imagine an educational setting where a classroom display shows the Eiffel Tower, a moustached man in a striped jumper, a baguette under his arm next to a bicycle. Consider:

- what stereotypes does this display inadvertently reinforce?

- does this display help children engage meaningfully with culture?

- how could we broaden learning to help children identify, compare and contrast cultures, empathise and critically engage, rather than focusing only on the *4 Fs* (food, fairs, folklore and facts)?

Alternatively, in a multicultural primary school in Birmingham, a Year 4 class learning French explored the theme of 'home and belonging' through a unit titled *Chez Moi*. Pupils read a bilingual story about a child living in Senegal who speaks French and Wolof. The teacher facilitated discussions about different types of homes, languages spoken at home and what 'belonging' means.

Pupils created posters in French describing their own homes and languages, using phrases like '*J'habite avec ma famille*' and '*Je parle anglais et arabe.*' The class then compared their posters with the story character's experiences, identifying similarities and differences. This approach allowed pupils to:

- practise target language vocabulary in meaningful contexts;

- reflect on their own cultural identities;

- develop empathy and curiosity about others' lives.

Educators should help pupils think deeply about cultural norms (their own culture included), question assumptions and appreciate diversity within cultures. Kramsch (1991) critiques superficial approaches and encourages treating ICU as a reflective and dialogic process. For further reading, Byram's (1997) framework of the *savoirs* – including *savoir comprendre* (interpreting), *savoir apprendre/faire* (discovery and interaction) and *savoir s'engager* (critical cultural awareness) – offers a strong model.

REFLECTION 14.4

- How do I help children reflect on their own cultural identities and assumptions in everyday classroom interactions?

- What opportunities do I provide for authentic intercultural dialogue, and how do I ensure these go beyond stereotypes or tokenistic representations?

- How do I select and use culturally diverse stories or texts to promote empathy, curiosity, and critical engagement with different worldviews?

- How do I celebrate and include pupils' home languages and cultural backgrounds in a way that is voluntary, respectful and empowering?

FINAL THOUGHTS

This chapter on foreign languages education has equipped you with a deeper understanding of the historical, political and pedagogical dimensions of primary language education across the UK and beyond. More importantly, it has provided practical, inclusive strategies that can be implemented straight away in your classroom.

The toolkit of ideas – from embedding language into daily routines and modelling metacognitive strategies, to using sound buttons, multilingual labels and storytelling to foster engagement and inclusion – can be used anywhere and with all learners. You also now have approaches to support both monolingual and multilingual pupils, scaffold language development across the four modalities (speaking, listening, reading and writing) and promote intercultural understanding in meaningful, respectful ways.

The children you work with, now and in the future, will benefit from your ability to make language learning inclusive, engaging and impactful.

FURTHER READING AND RESOURCES

Porter, A., Graham, S., Myles, F. and Holmes, B. (2022). Creativity, challenge and culture in the languages classroom: A response to the Ofsted Curriculum research review. https://doi.org/10.1080/09571736.2022.2046358

An academic article that provides a critical response to the Ofsted *Curriculum research review* (2021) in languages, advocating for the importance of creativity, challenge and cultural depth in the modern languages classroom.

Frisch, S. and Glaser, K. (Eds.) (2025). *Early language education in instructed contexts: Current issues and empirical insights into teaching and learning languages in primary school.* https://benjamins.com/catalog/lllt.62

A collection of chapters offering empirical research and current issues in the teaching and learning of languages in primary school settings.

Byram, M. (2021). *Teaching and assessing intercultural communicative competence: Revisited.* Multilingual Matters.

A key academic work that revisits and updates the influential concept of intercultural communicative competence (ICC), providing guidance on how to teach and assess it.

Association for Language Learning (ALL) Primary Languages Zone. www.all-languages.org. uk/primary-2/

The leading subject association's resource hub providing support, advocacy, news and resources specifically for primary modern foreign languages (MFL) teachers.

New CiLT: high-quality information and support for primary Modern Foreign Languages. www.new-cilt.org.uk

A resource that provides high-quality information and professional support for the teaching of primary MFL.

REFERENCES

Arunthawatchai, O. C., Jarunthawatchai, W. and Gilbert, L. (2025). Connecting reading and writing in foreign language instruction: A process-genre approach. *LEARN Journal: Language Education and Acquisition Research Network, 18*(2), 493–518. https://doi.org/10.70730/SOGP3675

Bruner, J. S. (1960). *The process of education.* Harvard University Press.

Byram, M. (1997). *Teaching and assessing intercultural communicative competence.* Multilingual Matters.

Collen, I. and Duff, J. (2024). *Language trends England 2024: Language teaching in primary, secondary and independent schools in England.* British Council. www.britishcouncil.org/sites/default/files/language_trend_england_2024.pdf

Council of Europe. (2022). *Recommendation CM/Rec(2022)1 of the Committee of Ministers to member States on the importance of plurilingual and intercultural education for democratic culture, and explanatory memorandum.* https://rm.coe.int/0900001680a563ca

Curtain, H. (2000). *Languages and children: Making the match.* Longman.

Department for Education (DfE). (2013). *National curriculum in England: Primary curriculum.* www.gov.uk/government/publications/national-curriculum-in-england-primary-curriculum

Department for Education and Skills (DfES). (2002). *Languages for all: Languages for life – A strategy for England.* www.gov.uk/government/publications

Doye, P. (1996). *Foreign language learning in the primary school: Intercultural learning and language awareness.* Council of Europe.

Ellis, S. and McCartney, E. (Eds.). (2011). *Applied linguistics and primary school teaching.* Cambridge University Press.

European Commission. (2024). *Europeans and their languages: Eurobarometer survey.* https://europa.eu/eurobarometer/surveys/detail/2979

Ginott, H. (1972). *Teacher and child: A book for parents and teachers.* Macmillan.

Holmes, B. and Myles, F. (2019). *Primary languages in practice: A guide to teaching and learning.* Routledge.

Johnstone, R., Cavani, J., Low, L. and McPake, J. (2000). *Assessing modern languages achievement: A Scottish pilot study of late primary and early secondary pupils* (Edited by L. Low). Scottish CILT.

Kramsch, C. (1991). Culture in language learning: A view from the United States. In K. de Bot, R. Ginsberg and C. Kramsch (Eds.), *Foreign language research in cross-cultural perspective* (pp. 217–232). John Benjamins.

Liddicoat, A. J., Scarino, A., Curnow, T. J., Kohler, M., Scrimgeour, A. and Morgan, A.-M. (2007). *Investigation of the state and nature of languages in Australian schools: RCLCES.* DfE, Employment and Workplace Relations.

Malone, E. (2015). Foreign languages in primary education in England: An ethnographic case study of three school contexts (Doctoral thesis). Liverpool John Moores University. https://researchonline.ljmu.ac.uk/id/eprint/4251/1/2016malonephd.pdf

Martin, C. (2000a). *An analysis of national and international research on the provision of modern foreign languages in primary schools.* QCA.

Martin, C. (2000b). Modern foreign languages at primary school: A three-pronged approach? *The Language Learning Journal, 22*(1), 5–10. https://doi.org/10.1080/09571730085200181

Martin, C. (2008). *Primary languages: Effective teaching and learning (Achieving QTS).* Learning Matters.

Murphy, V. A., Macaro, E., Alba, S. and Cipolla, C. (2014). The influence of learning a second language in primary school on developing first language literacy skills. *Applied Psycholinguistics.* https://doi.org/10.1017/S0142716414000095

Murray, E. (2017). Modern languages in Scottish primary schools: An investigation into the perceived benefits and challenges of the 1+2 policy. *Scottish Languages Review, 33*(Winter), 39–50. https://scilt.org.uk/Portals/24/Library/slr/issues/33/33-04%20Murray.pdf

Nikolov, M. (1999). Why do you learn English? Because the teacher is short. A study of Hungarian children's foreign language learning motivation. *Language Teaching Research, 3*(1), 33–56. https://doi.org/10.1177/136216889900300103

Nikolov, M. (2009). The age factor in context. In M. Nikolov (Ed.), *The age factor and early language learning* (pp. 1–38). Mouton de Gruyter. https://doi.org/10.1515/9783110218282.1

Nikolov, M. and Djigunović, J. (2006). Recent research on age, second language acquisition, and early foreign language learning. *Annual Review of Applied Linguistics, 26*, 234–260.

Ofsted. (2021). *Research review series: Languages.* www.gov.uk/government/publications/curriculum-research-review-series-languages

Porter, A., Graham, S., Myles, F. and Holmes, B. (2022). Creativity, challenge and culture in the languages classroom: A response to the Ofsted curriculum research review. *The Language Learning Journal, 50*(2), 208–217. https://doi.org/10.1080/09571736.2022.2046358

Renukadevi, D. (2014). The role of listening in language acquisition: The challenges and strategies in teaching listening. *International Journal of Education and Information Studies, 4*(1), 59–63.

Sharpe, K. (2001). *Foreign languages in the primary school: The what, why and how of early FL teaching*. Routledge.

Woodgate-Jones, A. and Grenfell, M. (2012). Intercultural understanding and primary-level second language learning and teaching. *Language Awareness*, *21*(4), 331–345. https://doi.org/10.1080/09658416.2011.609623

Xu, F. (2015). The priority of listening comprehension over speaking in the language acquisition process. https://files.eric.ed.gov/fulltext/EJ1066407.pdf

15
MUSIC

PHIL GRIFFITH

THIS CHAPTER

This chapter explores the ideas that:

- there is an argument for prioritising 'musicianship' over 'musical information' in primary music education

- positively acknowledging ourselves as musical beings (as opposed to the connotations of being 'a musician') is a necessity to teaching musicianship well

- encouraging pupils to explore the realms of performing, composing, listening and appraising is more engaging than mere musical information.

KEY TERMS FOR THIS CHAPTER

Performance: the process and/or product of playing or singing pieces of music.

Composition: the process and/or product of creating music.

Listening: the active moments of deliberately choosing to hear what is going on.

Appraising: making judgements about what has been heard, played or created.

Elements: basic building blocks of music, such as *pitch* (how high or low a musical sound is), *dynamics* (how loud or quiet the sound is), *timbre* (the distinctive quality of a sound that enables us to tell the difference, say, between a school bell and a church bell), or *tempo* (how fast or slow the music appears to be played).

Interrelated dimensions: next-level building blocks such as *texture* (how music might be layered), or *structure* (how pieces might be put together sequentially), which help us to describe the music which we hear.

Rhythm: the combination of notes of different duration which gives music its sense of style.

Harmony: the resultant sound when two or more lines of music are played and sung simultaneously. Sung *rounds* naturally create harmony with the entrance of each new part, while many songs deliberately employ a unique harmony line to support the main melody.

Notation: different methods of writing music down to enable it to be played again in similar or exact ways. These serve as visual representations, of which Western stave notation is just one kind.

Expression: the *way* in which something is sung or otherwise performed that helps the music convey a sense of meaning.

INTRODUCTION

First, 'Thank you' to all who are either already engaged in, or considering for the future, teaching music in the primary phase. The fact that you are turning to this chapter hopefully means that there is, at the least, a genuine concern and/or curiosity for music education and, at best, a firm commitment to learning how to teach music better. For those already involved in teaching music in some capacity in many varied settings to those just embarking on university study, it is hoped that this chapter will provide fresh impetus and perhaps an even fresher *way* of approaching music education. For music as a subject, I endeavour to highlight some of the tensions between musical information and musical skills, as this is the largest arena for reimagining what *subject knowledge* actually looks like. As a result, it should be possible, then, to approach lesson planning, delivery, content and skills development with a more narrow focus to ensure that quality, lasting subject knowledge is both held and developed by teachers and passed on to children.

I acknowledge that every school, and each school's context, is different. While many cover music education as a regular part of their school-specific curriculum, others adopt a carousel approach, where children may engage with music lessons in one term, then another creative discipline like art, drama or dance in the next. Many schools are rich with musical instrumental resources while others perceive a struggle to teach with very limited resources. The presence of a well-qualified music lead often enhances the musical provision of the whole school, while in other scenarios schools may simply defer the entire musical delivery to that music lead, with perhaps a few other willing, supportive staff. It is important to realise that while these differences exist, only in one context, that of the carousel, will this chapter highlight it as being wholly detrimental to the development of subject knowledge in music for children. True, a formal carousel might exist mainly in the secondary phase, but I use the term here to highlight any lack of continuity or purpose of curriculum provision.

As a result of this distinction, this chapter is not solely aimed at individual educators seeking to develop their own musical knowledge and pedagogy, but also to whole school leaderships whose decisions hugely impact the capacity for success for their teachers and children alike, with implications lasting well into the musical futures of the children they aim to support. Primarily the chapter is written for those who do *not* consider themselves to be music specialists. If this is you, then I hope you find what follows helpful.

THE BIG ISSUE

Okay, so let's deal with the main issue first! You *are* musical. The fact that many of you believe otherwise is not based on fact, but more likely on three restraints. The first restraint is simply *forgetting* or *not realising* that we all have innate musical skills. We become accustomed to taking so many things for granted. For example, consider the ability to hear – that most of us can take a moment to *actively* listen, hear and identify the noise of the breeze outside, the ticking clock, the passing lorry or a motorbike. We may even become aware again of the sound of our own breathing. These are musical skills.

Take the young mechanic friend of mine, who can identify certain cars by their sound, despite him being indoors and the car being one curtain, a closed double-glazed window and a whole road away. This is a musical skill. In other words, aural acuity, however it has been acquired or applied, is simply the ability to actively listen and discern what is going on. As Hallam (2006, p. 95) states, when commenting on historical studies of musical aptitude, 'Musicality has its basis in aural perception'. One hypothesis upon which this chapter is based is that we have forgotten how we learned to do these things. Becoming more musical is, to some degree therefore, a reversal of that forgetting process. We reacquaint ourselves with these mostly innate skills and, as we do so, we remind ourselves of our inner musicality. The more we do this, the more musical we become.

Those who can distinguish the sound of a fretless electric bass from an upright double bass are no more or less musical than my mechanic friend. It is just that they have applied their aural acuity more regularly to musical instruments rather than to car engines. The same could be said of health professionals who regularly use a stethoscope, or an ornithologist who can identify birds by their call or 'song'. The parents who vocally model and encourage their young child to mimic the sound of animals are indeed helping those children to develop musical skills. As Burke (2018, p. 1) states, 'All vocal communication is comprised of musical elements such as pitch, rhythm and timbre, demonstrating that musicality is an intrinsic part of being human.' It is this sound world that needs to be developed first. Odam (1995, p. 4) shares: 'Thinking in sound, imagining sound, constructing possible sounds in the head and improvising music all have to be established as skills before the symbols for these things are learned. When we eventually use the symbols we have already to know how they will sound.'

The second restraint is that it is commonly perceived that one has to be an accomplished singer or be able to play an instrument to be a music teacher. Consequently, the better one is at an instrument or voice, the more musical they must be. There *is* truth in that, but it does not automatically follow that those who do *not* currently play or sing lack musicality. Odam (1995, p. 5) describes this situation of such lack of confidence as a 'disincentive' to teach music and this issue still, naturally, exists for most people entering the profession. In one of my roles, therefore, as a music tutor for primary teacher trainees, I never model musical concepts using a piano, as this would simply serve to perpetuate this perception and further deepen the disincentive.

The third restraint exists for many, but, mercifully, not all. Regrettably, a number of people (you may even be one of them) have been told by friends and family that they *cannot* sing. Such statements are factually incorrect. What they *may* mean is that some voices are not to their preference, but so what! We are not designed to all sound alike. Such is the rich diversity of human vocal *timbres* where voices such as Bjork, Eartha Kitt, Shirley Bassey, Bryn Terfel, George Ezra are all not only acceptable, but actually celebrated. The issue should not be whether one *can* sing, but rather how well they can sing in tune with themselves and others; that issue is one of time and practice. But what happens when someone is insensitively told that they cannot sing? They stop. They no longer allow that innate sense of creative self to be explored, developed and heard by others. If that is you, may I simply say: 'I'm sorry'. *You were born to sing* so let no one stop you. A necessary step therefore in developing your singing will be to accept your own voice as is. If you like, find a patient teacher who can rebuild that lost confidence with you. Or join a community choir. Regain the full musical you. The main goal of primary music education is not to train the 30 children in the class to become opera singers, rock stars, professional choral scholars or concert pianists, but simply to encourage and allow children to find their *own* voice and to become more musical, on an instrument of their choice if they wish. This takes time, commitment, encouragement and regular opportunities. Space here does not permit a fuller exploration, but the above encouragements should be available to *all* children regardless of any perceived learning difference or physical disabilities. These issues are not barriers to musical learning (Music Mark, 2016).

The issue with all of these restraints is that they can so easily become internalised and believed; as I have stated, these internalisations are not based on fact. More accurately then, the person that states: 'Oh, I can't sing. I have an awful voice' is simply stating that they might have issues with accuracy of pitching the correct notes and have never been encouraged to develop any further. Tragically, it is not uncommon for the discouragement of being asked to mime to have come from a music teacher in one's past. My fervent plea to all teachers is to never tell anyone, *especially* a child, such nonsense. It is our privilege as teachers to help children develop their understanding of pitch, of dynamics, of timbres. To the child that struggles to stay in time with others, here's our opportunity to encourage their *development* of tempo and rhythm. For the child who struggles to temper their vocal volume to match that of the wider group, here is our clear opportunity to encourage *greater* exploration into dynamics. Changing our perceptions away from the notion that only some are musical and adopting an inclusive approach that offers opportunities for all to develop is crucial as a starting point to developing our subject knowledge. These developments and the practical progression enjoyed by children does not happen overnight. Such skills development requires huge amounts of practice time and regular attention. This is one reason why the carousel approach damages music education.

- To what extent do you recognise within yourself any reticence or lack of confidence which leads you to avoid wanting to teach music?

- Might it stem from your own school experiences?

- Have you considered discussing this with a school music lead or other music teacher for further support and guidance?

WHAT IS MUSIC AS A SUBJECT?

A wide range of perspectives must be narrowed in order to clarify the intentions of music education at primary level. I often start with the question 'What *is* music?' and it never fails to astonish how few people have ever considered the question! Does music warrant a scientific definition involving terminology around the physics of sound, sound creation and organisation? Or perhaps a more reactive, subjective approach around styles and different cultural ways of (and occasions for) music making? At a very practical level, do the printed dots and stems on the page (a system of writing down organised musical sounds that we refer to as notation) class as music, or does real music only exist when those intended sounds are performed and heard? What then of the songs and pieces that we recall only in our minds? Fundamentally, how do we collectively as educators agree what music is and where the curriculum focus should be with such a vastly creative, subjective, diversity of human expression?

These are complex questions into which Toyne (2021) (albeit referring mainly to the secondary phase) offers a succinct exploration; but as one looks at the varied curricula on offer for the UK's approach to music education, the main strands that make up this approach revolve around the abilities to perform music (through playing an instrument or singing), create music (through improvising ideas to methodically planning one's intent) and critically listen to and make judgements about music. The profession lists these *strands* as *performing, composing, listening* and *appraising* (hereinafter referred to simply as the strands), although the expectation is, especially as children progress through the year groups, that these strands are experienced and taught as integrated rather than separate disciplines. Note that I exclude here the function of background information relating to people and places and periods. These all have their place, but we shall see this information should support the strands and not replace them.

When we talk, then, of subject *development* in the teaching of music at primary level, we are not mainly talking about information about music history, composers, performers and other artists; instruments, orchestras, bands; individual pieces and songs. Rather, we are actively delving back into the skillsets that can help us become more musical. Similarly, we sometimes talk about classroom management, pedagogy and pupil engagement as though they are these insurmountable subject-specific issues for music. Certainly, yes, they present some challenges, but often these too are simply everyday skills and expectations being explored in a new context. Sitting down, sitting up straight, standing, smiling, frowning, making deliberately loud sounds, making deliberately quiet sounds – even listening – all are an adventure to be actively explored in ever-increasing levels of complexity. These are all musical skills, warranting regular practice. The ability to stand together, sit together, get louder or quieter together will all form part of the exploration and development of performance skills.

As previously stated, the ability to identify dozens of different instruments is not limited to those who are musical instrument experts. We all have (and regularly apply) these skills to the world around us. Applied to music, we rediscover these skills in the realm of timbres. This is what enables us to discern the sound of the dripping tap from the clock, or one person's voice from another. Again, these skills are innate – in varying degrees, musical. The real issue is whether we have re-gathered these seemingly disparate skills under this umbrella called *musicianship*.

At this stage, we can start to see that it is the *doing* music part that makes the difference. Reduced to mainly information, music as a subject comes with historical, biographical, geographical, cultural, theoretical and (to include an increasingly common threat) software/technical focus. My belief is that music (as a subject for both primary and secondary schools) should reside in the mainly practical aspects of the subject domain. Making music, listening to music, creating music, experimenting with music – all these activities help grow real, transferable musical learning. Then, we can deploy that learning across aspects involving software and significant technical tools with greater musical understanding. Developing subject knowledge should start with the doing. Stafford (2021) is highly reassuring in this aspect when she states, even while addressing music subject leads, 'All the knowledge and skills you need can be learned on the job!'

SO, WHAT IS THIS THING CALLED MUSICIANSHIP?

Consider for a moment your next dental visit. Will your confidence in the dentist lie in the fact that they have read a series of books on the subject of dentistry, or, rather, that they have had *extensive, regular practice*? Even better, then, when combined with the latest research theory? Similarly, we naively trust that, in addition to the mass of study, the airline pilot has undertaken a considerable amount of flying hours as part of the development process. We would not dream of entrusting ourselves to those who have just read the manual! Yet that manual might class as subject knowledge. Musicianship, as a word, defies strong definition, as the world of music is so vast. Some musicians might offer verbal definitions of musicianship as being or having a *skill* with a musical instrument or one's own voice; or a level of experience and proficiency in a particular musical field such as performing or composing. Hallam (2006) reports a similar difficulty in defining the word 'musicality'. However, it is much more encompassing than either of these. I therefore humbly offer a simplistic definition for our purposes here in that *musicianship is the cumulative and developing mix of musical skills and musical experiences that enables one to make appropriate musical choices or decisions for that moment. It is the confluence of both knowledge and practical skills.* I recognise that this too will be insufficient for other contexts, which may in turn offer additional or alternative understandings. As a result, musicianship can vary hugely in terms of natures and levels. Burke (2018, pp. 4–15) makes it clear that 'children develop at their own rates' and therefore these natures and levels of musical stimuli which children receive will have a direct impact on their development. Noteworthy here is that even in the Early Years context, Burke uses the title *musical development* as opposed to simply *music*.

The strands of performing, composing, listening and appraising, therefore, essentially provide both the arenas and continuity for the breadth of these natures and the depth of those levels, seeing children through to the end of the primary music phase (Year 6 in England and Wales, and Primary 7 (P7) in Scotland and Northern Ireland) and into the secondary school experience. But where does one go to discover what that combination should look and sound like? Herein lies the value of the wordings of the varied curricula. Although the English National Curriculum for Music (NCM) (DfE, 2013) does not refer explicitly to the word 'musicianship', its entire content serves as a fuller and more effective definition of what this concept of musicianship covers. Further, Ofsted's latest subject report for music states: 'Taught well, music gives children the opportunity to make music, think more musically and, crucially, become even more musical' (Ofsted, 2023).

This latter report does mention the word 'musicianship', but offers no succinct definition. What may clearly be inferred, however, is the focus on musical development – on children getting better at something. In this realm, the overarching purpose of a music curriculum is made clear. Children must be getting better within each of the strands. This is similarly highlighted by the curricula which use phrases such as *build on, improve, develop* (hwb.gov. Wales, 2008). The Northern Ireland Primary Curriculum repeatedly uses the terms 'develop' and 'increasingly' (CCEA, 2007, pp. 77–79). While, on paper, these points may be missed, Phillips made these emphases clear when personally addressing the Music and Drama Education Expo in 2021 (Phillips, 2021, 5m30–7m15). It is the *increase* in musical skills such as accuracy, 'fluency, control and expression' and an 'increasing aural memory' which demonstrates progression in musicianship and, despite other apparent differences in specifics across the curricula, the aspects of progression and development are shared.

WHY MAKE A DISTINCTION BETWEEN THE WORDS 'MUSIC' AND 'MUSICIANSHIP'?

Quite simply, I believe that we are less likely to drift into an over-focus on information, an over-reliance on technology and a poor balance between simply doing music regularly and actually learning and progressing. By constantly challenging the expectations of what content should be taught, we can better start to understand both the *what **and** the *how* for music education. A school may perceive that it is satisfying the aims of the music curricula and that regular concerts and the existence of ensembles and performance opportunities surely evidence this. However, is that focus on the increase in skills – the increase in fluency and accuracy? These increases in musical progression must be planned systematically across all the elements of music for the success of the school's published intent for music education to be realised fully. Therefore, if any music educator provides regular concerts (and other performing opportunities), these must show increased proficiency in dynamics, pitching and expressive control, whatever has been the focus of learning objectives. It is possible to do more and more of the same and never get better. In doing so, we are merely increasing repertoire. There *is* still a merit in this. But by deliberately seeking music with a slightly higher level of challenge we make our curriculum intent specific. Will the next song require an increase in the challenge of dynamic control, or clearer diction? Will that next piece demand a slightly more sophisticated understanding of expression or tempo? By looking at the actual skillsets required to perform, compose, listen and appraise better, these give us an indication as to how to word our learning objectives and focus our attention on the choice of warm-up activities suitable for that particular scheme of work. The resultant growth in musicianship should become increasingly evident.

THREATS TO MUSICIANSHIP: FOCUSING ON FACTS/FOCUSING ON TECHNOLOGY

An overly generalist approach to teacher training and schools adopting a generalist approach to their classroom teachers' pedagogies might both be counter-productive. With the cohorts I meet during teacher training, I have opportunities to 'teach' them information about music. In that space, I could cover lots of theory about music notation, the building blocks of composing, melody writing, accompaniment, harmony and so on. I could check their understanding with written tests to see what and how much they have remembered. I could even suggest 'best' resources to use. Such an approach could be assessed by students' proof of memory of facts. However, in *only* doing so, I would have squandered my opportunity to let them experience, explore, make creative choices, compose and perform; I would have robbed them of the opportunity to listen to each other's compositions and to offer constructive, musical feedback on those compositions (and, in turn, the very performances of those compositions). Fundamentally, I would not have modelled to them how they, in turn, can encourage their young children to experience and explore, and I would have missed the opportunity to develop their own musicianship.

It is possible for such threat to come also from school policies. Those that suggest a whole-school approach to lesson delivery, often involving recall and writing of facts, actually hamper the music-specific pedagogies and benefits of a good-quality music education.

Another threat to this developing nature of musicianship lies in when and how we employ the rich provisions of technology. This is a vast and rapidly developing issue, so let me offer just a couple of examples and leave you to consider how you apply this to your own teaching and in your own settings. Digital tuners have existed for a long time; in order to tune a guitar or a ukulele or some other, mainly electric instrument, one can turn on the tuner and the dial or the colours will indicate whether that particular string is 'in tune'. These are great devices! However, the human skill and opportunity is circumvented if the need to develop one's own listening skills has been ignored. Indeed, in some instances, the tuners can be plugged directly to the instrument, and one simply adjusts the strings and waits for the green light! Yes, it may take a few seconds longer to use our ears, but, over time, one gets better at it. Therein lies the *increasing* aural capability.

I recently watched a school colleague as we worked together to tune a class set of ukuleles. No electronic tuner in sight – and she was slick! Why? Excellent aural acuity, the result of regular practice and experience. It would clearly have taken more time to employ an additional device. There is a world of difference between learning musicianship and learning how to use technology.

Similarly, the most recent advances in digital apps enable children to teach themselves how to play instruments. Essentially the apps take the place of a teacher, offering options for increased difficulties over time. Surely this would be a good thing, freeing up teacher time when used in a classroom situation. Caution must be exercised, however, as if the human teacher is not involved in the process, potential misconceptions, errors of technique and the loss of humanity in a performance (expression is often evidenced by subtle nuances in speed and volume that cannot be picked up or appreciated by such apps). The burgeoning rise of the use of artificial intelligence (AI) software will make these discussions more challenging, but I maintain that you, the teacher, are the critical musical resource. It is in this realm of *human* creativity and exploration that all the basic elements of music now have more space to make sense.

REFLECTION 15.2

- If using music apps to support individual children's progress, to what extent might you be diverting time *away* from their *musical* understanding in preference to them learning how to use the apps?

CHALLENGES WITH MUSICAL SKILLS DEVELOPMENT

Developing musical skills in schools requires both a regularity of practice and a supportive curriculum. Coupled with a range of extra-curricular activities and opportunities to regularly perform, the breadth of musicianship can stem from the richly nourished soil of the school's individual support for the arts. A carousel or other intermittent timetabling system puts gaps in both learning opportunities and the flow of musical progression that makes recovery hard. Rather, regular music teaching has the capacity to support both literacy and numeracy. The damage done by the irregular timetabling of music cannot be easily undone and such repair takes time. The Covid-19 pandemic, for example, impacted our musical educational systems in ways from which we are still recovering, and its effect has continued to be felt into the quality of musicianship even at university levels. But this is not to say that these events and situations are insurmountable. We start from where we are and hit the challenges head on. It starts with us as individuals.

DEVELOPING YOUR OWN SUBJECT KNOWLEDGE

In the light of everything I have mentioned above, just try things out! Be curious. Remember that musical learning is best situated in the doing and in the exploration. What we want children to learn in a single session or over time should be clearly worded in objectives. Musical progression occurs when we make it our intent to get better over time and focus our classroom activities so that children increase their skills with greater and greater understanding.

REFLECTION 15.3

- To what extent have you undertaken some of the tasks which you are asking children to engage in? This is especially relevant when using bought packages to which schools and individual educators may have signed up.

- How might you develop your musicianship by making more selective pedagogical or content decisions?

Yes, we do have to know about pitch, dynamics, duration, tempo, structure, etc. How these interact and combine to make up our more developed musical concepts (interrelated dimensions) enables us then to explore things like rhythm, style and mood. It's all about exploration so that children can develop their own musical associations before we impose a strict terminology upon them. Here, the maxim *sound before symbol* is fundamental. Let children hear, create, perform, experiment. In this environment, there is much less of a need to worry about teachers not feeling able to manage noise in the music classroom. Indeed, we need to encourage more noise at the outset. Herein lies the more conscious start of our musical experiential learning, especially in dynamics! The theory, history and other subject information will make more sense when the main focus is on increasing the quality of these practical experiences. Regular and progressive warm-up activities are essential in this process.

WHAT COUNTS AS 'SUBJECT KNOWLEDGE' AS FAR AS IT APPLIES TO PRIMARY MUSIC?

It is commonplace for many subjects' schemes of work to be themed. This approach can be popular, effective and requires no further justification here. However, if we build music schemes with similar parameters and approach, one can again unwittingly reduce the music curriculum to factual information. Whether those facts are theoretical, historical and/or biographical is not an issue in its own right. Each has their place in offering background contexts and bigger pictures into which such knowledge may be acquired and built upon at a later date. What the approach cannot do is build real musical skills.

Such a question is difficult to address in any generic sense as each school brings their different mix of physical and human resources, demographic and musical legacy from previous cohorts and staffing. What each school has in common is the availability of children's own voices; therefore using the voice to develop fundamental understanding of musical skills is vital and central to every primary (and, indeed, secondary) curriculum. Here, the national curricula find agreement in the use of voice to develop musicianship. Each curriculum within the UK fundamentally focuses on musical skills across the strands and then, in supportive capacity, a developing understanding of some theoretical and historical facts.

THE TENSIONS BETWEEN INFORMATION AND SKILLS

If the areas of learning across the strands can only (and best) be achieved by the doing, then singing songs, playing pieces, using instruments and developing voices is what needs to happen, and regularly. But these activities in and of themselves are insufficient for skills building without specific, progressive learning objectives in place. Among other findings, Ofsted's 2012 report stated: 'Too much music teaching continued to be dominated by the spoken or written word, rather than by musical sounds. Lessons were planned diligently, but not always prepared for musically.' If children have successfully memorised the lyrics and the melody, this might merely be an outcome of a few weeks' rehearsals. The learning objectives must incorporate *increasing* layers of complexity. Similarly, and perhaps counter-intuitively, published schemes of work may appear to offer the required subject knowledge to deliver good and appropriate music lessons for children; however, the publishers of schemes are not there with your children in the classroom. You are the one who observes how children work on a task and you are the one who listens to them while they perform and compose. The bought packages cannot know the pupil who has just made an oblique response to a question, but, because you know the pupil, you understand why they have made such an association and offer individualised, encouraging feedback. Published or bought packages can only provide additional support; the best musical resources in your classroom are you and your children. I regularly say to my trainees at the end of the course: 'I expect you to trust your own developing musicianship and your knowledge of your classes to help you discern when or whether you should use a bought scheme or package. Certainly, do not be afraid to adapt them.' In terms of core music theory, again, this needs to be in the context of real, practical musical exploration.

REFLECTION 15.4

- Evaluate where your current (perhaps hitherto unquestioned) balance lies between your subject knowledge of music and your own musicianship.

- To what extent have you considered that your own engagement, enjoyment and subject development might be enhanced by interacting with children in their curious, creative moment?

TIPS FOR DEVELOPING SUBJECT KNOWLEDGE IN MUSIC

- Start from where you are, with no self-judgement.

- *Actively* listen more to the music you hear. Whatever you have on your usual playlist, regularly pick out a couple of pieces and deliberately think about what you are hearing. You might even go so far as to write it down, using terminology of basic music elements!

- Rediscover your creative curiosity: choose just one phrase of a piece you like and try and work it out on a piano, or guitar, or a ukulele, or a recorder ... whatever is to hand at school. If you can sing it, you're already halfway there!

- If you have never done so, simply go and observe part of a session taken by the music lead and join in as if you were a pupil!

- Develop your repertoire of vocal and rhythmic warm-ups. These are best learned by doing and there is no harm in learning from colleagues or finding some online. However, the most appropriate warm-ups are those that feed directly into the learning objective for that session, that module, that upcoming performance. If we want to teach children to sing clearly, we must use regular and progressive warm-ups that focus on diction. Similarly, if we want children over time to develop their range of vocal timbres, then encourage them to sing simple phrases, but pretending to be someone who is really overjoyed, or quite sad, or like a mouse, or Pavorotti! Ditch any concept of a 'rule' book. Make up your own metaphors or, better still, invite children to offer their own suggestions which, if appropriate, you can then enter into the ongoing canon of your own repertoire. The broader and more adventurous these warm-up games, the greater the level of understanding and skill when we later ask and encourage children to sing with expression.

- Set yourself a goal. This will help by enabling you to put yourself in children's shoes and help to set more realistic (or, indeed, more adventurous) learning objectives. *There is no obligation to do so, but if as you continue your own exploration, you find yourself being inspired to learn an instrument formally, then let nothing stop you. If you wish to sit a music theory or instrumental exam, far be it from me to dissuade you. Go for it!*

FINAL THOUGHTS

The mix of information and skillsets must be carefully curated by schoolteachers, home educators and other providers to give children transferable skills into higher and broader levels of musical understanding.

Developing pupil musicianship as an overarching aim helps to decide the key objectives for schemes of work and, in the day-to-day aspects, the learning objectives for every music session. Subject knowledge is one crucial aspect to these outcomes, but the best impact is found in the resultant musicianship of children, making small regular adjustments for great gains in progression.

Let us stop assuming that we all share common definitions for the term 'music' as a subject. It is too easily delivered as information. Perhaps a braver move would be to establish *musicianship* as our subject name throughout primary and secondary school phases, putting the growth of those musicianship skills front and centre of our curricula, where the very necessary background information can truly support rather than supplant.

Let us not overlook the simple skills. Practise regularly getting children to stand, sit, smile, not smile, breathe together. These skills, well developed and rehearsed, pay dividends when coordinating concerts and massed pupil involvement.

Let us not be afraid to learn from our children, who often have the curiosity to make and verbalise musical associations that display their own innate sense of musicianship.

Let us make the most of our opportunities to develop these musicianship skills in each of the strands. Vocal, clapping and other rhythmic warm-ups can be regular features which provide tools not only for longer-term musical development, but also for fun and engaging ways to promote positive musical classroom management. Where a carousel timetable is unavoidable, these short warm-ups help provide the continuity required to mitigate loss of musical progression.

FURTHER READING

Herein lies an irony: yes, having engaged with this chapter and by exploring some of the following you will gain a deepening academic insight into the backdrop against which we strive to deliver a truly musical curriculum, but it cannot stop with just the reading! The real adventure lies in the doing, so get out there and make more music with your children, all the while becoming even more musical yourself! Then read the national curriculum for music in the light of your own context.

Local music hubs. DS Music endeavour to keep a four-nation list of hubs updated. www.dsmusic.com/blogs/music-services-in-the-uk

Explore the practical support (e.g. group events, webinars, performing opportunities and instrument loan schemes) offered by your local music hub.

Audain, J., Lloyd, S. and Mead, H. (2023). Music. In N. Majid (Ed.), *Essential subject knowledge for primary teaching* (pp. 169–199). Learning Matters.

Their chapter offers a comprehensive look at background information and terminology.

Berryman, S. (2018). Knowledgeable skills or skilful knowledge? *Impact Magazine, Issue 4: Designing a Curriculum.* Chartered College of Teaching. https://my.chartered.college/impact_article/knowledgeable-skills-or-skilful-knowledge/

An article that explores the knowledge vs skills debate in curriculum design, questioning the emphasis placed on each and arguing for a deeper understanding of their relationship in effective teaching.

Daubney, A. and Fautley, M. (2025). *A framework for curriculum, pedagogy and assessment in primary school music.* ISM Trust. www.ism.org/wp-content/uploads/2025/01/ISM_Curriculum-for-Music-booklet_Primary_Digital.pdf

A proposed framework that offers a structured approach to defining the curriculum, teaching methods (pedagogy), and evaluation (assessment) specifically for primary school music.

Phillips, M. (2021). *The substance of music education: Music and Drama Education Expo.* YouTube. www.youtube.com/watch?v=wUWhqAn9yNY

A video presentation that discusses the core of music education.

REFERENCES

Audain, J., Lloyd, S. and Mead, H. (2023). Music. In N. Majid (Ed.), *Essential subject knowledge for primary teaching* (pp. 169–199). Learning Matters.

Berryman, S. (2018). Knowledgeable skills or skilful knowledge? *Impact Magazine, Issue 4: Designing a Curriculum.* Chartered College of Teaching. https://my.chartered.college/impact_article/knowledgeable-skills-or-skilful-knowledge/

Burke, N. (2018). *Musical development matters in the early years.* British Association for Early Childhood Education. https://early-education.org.uk/wp-content/uploads/2021/12/Musical-Development-Matters-ONLINE.pdf

Daubney, A. and Fautley, M. (2025). *A framework for curriculum, pedagogy and assessment in primary school music.* ISM Trust. www.ism.org/wp-content/uploads/2025/01/ISM_Curriculum-for-Music-booklet_Primary_Digital.pdf

Department for Education (DfE). (2013). *National curriculum for music: Music programmes of study: Key stages 1 and 2.* https://assets.publishing.service.gov.uk/media/5a7b7f8c40f0b645ba3c4b8a/PRIMARY_national_curriculum_-_Music.pdf

DfE. (2022). *The power of music to change lives: The new national plan for music education.* https://assets.publishing.service.gov.uk/government/uploads/system/uploads/attachment_data/file/1086619/The_Power_of_Music_to_Change_Lives.pdf

Education Scotland. (2017). *Benchmarks: Expressive arts*. https://education.gov.scot/media/mvddi43h/expressiveartsbenchmarkspdf.pdf

gov.Wales. (2022). *National plan for music education*. www.gov.wales/sites/default/files/publications/2022-05/national-plan-for-music-education.pdf

Hallam, S. (2006). Musicality. In G. McPherson (Ed.), *The child as musician*. Oxford University Press.

hwb.gov.Wales. (2008). *Music in the national curriculum for Wales*. Welsh Assembly Government. https://hwb.gov.wales/api/storage/558982ea-193c-4e72-9830-f51ad8230450/music-in-the-national-curriculum.pdf

Music Mark. (2016). *Ten things schools should know about music*. www.musicmark.org.uk/wp-content/uploads/10_things_booklet.pdf?x75066

Northern Ireland Curriculum for Primary (CCEA). (2007). *Music*. https://ccea.org.uk/key-stages-1-2/curriculum/arts/music

Odam, G. (1995). *The sounding symbol*. Nelson Thorne.

Ofsted. (2012). *Music in schools: Promoting good practice*. https://dera.ioe.ac.uk/id/eprint/16037/1/Music%20professional%20development%20materials.pdf

Ofsted. (2023). *Research review: Music subject report: Striking the right note*. www.gov.uk/government/publications/subject-report-series-music/striking-the-right-note-the-music-subject-report

Phillips, M. (2021). *The substance of music education: Music and Drama Education Expo*. YouTube. www.youtube.com/watch?v=wUWhqAn9yNY

Stafford, E. (n.d.). Curriculum for Wales: An innovation in music education. https://musiceducationsolutions.co.uk/news/curriculum-for-wales-an-innovation-in-music-education/

Stafford, E. (2021). *Primary music leader's handbook: Inspiring ideas*. Collins.

Toyne, S. (2021). Music. In A. S. Cuthbert and A. Standish (Eds.), *What should schools teach? Disciplines, subject and the pursuit of truth* (2nd ed., pp. 103–121). UCL Press.

16
PHYSICAL EDUCATION

JORDAN WINTLE

┌─ **THIS CHAPTER** ───

This chapter explores the ideas that:

- a physical literacy approach can make physical education a meaningful, inclusive and integral part of every child's education

- meaningful experiences and the development of fundamental movement skills are central to designing engaging and developmentally appropriate lessons

- a high-quality physical education curriculum, supported by clear progression and purposeful assessment, helps ensure all pupils build confidence, competence and enjoyment in movement.

┌─ **KEY TERMS FOR THIS CHAPTER** ───────────────────────────

Fundamental movement skills: basic movements like running, jumping, throwing and catching that form the foundation for more complex physical activities.

Motor competence: a person's ability to perform a wide range of movements with control and coordination.

Physical literacy: the motivation, confidence, physical competence, knowledge and understanding to value and take part in physical activity for life.

Meaningful Physical Education: an approach to physical education that prioritises experiences pupils find personally relevant, enjoyable and valuable, often focusing on features like fun, challenge and social connection.

INTRODUCTION

Physical education (PE) in the primary years occupies a unique and powerful position within the curriculum. Far more than a vehicle for physical activity alone, it offers rich opportunities to nurture the holistic development of every child, supporting physical competence, social connectedness, emotional wellbeing and cognitive growth. In this chapter, I explore how you can implement a high-quality, inclusive PE curriculum underpinned by the principles of physical literacy and meaningful experiences. I draw on current research, policy and pedagogy to show what children should learn, how they might learn it and how you can be supported to deliver PE with confidence, creativity and care. Together, we position PE as an essential contributor to lifelong health, positive identity formation and educational equity.

THE PURPOSE AND VALUE OF PHYSICAL EDUCATION IN THE PRIMARY YEARS

PE in the primary years holds a distinctive and essential place within a broad and balanced curriculum. Far more than a break from academic learning, primary PE provides opportunities for holistic development – physically, socially, emotionally and cognitively. When planned and delivered effectively, it becomes a powerful form of *education through movement*, enabling children to learn about themselves and the world in active, embodied ways (Pickup and Randall, 2022).

Physically, PE supports the development of *fundamental movement skills* (FMS), *motor competence*, coordination and physical confidence – key building blocks for participation in a broad range of activities, including active recreation, daily physical activity and various sports (Salters and Benson, 2025). Cognitively, children engage with problem-solving, tactics, sequencing and spatial awareness. Social and emotional learning is also central, as children collaborate with peers, learn to manage their emotions, experience challenges and successes and develop resilience (Wright et al., 2021). As such, PE contributes to children's identity, self-esteem and sense of belonging within the school environment (Bailey et al., 2009).

Enjoyment in PE matters, too. Many young children express a love for physical activity and movement-based learning (Domville et al., 2019). When PE lessons are meaningful and inclusive, they can create positive associations that last a lifetime. These experiences help form the basis for long-term engagement in physical activity, promoting healthy lifestyles and supporting mental and emotional wellbeing (Doherty and Brennan, 2014; Wintle, 2022). Conversely, poorly delivered or exclusionary experiences in PE can have enduring negative consequences. Research by Ladwig and colleagues (2018) revealed that childhood memories of embarrassment, marginalisation and punitive environments within PE are significantly associated with less favourable attitudes, lower intentions to engage in physical activity and increased sedentary time in adulthood. Their study indicates that the best PE memories – characterised by enjoyment, physical competence and supportive social interactions – positively correlate with adult activity. In contrast, the worst memories, including being picked last, feeling embarrassed, or experiencing anxiety, have the opposite effect (Ladwig et al., 2018).

In recognition of its significance, PE holds statutory status in the curricula of many nations. In England, for example, PE is a foundation subject within the National Curriculum, with aims including competence in movement, sustained physical activity and understanding the benefits of a healthy lifestyle (DfE, 2013). However, despite this formal positioning, PE often struggles for time, recognition and teacher confidence. Research highlights common challenges, including inconsistent delivery, lack of training in initial teacher education and the outsourcing of PE to external coaches (Griggs and Petrie, 2018).

I begin this chapter with a call to elevate the status of PE in primary education, not simply as sport or fitness, but as a unique and vital site for learning. I invite you to see PE as integral to the development of the whole child, offering opportunities to learn in, about and through movement. With the right approach, you can make PE a joyful, inclusive and purposeful part of every child's school experience, and a springboard for lifelong engagement in physical activity.

UNDERSTANDING PHYSICAL LITERACY AS A FOUNDATION FOR PHYSICAL EDUCATION

A growing body of research and curriculum guidance positions *physical literacy* as a foundational concept for PE, particularly in the primary years. Rather than viewing PE as a narrow focus on fitness or sports technique, the concept of physical literacy invites us to consider the broader, more human question: *what does it mean to be physically educated, confident and motivated to move for life?*

According to Margaret Whitehead, who introduced and developed the concept, physical literacy is 'the motivation, confidence, physical competence, knowledge and understanding to value and take responsibility for engagement in physical activities for life' (Whitehead, 2010, p. 11). This widely adopted definition acknowledges that physical literacy is not a fixed achievement, but a *lifelong journey* – one that evolves in response to context, opportunity and individual experience. In this way, physical literacy aligns closely with holistic education, recognising the role of the body in learning and the importance of meaningful, developmentally appropriate physical experiences. Physical literacy aligns closely with the goals of primary PE because both are concerned with the holistic development of the child – physically, cognitively, socially and emotionally. Positioning physical literacy as a vision for PE is important because it shifts the focus from short-term performance outcomes or sport-specific skills towards long-term engagement, wellbeing and personal growth. This perspective encourages educators to view PE not merely as preparation for competitive sport, but as a means of nurturing flourishing, embodied individuals (Durden-Myers et al., 2018).

At the heart of physical literacy are three core principles (Whitehead, 2021):

* respect for the holistic individual: educators should acknowledge and respond to each child as a whole person, recognising the interconnected nature of their physical, psychological and emotional development. This requires an inclusive outlook

that values diversity and ensures learning experiences are accessible and meaningful for all children, regardless of ability or background. Going beyond a focus on physical performance, educators should foster environments characterised by empathy, encouragement, humility and recognition of effort as well as achievement;

- *importance of varied movement experiences*: PE should offer students experiences across a range of movement forms, including adventure, aesthetic, competitive, fitness/health and relational activities. This emphasises the importance of broadening young people's movement experiences to lay the foundations for lifelong participation. It acknowledges that PE's historical narrow focus on competitive sports may not cater to all students and suggests that curricula should allow students to explore various forms of movement;

- *engagement with each and every child*: this principle highlights the importance of actively engaging with each pupil as a unique individual, aligning with inclusive pedagogical approaches and the foundations of physical literacy. It involves recognising and responding to children's varied experiences, valuing their efforts not just outcomes and adaptive teaching to ensure that all children are appropriately challenged and supported.

These principles speak directly to the aims of primary PE: to nurture well-rounded individuals who feel capable, included and inspired to move – now and into the future. As such, physical literacy is not a 'bolt-on' concept, but a powerful educational framework that underpins the curriculum, pedagogy and assessment in PE.

In the primary years, physical literacy should be recognised as a fundamental right and entitlement for every child. While the development of movement competence is essential, it must be accompanied by the intentional cultivation of positive dispositions such as joy, curiosity, persistence and self-belief. As Pickup and Randall (2022) note, 'the teaching and development of fundamental movement skills (the physical domain) should not be taught in isolation of the child's cognitive, affective or psychosocial understanding' (p. 21). When PE neglects these broader dimensions – leaving children feeling excluded, unsuccessful, or disconnected – it can diminish their sense of agency and intrinsic motivation. In turn, this risks weakening the foundations for lifelong engagement in physical activity, health and wellbeing.

Physical literacy provides a suitable vision to develop *inclusive, child-centred practice* in PE. From this perspective, the goal is not to prepare children for elite performance or rigid skill mastery, but to create opportunities for all learners to find success, meaning and enjoyment in movement (Lundvall, 2015). Importantly, this approach recognises and values diversity: every child's physical literacy journey is unique, shaped by their background, culture, abilities and prior experiences.

Physical literacy also provides a strong foundation for promoting inclusion and social justice. Children from different socioeconomic, cultural, or ability backgrounds may have unequal access to community sports, playgrounds, or positive role models. For many children, PE may be the only structured opportunity to explore physical activity in a safe and supportive way. Viewing PE through the lens of physical literacy reinforces the idea that every child *can* be a confident mover – and that it is the educator's role to nurture that potential, not to act as a gatekeeper.

Ultimately, physical literacy reminds us that movement matters, not just for physical health, but for identity, wellbeing, learning and life. In the primary years, educators have a unique opportunity to lay the foundations for this journey. By embracing physical literacy as a guiding principle, we can create a curriculum that supports the whole child, one that moves beyond narrow notions of performance or sport, and towards lifelong, joyful engagement with movement.

In summary, a physical literacy-informed approach encourages educators to:

- provide varied, developmentally appropriate opportunities for movement;
- celebrate effort, progress and creativity as much as outcomes;
- encourage children to reflect on their feelings, preferences and goals;
- ensure that learning environments are inclusive, supportive and challenging;
- connect movement experiences to children's lives beyond the school gates.

REFLECTION 16.1

- Reflecting on your own experiences of PE, how have these influenced your views on what makes movement meaningful and enjoyable?
- How could adopting a physical literacy-informed approach in primary PE support every child to feel confident, competent and motivated to move?

CORE ACTIVITY AREAS: DEVELOPING FUNDAMENTAL MOVEMENT SKILLS AND MOTOR COMPETENCE

Primary PE plays a critical role in developing children's *fundamental movement skills* (FMS), which include locomotor (e.g. running, hopping), stability (e.g. balancing, twisting) and object control (e.g. throwing, catching) abilities. These foundational skills underpin confident participation in a wide range of physical activities and sports, supporting the development of motor competence – a key driver of lifelong physical activity and motivation (Goodway et al., 2019). Sadly, there is growing global concern over declining levels of motor competence in children (O'Brien et al., 2016). Fewer than half demonstrate mastery in fundamental loco-motor and object-control skills, and just 11 per cent of 12- to 13-year-olds achieve advanced levels of proficiency. A more recent systematic review, encompassing 60 studies and data from over 21,000 children aged three to ten across 25 countries, reported that only 57–64 per cent of children demonstrated average proficiency in locomotor skills. Object-control skills showed slightly wider variability, with 51–69 per cent achieving average levels. When consid-ering overall FMS competence, the proportion of children meeting average proficiency ranged from just 34 per cent to 49 per cent (Bolger et al., 2021).

FMS do not always emerge naturally; structured, meaningful opportunities are needed to practise and apply them in diverse contexts. Within primary PE, a well-rounded cur-riculum should provide opportunities to develop these skills. In the early primary years, a well-designed curriculum should expose children to a range of FMS. A good example of a programme that supports FMS and is aligned to physical literacy is the Boing project (Roberts et al., 2019). The Boing programme aims to foster both a love of movement and the development of FMS in primary PE. It consists of play-based mini-games and activities that are fun, inclusive, age-appropriate and easy to set up, making them highly accessible for non-specialist teachers. This move away from traditional sports, or even mini versions of those, allows children to develop their FMS before being exposed to highly competitive environments that can leave some children feeling excluded.

As children progress through primary education, the curriculum content should encompass a broad range of activities from different activity areas, outlined below. Importantly, these activities should be adapted to be age-appropriate; this may involve working in smaller groups/teams, using modified equipment and utilising adapted spaces.

- *Games*: provides a dynamic environment for practising object-control and locomotor skills. Simplified, inclusive formats promote sending, receiving, travelling with equip-ment, teamwork and tactical awareness. Emphasis on purposeful play over technical perfection enhances success for all (e.g. football, rounders, tennis).

- *Dance*: encourages self-expression through movement. Develops creativity, rhythm, control, stability and locomotor skills. Strong potential for cross-curricular links and thematic learning (see Chapter 8).

- *Gymnastics*: emphasises control, balance, strength and sequencing. Activities like roll-ing, jumping and climbing support core stability, confidence and personal challenge.

- *Athletics*: focuses on running, jumping and throwing with a *personal best* ethos. Promotes goal-setting, persistence, technical understanding and self-improvement through measurement and reflection.

- *Outdoor and adventurous activities*: develops communication, teamwork and problem-solving. Tasks such as orienteering or group challenges build resilience, trust and social-cognitive skills.

- *Swimming and water safety*: builds aquatic competence and water confidence. Teaches survival skills and fulfils statutory requirements in many countries. A vital component for life safety and physical literacy.

A high-quality primary PE curriculum must strike a careful balance between breadth and depth. On the one hand, children must be exposed to a wide range of activity types, allowing them to experience diverse movement contexts and form preferences and positive associations with physical activity. However, breadth alone is insufficient. Without sufficient depth, children may encounter only surface-level experiences, which do not allow for meaningful skill development, confidence-building, or an understanding of the activity. Recent recommendations suggest ten lessons strike the right balance in this area (Whitehead, 2021); therefore, educators should look to plan exposure to different types of activities both within and across year groups.

TEACHING FOR MEANING: PEDAGOGICAL APPROACHES

For primary PE to be fully effective, creating meaningful and relevant experiences is critical. Beni et al. (2017) and Fletcher et al. (2021) emphasise that for learning to be meaningful, it must connect with children's values and interests. Children should be able to see purpose in what they are doing – whether that is expressing themselves through dance, working together to solve a problem, or achieving a personal best in running or jumping. Physical literacy flourishes when children are given an opportunity to see value in their experiences, which allows them to see them as personally significant.

An increasing number of researchers and practitioners argue that the true value of PE education lies not only in *what* we teach, but also in *how* and *why* (Beni et al., 2021; Wintle, 2022). The *Meaningful Physical Education* (MPE) approach offers a pedagogical framework that prioritises children's lived experiences in PE, placing value on connection, engagement and purpose. In doing so, it helps ensure that PE is not just enjoyable in the moment, but impactful and memorable over time (Fletcher et al., 2021).

MPE is rooted in the idea that movement becomes meaningful when it connects to children's lives, values and goals. Drawing from a large body of youth voice research, Beni et al. (2017) identified six features commonly associated with meaningful experiences in PE:

- *fun*: enjoyment and positive emotion;

- *social interaction*: collaboration, belonging, peer relationships;

- *challenge*: achievable but demanding tasks;

- *motor competence*: opportunities to improve skills and confidence;

- *personal relevance*: connecting to children's interests and lives;

- *delight*: moments of personal satisfaction or transcendence.

These features are not a checklist, but rather interrelated qualities that should guide curriculum planning, task design and reflection. For example, a gymnastics unit might emphasise challenge and delight through sequences that allow children to showcase creativity and progress. In games, personal relevance and social interaction could be foregrounded through cooperative formats or by choosing team roles.

A core principle of MPE is the promotion of choice and voice. Giving children agency – through selecting activities, equipment, or roles – builds ownership and engagement. This might involve children choosing between a set of challenges in an *outdoor and adventurous activities* (OAA) session or co-developing a warm-up routine in dance. Cardiff et al. (2024) emphasise the importance of educators making *space* for children's meaning-making, where children are not just performers, but co-constructors of learning.

Goal-setting is a core pedagogical strategy within the MPE framework, supporting the development of autonomy, motivation and personal relevance. Encouraging learners to create their own goals (or to select from a range of educator-provided options) allows for personalisation of the learning experience while still providing appropriate structure and support. This fosters a sense of ownership and ensures that goals are meaningful and attainable for each learner. Rather than centring on external outcomes such as winning or comparison with peers, this approach highlights effort, progress and self-improvement. It aligns with a mastery-oriented climate (valuing individual progress over peer comparison) and contributes to the development of reflective, confident learners who are more likely to maintain a positive relationship with physical activity throughout life.

Reflection is another key strategy in meaningful PE. Educators can use questions like 'What was challenging today?', 'What did you enjoy?' or 'How did you feel about that activity?' to prompt children to connect emotion and understanding. These reflections support metacognition and help children recognise their own growth, supporting both motivation and physical literacy (Whitehead, 2010).

Across all activity areas, MPE can be applied flexibly. In athletics, children might set personal goals and track progress, experiencing fun and challenge through improvement. In dance, they might create a routine that tells a personal story – connecting to identity and self-expression. In games, educators can adapt rules to encourage inclusion and creativity, fostering social interaction and confidence. In OAA, meaningfulness can emerge from trust-building or solving a team puzzle under time pressure.

However, making PE meaningful does not mean abandoning structure or progression. Rather, it involves designing lessons that are developmentally appropriate, inclusive and emotionally resonant. Fletcher et al. (2021) encourage educators to think of MPE as a 'lens' through which all content is taught, not a bolt-on or a separate programme. MPE also aligns with broader educational goals around pupil voice, wellbeing and holistic development.

Specifically, within primary settings, Cardiff et al. (2024) have contributed important insights by highlighting how meaningful PE pedagogy supports inclusion, voice and autonomy. Their work with primary teachers demonstrates that small pedagogical shifts, such as co-creating success criteria, offering task choices, or reflecting on what made a lesson meaningful, can transform engagement. Importantly, Cardiff et al. note that meaningful PE does not require a complete curriculum overhaul, but rather a shift in intentionality: designing lessons with the child's experience at the centre.

Implementing this approach requires educators to be reflective and flexible. Cardiff's work highlights common challenges, such as time pressures, varying pupil needs, or lack of confidence in giving autonomy, but also shows that teachers and other educators are well-positioned to embed MPE gradually. Even small shifts in language ('What do you think we should do next?'), structure (learner-led warm-ups), or assessment (reflective journals) can make a powerful difference.

Importantly, MPE is not just about what children remember, but what they take with them: confidence, motivation and a belief that movement can add value to their lives. In an era where physical inactivity and inequality are growing concerns, MPE provides a practical and principled approach to making PE more relevant, inclusive and impactful.

REFLECTION 16.2

- In what ways could prioritising fundamental movement skills over sport-specific skills shape more inclusive and positive PE experiences for pupils?

- Reflect on a time when physical activity felt personally meaningful to you – what features contributed to that sense of meaning and how might similar experiences be created for your pupils?

INCLUSION AND EQUITY IN PHYSICAL EDUCATION

A truly effective primary PE curriculum must be inclusive and equitable, ensuring that all children, regardless of ability, background, or identity, can engage meaningfully with physical activity. While inclusion is often referenced in policy and practice, it is not simply about access or participation; rather, it concerns whether children feel they belong, are valued and are afforded the opportunity to experience success (Stidder and Hayes, 2012). Increasingly, PE is being recognised as a critical space for advancing social justice, particularly in response to the structural inequalities that shape children's experiences both within and beyond the school environment.

Drawing on the work of Lynch et al. (2022), a *socially just* approach to PE is one that actively seeks to challenge systems of oppression, including ableism, racism, sexism and classism. This requires educators to engage in critical reflection about their assumptions and the normative practices embedded in curriculum design and delivery. Rather than adopting a deficit model that sees difference as a challenge to be managed, inclusive PE instead positions diversity as a strength and aims to create learning environments where all children can thrive.

One of the central strategies for achieving this is through the deliberate cultivation of a mastery climate (aligned with physical literacy and MPE) – an approach that values effort, improvement and personal growth over competition and comparison (Newton, 2022). This climate can be fostered through flexible lesson structures (with elements of choice and varying levels of challenge), differentiated outcomes and sensitive use of language. For example, praising persistence and creativity in movement, rather than just technical precision, helps create a safe environment for learners of all abilities. Newton's work on inclusion for children with *special educational needs and disabilities* (SEND) underscores the importance of meticulous planning, the use of visual prompts and consistent routines that facilitate participation without compromising challenge or dignity. In this sense, inclusion is not an 'add-on', but an embedded pedagogical stance.

Inclusive practice also involves being attuned to the intersectional identities of learners. Multiple, overlapping factors, including gender, ethnicity, socioeconomic status and physical ability, shape children's experiences of PE. A one-size-fits-all model not only risks alienating many learners, but also reinforces dominant cultural narratives that privilege certain forms of physicality. As Lynch et al. (2022) note, educators must critically reflect on how activities, expectations and pedagogical choices may either reproduce or resist exclusionary norms. For instance, overly traditional, sport-focused curricula may marginalise learners who do not see themselves represented or successful in these forms of activity.

To ensure all learners can access the curriculum meaningfully, educators can adopt the *STEP* framework – a practical tool that enables purposeful adaptive practice. Adjusting *space* (e.g. reducing playing area to support mobility), *task* (e.g. simplifying instructions or offering multiple ways to complete a challenge), *equipment* (e.g. using larger or softer balls for easier manipulation) and *people* (e.g. structuring group roles to promote cooperation or peer support) allows educators to remove barriers while maintaining high expectations. Used flexibly, STEP promotes inclusive environments that support both individual needs and collective engagement, aligning with Newton's view that inclusion must be both emotional and physical. Equally, for those who require higher levels of challenge, the framework can be used to increase difficulty. For example, reducing the space in a 3 v 3 football game will require higher levels of ball control and speed of action to be successful.

A socially just and inclusive PE curriculum also prioritises pupil voice and agency. Empowering children to co-construct elements of their learning – through choice of task, reflection on experiences, or negotiation of rules – enhances not only motivation, but also relevance. Creating space for young people to contribute meaningfully to lesson and/or curriculum design can disrupt traditional power dynamics and promote a more democratic and responsive learning environment. This, in turn, supports the development of personal relevance and self-efficacy, both key components of a meaningful PE experience. Therefore, please take some time to gather pupil feedback on their experiences in PE. This could be achieved by connecting their experiences in PE with other primary subjects – for example, through artwork depicting their favourite PE lesson or writing a letter to the headteacher on what they would like to see more of in their PE lessons.

Ultimately, the pursuit of inclusion and equity in PE is an ongoing process – one that demands reflexivity, adaptability and a deep commitment to social justice. By embracing inclusion not as a technical fix, but as a moral and educational imperative, educators can ensure that PE becomes a space of belonging, affirmation and opportunity for all learners where the foundations of a physically active lifestyle can be laid.

ASSESSING PROGRESS IN PRIMARY PHYSICAL EDUCATION

Despite its integral role in supporting learning, assessment in primary PE has historically been marginalised or treated superficially (Penney, 2020). Research suggests that assessment in PE is often limited to teacher observation of physical performance, with minimal attention given to learners cognitive, social, or affective development. As a result, opportunities to inform planning, personalise learning and support progress across the whole child are frequently missed. A more balanced and intentional approach to assessment is needed – one that captures the breadth of learning in PE and reinforces its educational value within the broader curriculum (Thompson and Penney, 2018).

One model that supports this holistic view is the *head, heart, hands* framework (Frapwell and AfPE, 2015) which encourages educators to think beyond physical execution when designing and assessing learning. The *head* represents cognitive development – what learners know and understand about movement, rules, tactics and health. The *heart* refers to the affective domain, encompassing motivation, confidence, enjoyment and social engagement. The *hands* symbolise physical competence – the skills, techniques and execution of movement. When assessment encompasses all three domains, it aligns with the concept of physical literacy, promoting balanced development rather than an overemphasis on physical performance alone (Whitehead, 2010). However, as the only subject that prioritises the physical domain, I would suggest placing greater emphasis on the physical capabilities of the child, especially given the pivotal role motor competence plays in long-term engagement in physical activity. Figure 16.1 supports this notion, with physical competence as the capstone of the cognitive and affective domains.

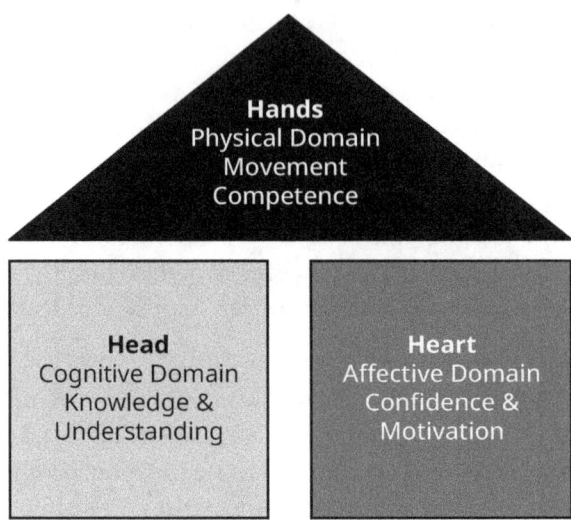

Figure 16.1   Assessment priorities within physical education

The head, heart and hands model also supports more inclusive and equitable assessment practices. By valuing effort, cooperation and personal growth alongside skill execution, it creates multiple pathways to success. A pupil who finds throwing difficult might still demonstrate tactical awareness (*head*) and persistence (*heart*) and should be recognised for those contributions. This reflects a broader move away from purely performance-dominated PE towards learning environments where all children can succeed in meaningful ways.

Assessment of FMS in primary schools should be prioritised as a key element of inclusive and effective PE. Early assessment helps identify children who demonstrate advanced motor competence and may benefit from enriched opportunities, while also recognising those who are struggling and require additional support. Without timely identification and intervention, gaps in motor proficiency can widen over time, leading to reduced confidence, disengagement from physical activity and long-term health implications. Early, targeted support ensures all children have the opportunity to build foundational skills essential for lifelong participation. Moreover, regular FMS assessment provides educators with meaningful insights to inform planning, differentiate instruction and promote equity in physical development.

While assessment must occasionally serve reporting and accountability purposes, the priority in primary PE should be on making it manageable and meaningful. Newton and Bowler (2021) warn against bureaucratising assessment to the point where it becomes a distraction from learning. Instead, it should be used to support future learning through the identification of current progress and identifying the next steps for learners to progress. Ultimately, assessment in PE should be seen as a form of feedback, not only for educators to adjust instruction, but also for children to better understand themselves as movers and learners. When assessment engages the head, heart and hands, it promotes physical literacy, deepens engagement and ensures that PE contributes meaningfully to the broader aims of education.

REFLECTION 16.3

How does a holistic approach to assessment in PE make you feel about your own confidence and ability in physical activities? Does this enable you to see progress in PE in a different light?

DEVELOPING TEACHER CONFIDENCE AND SUBJECT KNOWLEDGE

Many primary classroom teachers report feeling ill-equipped to teach PE, describing deficiencies in both subject knowledge and pedagogical confidence (Blair, 2018). Without a strong foundation in PE-specific knowledge, teachers are at risk of undervaluing its importance or marginalising it within the curriculum. Effective professional learning is therefore essential for teachers to build knowledge of the curriculum content (often the major concern) and pedagogies associated with primary PE.

Many primary teachers report that they feel ill-prepared to teach PE, with limited time spent on the subject within initial teacher education and varying levels of personal interest in the subject matter (Jess et al., 2016). Blair (2018) highlights ongoing concerns about the preparation and confidence of primary teachers in delivering PE effectively. The limited preparation leaves many feeling under-equipped and dissatisfied with their ability to teach the subject effectively. Confidence levels among preservice teachers tend to be moderate at best, with many expressing anxieties around managing physical environments, ensuring safety and delivering specific content. The increasing reliance on external sports coaches in primary schools has also raised concerns, as it reduces opportunities for class teachers to build their own pedagogical skills in PE. As this practice becomes normalised, teachers risk becoming deskilled and further removed from PE delivery. These challenges, when combined with the distinctive demands of class management, physical risk and content knowledge, contribute to PE being viewed as one of the most challenging subjects for primary teachers to teach.

To address these concerns, I propose three key recommendations for primary teachers and schools:

- *leverage internal expertise through mentoring*: one of the most effective approaches is to utilise existing expertise within the school. Identifying confident and competent staff to act as mentors for colleagues with less experience in PE can provide valuable peer support. Through observation, co-teaching and collaborative planning, mentoring helps demystify the subject and promotes confidence through shared practice;

- *prioritise staff development over external coaching*: where additional funding is available, such as through the Primary PE and Sport Premium, it should be strategically allocated to sustainable professional development. Rather than relying on external coaches for delivery, which may contribute to the de-skilling of teachers, investment in teacher training ensures long-term capacity-building and embeds knowledge within the school;

- *transfer pedagogical principles and build content knowledge gradually*: teachers should be encouraged to recognise that the foundational elements of good teaching – such as planning, scaffolding, adaptive teaching and assessment – are equally relevant in PE. Content knowledge can be developed progressively through collaboration with colleagues, independent study and support from PE specialists, including university staff and professional networks.

Ultimately, enhancing primary PE quality requires a systemic approach. Real transformation occurs when teachers are empowered to lead PE learning, supported by collaborative CPD structures that promote reflection, experimentation and professional enquiry. When external coaches are used strategically to support, rather than supplant, teacher development, a strong culture of teacher-led PE emerges, resulting in greater teacher confidence, curriculum ownership and improved learning outcomes for young people.

REFLECTION 16.4

What element of PE practice would you prioritise for your own professional development? What impact would you like this to have?

FINAL THOUGHTS

This chapter has explored the implementation of an effective primary PE curriculum through a holistic, inclusive and evidence-informed lens. It has emphasised that PE is not simply a vehicle for physical activity or sporting skill acquisition, but, in fact, a vital component of a balanced education.

At the heart of this vision is the concept of physical literacy, which frames children's engagement in PE as a lifelong journey marked by the development of motivation, confidence, physical competence, knowledge and understanding. Physical literacy provides a conceptual foundation for curriculum design and pedagogy that goes beyond transient performance outcomes. It encourages educators to view each child as a whole person, whose physical development is intertwined with identity, enjoyment, relationships and a sense of self-efficacy.

Central to the delivery of this vision is the intentional creation of meaningful experiences in PE. This chapter has explored how features such as fun, challenge, motor competence, social interaction, personal relevance and delight can be woven into lesson design and pedagogy. Meaningful PE is not a fixed model, but a way of thinking about how children experience movement and how educators can shape those experiences to foster lasting engagement.

A high-quality PE curriculum must also be grounded in subject knowledge and progression. Children require structured, varied and developmentally appropriate opportunities to build FMS across key activity areas. Importantly, these learning experiences must be connected to children's lives and be delivered in ways that promote confidence, competence and curiosity.

Teachers and other educators play a pivotal role in bringing this vision to life. As such, this chapter has highlighted the importance of ongoing professional learning, underpinned by collaboration, critical reflection and school cultures that value inclusive PE. Educators must be supported in developing both their pedagogical content knowledge and confidence, ensuring they feel equipped to lead PE lessons that are inclusive, purposeful and enjoyable for all learners.

Looking ahead, teachers are encouraged to adopt a bold and reflective stance towards their own PE practice. This means being willing to try new approaches, listen to pupil voice, challenge traditional assumptions about ability and performance, and centre inclusion in all aspects of curriculum design. PE holds immense potential to contribute to lifelong physical activity, personal development and the cultivation of positive identities.

FURTHER READING AND RESOURCES

Association for Physical Education (AfPE). www.afpe.org.uk

The UK's leading subject association for PE, providing high-quality CPD, resources and advice to promote safe and effective practice in PE.

PE Scholar. www.pescholar.com

A platform offering a wide range of educational content, resources and curriculum support to help PE teachers improve their practice and subject knowledge.

Fletcher, T., Ní Chróinín, D. N., Gleddie, D. and Beni, S. (Eds.). (2021). *Meaningful Physical Education: An approach for teaching and learning.* Routledge.

An academic text presenting the *Meaningful Physical Education* (MPE) framework, which focuses on creating rich, engaging and personally relevant experiences for all learners in PE.

Griggs. G. and Petrie, K. (2018). *Routledge handbook of primary physical education.* Routledge.

A comprehensive handbook that surveys key issues, debates and practices in primary PE, covering curriculum, pedagogy and research.

Griggs and V. Randall (2022). *An introduction to primary physical education* (2nd ed.). Routledge.

An introductory textbook providing an overview of the principles, practice and professional issues central to teaching primary PE.

REFERENCES

Bailey, R., Armour, K., Kirk, D., Jess, M., Pickup, I., Sandford, R. and BERA Physical Education and Sport Pedagogy Special Interest Group. (2009). The educational benefits claimed for physical education and school sport: An academic review. *Research Papers in Education, 24*(1), 1–27. https://doi.org/10.1080/02671520802355020

Beni, S., Fletcher, T. and Ní Chróinín, D. (2017). Meaningful experiences in physical education and youth sport: A review of the literature. *Quest, 69*(3), 291–312. https://doi.org/10.1080/00336297.2016.1224192

Beni, S., Ní Chróinín, D. and Fletcher, T. (2021). 'It's how PE should be!': Classroom teachers' experiences of implementing Meaningful Physical Education. *European Physical Education Review, 27*(3), 666–683. https://doi.org/10.1177/1356336X20986092

Blair, R. (2018). The deliverers debate. In G. Griggs and K. Petrie (Eds.), *Routledge handbook of primary physical education* (pp. 61–73). Routledge.

Bolger, L. E., Bolger, L. A., O'Neill, C., Coughlan, E., O'Brien, W., Lacey, S., Burns, C. and Bardid, F. (2021). Global levels of fundamental motor skills in children: A systematic review. *Journal of Sports Sciences, 39*(7), 717–753. https://doi.org/10.1080/02640414.2020.1841406

Cardiff, G., Bowles, R., Beni, S., Ní Chróinín, D. and Fletcher, T. (2024). Learning to facilitate student voice in primary physical education. *European Physical Education Review, 30*(3), 381–396. https://doi.org/10.1177/1356336X231209687

Department for Education (DfE). (2013). *The national curriculum in England: Physical education programmes of study: Key stages 1 and 2.* https://assets.publishing.service.gov.uk/media/5a7c4edfed915d3d0e87b801/PRIMARY_national_curriculum_-_Physical_education.pdf

Doherty, J. and Brennan, P. (2014). *Physical education 5–11: A guide for teachers.* Routledge.

Domville, M., Watson, P. M., Richardson, D. and Graves, L. E. F. (2019). Children's perceptions of factors that influence PE enjoyment: A qualitative investigation. *Physical Education and Sport Pedagogy, 24*(3), 207–219. https://doi.org/10.1080/17408989.2019.1571181

Durden-Myers, E. J., Whitehead, M. E. and Pot, N. (2018). Physical literacy and human flourishing. *Journal of Teaching in Physical Education, 37*(3), 308–311. https://doi.org/10.1123/jtpe.2018-0133

Fletcher, T., Ní Chróinín, D., Gleddie, D. and Beni, S. (2021). The why, what, and how of Meaningful Physical Education. In T. Fletcher, D. Ní Chróinín, D. Gleddie and S. Beni (Eds.), *Meaningful Physical Education: An approach for teaching and learning.* Routledge.

Frapwell, A. and Association for Physical Education (AfPE). (2015). *A practical guide to assessing without levels: Supporting and safeguarding high quality achievement in physical education.* AfPE.

Goodway, J. D., Ozmun, J. C. and Gallahue, D. L. (2019). *Understanding motor development: Infants, children, adolescents, adults.* Jones and Bartlett Learning.

Griggs, G. and Petrie, K. (2018). Introduction. In G. Griggs and K. Petrie (Eds.), *Routledge handbook of primary physical education.* Routledge.

Jess, M., McEvilly, N. and Carse, N. (2016). Moving primary physical education forward: Start at the beginning. *Education 3–13, 45*(5), 645–657. https://doi.org/10.1080/03004279.2016.1155072

Ladwig, M. A., Vazou, S. and Ekkekakis, P. (2018). 'My best memory is when I was done with it': PE memories are associated with adult sedentary behavior. *Translational Journal of the American College of Sports Medicine, 3*(16), 119–129. https://doi.org/10.1249/TJX.0000000000000078

Lundvall, S. (2015). Physical literacy in the field of physical education: A challenge and a possibility. *Journal of Sport and Health Science, 4*(2), 113–118. https://doi.org/10.1016/j.jshs.2015.02.001

Lynch, S., Walton-Fisette, J. and Luguetti, C. (2022). *Pedagogies of social justice in physical education and youth sport.* Routledge.

Newton, A. and Bowler, M. (2021). Assessment for and of learning in physical education. In S. A. Capel, J. Cliffe and J. Lawrence (Eds.), *Learning to teach physical education in the secondary school: A companion to school experience* (5th ed., pp. 144–161). Routledge.

Newton, F. (2022). *Inclusive PE for SEND children: A practical guide.* FB3.

O'Brien, W., Belton, S. and Issartel, J. (2016). Fundamental movement skill proficiency amongst adolescent youth. *Physical Education and Sport Pedagogy, 21*(6), 557–571. https://doi.org/10.1080/17408989.2015.1017451

Penney, D. (2020). Assessment in physical education. In S. A. Capel and R. Blair (Eds.), *Debates in physical education* (2nd ed., pp. 190–205). Routledge.

Pickup, I. and Randall, V. (2022). The importance of primary physical education. In G. Griggs and V. Randall (Eds.), *An introduction to primary physical education* (2nd ed., pp. 11–24). Routledge.

Roberts, W. M., Newcombe, D. J. and Davids, K. (2019). Application of a constraints-led approach to pedagogy in schools: Embarking on a journey to nurture physical literacy in primary physical education. *Physical Education and Sport Pedagogy, 24*(2), 162–175. https://doi.org/10.1080/17408989.2018.1552675

Salters, D. and Benson, S. S. (2025). Physical education-based interventions contribute to the development of fundamental movement skills in primary school-aged children: A systematic review. *Journal of Motor Learning and Development, 1*(aop), 1–26. https://doi.org/10.1123/jmld.2024-0012

Stidder, G. and Hayes, S. (Eds.). (2012). *Equity and inclusion in physical education and sport.* Routledge.

Thompson, N. and Penney, D. (2018). Assessment and standards. In G. Griggs and K. Petrie (Eds.), *Routledge handbook of primary physical education.* Routledge.

Whitehead, M. (2010). *Physical literacy: Throughout the lifecourse*. Routledge.

Whitehead, M. (2021). Enacting a physical literacy approach. In S. Capel, J. Cliffe and J. Lawrence (Eds.), *A practical guide to teaching physical education in the secondary school* (3rd ed., pp. 29–38). Routledge.

Wintle, J. (2022). Physical education and physical activity promotion: Lifestyle sports as meaningful experiences. *Education Sciences*, *12*(3), 181. https://doi.org/10.3390/educ-sci12030181

Wright, P. M., Gray, S. and Richards, K. A. R. (2021). Understanding the interpretation and implementation of social and emotional learning in physical education. *The Curriculum Journal*, *32*(1), 67–86. https://doi.org/10.1002/curj.50

17

RELIGIOUS EDUCATION

ELIZABETH YEOMANS

THIS CHAPTER

This chapter explores the ideas that:

- there is not a neutral, fixed body of subject knowledge in RE

- decolonising the curriculum requires us to move away from a transmission approach to teaching RE and towards a dialogic approach

- within RE we can encounter reality and engage with different perspectives.

KEY TERMS FOR THIS CHAPTER

Conscientisation: an ongoing critically engaged orientation towards the world, reached through a process of dialogic praxis.

Controversial issues: issues about which there is no fixed or universally held point of view and which may cause divisions in society.

Decolonisation: revealing the hidden narrative which runs contrary to the patriarchal Eurocentric dominant worldview.

Dialogic: a form of communication featuring exchange of ideas where transformation may be developed through interaction.

Engaged pedagogy – bell hooks (1994): teaching in a manner that respects and cares for the souls of our students.

Liberation: according to Freire (1970) the purpose of education was to become alive, to help people move from unquestioning beliefs and opinions to a critical stance where one finds one's place in the world and becomes free and fully human (no longer an oppressor or an oppressed person).

Life-worlds: the past, present and future contexts that we each bring to the classroom.

Transmission approach: otherwise known as the 'banking' approach, where the teacher deposits knowledge into the minds of the pupils (Freire, 1970).

INTRODUCTION

This chapter examines the concept of subject knowledge in RE from a dialogic approach. To teach RE well, it is important that we recognise the subject as living and breathing, constantly being *re*newed, *re*shaped and *re*purposed. RE does not consist of neutral subject knowledge which can be objectified or simplified, as it relates to human questions about life and purpose, which exist in time, place and culture. There is not a fixed body of knowledge in any religious or non-religious worldview.

Likewise, humans are not objects. We (teachers and pupils) are subjects in our own lives, and it is essential to recognise our own 'subject-ness' before we start to teach RE. Regardless of our own position, we are all humans with a worldview (religious or non-religious) which impacts upon the way we live. RE is not about the 'other' or the 'exotic'. Therefore, RE is not a subject which should objectify humanity.

ISSUES AND RECOMMENDATIONS

There is not a unified approach to RE in the UK, although all four nations agree that religious traditions are in the main Christian and this should be reflected. In Scotland, RE is prescribed by the Scottish parliament and is called *religion and moral education*. In England, the agreed syllabus is set by Standard Advisory Committees on RE (SACREs) in local areas. In Wales, the SACs are Standing Advisory Councils for Religion, Values and Ethics, due to the new curriculum (Curriculum for Wales, 2022). In Northern Ireland, RE has a core syllabus drawn up by the four main churches. In most cases in Northern Ireland, religions other than Christianity are not taught until Key Stage 3.

The diversity of RE provision across the four nations adds to the debate about the nature and purpose of RE. Helpfully, the Final Report by the Commission on RE (CoRE, 2018) recommended some important changes for England and Wales. One of these is to challenge the legal right which currently allows parents and carers to withdraw their child from RE lessons (although this is being phased out in Wales and is rarely exercised in Northern Ireland). Another recommendation is for a National Statement of Entitlement (NSE). Wales has already moved towards this recommendation, with their new curriculum which embeds *religion, values and ethics* (Curriculum for Wales, 2022). In England, although RE is mandatory, it is not on the national curriculum (DfE, 2013).

Another recommendation from the CoRE report (2018) is that RE should be renamed and taught from a *religion and worldviews* approach. This approach requires both pupils and teachers to recognise that we all have a worldview, whether religious or non-religious. It enables an interpretive experience of knowledge, actively engaging with living members of religious and non-religious traditions. This approach also embraces the diverse and complex ways in which humans make sense of life and rejects simplistic subject knowledge that classifies religions and worldviews into homogeneous groups. Beginning with the diverse beliefs and experiences of people allows for a *decolonial* approach to RE. By this I mean moving away from a claim to knowledge that is often linked to a patriarchal Eurocentric worldview. Traditionally in RE, information about the six major religions is packaged as knowledge representing each religion (Pett, 2024). However, in reality, religious and non-religious beliefs are diverse and often relate more to *sense* knowledge than *rational* knowledge (Salami, 2020). Teaching from a religion and worldviews approach promotes the often-hidden narrative of lived, sensory experience over organised religion. The CoRE report (2018) also found that many teachers feel a lack of confidence when teaching RE. Considering RE from a religion and worldviews approach means that we can dispel of the daunting concept of knowledge in RE as solely something which can be acquired or 'understood', and instead approach subject knowledge in RE as a dialogic connection with humanity, spirituality and self.

In this chapter I propose that teaching RE from a religion and worldviews approach gives us the opportunity to engage with the subject in a unique way. Recognising that RE is a subject which requires us to be engaged and 'awake' means that we can consider what Paulo Freire calls a process of 'conscientisation' (1970). Freire contrasts the *necrophilic* approach to teaching, where pupils are essentially asleep, passively regurgitating the answer that the teacher has already provided, with the *biophilic* approach, which is life-loving and expects pupils to be conscious, active and engaged (Friere, 1984). Rather than eloquent lectures from the teacher (Freire, 1973), pupils and teachers should be engaged in authentic dialogue, which requires reflection and action, affecting the interior of a human as well as the exterior. Freire called this approach *liberation pedagogy;* I want to set out in this chapter why this life-affirming way of teaching is essential to the subject of RE.

A CO-CREATED IMAGE

In this chapter I use an image (co-created with primary student teachers) as a starting point to explore dialogic teaching in RE. The image was the result of a participatory action research project. As a lecturer and RE subject lead in initial teacher education, I wanted to explore how to engage with student teachers in a deeper way, to model the process of developing conscientisation. I decided to critique an image with them, which eventually led to the co-creation of the image in Figure 17.1. For more information on the original image see Yeomans, 2025.

The co-created image represents the primary RE classroom, uses language from *Developing a religion and worldviews approach to religious education in England* (Pett, 2024) and challenges us to consider some key elements which are particularly important in RE. These will be outlined in the next section and then two of these areas (the role of the pupils and the role of the teacher) will be explored more thoroughly with reference to liberation pedagogy and engaged pedagogy. Regular questions will support you to actively reflect on your own practice.

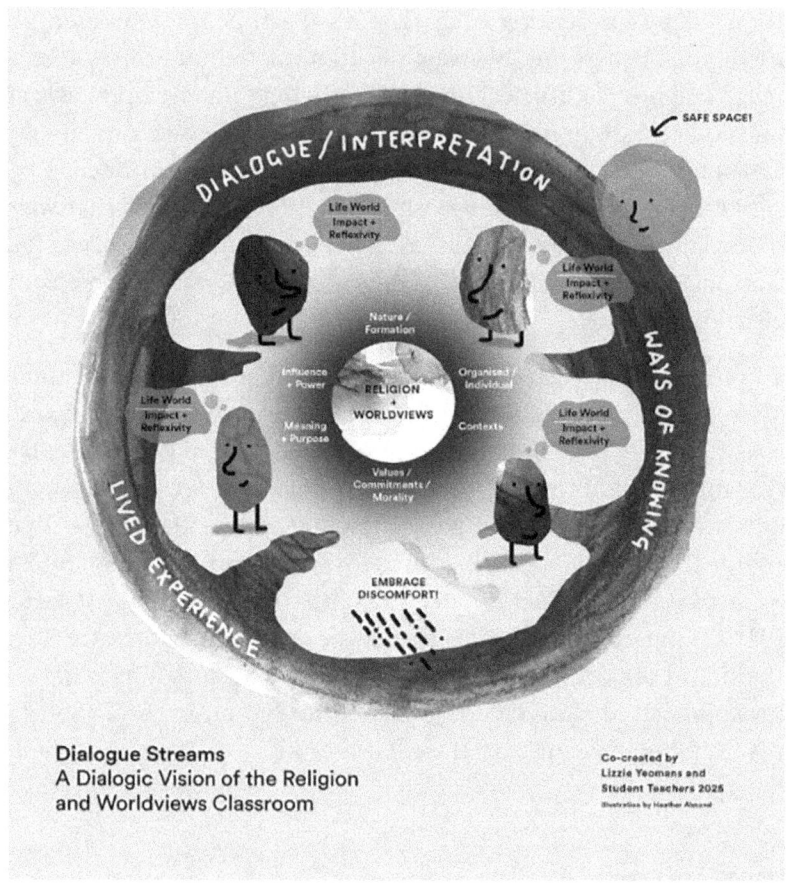

Figure 17.1   Dialogue streams: A dialogic vision of the religion and worldviews classroom

Source: Yeomans, 2025. Illustration by Heather Almond for author.

The co-created image shows four non-human figures which represent the teacher and pupils. It is not clear who is who. This highlights the need to reject a *transmission* approach to teaching, where the teacher is the holder of knowledge and the pupils are empty vessels, waiting to be filled (Freire, 1970). Instead, the teacher and pupils are positioned around the Earth, viewing RE as a problem-posing subject that they can engage with as equals, learning with and from one another through dialogue. This may require a renewed consideration of the role of the pupil and the role of the teacher in primary RE, which will be explored in more detail in the next section.

AN EX-CENTRIC APPROACH

The Earth is in the centre of the image, which echoes Gert Biesta's call for an *ex-centric* approach to education. He argues that the focus of education should be an encounter with reality (Biesta, 2016). This can sometimes be uncomfortable, and we may encounter resistance, but school should be a place where we are supported to practise how it feels to grapple with different perspectives through engaged pedagogy (more of this below).

Around the Earth is content knowledge. This progresses from the Early Years, through activities such as story, music, art and play. Content knowledge should not require pupils to memorise names of clothing or places of worship. Religious language can be embedded in lessons and used in stories and by people of faith, but when we start testing pupils on their memory of terms which may or may not be part of their lived experience, we run the risk of positioning them as 'high or low attainers'. Pupils do not need to memorise words to be good at RE. Indeed, for some people of faith, the language used to describe their practice does not align with their lived experience. Some Christians would not be able to define 'the Eucharist', as they may call it 'Communion' or 'The Lord's Supper' instead. Some Muslims would not be able to list the Five Pillars, as each component is part of their everyday life and not necessarily known as a 'pillar'. There is a broad spectrum of worldviews, both religious and non-religious. Often this is described as 'messy' (Cooling, 2020). This can be challenging for the RE teacher, but worldviews should not be simplified or generalised, as this does not represent the diversity of beliefs and practice.

Instead of a focus on terminology, RE lessons can explore concepts and beliefs such as the origin of the world, creation stories, questions of existence and diverse religious and non-religious responses to the meaning of life. Other topics may include the diversity of worldviews, and the recognition that a person may have a personal belief, but it might look very different to the organised religion of the same faith. There should not be a focus on debating the rights and wrongs or whether we agree or disagree with these beliefs.

LIFE-WORLDS

Above each figure is a bubble with 'life-world, reflexivity and impact' written inside. *Life-worlds* illustrate the historical, present and future context of each participant in the classroom. Reflexivity can be defined as reflection and action:

- how does the content knowledge impact a believer and their actions in the world?

- where does it come from and how may it be interpreted?

- how does the knowledge impact me and my personal beliefs?

These questions should be considered by both pupils and teachers from the Early Years onwards. In doing this, the subject is addressing the three forms of interconnected knowledge which Ofsted (2021) set out as 'substantive, disciplinary and personal'. The National Statement of Entitlement (see Pett, 2024, p.19) similarly classifies knowledge in RE into three forms: 'content, engagement and position'.

SHARED SEA

Behind each figure is a stream, leading to a 'shared sea' of dialogue. The flow of the stream represents the two-way process of dialogue. This two-way dialogue means that pupils and the teacher can relate their own concerns to the wider cultural community, and then back to themselves, and then out again, being both part of a culture and also independent from it (Leganger- Krogstad, 2003). They do not lose their individuality, but have an authentic connection with their school and community.

Within the shared sea are terms to describe how content knowledge is engaged with. Ways in which the content knowledge can be explored are varied. One example is using disciplinary approaches such as interpretation or hermeneutics: exploring authentic scripture, poetry and art. Another could be engaging in ethnographic research, interviewing people or visiting a place of worship. Personal knowledge (reflexivity and impact) can then be revisited, giving pupils time to express what they have found, felt or understood. Moving away from a reliance on written work helps to engage pupils who may have more confidence expressing themselves in another form, such as art, dance, drama or songwriting.

UNCOMFORTABLE WEATHER

The co-created image has a sun, which represents the *safe space* of the RE classroom, but also a thundercloud, to 'embrace the discomfort' (Yeomans, 2025, p. 397) that is sometimes felt when encountering controversial issues or questions that have many or no answers. *Discomfort* in the RE classroom is normal and should not be avoided or ignored if we are serious about decolonisation. For some pupils who belong to the dominant discourse, feeling uncomfortable in the classroom will be a new sensation. For others, feeling different, uncomfortable or 'other' may be a continually present feeling in the classroom. Subject knowledge that is not truly representative of pupils' life-worlds or of historical and cultural context will create a classroom where pupils do not feel they belong and therefore do not feel safe.

REFLECTION 17.1

Consider the often-used phrase 'safe space'.

Can you think of pupils who may not consider the classroom as safe? Why do you think this is?

We will explore this further in the next section.

RE can be the subject which forges connections while also recognising feelings of discomfort. Controversial issues are part and parcel of RE, defined as: 'Issues about which there are no fixed or universally held points of view. Such issues are those which commonly divide society and for which significant groups offer conflicting explanations and solutions' (Crick Report, 1998, paragraph 10.2, in Cooling, n.d.).

Embracing this definition can help us to be good teachers of RE. Exploring issues together within the context of a school community which values belonging and acceptance can support pupils to become global citizens in a pluralist society. However, this can be challenging for the teacher, especially if the teacher has never encountered education in this sense – that is, to encounter freedom through belonging and being seen. It requires time to explore what we mean by the role of the pupil and the role of the teacher in RE, and how the school can be a supportive community.

I will now explore these two themes in greater depth.

THE ROLE OF PUPIL LIFE-WORLDS IN RE

To avoid a transmission approach to teaching and learning in RE, where the teacher holds the knowledge and pupils passively acquire content to regurgitate, it is important that pupils and teachers work together as whole humans through engaged pedagogy (hooks, 1994). This requires the teacher to recognise that pupils are more than just individuals, they also have past, present and future lives, which are both physical and spiritual, and which are continually influenced by social connection. It is also essential that the teacher is able to understand knowledge in this sense, that their understanding of worldviews is not just based on content or 'pub quiz knowledge': 'We need an approach to knowledge that synthesises the imaginative and rational, the quantifiable and immeasurable, the intellectual and the emotional' (Salami, 2020, p.14).

Salami challenges us to move away from a patriarchal Eurocentric view of knowledge to one that she calls *sensuous knowledge*. This term embraces our wholeness, as beings who feel, sense and empathise as well as think, rationalise and determine. Nhất Hạnh, a Vietnamese Buddhist monk, also emphasised the non-duality approach which requires us to engage with one another holistically. In primary RE, this means that we need to recognise the intellectual, physical and spiritual world. We are more likely to find theological truth in the language of art than science (Pillay, 2002).

SPIRITUALITY

The English national curriculum states that every state-funded school must offer a curriculum which is balanced and broadly based and which: 'Promotes the spiritual, moral, cultural, mental and physical development of pupils at the school and of society' (DfE, 2013, p. 2).

It is important then to consider what *spiritual development* means in the context of RE. The Curriculum for Wales does this well, devoting over a page to unpicking a definition and making it clear that spiritual development may or may not include religion (Curriculum for Wales, 2022). The Scottish Curriculum states that one of its aims is to help pupils to explore significant questions about existence, values and the spiritual dimension of life (Scottish Government, 2011). The Core Syllabus for RE in Northern Ireland uses the term 'spiritual awareness' (2007).

Elton-Chalcraft, Hollander and Prescott (2024, p. 117) categorise the concept of spirituality as four dimensions:

1. the inner dimension, where you look inwards to yourself;

2. the social and moral dimension, where you look outwards to others;

3. the environmental dimension, where you look downwards to Earth;

4. the transcendental dimension, where you look upwards to God/the Transcendent.

The Curriculum for Wales emphasises the interconnectedness of education and the sense of self, and highlights this with the term 'cynefin', which is a feeling of belonging – not just in relation to a physical or geographical place, but also a historic, social and cultural place, which may be developed by the recognition of emotional or spiritual feelings (Curriculum for Wales, 2020).

Developing feelings of belonging in the classroom is essential in the primary school, especially in the context of social, racial and religious polarisation, which is on the rise (CPA, 2024), and when teaching from a trauma-informed approach (Bomber, 2020). bell hooks (1994, p. 13) promotes *engaged* pedagogy as a way to support all pupils to feel they belong in the classroom:

> *To teach in a manner that respects and cares for the souls of our students is essential if we are to provide the necessary conditions where learning can most deeply and intimately begin. Throughout my years as student and professor, I have been most inspired by those teachers who have had the courage to transgress those boundaries that would confine each pupil to a rote, assembly-line approach to learning. Such teachers approach students with the will and desire to respond to our unique.*

Building social connections among pupils and teachers rather than an individualised approach to teaching and learning allows for the classroom to be a space where we can all become fully human. It requires effort on the part of both the teacher and the pupils, and an expectation that all will participate in a variety of ways.

REFLECTION 17.2

- How are all pupils engaged in the classroom?
- How do they feel seen, heard and known?

The impact of engaging with pupils' life-worlds can be huge. Here are some memories from an RE teacher in a predominantly white primary school:

1. Muslim boy, Year 6, who taught his classmates the position of Salah;

2. Muslim girl, Year 6, who had been fasting for Ramadan, supported by her classmates, wanted to share Eid with her friends. The day after Eid, we had an Eid celebration. Her mum provided food! The same girl also taught me how to put on a hijab correctly – she laughed when I tried!

3. Christian girl, Year 3, shared about baptisms in her church;

4. a reception girl brought her Eid gift, a Muslim doll, to show her class;

5. Hindu boy, Year 4, wore his puja ash to school. His brother set up a Hindu shrine in his classroom, 'like the one at my home'.

All children should feel engaged in RE lessons. This emphasises the need to move away from the transmission approach to teaching, where learning is equated to passively acquiring information. For some children, religious worldviews will be completely alien to the way they view life, and learning about a new way to view the world may open a range of questions to engage with. For others, viewing the world through a religious lens is only usually done outside a school context; having the opportunity to share part of their life that is usually absent from school life can be freeing for them (like the boy in the example above who kept his puja ash on when he came to school instead of removing it like he normally would – he felt seen and known).

For other children, there can be potential barriers to education, such as having English as an additional language or having an educational need. Sometimes these children are taught from a deficit approach, they are given simplified worksheets or scaffolded word mats. Karisman (1997) shows how allowing space for pupils in a SEND school to authentically engage with big questions by drawing on their life experience can be empowering (and lead to what Freire would call liberation). She noticed that many of these children have had difficulties to overcome and can relate to the spiritual struggle evident in many big questions shared by humans. Treating all pupils as humans with a worldview promotes respect and trust. Correspondingly, Ipgrave (2013) built relationships with pupils through dialogue and assimilated their spiritual language into her teaching, to build bridges and make meaningful connections. Recognising the life-worlds of pupils who have English as an additional language can bring a range of communities into the classroom. Giving the class the opportunity to learn home languages can help pupils to feel seen and known in their classroom. Using other languages – listening to (or learning) an Arabic prayer, a Hebrew song, a Greek hymn or a Hindi mantra can bring religions alive.

Another excellent way to engage pupils in the primary classroom is to use religious and non-religious stories and sayings to connect to each life-world through dialogue. An aboriginal saying sums up beautifully the power of story: 'Stories takes you up, then down, leaving you in a place that is higher than before' (Daddow et al., 2019, p.1184).

REFLECTION 17.3

What story has 'taken you up, then down', leaving you in a place that was 'higher than before'?

THE ROLE OF THE TEACHER IN PRIMARY RE

So far in this chapter we have examined liberation pedagogy – teaching for critical consciousness where pupils are able to be truly 'alive' (Freire, 1970); and engaged pedagogy – where the teacher ensures that everyone in the classroom is involved, seen and known *holistically* (hooks, 1994).

However, if the teacher has not gone through a process of liberation, self-knowledge or transformation in their own education, either as a pupil or as a student teacher, it may be hard to begin to relinquish the control or power they believe an 'expert' teacher needs to have.

The unique position of an RE teacher in the primary classroom means that the teacher may not have studied RE for many years and may feel underqualified for teaching the subject. However, let's remove this idea that we need to know everything to be a good teacher of primary RE! The best teachers know that they do not know and recognise that they have a worldview which impacts the way that they live and teach.

As anthropologist and teacher educator Gloria Ladson-Billings (2004, p. 107) points out:

> *Most of my students are white, middle-class, monolingual Midwesterners. They are surrounded by people who look, talk, and perhaps think as they do. When I try to get them to think about their culture, they are stymied. They describe themselves as having 'no culture' or being 'just regular' or 'just normal.' When I point out the semantic challenge with their characterisations – by default people unlike them are 'irregular' or 'abnormal' – they fumble to correct that impression (my students are nothing if not polite).*

For teachers (like me) who belong to the dominant discourse of being a white, middle-class teacher, it is essential for decolonisation to recognise the influence and existence of culture. When you are part of a dominant discourse it is not usual to classify yourself as a cultural being as you are the 'norm'; culture belongs to the exotic 'other'. As Ladson-Billings states, 'culture' is understood by some as 'what it means to be non-white'.

REFLECTION 17.4

What does culture mean to you? Think of five aspects of your life that reflect your worldview.

Without what Ruth Flanagan calls a *worldview shock* (2020), teachers may never have questioned their identity within the dominant discourse. Being a white teacher in a majority white teaching profession gives an illusion of being 'just normal'. The classroom may be your safe space, where your worldview has never been challenged. However, RE may be the one subject where you feel vulnerable and scared of saying the wrong thing, so you learn some facts about a religion and transmit these facts to pupils, without giving any opportunities for discussions which may veer into 'unsafe' territories that you cannot control. This is not acceptable RE; it does nothing to promote spirituality, to help pupils feel they belong, to explore what it means to be human.

Therefore, teachers need to identify that they exist in a culture and have a worldview. This may only be possible through becoming an 'archaeologist of the self' (Ricouer, 1970, in Flanagan, 2020). Further, in order to truly know yourself, you may need to encounter radically different positions to the one you hold. As Gadamer (1975) points out, our own preconceptions cannot be known directly, and we need opportunities to be responsive to the unfamiliar.

In order to challenge the dominant discourse of education, it is essential to become self-aware: 'You can't change what you don't see' (Picower, 2013). RE is the ideal subject to raise awareness of ourselves and each other as non-neutral beings, connected and curious in an unknowable world. Rejecting teacher expertism and asserting true inclusivity by practising what it means to live together in the world (Biesta, 2016) allows us to become vulnerable participants alongside pupils in the classroom (Roebben, 2012).

bell hooks expresses this need for recognising the classroom as a place which does not always feel comfortable:

> *To some extent, we all know that whenever we address in the classroom subjects that students are passionate about there is always a possibility of confrontation, forceful expression of ideas, or even conflict. In much of my writing about pedagogy, particularly in classroom settings with great diversity, I have talked about the need to examine*

critically the way we as teachers conceptualize what the space for learning should be like. Many professors have conveyed to me their feeling that the classroom should be a 'safe' place; that usually translates to mean that the professor lectures to a group of quiet students who respond only when they are called on. The experience of professors who educate for critical consciousness indicates that many students, especially students of color, may not feel at all 'safe' in what appears to be a neutral setting. It is the absence of a feeling of safety that often promotes prolonged silence or lack of student engagement. Making the classroom a democratic setting where everyone feels a responsibility to contribute is a central goal of transformational pedagogy.

(hooks, 1994, p. 39)

The exciting challenge in RE is the opportunity to embed an anti-racist curriculum. The teacher is not the sole holder of knowledge, and the responsibility of the RE teacher to ensure that no black or brown child is discriminated against requires them to be aware of any unconscious bias they may hold (Elton-Chalcraft, Brown and Yates, 2024).

REFLECTION 17.5

Is there space for uncomfortable questions and feelings in the RE classroom?

FINAL THOUGHTS

In this chapter we have explored education primarily through the lens of Paulo Freire's liberation pedagogy. One of Freire's main aims was to challenge the dehumanising impact of education, both on the teacher as oppressor and the pupils as oppressed. He argued that the way to do this was to adhere to his *principles of dialogue*, which I have reinterpreted in the context of primary RE:

- *love*: be open to each other through authentic relational connection;

- *faith*: be aware of a spiritual dimension of existence that may exist regardless of your own belief. Consider the definitions of belief, opinion and fact;

- *hope*: humanity can be transformed through good RE; actively listening and responding to the wider community can bring a sense of belonging;

- *humility*: the teacher does not solely hold the power and the knowledge;

- *critical thinking*: what is my culture, identity and worldview? How does it influence how I teach RE, view my pupils and view myself? Dialogic RE can provide a space to delink from the colonial practice of the transmission approach.

Although many of the writers referred to in this chapter do not write specifically about RE, they all care about education being a place of freedom, of thought, of conscientisation, of transformation. As Gert Biesta argues, school can promote an 'ex-centric' way of trying to exist, placing the world or reality in the centre instead of ourselves (2016).

Biesta classifies education into three domains, the first of which is *qualification*. This type of knowledge is sometimes disproportionately promoted through testing, recall and exams. Biesta views the second domain of RE to be *socialisation*, which he relates to empowering pupils by cultivating the 'inner life' (Biesta, 2002, p. 345). Education is defined as 'Bildung' (formation of self through engaging with others), which should be a lifelong process.

Subjectification is Biesta's third domain of education; it can be equated to critical literacy, seeing oneself as a subject, which leads to liberation. It is a critical attempt to reveal reality and can lead to conscientisation if enacted through action and reflection (Friere, 1984). German pedagogy can explain the importance of connection through dialogue for subjectification, *Erziehung* (freedom through becoming known) (Biesta, 2016, p. 835). Another term, 'perspective sharing' (Rix and Paige-Smith, 2011) emphasises the need to build empathy and reduce stereotypes. This is challenging; to be an educator in RE could be redefined 'as leading out or leading away from oneself, towards the world' (Biesta, 2020, p. 18).

Refer back to the co-created image (Figure 17.1) now that you have come to the end of this chapter. The aim of this chapter, to recognise knowledge in RE as living and breathing, not static and dead, requires us as teachers to consider our own understanding of knowledge. Linda Whitworth (2020) explored this by engaging her student teachers in dialogue, finding that over-simplification of beliefs could lead to stereotypical descriptions, the very opposite of what is needed in our current climate. Approaching RE as a humanising subject requires 'Namaste', a Sanskrit term which can be translated as 'the sacred in me recognises the sacred in you'.

I hope this chapter will help you to feel full of confidence that you can teach RE in an inclusive way, being aware of your own vulnerability as a dialogic participant in the RE classroom, along with your pupils, as you practice what it means to encounter reality.

FURTHER READING

Chipperton, J. Georgiou, G. Seymour, O. and Wright, K. (n.d). Balanced RE. https://balance-dre.org.uk/

A website offering a structured, balanced approach to teaching RE that integrates both the personal worldviews of pupils and a study of religious and non-religious traditions.

Culham St Gabriel's Trust. Free e-learning courses. https://courses.cstg.org.uk/

Provides a range of free online professional development (CPD) courses for teachers to enhance their knowledge and pedagogy in RE.

Downe, E. (2021). *Nobody Stands Nowhere* (Worldviews Film). www.theosthinktank.co.uk/comment/2021/05/12/worldviews-film

A resource from Theos ThinkTank that discusses the concept of *worldviews* and the philosophical position that everyone holds a perspective, often in the context of RE.

NATRE Spirited Arts Annual Competition. www.natre.org.uk/about-natre/projects/spirited-arts/

An annual, national art and media competition for schools that encourages pupils to reflect creatively on religious, spiritual and moral themes.

Smith, L. J. The RE Podcast. www.therepodcast.co.uk/blog

A podcast offering insights, interviews and discussion on current issues, research and effective pedagogy in RE.

Yeomans, E. (2025). How a process of subjectification in ITE can challenge the paradigm of the expert teacher in primary RE. *Journal of Religious Education, 73*, 385–400. https://doi.org/10.1007/s40839-025-00278-z

An article exploring how initial teacher education (ITE) can use a subjectification process to challenge the concept of the expert teacher in primary RE.

REFERENCES

Biesta, G. (2002). Bildung and modernity: The future of Bildung in a world of difference. *Studies in Philosophy and Education, 21*, 343–351. https://doi.org/10.1023/A:1019874106870

Biesta, G. (2016). *The beautiful risk of education* (1st ed.). Routledge.

Biesta, G. (2020). Education, education, education: Reflections on a missing dimension. In G. Biesta and P. Hannam (Eds.), *Religion and education* (pp. 8–19). Brill. https://doi.org/10.1163/9789004446397

Bomber, L. M. (2020). *Know me to teach me: Differentiated discipline for those recovering from adverse childhood experiences*. Worth.

Cooling, T. (n.d.). *Controversial issues in RE*. www.natre.org.uk/resources/controversial-issues-in-re/

Cooling, T. (2020). Worldview in RE: Autobiographical reflections on The Commission on RE in England final report. *British Journal of Religious Education, 42*(4), 403–414. https://doi.org/10.1080/01416200.2020.1764497

Commission on Religious Education (CoRE). (2018). *Final report: Religion and worldviews: The way forward*. www.commissiononre.org.uk/final-report-religion-and-worldviews-the-way-forward-a-national-plan-for-re/

Crown Prosecution Service (CPS). (2024). *Racial and religious based offences drive increase in hate crime cases.* www.cps.gov.uk/cps/news/racial-and-religious-based-offences-drive-increase-hate-crime-cases

Curriculum for Wales. (2020). *Areas for learning and experience.* https://hwb.gov.wales/curriculum-for-wales/humanities/

Curriculum for Wales. (2022). *Religion, values and ethics guidance.* https://hwb.gov.wales/curriculum-for-wales/humanities/designing-your-curriculum/#religion,-values-and-ethics-guidance

Daddow, A., Cronshaw, D., Daddow, N. and Sandy, R. (2019). Strengthening inter-cultural literacy and minority voices through narratives of healthy religious pluralism in higher education. *International Journal of Inclusive Education, 25*(10), 1174–1189. https://doi.org/10.1080/13603116.2019.1600056

Department for Education (DfE). (2013). *National curriculum in England: Primary curriculum.* www.gov.uk/government/publications/national-curriculum-in-england-primary-curriculum

Department of Education, Northern Ireland (DoE, NI). (2007). *Religious education core syllabus.* www.education-ni.gov.uk/publications/religious-education-core-syllabus

Elton-Chalcraft, S., Brown, A. and Yates, J. (2024). Challenging discrimination and prejudice through creative and inclusive RE. In S. Elton-Chalcraft (Ed.), *Teaching religious and worldviews education creatively* (2nd ed.). Taylor & Francis. https://doi.org/10.4324/9781003361480

Elton-Chalcraft, S., Hollander, P. and Prescott, G. (2024). Spiritual development through creative RE. In S. Elton-Chalcraft (Ed.), *Teaching religious and worldviews education creatively* (2nd ed.). Taylor & Francis. https://doi.org/10.4324/9781003361480

Flanagan, R. (2020). Teachers' personal worldviews and RE in England: A way forward? *British Journal of Religious Education, 43*(3), 320–336. https://doi.org/10.1080/01416200.2020.1826404

Freire, P. (1970). *Pedagogy of the oppressed.* Seabury Press.

Freire, P. (1973). *Education for critical consciousness.* Seabury Press.

Freire, P. (1984). Education, liberation and the church. *Religious Education, 79*(4), 524–545. https://doi.org/10.1080/0034408400790405

Gadamer, H. (1975). *Truth and method.* Seabury Press.

hooks, B. (1994). *Teaching to transgress* (1st ed.). Routledge. https://doi.org/10.4324/9780203700280

Ipgrave, J. (2013). The language of interfaith encounter among inner city primary school children. *Religion and Education, 40*(1), 35–49. https://doi.org/10.1080/15507394.2013.745361

Karisman, A. (1997). *Speak from the heart: Exploring and responding to RE in the special school.* Farmington Institute for Christian Studies. https://farmington.ac.uk/scholars/tt16-speak-from-the-heart-exploring-and-responding-to-re-in-the-special-school/

Ladson-Billings, G. (2004). It's not the culture of poverty, it's the poverty of culture: The problem with teacher education. *Anthropology and Education Quarterly, 37*(2), 104–109.

Leganger-Krogstad, H. (2003). Dialogue among young citizens in a pluralistic religious education classroom. In R. Jackson (Ed.), *International perspectives on citizenship, education and religious diversity* (pp. 169–190). Routledge Falmer.

Ofsted. (2021). *Research review series: Religious education.* www.gov.uk/government/publications/research-review-series-religious-education

Pett, S. (2024). *Developing a religion and worldviews approach to religious education in England: A handbook for curriculum writers.* https://religiouseducationcouncil.org.uk/rec/wp-content/uploads/2024/04/24-25698-REC-Handbook-A4-DIGITAL-PAGES.pdf

Picower, B. (2013). You can't change what you don't see: Developing new teachers' political understanding of education. *Journal of Transformative Education, 11*(3), 170–189. https://doi.org/10.1177/1541344613502395

Pillay, G. J. (2002). Theology as a human science: Reflections on Gadamer's Truth and Method. *South African Journal of Philosophy, 21*(4), 345–358. https://doi.org/10.4314/sajpem.v21i4.31356

Rix, J. and Paige-Smith, A. (2011). Exploring barriers to reflection and learning: Developing a perspective lens. *Journal of Research in Special Educational Needs, 11*(1), 30–41. https://doi.org/10.1111/j.1471-3802.2010.01185.x

Roebben, B. (2012). Living and learning in the presence of the other: Defining religious education inclusively. *International Journal of Inclusive Education, 16*(11), 1175–1187. https://doi.org/10.1080/13603116.2011.552648

Salami, M. (2020). *Sensuous knowledge: A Black feminist approach for everyone.* Bloomsbury Academic.

Scottish Government. (2011). *Curriculum for excellence: Provision of religious and moral education in non-denominational schools and religious education in Roma Catholic schools.* www.gov.scot/binaries/content/documents/govscot/publications/advice-and-guidance/2011/02/curriculum-for-excellence-religious-and-moral-education/documents/curriculum-excellence-religious-moral-education-pdf/curriculum-excellence-religious-moral-education-pdf/govscot%3Adocument/Curriculum%2Bfor%2Bexcellence%2B-%2Breligious%2Band%2Bmoral%2Beducation.pdf

Whitworth, L. (2020). Do I know enough to teach RE? Responding to the Commission on Religious Education's recommendation for primary initial teacher education. *Journal of Religious Education, 68,* 345–357. https://doi.org/10.1007/s40839-020-00115-5

Yeomans, E. (2025). How a process of subjectification in ITE can challenge the paradigm of the expert teacher in primary RE. *Journal of Religious Education, 73,* 385–400. https://doi.org/10.1007/s40839-025-00278-z

18
SCIENCES

MATT BORG AND MARC TURU PORCEL

THIS CHAPTER

This chapter explores the ideas that:

- primary science teaching must develop scientific thinking, literacy and capital through inclusive pedagogies and adaptive teaching, not just transmit facts
- effective teaching addresses misconceptions, recognises historical biases and links enquiry-based learning to real-world contexts
- when children understand what, how and why they're learning, they become critically engaged citizens capable of scientific discourse and democratic decision-making.

KEY TERMS FOR THIS CHAPTER

Science capital: the knowledge, attitudes and experiences that influence engagement with science.

Scientific literacy: the ability to apply scientific knowledge and reasoning in everyday life.

Substantive knowledge: the factual content of science (concepts, theories, laws).

Disciplinary knowledge: the methods and practices of doing science (enquiry, investigation).

Working scientifically: a pedagogical approach combining substantive and disciplinary knowledge through enquiry.

Scientific enquiry types: includes pattern-seeking, fair testing, classifying, observing over time and research.

Rich immersive scientific experiences (RISEs): thoughtfully designed activities that engage all learners and encourage exploration.

Adaptive teaching: tailoring instruction to meet diverse learner needs without fixed ability labels.

Diversity in science: recognising and integrating contributions from historically marginalised groups.

WHY TEACH SCIENCE?

A recent study on public perception of climate change showed that across several European countries people heavily underestimated the consensus among the scientific community on the causes of climate change (Duffy, 2022). This research found people believed that two-thirds of the evidence supports human-caused climate change and a third does not. However, consensus among the scientific community is 99 per cent (Lynas et al., 2021). Similarly, there is a growing distrust of well-grounded and evidence-based scientific knowledge such as on vaccines, and even human evolution.

How is this possible? How can people who have gone through science education hold these beliefs? What should the role of science education be?

THE ROLE OF SCIENCE IN PRIMARY EDUCATION

At the most basic level, science is a discipline grounded in objectively analysing evidence through systematic enquiry. Science education in primary schools should support the development of children in becoming informed, critical citizens who are equipped to navigate an increasingly complex and interconnected world by introducing pupils to the ways of scientific enquiry, including scientific concepts, methods and ways of thinking scientifically. This disciplinary foundation helps pupils become critical thinkers and understand how scientific knowledge is produced and why it is reliable, enabling them to discern between evidence-based facts, opinions and outright lies. As Rudolph (2023) argued, science education must not only focus on *technical training* (preparing scientists, learning about biology, physics, chemistry knowledge), but also on *general education* (preparing for meaningful citizenship). The purpose of science education, therefore, goes beyond the acquisition of isolated facts to engage in disciplinary understanding and the development of science capital and scientific literacy.

THE MULTIFACETED PURPOSES OF SCIENCE EDUCATION

The purposes of primary science education extend beyond simple content acquisition, embracing multiple interconnected dimensions that not only serve individual children, but also broader societal needs. These purposes range from acquiring science capital and producing future scientists to promoting critical thinking and developing informed citizens.

The purposes of science education have been traditionally captured under three overarching categories.

BUILDING SCIENCE CAPITAL AND ASPIRATIONS

Science education aims to help pupils build their *science capital*. Science capital can be described as all those resources that individuals possess and are able to use to succeed in life. Examples include science-related knowledge, attitudes and ways of thinking about science, experiences and personal relations with others involved in science. The more science capital young people possess, the more likely they are to engage with science in the future, study scientific subjects and aspire to work in science and technology jobs (Archer Ker et al., 2013). Science capital is composed of eight dimensions (Archer et al., 2015):

- *scientific literacy* is the ability to use scientific knowledge and understanding of how science works and apply it in daily life for personal and societal benefit;

- *scientific-related dispositions/preferences* are the pupils' attitudes and beliefs about the relevance of science to their everyday life;

- *knowledge about the transferability of science* encapsulates pupils' appreciation of the transferability of science knowledge and skills to other areas in life and work;

- *consumption of science-related media* is the extent to which pupils engage with science through different forms of media (TV, social media, books/magazines, online);

- *participation in out-of-school science learning contexts* captures pupils' engagement with science learning outside school, such as museums, clubs and other events;

- *knowing someone who works in a science job* reflects the social contacts and network pupils are exposed to that contribute to their scientific development;

- *parental science qualifications* is the extent to which pupils' parents and carers have science-related skills and knowledge;

- *talking to others about science* captures how often pupils talk about science with people in their lives.

PRODUCING FUTURE SCIENTISTS

Science education offers a critical foundation for preparing pupils to navigate an increasingly technology-driven work environment. On the one hand, as Rudolph (2023) explained, a key purpose of science education is what he calls *technical training* which is concerned with those who will enter science-related jobs and therefore with developing pupils for careers in STEM (science, technology, engineering and mathematics). In the UK, for example, it is projected that 1.9 million new STEM professionals will be needed by 2035 (DfE, 2024a). On the other hand, as economies worldwide shift to knowledge-based industries, the demand for scientifically educated professionals has expanded beyond traditional STEM fields. Modern industries increasingly value scientific skills and attitudes. These cognitive skills are valued in fields ranging from healthcare and education to finance and marketing, where professionals must solve complex problems using analytical approaches.

FOSTERING CRITICAL THINKING AND ANALYTICAL SKILLS

Science education also aims to develop pupils' cognitive skills, especially those associated with problem-solving, analysis, observation enquiry and critical thinking. Osborne (2010) showed that engaging pupils in scientific practices, such as evidence-based argumentation and hypothesis generation, enhances their ability to reason logically and evaluate claims critically. Furthermore, the development of scientific practices alongside the integrated nature of primary education provides opportunities to contribute to other disciplines. For example, mathematical knowledge and skills can be developed in scientific investigations through data collection and analysis, enhancing argumentation skills develops communication skills, and critical thinking supports the identification of mis- and dis-information.

SCIENCE EDUCATION FOR DEMOCRATIC PARTICIPATION IN CONTEMPORARY GLOBAL CONTEXTS

In a time of global mobility and interconnectedness, science education must transcend the transmission of disciplinary knowledge to support pupils' ability to engage in democratic processes. Primary science education increasingly serves the purpose of preparing pupils to understand and respond to global challenges such as sustainability, climate change and artificial intelligence. Global challenges require citizens capable of understanding and judging complex issues which are often heavily politicised and debated.

As Osborn and Allchin (2024) argued, science education should develop *competent outsiders* capable of making judgements on the credibility of claims and sources. These skills are especially vital in an age characterised by misinformation and *post-truth* discourse. Current international initiatives capture this need, such as the PISA science framework (OECD, 2023) which emphasises competency-based science education that develops students' abilities to evaluate scientific evidence, understand the nature of scientific enquiry and apply scientific reasoning to real-world problems. The framework reflects the need for scientifically literate citizens to engage in national and international contemporary challenges that require a level of scientific analysis and evidence-based decisions. Similarly, the UNESCO Sustainable Development Goal 4 (United Nations, 2017) on quality of education, with its emphasis on global citizenship education, places science education as critical to promoting informed citizens who are capable of actively engaging with local and global challenges.

Children are now living in a world increasingly characterised by complexity and uncertainty. They are growing up in a context saturated with digital information and social media and are often presented with narratives with competing claims about truth. Issues such as climate change denial, misinformation and public mistrust about AI and new technologies show the need for children to develop what Zetterqvist and Bach (2023) call *epistemic knowledge* – knowledge of how scientific knowledge is constructed, validated and developed – alongside the acquisition of disciplinary knowledge. The research study we opened this chapter with on people's climate change understanding (Duffy, 2022), or the Covid-19 pandemic and how infections propagate highlight the importance of people being able to assess scientific evidence and weigh expert advice (Lewandowsky et al., 2017). Similarly, Roth and Lee (2004) argued that science education and scientific literacy must be also understood as social practice, enabling children to critically engage with scientific claims in media, policy and everyday contexts.

REFLECTION 18.1

- What does your own science capital consist of? What exposure did you have to science teaching before this stage in your career? Do you know friends and family in science roles? How do you consume science news?

- How do you think this compares to how children today grow their science capital?

SUBJECT KNOWLEDGE AND CONCEPTUAL UNDERSTANDING IN SCIENCE

We have seen then why we should teach science, and the purposes of science education. To fully understand and appreciate how we develop subject knowledge in the sciences, it is important to spend some time looking at the types of knowledge that teachers and children encounter in this discipline. Subject knowledge in science can be organised into *substantive* knowledge and *disciplinary* knowledge.

Substantive knowledge is the collection of facts, concepts and theories that have been discovered and verified though scientific investigation. Disciplinary knowledge focuses on how learners can acquire the methods and practices of carrying out science.

KNOWLEDGE TYPES AND CURRICULA

In the UK, the four nations' curricula outlining science content all discuss substantive and disciplinary knowledge (Education Scotland, 2023; HWB, 2020; CCEA, 2019; DfE, 2013). Although there is variation in key terms used, an important principle is that teaching of disciplinary knowledge should go in tandem with substantive subject knowledge. Ofsted is clear that high-quality science education includes the explicit teaching of disciplinary knowledge (2021); it also emphasises how a mix of foundational knowledge and skills is crucial in ensuring a smooth transition through the primary phases (2024).

It is useful to acknowledge that as educators we will also encounter this distinction between two types of subject knowledge in other primary subjects, though it can manifest itself differently. For example, in history, substantive knowledge in older primary phases may include knowledge of historical dates, events and people. This would be taught alongside the disciplinary knowledge of historical thinking, analysing sources, understanding causation, recognising bias and using historical evidence to construct arguments.

Despite the combination of substantive and disciplinary subject knowledge being crucial, research shows that curricula disproportionately favour one over the other. Wyse and Manyukhina's analysis of the curriculum output of three countries (England, Canada and Australia) showed on average that 82.8 per cent of knowledge mentioned was disciplinary (2018). This suggests it could be too easy to focus just on one type of subject knowledge. However, when considering the eight dimensions of science capital, it is important to know that it is the *combination* of both types of knowledge that help learners develop those important scientific literacy and critical thinking skills (Thornton and Borg, 2025). It is therefore imperative that we as educators embrace the construction of subject knowledge in the sciences through understanding and effective teaching of both knowledge types and be explicit with our learners about what they are learning. This will help our learners develop their conceptual understanding of this important subject and mitigate against misconceptions.

WORKING SCIENTIFICALLY AND ENQUIRY TYPES

In practice then, national curricula can be used as a foundation on which to build the delivery of subject knowledge across all domains in the sciences, and this disciplinary knowledge must be delivered alongside substantive knowledge. When we as educators are delivering these two types of subject knowledge together, we are teaching children the fundamentals of *working scientifically*. Working scientifically is a way we can ensure that all children develop scientific subject knowledge alongside a strong conceptual understanding.

The development of subject knowledge is dependent on understanding the distinct types of scientific enquiry that educators can teach and that children can engage with. It is these enquiry types that demonstrate how subject knowledge in science comes together and can be structured, built on and scaffolded for all learners to access. There are distinct enquiry types, and it is useful to reflect on research that identifies the different purposes that enquiry types can serve in developing children's scientific understanding, in turn adding to their science literacy and capital. Each enquiry type contributes differently to children's developing scientific understanding, and effective science teaching incorporates a range of these approaches.

- *Pattern-seeking* enquiries involve children looking for relationships and connections in data – for example, investigating whether there is a relationship between hand span and height. These enquiries develop children's ability to identify variables, collect systematic data and recognise patterns (disciplinary subject knowledge) while building substantive knowledge about what is being studied.

- *Comparative and fair testing* enquiries focus on changing one variable while keeping others constant to determine cause and effect. A classic example is investigating which material provides the best thermal insulation by testing different materials while keeping all other factors the same. This type of enquiry particularly develops children's understanding of variables and control, important aspects of disciplinary knowledge.

- *Classifying and identifying* enquiries involve sorting and grouping objects, materials, or living things based on their properties or characteristics. Children might classify rocks by their properties or identify different types of plants in the school grounds. These activities build substantive knowledge about the characteristics of different materials or organisms while developing disciplinary skills in observation and classification.

- *Observing over time* enquiries track changes that occur naturally over extended periods. Examples include monitoring how shadows change throughout the day, observing plant growth over several weeks, or tracking weather patterns. These enquiries develop children's skills in systematic observation and data collection while building substantive knowledge about natural processes and changes.

- *Research* enquiries involve children using secondary sources (the internet, textbooks, teacher-prepared material) to research a specific topic – for example, using secondary sources to identify structures of plants and trees. This enquiry enables children to ask simple questions (disciplinary knowledge) and identify and describe plants (substantive knowledge).

As educators, we need to rely on our subject knowledge to match the enquiry type with the substantive knowledge and ensure that the children understand not just *what* they are learning, but *how* they are investigating it and *why* this method is appropriate.

EXAMPLES FROM ACROSS PRIMARY PHASES

What might this combined, working scientifically approach look like across the primary age range?

- *Three to five years*: children exploring 'floating and sinking' by testing different objects in water. The substantive knowledge includes understanding that some materials float while others sink, and properties like weight and material type matter. The disciplinary knowledge involves making predictions ('I think the wooden block will float'), conducting fair tests by trying objects one at a time, observing carefully what happens and discussing their findings with others. Children learn both the science content and how to think and work like scientists.

- *Five to seven years*: investigating plant growth by planting seeds in different conditions – some with light, some without, some with water, some without. The substantive knowledge covers what plants need to grow and survive (light, water, nutrients). The disciplinary knowledge includes asking investigable questions ('What happens if we don't give plants water?'), planning a fair test by changing only one variable, making systematic observations over time, recording results through drawings or simple charts and drawing conclusions from evidence about plant needs.

- *Seven to 11 years*: exploring electrical circuits to understand how to make bulbs brighter or dimmer. The substantive knowledge encompasses concepts about electrical current, resistance and how components affect circuit behaviour. The disciplinary knowledge involves forming hypotheses about what will happen when components are added or changed, designing controlled experiments with multiple circuits, measuring and recording data systematically, analysing patterns in results and using evidence to explain why certain configurations produce brighter or dimmer bulbs.

In all cases, this working scientifically also includes elements of *procedural* knowledge. This is the 'how to' of practical skills like using equipment, measuring accurately, drawing diagrams and would also include explicitly taught safety aspects.

For example, in the earliest year groups, pupils begin to use simple tools such as magnifying glasses and egg timers. As they progress through their science education, they learn to take accurate measurements with more sophisticated equipment such as thermometers and data loggers. At the upper end, pupils use sophisticated equipment to take multiple readings, calculate averages where necessary and present results in detailed tables and graphs. This progression means that procedural knowledge can be built up systematically alongside the rest of their science education.

REFLECTION 18.2

- How clearly can you distinguish between substantive and disciplinary knowledge in your own science teaching?

- Consider a recent lesson you have taught or observed – what evidence was there that both types of knowledge were being developed?

- Which type of knowledge (substantive or disciplinary) do you feel more confident teaching, and why?

- How might you strengthen your approach to the area you find more challenging?

HISTORICAL DOMINANCE AND THE SHAPING OF SCIENTIFIC KNOWLEDGE

For decades, medical research only studied male subjects, leading to dangerous misconceptions about women's bodies and health. Heart disease symptoms were historically defined based on male patients (chest pain, left arm numbness) although women often experience completely different symptoms (fatigue, shortness of breath, nausea and jaw pain). This male-centric research bias led to women's heart attacks being misdiagnosed for decades as anxiety, contributing to higher mortality rates. Dr Bernadine Healy coined the term '*Yentl* syndrome' (Healy, 1991) which refers to the phenomenon where women's health symptoms are often taken less seriously and are overlooked because they do not align with men's symptoms. Her work led to mandating the inclusion of women in clinical trials which contributed to a better understanding of women's bodies and a reduction in mortality.

The construction of scientific knowledge has been profoundly shaped by the historical dominance of Eurocentric white male perspectives within science that continue to impact current science education. This historical pattern has a direct influence in primary education, where pupils are often presented with an unusually narrow canon of scientific achievements and discoveries. It takes 'strong objectivity' (Harding, 2008, p. 121) to recognise that dominant social positions can limit the construction of scientific knowledge by narrowing the questions explored, the methodologies accepted and interpretations considered valid.

Contemporary science curricula largely only present canonical experiments and discoveries attributed to white Western men, from Galileo, to Newton, Darwin and Edison. These scientists are often featured as geniuses who made the discoveries on their own instead of acknowledging the collaborative nature of scientific development which often marginalises the contributions of women, non-Western scientists and indigenous people. For children this can become problematic; not only are they being presented with a narrow and very selective perspective of science discoveries, but also the associations they can make between the scientists they learn about and their demographics are limited, thus affecting their aspirations and engagement with science.

The marginalisation of diverse perspectives and exclusion of seminal historical scientific figures shapes not only the content delivered in science education, but also the methodologies accepted as scientific. For example, indigenous knowledge often uses holistic approaches that integrate ecological, political and religious dimensions to science which traditional global North scientific perspectives have marginalised despite their proven effectiveness (Black and Tylianakis, 2024). Similarly, women's contributions to scientific development have been historically undervalued, as known in cases ranging from Rosalind Franklin's work on understanding the structure of DNA, Lise Meitner and Chien-Shiung Wu's contribution to nuclear physics, to Dorothy Crowfoot Hodgkin, the only British woman to receive a Nobel Prize for science.

STRATEGIES FOR INCLUSION

Helping children appreciate how knowledge is created is essential for developing critical and curious learners. Teachers can use multiple strategies to diversify scientific narratives and support pupils to develop a more nuanced understanding of scientific knowledge. In primary science education, this involves moving beyond presenting facts as universal, unchanging truths towards acknowledging the collaborative and culturally embedded processes through which knowledge is produced.

- *Historical marginalised figures*: historical narratives illustrate that science develops over time through trial, error and debate. Stories such as the shift from *geocentric* to *heliocentric* models of the solar system, or Franklin's contribution to understanding DNA, show how new evidence challenges previous ideas and how collaboration shapes scientific progress. Presenting lesser-known scientists and examples from non-global North contexts helps challenge the narrow perspective of science as the work of a handful of scientific geniuses.

- *Contemporary scientists*: incorporating contemporary diverse scientists and their research can make scientific careers more accessible and engaging to all students. Highlighting scientists like Maggie Aderin Pocock, Brian Cox, Hannah Fry and Jocelyn Bell Burnell alongside their research and collaborations can demonstrate the diversity of contemporary scientific work. Similarly, inviting local scientists from diverse backgrounds can provide authentic and meaningful role models for pupils from diverse contexts.

- *Standing upon the shoulders of giants*: presenting scientific discoveries as cumulative and collaborative endeavours that build upon diverse communities, across cultures and over time can be an effective inclusive strategy. For example, ancient Chinese astronomers mapped constellations, Islamic scientists preserved and expanded this knowledge by developing advanced mathematics, European navigators used this knowledge for world exploration and modern space agencies use accumulated astronomical knowledge from all cultures for satellites and space exploration.

- *Embracing criticality and scepticism*: the critical analysis of scientific claims can help pupils develop a more sophisticated understanding of how biases can shape science. Age-appropriate debates and discussions on how biases affect research methodologies, interpretation of data and even publication and acceptance of results can build scientific criticality without undermining confidence in science. We opened this section with Healy's example on the over reliance on male subjects in medical trials. Similarly, medical trails are often skewed by over-representing white populations which affects the effectiveness of certain medicines on non-white patients. A third example is the lack of female crash test dummies to test car crashes until 2022 which effectively made cars less safe for women. Examining case studies like these, as well as incorporating and listening to diverse perspectives, can potentially correct and advance knowledge, supporting children to understand the importance of diversity.

- *Local science*: project-based learning focusing on local issues and needs can engage pupils in authentic scientific work while emphasising the relevance of science. Pupils might want to investigate the quality of the water in their local rivers and reservoirs, the effects on life of building in green belts, or air pollution near busy roads using scientific methods. Experiences such as these can support pupils not only in doing science that has the potential to have an impact on their local community, but also to see themselves as future scientists.

REFLECTION 18.3

- To what extent might your selection of examples, contexts and methods of investigation acknowledge diverse cultural contributions to scientific understanding?

- What notable scientists and canonical experiments were you exposed to in your own education? How might this have influenced your own worldview?

PEDAGOGY AND SUBJECT KNOWLEDGE IN SCIENCE

How then do we deliver the subject knowledge necessary? To make decisions about how to teach primary science subject knowledge, it is important to consider how children learn. The role that cognitive science plays in education has become influential in terms of applied research (EEF, 2023) and national policy documents such as the *Initial teacher training and early career framework* in England (ITTECF) (DfE, 2024b).

In terms of science education across primary settings, we are going to look at how staged retrieval and a dialogic pedagogy can support our learners in accessing, understanding and retaining subject knowledge in science. In addition to practising a sound pedagogy, we know also that educator subject knowledge is an important consideration. In addition to practising a sound pedagogy, research has shown that educator subject knowledge can be one of the most important factors in learners' progress (Coe et al., 2014). It is important therefore that we develop our own subject knowledge and use resources available to make sure this knowledge is up to date and relevant – not least so that we can deliver confident, engaging lessons, but crucially so that we can also deal with misconceptions in science.

Misconceptions in science rarely sit alone. Take, for example, the idea that all metals are magnetic. Here, a child who encounters a new metal will assimilate this into previous knowledge from examples such as fridge magnets at home. Their schema regarding metal has no differentiation. Without explicit teaching here, this misconception will stay with the child. Strong subject knowledge is essential to spot and detangle misconceptions and teach the correct ideas.

This section will offer some practical examples of how to use staged (spaced) retrieval and how a dialogic pedagogy can support and scaffold all learners in the classroom. A strong pedagogy combined with secure subject knowledge is foundational to improving outcomes and, perhaps more importantly given the role that scientific literacy can play, engagement in science.

DIALOGIC PEDAGOGY AND VOCABULARY DEVELOPMENT

A dialogic pedagogy strongly complements the delivery of science subject knowledge. Alexander suggests that *dialogic* refers to 'genuinely reciprocal talk' (2020, p. 22), and it is our assertion that this dialogic approach is the best way to ensure that children engage with science, build on existing science knowledge and understand the conceptual nature of the subject. As educators, we know that great learning experiences are rich in discussion. This is especially true in primary science education. One reason that the dialogic approach is so crucial is the way that both types of subject knowledge in science can depend on understanding and using terminology correctly. This is especially true given that some of the subject knowledge vocabulary that children need in science will have already been encountered, often with similar but different meanings. The importance of explicitly teaching scientific vocabulary is highlighted by the Education Endowment Foundation (EEF) (2023) which categorises vocabulary into groups.

Table 18.1   Types and examples of scientific vocabulary

Tier 1	Words that are encountered every day	push, pull, metal, object
Tier 2	Words that are used across science subject knowledge	predict, compare, observe, describe
Tier 3	Words specific to a science topic	magnetic, non-magnetic, bar magnet, horseshoe magnet
Polysemous	Words that have everyday and scientific meanings	attract, repel, force, slide, pole

ADAPTIVE TEACHING AND RISE ACTIVITIES

Consider the wealth of planning schema available to us as educators. What proportion of these resources are still structured and labelled as to whether they are suitable for 'low' or 'high' achievers? Differentiating subject knowledge teaching experiences in this way does not help us create the scientifically literate citizens we have been discussing. We now know as educators that adaptive teaching is a more suitable practice that is better placed to scaffold, support and help all the children we are teaching to embed knowledge in their long-term memory. Moving beyond a one-size fits all approach in science enables us as educators to move to responsive, adaptive teaching that scaffolds and supports all learners.

Practising adaptive teaching in science means that we can help children overcome potential barriers to learning in science, including, but not limited to:

- *cognitive development barriers*: the mismatch between abstract nature of science concepts and developmental stage of young learners;

- *sociocultural factors*: how young learners develop science capital;

- *social and emotional barriers*: factors that affect learner's confidence and willingness to participate;

- *contextual barriers*: resource and pedagogical barriers such as inadequate equipment and time for investigation.

(Adapted from Thornton and Borg, 2025)

In practice, this requires us as educators to plan more, not less. It means using our own robust subject knowledge to create teaching experiences that align with children's cognitive development. It requires the explicit teaching of science vocabulary and encouraging enquiry-based learning through variety of means, including what we call *rich, immersive scientific experiences* (RISEs).

RISEs in primary science refer to thoughtfully designed activities that immerse pupils in meaningful scientific enquiry and thought. These experiences are hands-on, curiosity-driven and rooted in real-world contexts, allowing children to actively explore scientific concepts while developing both substantive and disciplinary subject knowledge.

RISEs are characterised by:

- *active participation*: pupils manipulate materials, observe phenomena and conduct investigations;

- *dialogic interaction*: teachers and pupils engage in reciprocal talk to deepen understanding;

- *conceptual clarity*: activities are structured to explicitly connect what is being learned with how and why it is being investigated;

- *inclusivity*: tasks are accessible to all learners through adaptive teaching, not ability grouping;

- *real-world relevance*: links to everyday life and local contexts help build science capital and motivation.

These experiences foster scientific literacy, critical thinking and long-term retention of knowledge by making science both accessible and meaningful.

CASE STUDY: MR HERATY'S MAGNETS LESSON

To illustrate some of the points that we have mentioned in this chapter, we present a case study. As you read through, try to identify how Mr Heraty considers subject knowledge – both his own and the subject knowledge of the class.

He teaches a mixed Year 3/4 class of 28 children aged seven to nine in a one-form entry primary school in England. He is delivering a lesson on magnets from the English Key Stage 2 national curriculum, specifically focusing on the statutory requirement that pupils should be taught to 'observe how magnets attract or repel each other and attract some materials and not others'.

PLANNING PHASE

There are several aspects of the planning phase.

SUBJECT KNOWLEDGE PREPARATION

Mr Heraty begins his planning by reviewing both substantive and disciplinary knowledge requirements. The substantive knowledge includes that magnetic forces can act at a distance, and that magnets have poles that attract and repel. The disciplinary knowledge focuses on fair testing skills: controlling variables, making systematic observations and drawing conclusions from evidence. He considers what prior knowledge children might have (e.g. seeing fridge magnets at home) and plans to incorporate these real-world examples into the lesson. He identifies potential misconceptions, particularly that all metals are magnetic. Mr Heraty plans to address this through carefully structured enquiry work.

LEARNING OBJECTIVES

* I know that magnetic forces can act at a distance.

* I know that magnets have poles that attract and repel.

* I can classify and identify magnetic and non-magnetic materials.

* I can present my results in a table.

ASSESSMENT STRATEGY

Mr Heraty plans formative assessment through observation during group work, questioning during dialogic discussion and a practical assessment where children predict outcomes for new surface combinations. He designs a simple recording sheet that captures both children's predictions and results, allowing him to assess understanding of fair testing principles.

TEACHING

Step-by-step through the lesson.

SPACED RETRIEVAL

Mr Heraty begins with spaced retrieval to strengthen previous learning in science forces. He has created a sheet called a *do now activity* (DNA) which is how he begins every science lesson. This sheet has four questions – one relating to substantive knowledge that children learned in the previous lesson, one from the previous science topic, one from a previous year's topic and a question about disciplinary knowledge. He knows the children will be using equipment to measure distance in subsequent lessons, so this question is about what scientific equipment would be suitable to measure the height of children in class.

This retrieval practice strengthens schema and links that children have already made, while providing Mr Heraty with diagnostic information about children's starting points for today's lesson.

RISE

Mr Heraty holds up a printed-out, paper bar magnet. He asks 'Does anyone know what this is called? Talk to your partner.' He listens for possible correct answers while children talk. He then explains that this is a bar magnet. He also asks why there might be two colours, which gives him an informal assessment for learning opportunity. Mr Heraty then gives each child their own printed-out paper bar magnet and a piece of sticky-tack. The children are asked to move around the class and just think about where their magnet belongs. He is careful not to use the word 'stick' as he is aware that children will have a misconception that magnets 'stick' rather than being *attracted* to magnetic material.

As the children wander around the classroom affixing their magnets to different materials (the metal edge of a table, the glass of the windows, Mr Heraty's coffee mug) he asks them 'Why did you put it here?', enacting a dialogic pedagogy.

INTRODUCTION

'Today, we're going to be materials detectives,' Mr Heraty begins, holding up two bar magnets. 'These magnets will help us discover something special about objects.' He gives each pair of children bar magnets and asks them to explore. He gives a few minutes and watches as the children start seeing what the magnets do, watching and asking questions as the children experience like poles repelling and different poles attracting.

He then explicitly teaches that the two ends are called poles and that different poles attract. He reminds children about the forces lesson they did the previous week and explains that magnetism is another type of force.

PLANNING THE INVESTIGATION

Mr Heraty places everyday objects on each table: paper clips, copper coins, aluminium foil, iron nails, plastic buttons and steel washers. He does not reveal what materials they are made from initially. Mr Heraty explains: 'We'll use magnets to classify these mystery objects. We need a fair test to discover which are magnetic.' He guides children through planning. This is done as a whole-class activity, to ensure all children can access. He uses questions to structure:

- what are we investigating? (which materials are magnetic);

- what will we change? (different test objects);

- what will we measure? (whether they are magnetic or not magnetic);

- what stays the same? (same magnet, measuring method, starting distance);

- working scientifically.

Mr Heraty creates mixed-age and mixed-ability groups. Different abilities are then supported by more confident children in their group. They then systematically test each object. They discover some materials that are attracted to the magnet while others show no response. Children record their findings in tables.

REAL-WORLD APPLICATIONS

Mr Heraty connects their discoveries to everyday situations, this links their learning with the real-world and adds to their growing science capital. For example, recycling centres using powerful magnets to separate iron and steel from other materials and scrapyards using magnets to move iron and steel items.

FORMATIVE ASSESSMENT DURING LEARNING

Throughout the lesson, Mr Heraty conducts ongoing assessment through:

- *observation*: noting which children can identify variables to control and which need support;

- *questioning*: using dialogic techniques to probe understanding without leading children to specific answers;

- *listening*: identifying misconceptions and partial understandings through children's discussions.

MR HERATY'S REFLECTION

The combination of spaced retrieval, dialogic pedagogy and hands-on enquiry proved effective. Children demonstrated growing confidence in using scientific vocabulary and fair-testing principles. The spaced retrieval successfully activated prior learning, while dialogic approaches encouraged deeper thinking and collaborative construction of understanding. Importantly, the RISE meant that all children could access this task; he considers that it would have been useful for children to write their names on the paper magnets; after the learning, he could have asked them whether they would move their magnets. This would have acted as an additional RISE and as an assessment opportunity. Next time!

FINAL THOUGHTS

Primary science teaching must be more than just preparing children for what happens in subsequent educational stages. We have seen how a solid grasp of subject knowledge in science can play a vital role in informed, curious and critically engaged citizens. It must go beyond the transmission of facts to include the development of disciplinary thinking, scientific literacy and science capital. By integrating substantive and disciplinary knowledge through inclusive pedagogies, such as dialogic teaching, adaptive strategies and RISEs, educators can foster deep conceptual understanding and equip children to navigate complex global challenges.

Recognising the historical biases in science and embracing diverse contributions helps broaden pupils' perspectives and aspirations. Effective science teaching also involves addressing misconceptions, explicitly teaching vocabulary and creating opportunities for enquiry-based learning that connects with real-world contexts. When the children we are teaching understand not just what they are learning, but how and why, they become empowered to think scientifically and engage meaningfully with the world around them. Ultimately, primary science education must prepare learners for lifelong participation in scientific discourse and democratic decision-making.

FURTHER READING AND RESOURCES

STEM Learning. www.stem.org.uk/

Provides free, quality-assured resources and CPD to improve teaching and learning across all STEM subjects in the UK.

Primary Science Teaching Trust. https://pstt.org.uk/

A charity dedicated to enhancing primary science education through professional development, resources and encouraging children's curiosity (e.g. Explorify).

The Royal Society. https://royalsociety.org/news-resources/resources-for-schools/

Offers a collection of educational resources for schools focused on engaging topics like climate change and machine learning, promoting science careers.

Steps into Science. https://edu.rsc.org/primary-science

Resources from the Royal Society of Chemistry providing hands-on primary investigations emphasising core chemistry concepts like materials and reactions.

Australian Academy of Science. https://education.science.org.au/our-programs/primary-connections

Flagship primary science program utilising a guided-enquiry approach to build student knowledge and teacher confidence in science teaching.

Wellington, J. and Ireson, G. (2017). *Science learning, science teaching* (4th ed.). Routledge.

A comprehensive, practical guide covering creative classroom teaching, curriculum changes, planning and contemporary issues for secondary science teachers.

Windschitl, M., Thompson, J. and Braaten, M. (2018). *Ambitious science teaching*. Harvard Education Press.

Outlines a powerful framework of four core teaching practices to ensure rigorous and equitable science instruction for all students.

Hoath, L. and Rogers, B. (2025). *Primary science in a nutshell*. Millgate.

A concise guide designed to boost primary teachers' confidence and subject knowledge by clearly explaining key concepts and addressing student misconceptions.

REFERENCES

Alexander, R. J. (2020). *A dialogic teaching companion*. Routledge.

Archer, L., Dawson, E., DeWitt, J., Seakins, A. and Wong, B. (2015). 'Science capital': A conceptual, methodological, and empirical argument for extending Bourdieusian notions of capital beyond the arts. *Journal of Research in Science Teaching, 52*(7), 922–948. https://doi.org/10.1002/tea.21227

Archer Ker, L., DeWitt, J., Osborne, J. F., Dillon, J. S., Wong, B. and Willis, B. (2013). *ASPIRES report: Young people's science and career aspirations, age 10–14*. King's College London.

Black, A. and Tylianakis, J. M. (2024). Teach Indigenous knowledge alongside science. Science, 383(6683), 592–594. https://doi.org/10.1126/science.adk4567

CCEA. (2019). *The Northern Ireland curriculum primary*. https://ccea.org.uk/downloads/docs/ccea-asset/Curriculum/The%20Northern%20Ireland%20Curriculum%20-%20Primary.pdf

Coe, R., Aloisi, C., Higgins, S. and Major, L. E. (2014). *What makes great teaching? Review of the underpinning research*. Sutton Trust. www.suttontrust.com/wp-content/uploads/2014/10/What-Makes-Great-Teaching-REPORT.pdf

Department for Education (DfE). (2013). *Science programmes of study: Key stages 1 and 2*. https://assets.publishing.service.gov.uk/government/uploads/system/uploads/attachment_data/file/425618/PRIMARY_national_curriculum_-_Science.pdf

DfE. (2024a). *Labour market and skills projections: 2020 to 2035*. www.gov.uk/government/publications/labour-market-and-skills-projections-2020-to-2035

DfE. (2024b). *Initial teacher training and early career framework*. https://assets.publishing.service.gov.uk/media/661d24ac08c3be25cfbd3e61/Initial_Teacher_Training_and_Early_Career_Framework.pdf

Duffy, B. (2022). *PERITA: Public perceptions on climate change*. King's College London. www.kcl.ac.uk/policy-institute/assets/peritia-climate-change%E2%80%8B.pdf

Education Scotland. (2023). *Curriculum for excellence: Sciences. Principles and practice*. https://education.gov.scot/media/111nhizk/sciences-pp.pdf

Education Endowment Foundation (EEF). (2023). *Improving primary science*. https://educationendowmentfoundation.org.uk/education-evidence/guidance-reports/primary-science

Harding, S. (2008). *Sciences from below: Feminisms, postcolonialities, and modernities*. Duke University Press.

Healy, B. (1991). The Yentl syndrome. *New England Journal of Medicine, 325*(4), 274–276. https://doi.org/10.1056/NEJM199107253250411

HWB. (2020). *Curriculum for Wales: Science and technology*. https://hwb.gov.wales/curriculum-for-wales/science-and-technology/

Lewandowsky, S., Ecker, U. K. H. and Cook, J. (2017). Beyond misinformation: Understanding and coping with the 'post-truth' era. *Journal of Applied Research in Memory and Cognition, 6*(4), 353–369. https://doi.org/10.1016/j.jarmac.2017.07.008

Lynas, M., Houlton, B. Z. and Perry, S. (2021). Greater than 99% consensus on human-caused climate change in the peer-reviewed scientific literature. *Environmental Research Letters, 16*(11), 1–7. https://doi.org/10.1088/1748-9326/ac2966

OECD. (2023). *PISA 2025 science framework*. https://pisa-framework.oecd.org/science-2025/

Ofsted. (2021). *Research review series: Science*. www.gov.uk/government/publications/research-review-series-science/research-review-series-science#organising-knowledge-within-the-subject-curriculum

Ofsted. (2024). *Strong foundations in the first years of school*. www.gov.uk/government/publications/strong-foundations-in-the-first-years-of-school/strong-foundations-in-the-first-years-of-school

Osborne, J. (2010). Arguing to learn in science: The role of collaborative, critical discourse. *Science, 328*(5977), 463–466. https://doi.org/10.1126/science.1183944

Osborne, J. and Allchin, D. (2024). Science literacy in the twenty-first century: Informed trust and the competent outsider. *International Journal of Science Education*, 1–22. https://doi.org/10.1080/09500693.2024.1234567

Roth, W. M. and Lee, S. (2004). Science education as/for participation in the community. *Science Education, 88*(2), 263–291. https://doi.org/10.1002/sce.10113

Rudolph, J. L. (2023). *Why we teach science (and why we should)*. Oxford University Press. https://doi.org/10.1093/oso/9780192867193.003.0004

Thornton, A. and Borg, M. (2025). Science. In C. Mosey and J. Stothard (Eds.), *Planning for adaptive teaching in the primary curriculum* (pp. 199–222). Learning Matters.

United Nations. (2017). *Sustainable development goals*. https://sdgs.un.org/goals

Wyse, D. and Manyukhina, Y. (2018). The place of knowledge in curricula: A research-informed analysis. University College London, Institute of Education. https://ncca.ie/media/4424/the-place-of-knowledge-in-a-redeveloped-curriculum.pdf

Zetterqvist, A. and Bach, F. (2023). Epistemic knowledge: A vital part of scientific literacy? *International Journal of Science Education*, *45*(6), 484–501. https://doi.org/10.1080/09500693.2023.2174567

19

SUSTAINABILITY AND CLIMATE CHANGE

CATHERINE FOLEY, MATTHEW KNIGHT, JO ANNA REED JOHNSON, PHILIPPA HEATH AND SARAH MARSTON

THIS CHAPTER

This chapter explores the ideas that:

- educating about climate and sustainability goes beyond subject-specific knowledge into developing an informed, critical and ethical stance

- learners take away more than curriculum content from their educators, learning from the language used, examples explored and values displayed in addition to the taught content

- powerful learning on climate and sustainability is achievable across contexts and curricula.

KEY TERMS FOR THIS CHAPTER

Climate: the long-term average of weather patterns, such as temperature and rainfall, in a particular region.

Climate action: practical steps to reduce greenhouse emissions and prepare for climate impacts.

Climate advocacy: speaking up and pushing for policies to tackle climate change.

Climate change: long-term shifts in temperature and weather patterns, mainly caused today by human activities such as burning fossil fuels.

Climate justice: the idea that climate change is a fairness issue as well as an environmental problem – often the people who have done least to cause climate change suffer most from it.

Climate- or ecoanxiety: can range from mild stress to clinical disorders and defined by the American Psychological Association (APA) as 'a chronic fear of environmental doom' (APA, 2017, p. 68).

(Continued)

Education for sustainable development (ESD): teaching and learning that gives people the knowledge, skills and values to make decisions and take actions for a fairer, greener and more sustainable future (UNESCO, n.d.).

Fossil fuels: non-renewable energy sources, such as coal, oil and natural gas, formed from the remains of plants and animals that died millions of years ago.

Greenhouse gases: gases in the atmosphere such as water vapour, carbon dioxide and methane, that absorb and trap heat energy from the sun, warming the planet.

Greenwashing: a deceptive practice where companies or other institutions falsely portray their products, services or approaches as more environmentally friendly than they are.

Sustainability: living in a way that meets our needs today without stopping future generations from meeting theirs (this includes protecting nature, people and the economy).

Systems thinking: an approach to understanding complex problems through recognising the interconnected parts of a system including root causes and unintended consequences.

INTRODUCTION

The Intergovernmental Panel on Climate Change (IPCC) in 2022 highlighted the importance of education in dealing with the challenges of *climate change* (IPCC, 2022). While climate change has a global impact, some parts of the world, and some people, are impacted more than others. This sets the scene for the importance of developing both a broad and deep understanding of the wider issues of sustainability and climate justice, going beyond a simple focus on climate 'facts'. Educators need to be able to embed learning about climate and sustainability into their teaching. To do that you will need to reflect on your own teacher positionality and the things that impact the ways that you teach or how you view the world. You will also need to be able to draw on localised examples as well as the global picture.

In this chapter we start by positioning climate and sustainability in the curriculum, defining terms and key ideas and establishing a shared language, then exploring curricular approaches.

Next, we explore the idea of 'knowledge' in this complex and contested area, including ideas of trust and authenticity, then examine key pedagogical issues in developing knowledge around climate change, including how to make difficult ideas accessible to children. Two detailed case studies prompt reflection on how climate and sustainability can be embedded within the context of different educational environments – an innovative primary school and a museum which has education for sustainability at its heart.

Finally, we provide opportunity for reflection, further reading and starting points for exploration.

CLIMATE AND SUSTAINABILITY IN THE CURRICULUM: DEFINITIONS, TERMINOLOGY AND POSITIONING

To be able to discuss the development and implementation of subject knowledge for teaching *climate and sustainability education* (CASE), we will find it helpful to have a shared frame of reference and establish some basic principles.

The first of these is that the idea that CASE goes beyond simply teaching about climate change into the realm of sustainability. A key overarching concept is the idea of *education for sustainable development* (ESD). The United Nations Educational, Scientific and Cultural Organisation (UNESCO) states that ESD 'empowers people with the knowledge, skills, values, attitudes and behaviours to live in a way that is good for the environment, economy, and society. It encourages people to make smart, responsible choices that help create a better future for everyone' (UNESCO, n.d.). This broader concept of climate change education underpins this chapter.

Thinking in this more holistic way about CASE leads us to a second key idea, that of educational competencies, or the 'knowledge, skills, understanding, attitude and values compatible with sustainable development' (UNESCO, 2017). These competencies go beyond an emphasis on knowledge, into how educators and learners can apply their understanding to tackling the unsustainable nature of our current ways of living. The competencies are pertinent across all types of education and consider:

- *ways of practising*:
    - o   strategic (effective strategies for collective action)
    - o   collaboration (working empathetically with others)
    - o   integrated problem-solving (applying problem-solving approaches to complex issues);
- *ways of thinking*:
    - o   systems thinking (understanding connections and influences)
    - o   anticipatory (future thinking and negotiating uncertainty)
    - o   critical thinking (questioning and analysis);
- *ways of being*:
    - o   self-awareness (understanding our own role, feelings and actions)
    - o   normative (capacity to reflect on and negotiate our own norms and values).

Grappling with CASE is complex and requires a constant process of self-reflection and critical engagement along with a shared vocabulary. It is through CASE that learners can develop a clearer understanding of the different dimensions of education for sustainable development such as *climate justice, climate education* and *climate action.*

CLIMATE AND THE CURRICULUM

Any country's educational curriculum can be seen as reflecting its prevailing societal priorities and norms (Ring et al., 2018). This applies equally to the field of climate and sustainability, where approaches to curriculum, content and assessment vary wildly between different countries and over time. Alongside the statutory curriculum, which may or may not contain explicit references to ideas of climate and sustainability, a key idea here is that of the *hidden* curriculum. This is the idea that education is about much more than what is explicitly codified in the curriculum. Instead, interactions, choices of resources, classroom environments and adult behaviours can establish deeply held assumptions about what is and is not valued by society (OECD, 2021).

Here we can also see the difference between the *espoused* curriculum – what institutions say they will teach – and the *enacted* or implemented curriculum, what children actually experience, which is shaped by teachers' day-to-day decisions (Porter and Smithson, 2001). No matter where CASE sits in your own curriculum, as an educator you have the power to make a positive difference.

In terms of climate and sustainability, then, we can think of the curriculum in terms of explicit curricular objectives, opportunities to use other curricular topics as a vehicle to explore sustainability, or the wider picture of how the classroom or school operates. Examples of these are given in Table 19.1.

Table 19.1   Curricular experiences of climate and sustainability

Positioning within the curriculum	Experience of the learner	Example
Explicit curricular aim	Today we are learning about climate change	Learning about different biomes as part of a geography lesson, and how these have changed over time
	Today we are learning about biodiversity	Naming different minibeasts and describing how they are suited to different habitats
Providing a context for exploring other areas of the explicit curriculum	Today we are learning how to represent data in graphs and charts	Carrying out surveys of butterflies and bees observed in an area of the school grounds before and after a project to introduce pollinator-friendly plans
	Today we are learning about expanded noun phrases	Writing poetry from the perspective of the ocean to encourage people to stop throwing their 'smelly, discarded wipes' into the sea

Positioning within the curriculum	Experience of the learner	Example
Integrated into the way the class or school operates	I know that I am expected to be mindful of the energy footprint of my classroom	Class rules that encourage 'last out, lights out', using both sides of all pieces of paper, wearing a jumper to turn the thermostat down by one degree, recycling any used paper or cardboard or composting food waste
	I know that my teacher cares about wildlife	Seeing that the teacher hangs up bird feeders or puts out water for birds in hot weather, sharing enthusiasm for wild animals seen on the way home, having books about nature and animals on the bookshelves to borrow

INTERNATIONAL COMPARISON

In developing our understanding of subject knowledge as it relates to the primary curriculum, we are going to look at curriculum implementation across some contrasting locations: England, Kenya and Finland.

ENGLAND (NATIONAL CURRICULUM, AGES FIVE TO 11)

Most relevant content is implicit, such as coverage of habitats, food change and climate zones, rather than explicit. Instead, the policy push of the early 2020s has come from the DfE's *Sustainability and climate change* strategy (DfE, 2023), which led to initiatives such as the National Education Nature Parks. There is no stand-alone assessment of climate knowledge, although some ideas are assessed by teachers within the geography and science curriculum. With a largely knowledge-led approach, the statutory curriculum does not include aspects such as eco-anxiety or advocacy. There is a commitment to strengthening initial teacher training on CASE, but at the time of writing this is not yet reflected in the accreditation criteria or statutory teacher training curriculum.

KENYA (COMPETENCY-BASED CURRICULUM, GRADES 1–6)

In contrast to the curriculum in England, the Kenyan curriculum makes clear that *pertinent and contemporary issues* (PCIs), including environmental conservation and climate change, must be integrated across learning areas (environmental activities, science and technology) (KICD, 2017). These areas are incorporated within expectations of assessment. There is a strong emphasis on competency and action alongside knowledge and values and, while eco-anxiety is not mentioned explicitly, the competency-based curriculum includes fundamental requirements for climate and sustainability action such as self-efficacy. Training teachers are taught to integrate the PCIs into their teaching, although the implementation of this can vary by provider.

FINLAND (NATIONAL CORE CURRICULUM FOR BASIC EDUCATION 2014, GRADES 1–6)

In Finnish education, building a sustainable future receives statutory status. Competences seen as cutting across all subjects are assessed *formatively* and *summatively* within subjects rather than in separate examinations. Knowledge, values and actions are linked, with curriculum language focusing upon participation, wellbeing and agency. This means that schools often address climate emotions within wider work on wellbeing. Teaching is a master's level profession, with official guidance linking sustainability to practical schoolwork alongside knowledge, values and attitudes.

REFLECTION 19.1

- How does what you have read correspond with your own experiences of education?

- Did you learn explicitly or implicitly about the climate and sustainability?

- Looking back, were you influenced by any teacher's orientation towards sustainability? What did they do that made a difference?

KNOWLEDGE, FACTS AND COMPETENCIES IN CLIMATE AND SUSTAINABILITY

As we have seen, climate and sustainability is a vast topic which spans across the curriculum. With a myriad of resources available to the educator, the prospect of teaching CASE can seem overwhelming. It might help to consider three key components: *knowledge, facts* and *competencies*. This can help you to decide upon which resources to use, which questions to ask, how prior learning will be built upon, how misconceptions can be addressed and how new learning can be assessed. Knowledge associated with CASE should always be viewed through a critical lens to promote the development of curriculum thinking skills and be sure of what is fact and what is opinion, teaching the learner how to make sense of this themselves. CASE exists in a world of both misinformation, arising from genuine misunderstandings or incomplete information, and disinformation, where individuals and institutions try to protect their own interests – for example, by *greenwashing* their environmental impact or casting doubt on the severity of the impacts of climate change.

When considering resources to support teaching, a key consideration is *trustworthiness*. Within the field of research, policy and practice should always be based upon evidence that is trustworthy, meaning that the research undertaken has been transparent, open, ethical and reproducible. Trustworthiness in research implies that the findings have been gained based on a robust research design and credible, high-quality research methods (Nowell et al., 2017).

The following questions can be used, either by the teacher or with learners, to appraise the robustness of the resource and to assess the extent to which it is evidence-informed.

- Is the information up to date?

- Who is the author and what qualifications do they hold on the particular topic?

- Who is the intended audience?

- Is it directly relevant to your topic?

- Is it supported by evidence?

- Is the information factually correct?

- Why was the article published?

- Are there any clues to potential biases?

- Are other perspectives offered?

The type of knowledge to be taught is also a key factor in the decision-making process. There are many different types of knowledge within CASE, ranging from scientific facts to feelings evoked by climate anxiety. Knowledge can be local, national or global, relating from the weather to education and climate injustice. To aspire to effective climate action and to reduce the climate divide in marginalised communities, we arguably need to know it all – scientific knowledge about climate change, practical *how-to* knowledge for implementing solutions, local knowledge for context adaptation, social science to understand and guide human behaviours and justice knowledge to ensure fair distribution of responsibilities and benefits. Indeed, having diverse forms of knowledge is vital because climate change is such a multifaceted problem needing diverse perspectives and *systems thinking* to create solutions. Issues relating to climate change are complicated, brought together by our interconnected economic, political, social and environmental systems (Majid et al., 2023). So, breaking this down into a coherent curriculum is an ongoing challenge.

Clearly, it is important to understand the *what* of climate change and build concepts of *how* to approach this in a manner which increases individual agency. Using global frameworks such as the United Nations Sustainable Development Goals (SDGs) can promote discussion of what global citizenship values are and what behavioural changes can look like. Moreover, work such as the BERA Manifesto for environmental sustainability demonstrates a values-based and youth-informed approach for ESD (Dunlop et al., 2022).

Who the knowledge belongs to, and who decides what is 'right', is also a key strand in the teaching of CASE. To facilitate effective climate action, there needs to be diverse, interdisciplinary knowledge from a variety of people, such as climate and social scientists, practitioners, indigenous and affected communities, policy-makers, business leaders and young people. Indeed, this evolution of knowledge also depends on the way in which it is communicated.

Understanding the competencies underpinning climate and sustainable literacies and teaching these implicitly to the learner can enhance the impact and effectiveness of climate change education. In order to do this, our team at the University of Reading created and embedded a framework to teach CASE to pre-service teachers, enabling the teaching of climate and sustainability in busy teacher training programmes (Majid et al., 2023). This framework uses knowledge adapted from the UNESCO's competencies for CASE (UNESCO, 2017), which embrace different ways of thinking, participating and being (Advance HE, 2021). The framework empowers pre-service teachers to conceptualise CASE using key questions based around positionality, climate justice and climate action to promote *critical thinking* techniques to explore different elements of our future life, provoking *anticipatory thinking.*

In addition to systems thinking, anticipatory thinking and critical thinking, competencies of climate education also include:

- *climate literacy*: aids understanding of climate science through comprehension of *climate-related vocabulary*;
- *advocacy and collaboration*: enables sustainable solutions through joint understanding and teamwork;
- *adaptability and resilience*: prepares us for climate-induced events;
- *ethical reasoning*: highlights climate injustice;
- *practical skills*: facilitates green jobs and future sustainable living.

Together, these competencies provide a toolkit for people to understand, respond to and create change for a better future while alleviating climate anxiety.

REFLECTION 19.2

- What do I understand about systems thinking in relation to my educational context?
- How can I provide activities which promote anticipatory thinking?
- Does my approach develop critical thinking in my learners?
- Can I explain climate-related vocabulary?
- Do resources I use as an educator provoke discussion on climate justice?
- To what extent are future jobs in sustainability highlighted in my organisation and how?

PRINCIPLES AND PRACTICE IN DEVELOPING AND APPLYING SUBJECT KNOWLEDGE IN CASE

Having explored the nature of CASE within the curriculum, and a sense of what 'knowledge' means in this context, we now turn to exploring key challenges and evidence-informed approaches in developing and applying subject knowledge in the context of CASE. Four aspects of subject knowledge are considered – think about how you might deepen and extend your knowledge in each of these areas.

MAKING THE ABSTRACT CONCRETE

One of the challenges in education around climate and sustainability is that the ideas are big, complex and abstract. Climate changes happen over scales that are very hard to understand for young children and in any one location or point in time global 'warming' may actually mean a child's experience of weather may be colder, or wetter – so the big, abstract ideas seem to contradict their day-to-day experience. Similarly, attempts to make ideas tangible can lead to over-simplification. Here are three examples of how abstract ideas can be made accessible for learners.

AN INTERNATIONAL EXAMPLE: THE CASE OF THE CLIMATE STRIPES

The *climate stripes* were created by Professor Ed Hawkins at the University of Reading in 2018. They use vertical, coloured bars to show the progressive heating of our planet in a single image, without the need for words, numbers or graphs. A strength of the climate stripes image is how they convey complex information in a readily accessible format. The

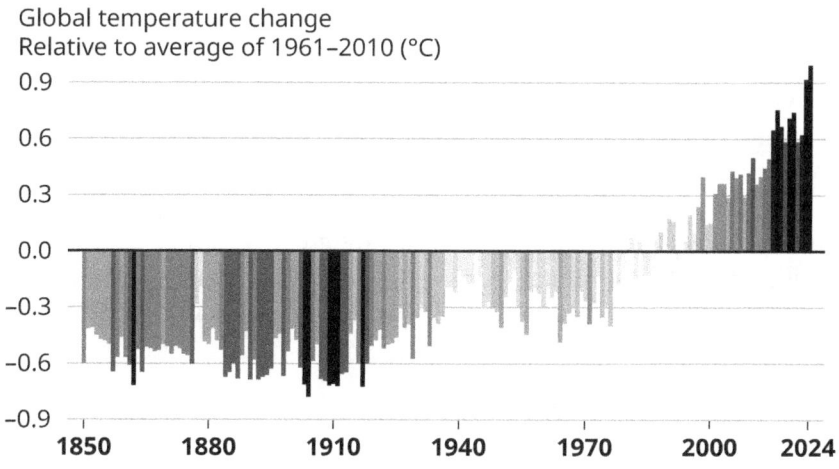

Figure 19.1   Climate stripes (Hawkins, 2018)

version here is in grey scale, but you can really see the full impact in the colour versions available online (Hawkins, 2018).

PRACTICAL EXPERIENCES EMBEDDED IN NATURE

Children can explore how to reduce waste by taking part in trash-to-treasure challenges, turning recyclables into items like bird feeders, growing herbs and vegetables, making bug hotels or going on a nature walk. Seeing their local parks after a drought or the difference compost and leaving leaf litter makes to the biodiversity of the school garden can bring home the value of small steps.

STARTING A DIALOGUE

One class of eight-year-olds brought into school plastic packaging from fruit, salad and vegetables consumed at home. Mapping the journeys of some of this produce (fresh basil brought in from Morocco to England was a notable example), particularly when the same produce grows well on the school's own site, helped children to understand the idea of carbon footprints and a sustainable approach to life on land.

EXPLORING COMMON MYTHS AND CONCEPTIONS

In an area as contentious as climate and sustainability, myths and misconceptions abound. The good news is that in terms of learning theory, the power of learning through exploring and challenging misconceptions is well-established, as is the idea is that hard thinking is beneficial because *memory is the residue of thought* (Willingham, 2009). The key to unlocking these powerful approaches to learning is knowing reputable sources and seeing misconceptions and myths as a positive catalyst for starting a productive dialogue. Here are some examples, and how they might be challenged or explored.

- *The climate has always changed over time – we're just coming out of the last ice age*

- Scientific consensus and authoritative assessments provide the strongest sources to counter this myth. NASA's review of global climate change knowledge shows the overwhelming consensus on human impact on the warming of Earth's surface and oceans, and the knock-on impact on oceans (NASA, 2024). The IPCC (2022) is 'unequivocal that human influence has warmed the atmosphere, ocean and land'. However, some people will find exploring models such as those comparing greenhouse gas concentrations or visual representations more effective. For others, self-interest (remember what it was like in the drought last year?) is a more powerful conversation starter.

- *The most important thing you can do is recycle*

- Recycling is good for the climate and can undoubtedly cut climate emissions. However, recycling processes generate emissions of their own, and there is a danger that recycling can perpetuate an unsustainable approach to buying unnecessary products or accepting unlimited packaging. Statistics around the effectiveness of recycling vary, with perhaps 5 per cent of plastics actually ending up being recycled (Verma, 2024); other strategies can be much more effective. Instead, some advocate groups refer to the *6 Rs of sustainability*: *reduce, reuse, recycle, refuse, rethink, repair.*

- *We need more honeybees, so we need more flowers*

- Well yes, and no. Or rather – not so simple. In the UK, honeybees are only responsible for around 5–15 per cent of total pollination. There are over 1,500 pollinating insect species, including wild bees, moths, butterflies, wasps, flies, hoverflies and beetles. This means that plants that support larval stages – for example, nettles – are just as important as flowers containing nectar. Pollinating London Together (2025) sets out to help individuals and organisations across London develop a pollinator-friendly urban environment.

SCALES OF KNOWLEDGE

The idea of *think global, act local* is controversial. For some, it provides a practical way for individuals to feel empowered and make a difference – 'I can't change my government's policy, but I can make the environment better in my own school yard.' For others, it gives global corporations and governments a way out of their responsibilities, by shifting accountability to individuals. Taking an idea like *biodiversity loss*, you might seek to understand global issues such as rainforest destruction, regional factors such as the Great Green Wall African Union-led initiative aiming to restore 100 million hectares of degraded land in the Sahel by 2030, a local re-wilding project such as the Knepp Wildland Project in West Sussex (Tree, 2018) or a small-scale project to improve an area of the school grounds.

Developing knowledge at a local, regional, national and international level will help you to have firm foundations for embedding climate and sustainability into the curriculum.

THE SPILLOVER EFFECT: IS A LITTLE KNOWLEDGE A DANGEROUS THING?

In terms of CASE, this relates to the idea that adopting one sustainable behaviour may make someone more likely to adopt others. Although we have explored the limitations of recycling above, proponents of the *spillover effect* would suggest that someone who starts recycling might build a positive self-image as being environmentally responsible and therefore start eating less meat or cycling to work. However, impacts can be negative as well as positive (Nash et al., 2017) – we might think that we are justified in making multiple long-haul flights in the year if we drive an electric car, or that we can buy and throw away clothing after using it a handful of times if it is responsibly sourced.

SUMMARY: PRINCIPLES AND PRACTICE IN KNOWLEDGE DEVELOPMENT

Perhaps the biggest takeaway from this section is to see developing subject knowledge as a dynamic, social and complex process in which understanding of pedagogy (how to make ideas relatable for children), content (how to get and stay well informed) and curriculum (how to link knowledge with existing ideas, local context and progression in skills and understanding) are intertwined.

APPLYING SUBJECT KNOWLEDGE TO THE PRIMARY CURRICULUM

By exploring case study examples, we are able to draw out key themes and lessons in relation to formal and informal learning around ESD. This section presents two examples. The first case study is based on work taking place at a junior school in the south east of England. The second case study focuses upon the activities that take place in the Museum of English Rural Life, part of the University of Reading.

Each of these settings has connected their learning to the United National SDGs (UN, n.d.).

CASE STUDY 1: SHINFIELD ST MARY'S JUNIOR SCHOOL, ENGLAND

Shinfield St Mary's Junior School is located in Berkshire, England, and has 12 classes of 30 pupils (360 pupils) aged between seven and 11 years.

BACKGROUND

The school has been teaching ecology and sustainability to pupils since 2014. Seen as a beacon of good practice in the local area, the school has designed its own sustainability curriculum; each week, two classes spend half a day engaging in this curriculum. SDGs 11 (Sustainable Cities and Communities), 13 (Climate Action) and 15 (Life on Land) are a central part of the curriculum.

LEARNING IN ACTION

By recognising the vital role that biodiversity plays in sustaining ecosystems, the school has developed hands-on initiatives to immerse children in conservation efforts, tree planting and sustainable land management practices. It has promoted biodiversity through enhanced green spaces and restoring degraded habitats. These activities foster environmental awareness, ecological responsibility and practical knowledge, ensuring that pupils understand how their actions impact the natural world. The children are engaged in conservation through direct hands-on experiences. This ensures that the learning is contributing meaningfully to local biodiversity efforts. By creating green spaces, planting native tree species and restoring habitats, the school provides a living example of sustainability in action, reinforcing the principles of Life on Land (SDG 15).

At the same time specific ecology teaching throughout the curriculum is linked to Climate Action (SDG 13) where the children are empowered as horticulturists to develop the school grounds. For example, they grow food in raised beds and aquaponic biodomes which is then donated to foodbanks; they also grow tree saplings in their community nursery which are planted throughout the local region to improve the environment. This connects their learning to Sustainable Communities (SDG 11), strengthening community collaboration and working alongside environmental organisations and charities in the UK such as the Tree Council, Ministry of Eco Education and Freely Fruity.

Learning is through doing: being outside as well as experiencing the indoor taught curriculum; making use of aquaponics, a biodome, raised beds, a recycled book dispenser and food composting all serve to make the abstract concrete for learners. These are some examples of how the learning environment supports both the implicit and explicit curriculum, going beyond statutory requirements. The objective is to ensure that young learners develop a deeper appreciation of nature and natural ecosystems while actively contributing to preservation. By instilling sustainable values early on in life, Shinfield St Mary's prepares students for the future as potential environmental stewards at the same time, managing their own eco-anxiety.

ADDITIONAL IMPACT

The integration of Life on Land (SDG 15) into the school's curriculum has resulted in measurable benefits, including:

- *increased biodiversity*: the introduction of pollinator habitats has led to a visible rise in bee and butterfly populations, demonstrating habitat success;

- *greater student engagement*: pupils actively participate in conservation efforts, organising campaigns for expanded green initiatives within the school;

- *lower carbon footprint*: through tree planting and sustainable land practices, the school has enhanced carbon capture, contributing to climate resilience;

- *wider community recognition*: Shinfield St Mary's has become a local model for environmentally conscious primary education, inspiring other schools to adopt similar initiatives.

WIDER BENEFITS AND THE ROLE OF SUBJECT KNOWLEDGE

Beyond immediate impact, the team at Shinfield St Mary's reflect that:

- early exposure fosters long-term ecological responsibility and environmental awareness;

- practical learning enhances knowledge retention through hands-on engagement;

- community partnerships with councils and charities amplify impact;

- going beyond the statutory curriculum makes learning more holistic.

In order to teach this content and make cross-curricular links, teachers need to engage in ongoing professional development. As well as working together, they explore resources from trusted charitable organisations. Continually embedding subject knowledge and ensuring that the ecology curriculum is sustainable rather than situated with 'enthusiasts' is a next step of development for the school.

CASE STUDY 2: MUSEUM OF ENGLISH RURAL LIFE, ENGLAND

The Museum of English Rural Life (MERL), based at the University of Reading, houses a nationally important, designated collection charting the history of food, farming and the countryside.

BACKGROUND

Founded in 1951, MERL's collections speak to the lives and diverse experiences of people who have lived and worked in the countryside. They can also be used as a powerful window through which to explore issues of contemporary concern, including sustainability and climate.

We know that museums have the potential to play an important role in supporting sustainability and climate education: 'Museums are perfectly positioned to address and enhance sustainability as they are able to work with communities to raise public awareness, support research and knowledge creation to contribute to the wellbeing of the planet and societies for future generations' (ICOM, n.d.).

In many ways, the MERL collection reflects a traditional, arguably more sustainable way of life including approaches to growing food before the dramatic uplift in intensive and mechanised farming from the Second World War onwards. We can draw on this evidence and explore intangible heritage in a process of active learning:

- hands-on exploration of objects and tools which have been used in the past provides an insight into our relationship with the land;

- archive documentation shows people's attitudes to the environment and how they have changed, alongside seasonal and climate change;

- collections hint at traditional growing techniques and knowledge.

This process of active learning extends to the museum garden which has become a place to champion rural heritage and for local communities to grow. The garden has evolved with increasing focus on biodiversity and habitat management for different purposes: shady areas for wildlife, planting designed to support insect life, areas to pilot wellbeing programmes and plantings designed to encourage healthy living and sustain the natural environment. Meanwhile the museum's Learning and Engagement programmes offer visitors of all ages the chance to experience the outdoors to develop knowledge, skills, green health and wellbeing.

REAPPRAISING COLLECTIONS AND THEIR MEANINGS BY CONNECTING THEM TO THE SDGS

One of MERL's first tasks was to undertake a remapping of collections through the lens of the SDGs. This programme of work, Our Green Stories, has formed the basis of many of the schools' programmes, with objects and archives acting as *learning hooks* enabling learners to think critically about what museums can tell us about sustainability and climate. For those leading this work, undertaking the mapping developed a deep knowledge of the Sustainability Goals and how to make links between these, curriculum and learning hooks explicit.

SPACES FOR BIODIVERSITY AS WELL AS COLLECTIONS

Having a garden space which can be used as a forum for learning alongside the heritage collections is a powerful combination which maximises the potential for a diverse delivery of sustainability and climate education. The garden speaks to and makes real the historic collections, as well as acting as a jumping off point into the contemporary, exploring what is happening now in our garden setting in relation to biodiversity, habitats and climate. It locates knowledge and understanding of climate and sustainability in a real-life, tangible setting.

IMPACT

The programmes provide learners with the opportunity to think about sustainability and climate through the lens of the past which can, therefore, make real and tangible concepts which might otherwise feel abstract. With seven out of ten young people worried about climate change (Woodland Trust, 2023) it can be beneficial to critically explore artefacts from the past which speak to our real-world relationship with the environment. This can hint at the ability for people to overcome challenges and concerns or make tangible contributory factors for our climate crisis – objects from our post-industrial age which might represent the mechanisation and intensification of agriculture. Collections can therefore provide a useful real-world and engaging learning hook.

SECRETS OF SUCCESS

You will notice some common features across these two case studies:

- the SDGs provide a lens through which to frame meaningful learning;

- whole-school and system approaches;

- engagement in wider community and use of school grounds;

- fostering critical thinking and hope;

- engaging in reflection and evolution;

- partnerships and collaboration.

Shinfield St Mary's Junior School has demonstrated how the SDGs can be integrated effectively into primary education, providing students with both theoretical knowledge and practical experience in conservation. Through initiatives like tree planting, pollinator habitat development and sustainable land management, pupils engage with real-world environmental challenges, learning the value of biodiversity and ecological responsibility. By nurturing young conservationists, the school has set a precedent for nature-focused education, proving that sustainability principles can be embedded into everyday learning.

MERL demonstrates the value that museums and heritage collections can bring to our understanding of sustainability and climate. It enables learners to consider where we are now and how we got here while also allowing us to explore evidence from the past to consider our imagined futures. Appraising collections through the lens of the SDGs has formed a foundation for many of its learning programmes and acts as a useful resource or learning hook for schools. MERL's continued use and development of the garden has provided a space of active learning to connect back to the heritage collections and allows students to make links, develop their own skills and build their confidence in the outdoors.

REFLECTION 19.3

As we come to the end of the chapter, you might like to pause and consider:

- what assumptions was I making about the nature of knowledge in relation to climate and sustainability? How have these assumptions changed?

- what do I know about local, regional, national and international perspectives on the environment? What do I now want to find out more about?

- what have I learned about the links between climate education, climate justice and climate action? What is my own positioning, and has this changed?

FINAL THOUGHTS

Throughout this chapter we have explored the idea that rather than fitting into any one subject area, developing the competence and confidence to teach about climate and sustainability requires subject knowledge that cuts across the curriculum, involves critical thinking and goes beyond facts and figures into developing an informed, ethical stance on climate justice, environmental sustainability and advocacy. By considering ways of practising, thinking and being, we have sought to establish a shared language, principles about the nature of knowledge and an insight into how this knowledge might be implemented with learners. Children learn more than curriculum content from their educators; this chapter aims to encourage you to reflect on your own positionality, knowledge-base and curricular assumptions.

In the words of internationally renowned broadcaster, biologist, natural historian and writer Sir David Attenborough (2021) speaking to COP26: 'If working apart we are a force powerful enough to destabilise our planet, surely working together we are powerful enough to save it.'

FURTHER READING AND RESOURCES

The UN Sustainable Development Goals. https://sdgs.un.org/goals

These are core to understanding how climate and sustainability impacts every facet of our current and future lives: United Nations Department of Economic and Social Affairs: Sustainable Development.

UNESCO Education for sustainable development. www.unesco.org/en/sustainable-development/education

Learning to act for People and Planet. This will give you an international perspective on all aspects of education for sustainability.

International Council of Museums: Sustainability. https://icom.museum/en/research/sustainability-and-local-development/

This might be the source for you if you are interested in climate and sustainability beyond a primary school context.

NASA: Climate Change. https://science.nasa.gov/climate-change/

This website combines a unique perspective on long-term observations of planet Earth from space with up-to-date information, allowing you to link teaching with current global issues.

REFERENCES

Advance HE. (2021). *Education for sustainable development guidance.* www.advance-he.ac.uk/guidance/education-sustainable-development

American Psychological Association (APA). (2017). *Mental health and our changing climate: Impacts, implications, and guidance.* www.apa.org/news/press/releases/2017/03/mental-health-climate.pdf

Attenborough, D. (2021). COP26: 'Not fear, but hope' – Attenborough speech in full [Video], 1 November. BBC. www.bbc.co.uk/news/av/science-environment-59121615

Department for Education (DfE). (2013). *National curriculum.* www.gov.uk/government/collections/national-curriculum

DfE. (2023). *Sustainability and climate change: A strategy for the education and children's services systems.* www.gov.uk/government/publications/sustainability-and-climate-change-strategy

Dunlop, L., Rushton, E., Atkinson, L., Ayre, J., Bullivant, A., Essex, J., Price, L., Smith, A., Summer, M., Stubbs, J., Turkenburg-van Diepen, M. and Wood, L. (2022). Teacher and youth priorities for education for environmental sustainability: A co-created manifesto. *British Educational Research Journal.* https://doi.org/10.1002/berj.3803

Hawkins, E. (Climate Lab Book). (2018). *Warming stripes.* www.climate-lab-book.ac.uk/2018/warming-stripes/

Intergovernmental Panel on Climate Change (IPCC). (2022). *Climate change 2022: Impacts, adaptation and vulnerability.* www.ipcc.ch/report/ar6/wg2/

International Council of Museums (ICOM). (n.d.). *Sustainability.* https://icom.museum/en/activities/sustainability/

Kenya Institute of Curriculum Development (KICD). (2017). *Basic education curriculum framework.* KICD.

Majid, N., Marston, S., Reed Johnson, J. A. and Happle, A. (2023). Reconceptualising pre-service teachers' subject knowledge in climate change and sustainability education: A framework for initial teacher education from England, UK. *Sustainability, 15*(12237). https://doi.org/10.3390/su151612237

NASA. (2024). *Scientific consensus.* https://science.nasa.gov/climate-change/scientific-consensus/

Nash, N., Whitmarsh, L., Capstick, S., Hargreaves, T., Poortinga, W., Thomas, G., Sautkina, E. and Xenias, D. (2017). Climate-related behavioural spillover and the potential contribution of social practice theory. *Wiley Interdisciplinary Reviews: Climate Change.* https://doi.org/10.1002/wcc.481

Nowell, L. S., Norris, J. M., White, D. E. and Moules, N. J. (2017). Thematic analysis: Striving to meet the trustworthiness criteria. *International Journal of Qualitative Methods, 16*(1). https://doi.org/10.1177/1609406917733847

Organisation for Economic Co-operation and Development (OECD). (2021). *Embedding values and attitudes in curriculum: Shaping a better future.* www.oecd.org/en/publications/embedding-values-and-attitudes-in-curriculum_aee2adcd-en.html

Pollinating London Together (PLT). (2025). www.pollinatinglondontogether.com/

Porter, A. and Smithson, J. (2001). *Defining, developing and using curriculum indicators.* CPRE Research Report Series. www.researchgate.net/publication/252368536_Defining_Developing_and_Using_Curriculum_Indicators

Ring, E., O'Sullivan, L., Ryan, M. and Burke, P. (2018). A mélange or a mosaic of theories? How theoretical perspectives on children's learning and development can inform a responsive pedagogy in a redeveloped primary school curriculum. *Irish Educational Studies*, *37*(3), 343–356. https://doi.org/10.1080/03323315.2018.1484292

Tree, I. (2018). *Wilding: The return of nature to a British farm.* Picador.

UNESCO. (n.d.). *Education for sustainable development.* www.unesco.org/en/sustainable-development/education

UNESCO. (2017). *Education for sustainable development goals: Learning objectives.* http://unesdoc.unesco.org

United Nations (UN). (n.d.). *Sustainable development goals.* https://sdgs.un.org/goals

Verma, S. (2024). Recycling isn't the solution to the climate crisis. *Yale Climate Connections.* https://yaleclimateconnections.org/2024/09/recycling-isnt-the-solution-to-the-climate-crisis/

Willingham, D. (2009). Why don't students like school? *American Educator*, Spring, 4–13.

Woodland Trust. (2023). *Young people's climate anxiety soaring.* www.woodlandtrust.org.uk

PART 3

TAKING YOUR SUBJECT KNOWLEDGE FURTHER

20
CONCLUSION: THE SUBJECT KNOWLEDGE DEVELOPMENT CYCLE

JEN AGGLETON

One of the strongest tools that an educator can have when developing the subject knowledge of others is to actively and continually develop their own knowledge. In a wide-ranging, international review of research, Coe et al. (2014) concluded that teachers' own subject and pedagogical content knowledge has a significant impact on learner outcomes:

> *The most effective teachers have deep knowledge of the subjects they teach, and when teachers' knowledge falls below a certain level it is a significant impediment to students' learning. As well as a strong understanding of the material being taught, teachers must also understand the ways students think about the content, be able to evaluate the thinking behind students' own methods, and identify students' common misconceptions.*
>
> (Coe et al., 2014, p. 2)

To achieve and maintain an effective level of knowledge in a world where knowledge is rarely static for long requires a commitment to professional development. This includes continual, purposeful reflection on our own knowledge and how it impacts our practice. As Simon C. Ripley argues in Chapter 5 of this book, taking time to reflect and then act on those reflections is a powerful tool which can demonstrably improve educational outcomes. However, educators do not always have the skills or time to engage in reflective practice as effectively as they could.

In response to that difficulty, I present here a model of how you might effectively engage in the continuous development of your own subject knowledge. This model draws on the work of previous scholarship on reflective practice, including that of Andrew Pollard (2023), Ronél Ferreira (2021), Fiona Timmins (2015), John Driscoll (2007), Graham Gibbs (1988), David Boud, Rosemary Keogh and David Walker (1985) and Terry Borton (1970). You can find details of all of these works in the References; you may find it valuable to explore them for yourself.

Like many models of reflection, I have chosen the form of a cycle. This is to highlight not only the continuous nature of both reflective practice and knowledge development, but also to represent one common pattern of progression through a knowledge development event. However, in practice you may find that you adopt a different pathway, or engage in two phases simultaneously.

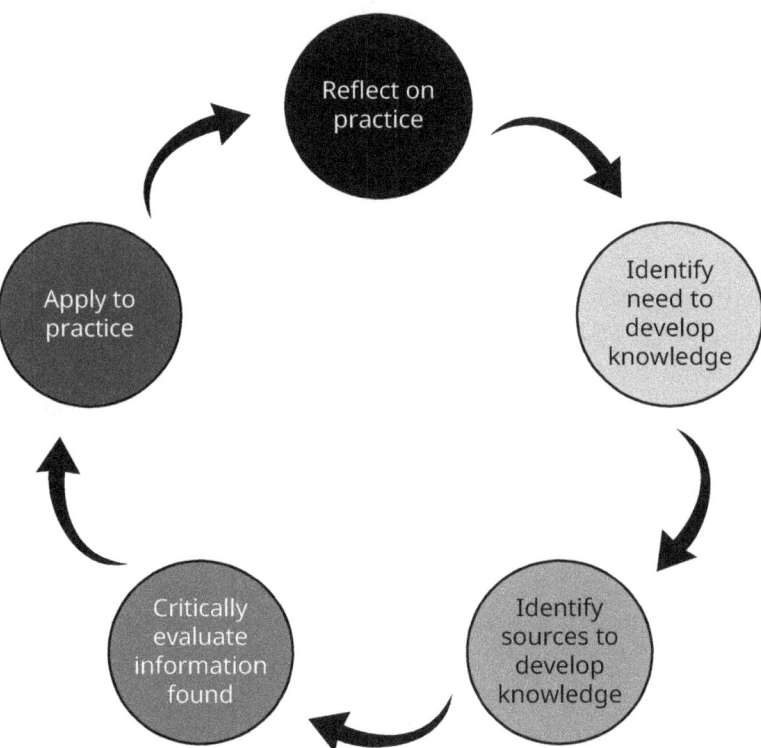

Figure 20.1   The subject knowledge development cycle

However, regardless of the order in which you engage with the phases, it is important that you do engage with each one. Each completion of the cycle should also conclude (it may also begin) with a reflection on practice. While I firmly believe that knowledge is valuable for its own sake, as education professionals it is essential that we constantly review the impact that our practice has and consider what we might change to ensure good outcomes for the children we teach. Those children are growing and changing all the time, and so is the world that we live in, so we must be constantly adapting too.

As you can see from the cycle, the development of knowledge requires action at each phase: *reflect, identify, evaluate, apply*. Below I have provided some examples of how you might undertake these actions, alongside resources or other elements that might be catalysts at each phase. These are not exhaustive examples, but rather indicative of the kinds of actions or catalysts that you may find useful.

REFLECT ON PRACTICE

When reflecting on your teaching practice, you may find it useful to assess the following elements and use these assessments to identify what changes you need to make, or the impacts of changes you have already implemented.

- What are the outcomes children are achieving and are these appropriate for each child?

- What progress are children making and is this appropriate for each child?

- How motivated are the children you are teaching?

- How is the wellbeing of the children you are teaching?

- How is your practice impacting your own workload and wellbeing?

- What misconceptions do the children hold?

- What do the children already know that you can build on?

- Are the children able to see the significance of what they are learning?

- Are the children enjoying learning?

- Are you enjoying how you are teaching?

- What questions are the children asking?

- What questions are you asking?

IDENTIFY NEED TO DEVELOP KNOWLEDGE

As well as (and sometimes as part of) reflecting on your practice, there are various elements which might make you realise that you need to develop your knowledge further. Identifying what these elements are can help you to notice them when they occur, as well as to reflect on their implications for your own professional development. These include:

- *questions raised*: either from children, your own questions, or those from other members of the learning community such as colleagues or caregivers;

- *working with new children*, who will have different knowledge development needs and interests;

- *the development of human knowledge*: when discoveries are made, ideas are reconceptualised or new information is revealed;

- *working with a new curriculum*, such as when moving schools or year groups, or when there are statutory changes;

- *local or global events;*

- *professional conversations* with colleagues.

IDENTIFY SOURCES TO DEVELOP KNOWLEDGE

Once you have identified the need to develop your knowledge, you will require sources that will help you to learn. This process can be highly interactive with the 'Identify need to develop knowledge' phase, as engaging with sources of knowledge can make you realise that you need to learn more – often you don't know what you don't know, until you realise that you don't know it! Useful activities and sources for the development of your knowledge include:

- attending professional conferences;

- engaging in continuing professional development (CPD) training;

- visiting or using resources from museums, charities, or other non-governmental organisations (NGOs);

- reading academic publications;

- engaging with blogs, podcasts and social media;

- joining subject associations or using their resources;

- collaborating with learning community you work in – the children, your colleagues, children's caregivers, local experts;

- undertaking investigations – sometimes the best way to learn about something is through experiential learning. This can be especially effective if done with your learning community as you can pool your experiences and expertise to build a more complete understanding. Some subjects and topics lend themselves particularly well to investigative types of knowledge development, such as design and technology and applied arts.

CRITICALLY EVALUATE INFORMATION FOUND

Once you have found information that can help you to develop your knowledge, it is essential that you critically assess it to ensure that it is relevant and reliable, and to consider how it might relate to the individual context you are working in. Our current information environment is highly volatile. While many of us now have an unprecedented level of access to information, this unfortunately comes with a great deal of misinformation (information spread due to a mistake) and disinformation (information which is intentionally inaccurate). The following criteria can help you to evaluate the information you find:

- *authorship*: who has provided the information? Do they have expertise in the topic? Do they have a vested interest in a particular viewpoint or approach (such as to sell an educational programme, gain advertising revenue through clicks, or push a political agenda)?

- *evidence*: how are the arguments justified? Is there clear evidence for what is being stated, or is it someone's uninformed opinion? Have they over-claimed based on the evidence provided, or might there be a different way to interpret something?

- *similarity*: how does this information relate to other information you have found on the topic? You may come across a source that really does represent a new idea or a significant revision of something previously understood. However, you should carefully evaluate the evidence presented if an argument seems to be wildly different to what most other information says. This is especially the case if the information is authored by someone without demonstrable expertise or with a vested interest;

- *values and attitudes*: the vast majority of information we engage with comes from people, and is therefore influenced by their values and attitudes – which are at least partly based on their lived experiences. Our own values and attitudes influence the way we then respond to that information. Important questions to ask here are: whose experiences, knowledge and lives are being valued here, and whose are not? What are the other ways of looking at this, or how might it be experienced in a different context? What are my own experiences and values that might prevent me from engaging with this fully, or encourage me to accept it without fully evaluating it?

- *context*: what context was the knowledge generated in? How old is it? What might have changed since then? How similar or different is that to your own context? How might you adapt what you have learned to your context?

- *relevance*: is this information going to help you achieve your aims? You and the children you teach are busy, so while something might be interesting, it is worth being reasonably sure it is likely to be useful before spending too much time trying to incorporate it into your practice.

APPLY TO PRACTICE

Once you have developed your knowledge in an appropriately critical manner, you will need to apply it to your practice. When exploring how your new knowledge might change your teaching, you may wish to consider the following elements:

- *curriculum design*: how might what you have learned influence what you teach, what links you make to other topics, what elements you prioritise or deprioritise?

- *pedagogy*: how might what you have learned influence how you teach?

- *individual learners*: how might you adapt what you have learned to support individual learners?

- *whole school*: how might you share what you have learned across the school, or apply it to whole-school activities rather than just the teaching and learning in individual classes?

- *enrichment*: how might what you have learned be used for enrichment activities beyond the formal curriculum?

- *hidden curriculum*: how might what you have learned influence elements of the hidden curriculum, such as behavioural expectations?

- *collaboration*: how might you use what you have learned to collaborate with other members of the learning community, including children, colleagues, caregivers and local community members?

Once you have applied your new knowledge to your practice, it is time to return to the beginning of the cycle and reflect on the impact that knowledge has had on your practice.

While it can seem daunting to know that the process of developing subject knowledge is never done, it is also part of what makes education such an incredibly exciting and dynamic profession to work in. Hopefully you will find this cycle, and this book more broadly, a useful tool to help you to engage in that continual process in a way that you find both professionally and personally satisfying and meaningful. Educators have the power and privilege to transform not only their learners, but also themselves and their societies. Go make change.

REFERENCES

Borton, T. (1970). *Reach, touch and teach*. Hutchinson.

Boud, D., Keogh, R. and Walker, D. (Eds.). (1985). *Reflection: Turning experience into learning*. Kogan.

Coe, R., Aloisi, C., Higgins, S. and Major, L. E. (2014). *What makes great teaching? Review of the underpinning research*. Sutton Trust. www.suttontrust.com/wp-content/uploads/2014/10/What-Makes-Great-Teaching-REPORT.pdf

Driscoll, J. J. (2007). Supported reflective learning: The essence of clinical supervision? In *Practising clinical supervision: A reflective approach for healthcare professionals* (2nd ed., pp. 27–50). Bailliere Tindall.

Ferreira, R. (Ed.). (2021). *Teacher identity development within a community of practice*. Nova Science.

Gibbs, G. (1988). *Learning by doing: A guide to teaching and learning methods*. Further Education Unit.

Pollard, A. (2023). *Reflective teaching in primary schools* (6th ed.). Bloomsbury.

Timmins, F. (2015). *A–Z of reflective practice* (1st ed.). Bloomsbury Academic.

INDEX

Page numbers followed by "f" indicate figures; those followed by "t" indicate tables.